THE CAMBRIDGE COMPANION TO JACK KEROUAC

Jack Kerouac is among the most important and influential writers to emerge from mid-twentieth-century America. Father of the Beat Generation literary movement, Kerouac's most famous novel, *On the Road*, was known as the bible of this generation, and inspired untold people to question the rigid social and cultural expectations of 1950s America. And yet despite its undeniable influence, *On the Road* is only a small piece of Kerouac's literary achievement, as more than forty other books by him have been published. The centerpiece to this work is Kerouac's multivolume Duluoz Legend, named for his fictional alter ego, Jack Duluoz, and comprising numerous books written over decades that together tell the story of Duluoz's life and times. This *Companion* offers fresh perspectives on Kerouac's multifaceted body of work, ranging from detailed analyses of his most significant books to wide-angle perspectives that place Kerouac in key literary, theoretical, and cultural contexts.

STEVEN BELLETTO is the author of *The Beats: A Literary History* (2020) (named a *Choice* Outstanding Academic Title) and *No Accident, Comrade: Chance and Design in Cold War American Narratives* (2012). He is the editor of *The Cambridge Companion to the Beats* (2017) and *American Literature in Transition, 1950–1960* (2018), among other books. He is a professor of English at Lafayette College.

A complete list of books in the series is at the back of the book.

THE CAMBRIDGE COMPANION TO JACK KEROUAC

EDITED BY

STEVEN BELLETTO

Lafayette College

Shaftesbury Road, Cambridge CB2 8EA, United Kingdom

One Liberty Plaza, 20th Floor, New York, NY 10006, USA

477 Williamstown Road, Port Melbourne, VIC 3207, Australia

314–321, 3rd Floor, Plot 3, Splendor Forum, Jasola District Centre, New Delhi – 110025, India

103 Penang Road, #05–06/07, Visioncrest Commercial, Singapore 238467

Cambridge University Press is part of Cambridge University Press & Assessment, a department of the University of Cambridge.

We share the University's mission to contribute to society through the pursuit of education, learning and research at the highest international levels of excellence.

www.cambridge.org
Information on this title: www.cambridge.org/9781009423601

DOI: 10.1017/9781009423571

When citing this work, please include a reference to the DOI 10.1017/9781009423571

First published 2024

A catalogue record for this publication is available from the British Library

Library of Congress Cataloging-in-Publication Data
NAMES: Belletto, Steven, editor.
TITLE: The Cambridge companion to Jack Kerouac / edited by Steven Belletto.
DESCRIPTION: Cambridge ; New York, NY : Cambridge University Press, 2024. | Series: Cambridge companions to literature | Includes bibliographical references and index.
IDENTIFIERS: LCCN 2023054386 (print) | LCCN 2023054387 (ebook) | ISBN 9781009423601 (hardback) | ISBN 9781009423571 (ebook)
SUBJECTS: LCSH: Kerouac, Jack, 1922–1969 – Criticism and interpretation. | American literature – 20th century – History and criticism. | Beats (Persons)
CLASSIFICATION: LCC PS3521.E735 Z587 2024 (print) | LCC PS3521.E735 (ebook) | DDC 813/.54–dc23/eng/20240220
LC record available at https://lccn.loc.gov/2023054386
LC ebook record available at https://lccn.loc.gov/2023054387

ISBN 978-1-009-42360-1 Hardback
ISBN 978-1-009-42356-4 Paperback

Contents

Notes on Contributors

STEVEN BELLETTO is the author of *The Beats: A Literary History* (2020) – named a *Choice* Outstanding Academic Title – and *No Accident, Comrade: Chance and Design in Cold War American Narratives* (2012). He is the editor of *American Literature in Transition, 1950–1960* (2018) and *The Cambridge Companion to the Beats* (2017); and the coeditor of *Neocolonial Fictions of the Global Cold War* (2019) and *American Literature and Culture in an Age of Cold War: A Critical Reassessment* (2012). He is Professor of English at Lafayette College and an editor of *Contemporary Literature*. He is currently writing a critical biography of Ted Joans, to be published in 2025.

FRANCA BELLARSI is an Associate Professor at the Université libre de Bruxelles. Her research is equally divided between the Beat Generation, ecocriticism and ecopoetics, and English Romanticism. She devoted her PhD to Allen Ginsberg as a poet of the "Buddhist Void" and has been interested in the Beats' syncretic mysticism and ecospirituality as well as in the countercultural resurgences of Romanticism in Beat writing. Her chapters/articles include contributions to *The Routledge Handbook of International Beat Literature* (2018), *The Reception of William Blake in Europe* (2019), *The Artist of the Future Age: William Blake, Neo-Romanticism, Counterculture and Now* (special issue of the Bulletin of the John Rylands Library, 2022), and *The Beats and the Academy: A Renegotiation* (2023). Within ecocriticism, she has guest-edited four special issues on topics ranging from "Ecospirit" to "Towards an Ecopoetics of Randomness and Design." She is currently preparing a Jack Kerouac special issue for *Europe*, an international 100-year-old francophone *belles lettres* journal of reference.

DAVID STEPHEN CALONNE is the author of *William Saroyan: My Real Work Is Being* (1983), *Charles Bukowski* (2012), *Henry Miller* (2014), *The*

Spiritual Imagination of the Beats (2017), *Diane di Prima: Visionary Poetics and the Hidden Religions* (2019), *R. Crumb: Literature, Autobiography and the Quest for Self* (2021), and *The Beats in Mexico* (2022). He has edited five volumes of unpublished prose by Charles Bukowski for City Lights and also *Conversations with Gary Snyder* (2017), *Conversations with Allen Ginsberg* (2019), and *Conversations with Diane di Prima* (2022). He is currently writing a monograph exploring the relationship between jazz, the counterculture, and spirituality to be published by Oxford University Press. Calonne has taught at the University of Texas at Austin, the University of Michigan, and the University of Chicago, and he currently teaches at Eastern Michigan University.

ANN CHARTERS received her BA from the University of California, Berkeley, in 1957 and her PhD from Columbia University in 1965. She retired as Professor of American Literature from the University of Connecticut in Storrs in 2017. Her *Jack Kerouac: A Bibliography* (1967) initiated the scholarly study of Jack Kerouac, and she is the author of *Kerouac* (1973), the first biography of Kerouac, and the coauthor, with her husband, Sam Charters, of *Brother Souls* (2010), the story of the friendship between Jack Kerouac and John Clellon Holmes. She is also the editor of several books, including *The Portable Beat Reader* (1992), *The Portable Jack Kerouac* (1995), *The Selected Letters of Jack Kerouac* (1995, 1999), and ten editions of the textbook anthology *The Story and Its Writer* (2024).

JEAN-CHRISTOPHE CLOUTIER is Associate Professor of English and Comparative Literature at the University of Pennsylvania, where he teaches twentieth- and twenty-first-century American literature, comics, and graphic novels and archival research methods. He is the author of *Shadow Archives: The Lifecycles of African American Literature* and the coeditor of Claude McKay's *Amiable with Big Teeth.* He is the editor of *La vie est d'hommage*, which gathers the original French writings of Jack Kerouac, as well as the newly released *Sur le chemin*, for Gallimard's *Le Monde Entier* collection. He translated into English two of Kerouac's French novels for the Library of America's *The Unknown Kerouac* and is currently completing an extensive study of Kerouac's oeuvre that explores the writer's practices as a novelist, translator, and archivist.

DOUGLAS FIELD is Senior Lecturer in Twentieth-Century American Literature at the University of Manchester. He is the author of two books on James Baldwin and the editor and coeditor of volumes on

American Cold War culture, Harold Norse, William Blake, and the Mimeograph Revolution. He is the co-founding editor of *James Baldwin Review* and a series editor for the British Pop Archive. His writing has been published in *African American Review*, *English Literary History*, the *Guardian*, and the *Times Literary Supplement*. *Walking with James Baldwin* will be published in 2024.

NANCY M. GRACE is Virginia Myers Professor of English (emerita) at The College of Wooster, Ohio. She is a founding member of the Beat Studies Association and the former coeditor and founding editor of *The Journal of Beat Studies*. She is the editor of *The Beats: A Teaching Companion* (2021), coeditor of the *Transnational Beat Generation* (2012), and author of *Jack Kerouac and the Literary Imagination* (2007) and *The Feminized Male Character in Twentieth-Century Literature* (1995). She also coauthored *Breaking the Rule of Cool: Interviewing and Reading Beat Women Writers* (2004) and coedited *Girls Who Wore Black: Women Writing the Beat Generation* (2002). She has also written articles on Diane di Prima, William S. Burroughs, ruth weiss, Joni Mitchell, George Olson, and Ed Sanders.

SARAH F. HAYNES is Professor of religious studies and anthropology at Western Illinois University, where she is the cofounder of the cannabis and culture program. Her primary research interests are Buddhism in America, ritual studies, and religion and drugs. She is the author of *Jack Kerouac's Buddhism and the American Search for Enlightenment* (2024).

KURT HEMMER is the editor of the *Encyclopedia of Beat Literature* (2007) and Professor of English at Harper College. With filmmaker Tom Knoff, he produced several award-winning films: *Janine Pommy Vega: As We Cover the Streets*, *Rebel Roar: The Sound of Michael McClure*, *Wow! Ted Joans Lives!*, *Keenan*, and *Love Janine Pommy Vega*. His essay on the Beats appears in *A History of California Literature* (2015).

MICHAEL HREBENIAK is Lecturer in Film Poetics at University College London and the convener of the New School of the Anthropocene, a higher-educational experiment dedicated to confronting biopolitical emergency through the arts. He previously taught at Cambridge University and the Royal Academy of Music and has worked as a documentary film producer and jazz journalist. His first book, *Action Writing: Jack Kerouac's Wild Form*, was published in 2006, and he has continued to write on the Beats as well as contributing chapters to edited collections on cinema, visual culture, jazz, ecopoetics, and the 1968 uprisings. He is currently writing a book for the BFI on the BBC Arena strand, and his first feature-length film, *Stirbitch: An Imaginary*, was premiered at the Heong Gallery in Cambridge in 2019.

TIM HUNT is the author of *Kerouac's Crooked Road: Development of a Fiction* (originally published by Archon Books, 1981, and republished by University of California Press, 1996, and Southern Illinois University Press, 2010) and *The Textuality of Soulwork: Kerouac's Quest for Spontaneous Prose* (2014). He is also the editor of the five-volume *Collected Poetry of Robinson Jeffers*. His six collections of poetry include *Voice to Voice in the Dark* and *Western Where* (both Broadstone Books). His final teaching post was at Illinois State University.

RONNA C. JOHNSON is Lecturer in English and American Studies at Tufts University, where she has been Director of Women's Studies. She has written about Jack Kerouac, Joyce Johnson, Lenore Kandel, Brenda Frazer, and Gregory Corso and presented papers on Diane di Prima, emphasizing gender, ethnicity, and postmodern effects in Beat movement literature. She is writing *Inventing Jack Kerouac: Reception and Reputation 1957–2007* and editing the collected correspondence of Jack Kerouac and John Clellon Holmes, 1948–1968. She has coauthored *Breaking the Rule of Cool: Interviewing and Reading Women Beat Writers* (2004) and coedited *Girls Who Wore Black: Women Writing the Beat Generation* (2002). Johnson is a cofounder of the Beat Studies Association, coeditor of the *Journal of Beat Studies*, and series coeditor of the Beat Studies Book Series at Clemson University Press/Liverpool University Press. Recent essays are "From Beat Bop Prosody to Punk Rock Poetry: Patti Smith and Jack Kerouac; Literature, Lineage, Legacy" and "Gender, Race, and Narrative in *On the Road*." She edited, with Tim Hunt, volume 10 of the *Journal of Beat Studies*, The Special Kerouac Centenary Issue.

AMOR KOHLI is an Associate Professor and the chair of the Department of African and Black Diaspora Studies at DePaul University. He received his PhD in English from Tufts University. Kohli's publications include essays on Black writers in scholarly journals such as *Callaloo*, *MELUS*, and *Journal of Commonwealth Literature*. His work has also appeared in edited collections, including *Beat Drama: Playwrights and Performances of the "Howl" Generation* (2016) and *The Black Imagination, Science Fiction, and the Speculative* (2011). He most recently edited the book *A*

Beat Beyond: Selected Prose of Major Jackson (2022) and has an essay on jazz slang in *Jazz and American Culture* (2024).

HASSAN MELEHY teaches French, English, and comparative literature at the University of North Carolina at Chapel Hill. His 2016 book, *Kerouac: Language, Poetics, and Territory*, is the first full-length study of the author's French-language heritage and its immense role in his writing. He also writes about the European Renaissance, critical theory, and cinema. His translations of French critical theory include Jacques Rancière's *The Names of History*. Melehy is also a poet: his first collection, *A Modest Apocalypse*, was published in 2017.

ERIK MORTENSON is a faculty member in English at Lake Michigan College in Benton Harbor, Michigan. He has published numerous journal articles and book chapters as well as several books: *Capturing the Beat Moment: Cultural Politics and the Poetics of Presence* (2011), which won a *Choice* Outstanding Academic Title award; *Ambiguous Borderlands: Shadow Imagery in Cold War American Culture* (2016); and *Translating the Counterculture: The Reception of the Beats in Turkey* (2018). He has also published *The Beats and the Academy: A Renegotiation* (2023), coedited with Tony Trigilio, along with the memoir *Kick Out the Bottom* (2023), cowritten with Christopher Kramer. Mortenson is also a translator whose work has appeared in journals such as *Asymptote*, *Talisman*, and *Two Lines*.

GEORGE MOURATIDIS is a research associate in the School of Culture and Communication at the University of Melbourne, where he coordinates the Beat and Counterculture reading group for researchers. He was a contributing editor of Jack Kerouac's *On the Road: The Original Scroll* (2007) with Howard Cunnell, Joshua Kupetz, and Penny Vlagopoulos. He is also the English translator of Greek Australian poet Nikos Nomikos' *Noted Transparencies* (2016), author of the poetry collection *Angel Frankenstein* (2018), and cofounder and editor of the online literary journal *Kalliope X*. He is currently working on a monograph, *Becoming Beat*, which reconsiders Beat's literary and cultural identity as a search for authenticity.

BRETT SIGURDSON earned his PhD in English Literature at the University of Minnesota, where he completed a dissertation on Jack Kerouac's posthumous reputation, *We Know Jack: On the Road with the Influencers Shaping the Legacy of America's Most Iconic Author.* He is currently revising the project for a book. He has taught courses on the Beats in Minnesota, Utah, and Vermont.

MATT THEADO is Professor of American cultural studies at Kobe City University of Foreign Studies. He is the author of *Understanding Jack Kerouac* (2000) and editor of *The Beats: A Literary Reference* (2003) and *The Beats, Black Mountain, and New Modes in American Poetry* (2021). He is a member of the editorial board for the *Journal of the American Literature Society of Japan* and serves as the President of the Beat Studies Association.

STEVEN WATSON is a cultural historian who is particularly interested in constellations of the American avant-garde. Among his published books are *The Birth of the Beat Generation* and *Factory Made: Warhol and the Sixties* (Pantheon). He has curated exhibitions at the National Portrait Gallery, notably *Rebels: Painters and Poets of the 1950s,* and directed a PBS documentary film, *Prepare for Saints: The Making of a Modern Opera*. He is currently creating a website, Artifacts movie, that features his video interviews over the past 30 years of pioneers of avant-garde and queer culture.

REGINA WEINREICH is a coproducer/director of the award-winning documentary *Paul Bowles: The Complete Outsider* and a writer for *The Beat Generation: An American Dream* (1986). She is the author of the critical study *Kerouac's Spontaneous Poetics* (1987; 2003), and she has also edited and compiled Kerouac's *Book of Haikus* (2003) and wrote the introduction for Kerouac's *You're a Genius All the Time* (2009). A leading scholar of the Beat Generation, she has contributed to numerous essay collections and literary journals, including *The Paris Review*, *Five Points*, and *The Review of Contemporary Fiction*.

A Kerouac Chronology

Brett Sigurdson

1922	Jean Louis Kérouac is born on March 12 in Lowell, Massachusetts, to Gabrielle (née Lévesque) and Joseph Alcide Leon (Leo) Kerouac, immigrants from Quebec. Ti Jean, as he is variously called, joins siblings Gerard (b. 1916) and Caroline, or Nin, (b. 1918) in the French-speaking home.
1923–1925	In 1923, Leo Kerouac (b. 1889) opens Spotlight Print in Lowell. A trained linotypist who learned the craft in Nashua, New Hampshire, Leo had managed and printed *L'Etoile*, a French-language weekly newspaper, in Lowell. Gabrielle Kerouac (b. 1895), who had been orphaned at sixteen and was working in a Lowell shoe factory when she married Leo in 1915, spends these years caring for the children. In 1925, Gerard, then nine, contracts rheumatic fever.
1926	Gerard dies on June 2 of purpura hemorrhagica, endocarditis, and myocarditis. Gerard's illness, death, and burial in Nashua would have a profound influence on Kerouac, who would revisit his memories of this period throughout his life, most notably in *Visions of Gerard* (1963).
1927–1932	After moving to three houses in Kerouac's first four years, the family would move four more times in and around Lowell during this period, settling, in 1932, in the city's middle-class Pawtucketville neighborhood. There, Leo manages the Pawtucketville Social Club, which Kerouac frequents to bowl and shoot pool. In fifth grade at St. Joseph's Parochial School, Kerouac begins to learn English.
1933–1935	In 1933, Kerouac enters Bartlett Junior High School, where his classes are taught exclusively in English. The next few years would see his athletic abilities flourish on

sandlot football fields (he scored nine touchdowns in one game in 1935) and his imagination take flight, fed in part by a voracious reading habit. In his room, Kerouac creates a fantasy baseball game played with cards, dice, and marbles. Inspired by radio shows and comics like *The Shadow*, Kerouac sketches cartoons, scribbles short stories, and creates a fantasy horseracing and boxing periodical called *The Turf* in his notebook, commencing a lifelong practice of keeping a journal.

1936–1937 A week after Kerouac's fourteenth birthday in 1936, a deluged Merrimack River extensively damages Leo's print shop. In debt, Leo is forced to sell the business in 1937, pushing the family into financial turmoil compounded by Leo's gambling and drinking troubles. He becomes an itinerant printer while Gabrielle takes a job in a shoe factory. In his journal, Kerouac describes 1937 as a traumatic year for his family.

1938 Despite family traumas, Kerouac's athletic triumphs and artistic explorations at Lowell High School set the course of his life in the short and long term. His gridiron prowess, manifested in his scoring the decisive touchdown against rival Lawrence High School in the annual Thanksgiving football game, garners attention from college coaches. Through his friendship with Sebastian Sampas and others who call themselves the Young Prometheans, he explores philosophy, politics, and literature.

1939 Kerouac graduates from Lowell High School on June 28. He lives with Gabrielle's stepmother in Brooklyn to attend Horace Mann Preparatory School in New York City before matriculating to Columbia University on a football scholarship. His creative development is nurtured in Harlem jazz clubs and Times Square theaters. He publishes his first piece, "The Brothers," in *Horace Mann Quarterly*.

1940 In spring, Kerouac publishes his second story in *Horace Mann Quarterly* and takes one-time Lowell girlfriend Mary Carney to the school's spring prom. That summer, he composes a spate of short stories. In September, Kerouac enters Columbia University. A month later, he fractures his tibia during a freshman squad game. While recuperating, he spends time voraciously reading and writing, including drafting an incomplete novella about football.

1941 After the school year, Kerouac travels with his family to New Haven, Connecticut, where Leo and Gabrielle relocate. To his father's disappointment, Kerouac leaves Columbia due to discord with his coach over playing time. After a brief trip to the South, he moves to Hartford, Connecticut, and composes short stories while working at a gas station. Later that winter, Kerouac returns to Lowell, where he drafts a short story, "Search by Night," in response to the Pearl Harbor invasion. He enlists as a Navy pilot and awaits orders to attend basic training.

1942 To bide time, Kerouac joins the *Lowell Sun* as a sports reporter and begins composing *Vanity of Duluoz*, the first in a planned trilogy about a character named "Jack Duluoz." He quits the *Sun* in March and travels to Washington, DC, to help work on construction of the Pentagon. Upon his return to the Northeast, he forgoes Navy enlistment and joins the Merchant Marine, sailing to Greenland on the *S.S. Dorchester*. After discharge in the fall, Kerouac accepts an invitation to rejoin the Columbia football team, but he soon quits again. He stays in New York and begins work on a novel, *The Sea Is My Brother*, and another short story, "The Wastral," featuring the character Duluoz. In journal entries, Kerouac dedicates himself to cultivating a life as a writer and sophisticate.

1943 After returning to Lowell at the end of 1942, Kerouac fails naval flight training and is sent to boot camp in Newport, Rhode Island. There, repeated insubordination consigns him to the hospital. Transferred to a base in Bethesda, Maryland, Kerouac is diagnosed with "schizoid tendencies" and is discharged from the military. He rejoins the Merchant Marine and sails aboard *S.S. George Weems*, a Liberty ship bound for Liverpool. After its return to New York, Kerouac moves in with his parents, now living in Queens. He continues to write, including a 158-page handwritten novel called *Merchant Mariner* (published in 2011 as *The Sea is My Brother*). He also frequents an apartment shared by Edie Parker and Joan Vollmer Adams. He meets Lucien Carr, a Columbia student, that fall.

1944 A watershed year in Kerouac's life. In February, Carr introduces Kerouac to William S. Burroughs and Allen Ginsberg. In March, Kerouac receives news that Sebastian Sampas, deployed as an Army medic, is killed in action in Italy. Later that summer, Carr stabs and kills David Kammerer, his infatuated, imperious former scoutmaster. Kerouac helps Carr dispose of the knife, becoming a material witness to the murder. When Leo refuses to pay his bail, Kerouac marries Edie Parker to receive $500 from her trust fund. They move to Grosse Point, Michigan, with her family, and Kerouac works in a ball-bearing factory to repay his debt. He soon quits and leaves Edie to join the crew of *S.S. Robert Treat Paine* but disembarks in Norfolk, Virginia. He reunites with Edie, and they move into an apartment with Joan Vollmer Adams on West 115th Street, which is frequented by Ginsberg, Burroughs, and Herbert Huncke, a drug addict and Times Square hustler. Throughout the year, Kerouac continuously writes, including "Galloway," a precursor to *The Town and the City*.

1945 Family and health issues plague him: he separates from Edie that summer, applies to the University of California, Los Angeles, but is denied admission, and begins caring for Leo, who is diagnosed with stomach cancer. Kerouac is also hospitalized with thrombophlebitis. Through it all, he continues to write. Guided by Burroughs and Huncke, Kerouac explores the Times Square underworld. He and Burroughs collaborate on a novel, *And the Hippos Were Boiled in Their Tanks*, inspired by the Carr–Kammerer incident. He also completes a novella, *Orpheus Emerged*. Publishers, though, reject the manuscripts.

1946 Kerouac's family splinters again. In May, he witnesses his father die at home. Leo is buried next to Gerard in Nashua. Later that year, Edie files an annulment in

Michigan. Creatively, Kerouac experiences two momentous beginnings: he begins work on what would become his first published novel, *The Town and the City*, a "novel of facts" written by a confessional narrator, and he meets Neal Cassady when Cassady arrives in New York from Denver with his wife, LuAnne Henderson.

1947 By May, Kerouac has written 175,000 words of *The Town and the City*. But throughout the year he struggles with the drive and direction to complete the novel, writing in great bursts of prose some nights and typing uninspired pages others. That summer, Kerouac begins the cross-country travel experiences that would later inspire the narrative of his second novel, *On the Road*. He travels from New York to Chicago by bus and then hitchhikes to Denver, where he reunites with Cassady. Later, he travels to San Francisco and becomes a security guard in Marin City with his friend Henri Cru, with whom he writes a movie script to sell in Hollywood. In early October, Kerouac takes a bus to Los Angeles, where he meets Bea Franco. He spends two weeks living and working with her family of migrant farmworkers near Selma, California. Gabrielle wires him bus fare to New York, where he returns to work on *The Town and the City*.

1948 Kerouac finishes *The Town and the City* – an 1,100-page, 350,000-word manuscript – in May, but multiple publishers reject the novel. He travels with his mother – who the family begins calling Mémère – to visit Nin in Rocky Mount, North Carolina, for the birth of a son, Paul Blake Jr., with her second husband, Paul Blake Sr. In July, Kerouac meets John Clellon Holmes, a fellow writer and intellectual, to whom Kerouac says in November, "So I guess you might say we're a beat generation." That fall, Kerouac begins taking courses at the New School for Social Research in New York and begins experimenting with a novel he calls *On the Road*. After Christmas, Cassady, LuAnne, and their friend Al Hinkle surprise Kerouac and family when they arrive in Rocky Mount unannounced after a manic cross-country trip. The trio transports Kerouac to New York City.

1949 In January, Kerouac leaves New York with Cassady, LuAnne, and Hinkle for Algiers, Louisiana, where Burroughs is living with Joan Vollmer Adams. With Cassady and LuAnne, Kerouac travels to San Francisco and then returns to New York by bus. The trip would inspire the second section of *On the Road.* That March, Mark Van Doren, a Columbia professor, recommends *The Town and the City* to Robert Giroux at Harcourt Brace, which agrees to publish the novel for a $1,000 advance. In May, Kerouac convinces his family to move with him to Denver. As he waits for their arrival, he continues composing *On the Road.* His family stays only for a few months before returning east. Kerouac travels to San Francisco and then drives with Cassady – now married to Carolyn Robinson – back to New York, visiting Chicago and Grosse Pointe along the way. He moves to an apartment with Mémère in Queens.

1950 Published in March, *The Town and the City* receives lukewarm reviews and little attention. Cassady meets Kerouac in Denver in June, and together they drive to Mexico, where Kerouac develops dysentery. When his health improves, Kerouac hitchhikes to New York and continues writing feverishly. He calls the period from July to September a "derangement des sens" during which he writes 25,000 words of prose that constitute new incarnations of *On the Road.* In November, he meets Joan Haverty, and they marry weeks later. At the end of December, Kerouac receives what becomes known as the "Joan Anderson Letter" from Cassady, which Kerouac later attributes as the inspiration for his evolving Spontaneous Prose style.

1951 Kerouac and Joan move into a new apartment on West 20th Street. He initiates an extensive correspondence with Cassady about his childhood memories. In April, Kerouac places a 120-foot-long roll of paper in his typewriter and, over three weeks, types what becomes known as the scroll version of *On the Road.* Robert Giroux rejects the draft. Kerouac separates with Joan, who is pregnant with Kerouac's child. While visiting Nin in North Carolina, Kerouac suffers severe thrombophlebitis and stays at a VA Hospital in the Bronx for three weeks. He begins rewriting *On the Road* using his Spontaneous Prose "sketching" method (parts of which would become *Visions of Cody*). In December, he moves to San Francisco to live with the Cassady family.

1952 While Kerouac works as a baggage handler for Southern Pacific Railroad, his daughter Jan is born in New York. Kerouac leaves the Cassady family to live with William S. Burroughs in Mexico City for the summer. In a rooftop shack, he writes *Doctor Sax*. In the fall, he briefly returns to North Carolina to live with Nin and Mémère and then travels back to San Jose to again live with the Cassadys. After an affair with Carolyn Cassady, Kerouac moves into a skid row hotel in San Francisco. Throughout these travels, he practices Spontaneous Prose sketching, particularly about Neal Cassady as an archetypal American hero. Meanwhile, the Beat Generation coalesces publicly thanks to John Clellon Holmes, whose first novel, *Go*, was inspired by the scene and whose *New York Times Magazine* article, "This is the Beat Generation," names Kerouac as the movement's progenitor.

1953 Living with his mother in New York, Kerouac drafts the novel *Maggie Cassidy*. He meets the writer and critic Malcolm Cowley, an editor at Viking Press, who encourages him to write "naturalistic fiction" in order to make a living as a writer. Kerouac responds by writing "Lucien Midnight," an impressionistic sketch intended to, as he writes, "free myself of the writing of fiction." He returns to California and resumes work for Southern Pacific. After returning to his mother's apartment in Queens in June, he has an affair with Alene Lee. After their breakup in the fall, Kerouac drafts *The Subterraneans* in three days. He also composes "Essentials of Spontaneous Prose," a treatise on his composition philosophy, upon prompting from Ginsberg and Burroughs. In November, he switches agents from MCA to Lord & Gilbert. Sterling Lord will represent him for the remainder of his career.

1954 Kerouac again moves in with the Cassadys in San Jose, where he's employed as a parking lot attendant. He discovers Dwight Goddard's *A Buddhist Bible* and begins an extensive study of Buddhism, keeping notes in a collection of journals he titles *Some of the Dharma*. That fall, he returns to Lowell and sneaks into his birth home on one of his many rambles around the city. At Lowell's Ste-Jeanne d'Arc Church, Kerouac has a vision of the Beat Generation as a "beatific" movement. Malcolm Cowley describes Kerouac's concept of the Beat Generation in a *Saturday Review* article. Despite Cowley's approbation, *On the Road* remains unpublished. During the year, Kerouac also writes *San Francisco Blues*, *Book of Dreams*, and the sci-fi short story "cityCityCITY."

1955 Joan seeks child support from Kerouac, who alleges he's unable to work because of his phlebitis, delaying the trial for a year. While *On the Road* is rejected by Alfred A. Knopf – and potential libel issues continue to present publication concerns for Viking – Cowley's advocacy leads to excerpts from the novel and *Visions of Cody* appearing in *New World Writing* ("Jazz of the Beat Generation") and *The Paris Review* ("The Mexican Girl"). Kerouac travels to Mexico during the summer, where he meets Esperanza Zaregoza (who is later often identified as Esperanza Villanueva or Esperanza Tercerero). There, he begins *Tristessa* and *Mexico City Blues*. In the fall, he travels to San Francisco and meets the poets of the San Francisco Renaissance, including Gary Snyder, Michael McClure, and Philip Whalen. On October 7, he attends the Six Gallery reading, where Ginsberg debuts "Howl." Kerouac travels back to North Carolina to live with his family and, after Christmas, begins composing *Visions of Gerard*.

1956 Kerouac completes *Visions of Gerard* during the first weeks of January. In March, he hitchhikes to California and lives with Gary Snyder in a Mill Valley cabin. He writes *The Scripture of the Golden Eternity* and completes *Old Angel Midnight*. In June, Kerouac hitchhikes to northern Washington to work as a fire lookout atop Desolation Peak in Mount Baker National Forest. He writes "Ozone Park" and numerous haikus in the cabin, where he stays for two months. In September, he returns to San Francisco and then journeys to Mexico

City. There, he writes what will become part one of *Desolation Angels* (1965). Upon his return to New York in November, he learns that Viking will publish *On the Road.* In December, he joins Mémère in Orlando, where she's moved to be closer to Nin's family.

1957 After Kerouac makes final revisions to *On the Road*, which involve changing character names at the behest of Viking, he spends the spring traversing through Tangier, Paris, and England. In Tangier, he stays with Burroughs and transcribes his *Naked Lunch* manuscript. Back in the United States, Kerouac and Mémère move to Berkeley, California. But after only a few months, they return to Orlando and Kerouac departs for Mexico City. There, he writes "The Philosophy of the Beat Generation," published in *Esquire* in 1958. He arrives in New York on the eve of *On the Road*'s publication on September 5. In a *New York Times* review, Gilbert Millstein raves about the book, which catapults Kerouac into fame and notoriety. In the fall, he returns to Orlando and writes a play, *Beat Generation*, and a novel, *The Dharma Bums.* When he returns to New York that winter, he begins reading poetry accompanied by jazz musicians such as David Amram. Despite his success, Kerouac begins to fear he's losing his writing ability.

1958 Both *The Dharma Bums* (Viking) and *The Subterraneans* (Grove) are published – the latter of which is sold to MGM Studios for a film adaptation. Kerouac also sells *On the Road*'s film rights to Tri-Way Productions for $25,000, though he'll only see part of that money before the film company dissolves. Kerouac buys a house in Northport, Long Island, to escape New York City – where he is beaten outside the Kettle of Fish bar in April – and the increasingly bright spotlight of notoriety that accompanies the appellation "King of the Beats." At times, Kerouac plays along by consenting to interviews with Mike Wallace and a speech at a Brandeis University-sponsored symposium titled "Is There a Beat Generation?" The demands of fame and near-constant criticism – such as Norman Podhoretz's essay "The Know-Nothing Bohemians" – compel him to drink more.

1959 A prolific year for Kerouac. Three of his novels see publication: *Doctor Sax* (Grove), *Maggie Cassidy* (Avon), and *Mexico City Blues* (Grove). He also narrates *Pull My Daisy*, a short film directed by Robert Frank and produced by Alfred Leslie. He begins a monthly column for *Escapade* magazine. In November, he appears on *The Steve Allen Show* and reads a selection from *Visions of Cody*. But just as many projects fall apart: Dot Records withdraws an album recorded with Steve Allen because of its "Anglo-Saxonisms." Invitations to Harvard, Phillips Exeter, and the local Rotary club fall through. Kerouac receives a proposal for a radio series based on his characters, but it fizzles. The backlash against the Beats intensifies. While Kerouac watches on television, Truman Capote utters the famous barb, "That's not writing, it's typing." After a six-day drinking binge that almost kills him, he and Mémère decide to move to Florida. He agrees to build a home with Nin's family in an Orlando-area development, but disagreements over money sink the project and he remains in Northport.

1960 Publishers continue to release Kerouac books: Avon prints *Tristessa*; Corinth issues *The Scripture of the Golden Eternity*; New Directions publishes an excerpt of *Visions of Cody*; and McGraw-Hill distributes *Lonesome Traveler*. But critics – like John Ciardi ("Epitaph for the Dead Beats," *Saturday Review*) – continue to condemn him. He spends time poring over his old notebooks to reconnect with his younger self. To create and convalesce, Kerouac takes a train to San Francisco and then treks to Big Sur, where his attempts at self-care are thwarted by too many friends and too much alcohol. His experience would provide fodder for the novel *Big Sur*, which he'd compose the following year.

1961 Kerouac moves with Mémère from Northport to Orlando to live near Nin and her family. In what would be a productive year for Kerouac, he departs for Mexico that summer to draft part two of *Desolation Angels*. In ten days that fall, he writes *Big Sur*. But personal travails continue. Joan Haverty presses him for child support.

In need of money, Joan adds her name to a ghostwritten story in *Confidential* magazine titled "My Ex-Husband Jack Kerouac Is an Ingrate." On Christmas Day, Kerouac and Paul Blake Sr. get into a physical altercation over a personal loan the Blakes stopped paying.

1962 In early 1962, Kerouac discovers that half the savings he shared with Mémère were, without his knowledge, put in a trust for Paul Blake Jr. In February, he meets Jan, now ten, for the first time. After a blood test proves he is her father, Kerouac is court-ordered to pay $12 a month in child support. Farrar, Straus, and Cudahy, which will publish *Big Sur* in the fall, accepts *Visions of Gerard* for publication. Kerouac travels to Old Saybrook, Connecticut, to visit Holmes and to search for a new house, but his plans are thwarted by too much drinking. He takes a taxi to Lowell, where his misadventures with friends and onlookers are detailed in the *Lowell Sun*. In December, he moves with Mémère from Orlando to Northport.

1963 Kerouac successfully sobers for part of the year, but circumstances compel him to resume drinking again. Farrar, Straus, and Cudahy publishes *Visions of Gerard* to mostly negative reviews. Fans and hangers-on increasingly distract him, and some become confrontational – one draws a gun on him in his Northport home. Even old friends represent an intrusion. When Cassady visits that summer, he brings two "sneery" beatniks who consume all the Kerouacs' food. When Gregory Corso drops by, he begs for money then steals Kerouac's checkbook and the manuscript for *Vanity of Duluoz*.

1964 That spring, Kerouac gives readings at Harvard and the Northport Library. In July, he sees Neal Cassady for the final time when he travels to New York City for a party attended by Ken Kesey and the Merry Pranksters. In August, Kerouac sells his house in Northport and buys a home in St. Petersburg, Florida. Only a few days after she visits the new home, Nin dies of a heart attack in her Orlando apartment. Too distraught, Kerouac doesn't attend her funeral.

1965 Coward-McCann publishes *Desolation Angels* with an introduction by Seymour Krim. Kerouac journeys to Paris and Brittany in June to research his ancestry. Though he plans to travel for much longer, he runs out of money and returns after only a few weeks. Almost immediately upon return, Kerouac drafts *Satori in Paris* in a notebook. He later sells the novel to Grove.

1966 Kerouac leaves St. Petersburg and moves with Mémère to Hyannis, Massachusetts. Grove Press publishes *Satori in Paris* to generally unfavorable reviews. That summer, Ann Charters visits Kerouac to compile his bibliography. In the fall, Kerouac's plans to travel to Italy are delayed when Mémère suffers a stroke, leaving her partially paralyzed and needing constant care. After years of corresponding with Stella Sampas – sister of his childhood friend Sebastian – Kerouac proposes marriage to her. They are wed in Kerouac's Hyannis home in November.

1967 In January, Kerouac, Stella, and Mémère move to Lowell. Working from old notebooks and journals, he spends the year composing *Vanity of Duluoz*. In October, Kerouac gives an interview to poets Ted Berrigan, Aram Saroyan, and Duncan McNaughton for *The Paris Review*. Jan Kerouac visits him before traveling to Mexico, where she gives birth to a stillborn child and writes a novel. It would be the last time they meet.

1968 *Vanity of Duluoz* is published in February to tepid reviews. A month later, he voyages to Europe with Stella's brothers. His alcoholism, now a constant concern, is evidenced in a Lowell arrest for public intoxication and his inebriated performance as a panelist on *Firing Line* with William F. Buckley. In need of money to fund a move to Florida, Kerouac sells his correspondence with Cassady and Ginsberg to the University of Texas and letters from Burroughs to Columbia University. In the fall, he moves with Stella and Mémère to 5169 10th Avenue North in St. Petersburg.

1969 Though he feels a growing lack of interest in writing, Kerouac needs money to pay his mortgage and an unexpected tax bill. He revises *Pic*, a novella he began in 1950, but it is rejected by publishers. On invitation from the *Chicago Tribune Magazine*, Kerouac writes "After Me, the Deluge," distancing himself from the counterculture generation he inspired. In September, he suffers a severe beating at a bar in St. Petersburg hours after changing his will to leave his estate to Mémère, something he underscores in a letter to Paul Blake Jr., written October 19. The following morning, Kerouac begins vomiting blood and is taken to the emergency room, where he succumbs to massive internal bleeding caused by cirrhosis of the liver on October 21. After a wake in St. Petersburg and again in Lowell, a requiem mass is held on October 24 at St. Jean Baptiste Church in Lowell. He is buried in the Sampas family plot. In December, Grove Press contracts with Barnett Bank of St. Petersburg, Kerouac's estate executor, to reprint *Mexico City Blues*, *Doctor Sax*, and *Lonesome Traveler*. Meanwhile, his vast archive is transported from Florida to Lowell for safe keeping.

1970 Representatives from Barnett Bank of St. Petersburg work to republish Kerouac's novels while providing Stella and Mémère a meager $100 monthly allowance. Grove Press arranges to publish *Pic* for a $2,500 advance. Seeking a biography of Kerouac, Sterling Lord and Grove's editors approach both Joe McGinness and Dan DeSole, a friend to Kerouac in the last years of his life. Ann Charters proposes a study of Kerouac's literature to Stella, who refuses. Charters begins research on Kerouac's biography without Stella's participation.

1971 In April, Aaron Latham signs a contract to write a biography of Kerouac with the encouragement of Barnett Bank of St. Petersburg and Sterling Lord, though Stella resists repeated attempts by Latham – and all other researchers – to view Kerouac's archive. The book is never released after Random House decides to withhold the manuscript and his contract expires. Grove publishes *Pic*.

1972 *Visions of Cody* is published by McGraw-Hill. In July, Barnett Bank of St. Petersburg turns over Kerouac's estate to Gabrielle Kerouac. To help raise money for Stella and Mémère, Sterling Lord sells the Kerouac manuscripts in his possession.

1973 In February, Gabrielle Kerouac creates a new will that leaves Kerouac's estate to Stella. That spring, Salem State University hosts a Jack Kerouac Symposium. Months later, Ann Charters publishes *Kerouac: A Biography*, the first treatment of the writer's life. Gabrielle Kerouac dies in October of a severe cerebral vascular occlusion, leaving Stella in charge of Kerouac's estate. Sterling Lord tells Stella he sees growing interest in Kerouac and his work, though she is reluctant to publish anything new because she believes his publications manifestly represent his artistic vision.

1974–1979 The latter half of the 1970s confirms Lord's belief in a Kerouac revival, as evidenced by several biographies and monographs, including *Jack Kerouac: Prophet of the New Romanticism* by Robert Hipkiss (1976); *Jack's Book: An Oral Biography* by Barry Gifford and Lawrence Lee (1978); *Desolate Angel: Jack Kerouac, the Beat Generation, and America* by Dennis McNally (1979); and *On the Road: Text and Criticism* edited by Scott Donaldson (1979). In 1974, Allen Ginsberg and Anne Waldman found the Jack Kerouac School of Disembodied Poetics at Boulder's Naropa Institute.

1980s A reassessment of Kerouac continues, beginning with the Jack Kerouac Conference at Naropa in 1982, attended by Beat writers and scholars who publish important work about Kerouac in subsequent years: Tim Hunt, Ronna C. Johnson, Regina Weinreich, Gerald Nicosia, and many others. In 1985, Stella signs an agreement with Jan Kerouac to apportion income from future copyright renewals of Kerouac's books. In 1988, Lowell unveils the Jack Kerouac Commemorative, and Jack Kerouac Alley is dedicated in San Francisco. Throughout the decade, a series of fan-run publications – *Moody Street Irregulars*, *Kerouac Connection* – contribute to a thriving community of Beat fans and scholars.

1990s Stella Sampas dies in February 1990, distributing Kerouac's estate among her remaining siblings. Her youngest brother, John Sampas, is named estate executor. Largely through Viking Press, and coinciding with a revival of interest in the Beat Generation in the mid-1990s, Kerouac's letters (edited by Charters) and a selection of unpublished manuscripts (*Some of the Dharma, Book of Blues*) are released. At a New York University Conference on the Beat Generation in 1994, Jan Kerouac and biographer Gerald Nicosia announce a lawsuit that alleges Gabrielle Kerouac's will was forged and the Sampas family was selling portions of Kerouac's archive to collectors. After Jan dies of kidney failure in June 1996 – two months before the trial is set to begin – the lawsuit wends through Florida and New Mexico court systems for the rest of the decade as Nicosia, Paul Blake, Jr., and Jan's ex-husband make claims to the estates of Jan and her father. The lawsuit would be eventually resolved in 2009, resulting in clarity over the division of Kerouac's copyright ownership.

2000–present Several unpublished Kerouac works are released throughout the 2000s. Coupled with film and album adaptations of *On the Road* and *Big Sur*, this illustrates Kerouac's continued relevance. (So too does the $2.3 million paid by Jim Irsay, the owner of the Indianapolis Colts, for Kerouac's *On the Road* scroll.) John Sampas dies in 2018. During his tenure as executor, twenty-four Kerouac books are published, more than during Kerouac's lifetime. His nephew, Jim Sampas, becomes the executor of the estate and begins a publishing venture called Sal Paradise Press. The first project is an edited collection of Kerouac's writing atop Desolation Peak in 1956. With a new anthology of unpublished writings slated for 2024, an authorized biography scheduled for 2026, and plans for a feature-length documentary, there's ample evidence that interest in Kerouac remains robust despite contemporary reservations about problematic aspects in his life and work.

Jack Kerouac

New York

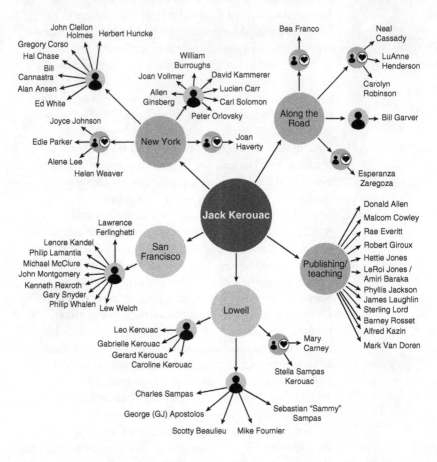

John Clellon Holmes
Herbert Huncke
Gregory Corso
Hal Chase
Bill Cannastra
Alan Ansen
Ed White

William Burroughs
Joan Vollmer
David Kammerer
Allen Ginsberg
Lucien Carr
Carl Solomon
Peter Orlovsky

Joyce Johnson
Edie Parker
Alene Lee
Helen Weaver

Joan Haverty

Along the Road

Bea Franco

Neal Cassady
LuAnne Henderson
Carolyn Robinson

Bill Garver

Esperanza Zaregoza

San Francisco

Lawrence Ferlinghetti
Lenore Kandel
Philip Lamantia
Michael McClure
John Montgomery
Kenneth Rexroth
Gary Snyder
Philip Whalen
Lew Welch

Publishing/ teaching

Donald Allen
Malcom Cowley
Rae Everitt
Robert Giroux
Hettie Jones
LeRoi Jones / Amiri Baraka
Phyllis Jackson
James Laughlin
Sterling Lord
Barney Rosset
Alfred Kazin
Mark Van Doren

Lowell

Leo Kerouac
Gabrielle Kerouac
Gerard Kerouac
Caroline Kerouac

Mary Carney
Stella Sampas Kerouac

Charles Sampas
George (GJ) Apostolos
Scotty Beaulieu
Mike Fournier
Sebastian "Sammy" Sampas

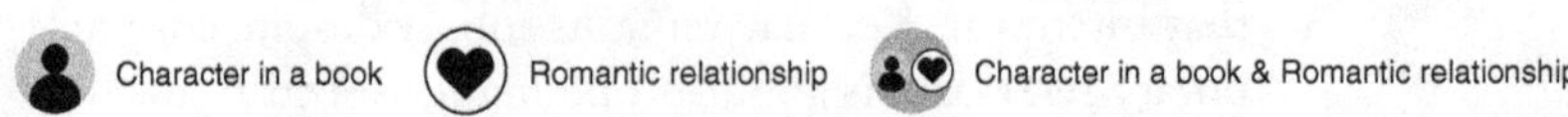

Jack Kerouac Sociogram by Steven Watson

Introduction

Steven Belletto

In 2022, the centenary of Jack Kerouac's birth, the Beat Studies Association marked the occasion with a conference devoted to his work. Gathered at this conference were scholars who had been pioneers in Kerouac studies, including Ann Charters and Dennis McNally, authors of early biographies of him, published in 1973 and 1979, respectively. These scholars were joined by other members of an old guard of Kerouac studies, as well as younger generations of scholars interested in understanding his life and literary legacy in fresh and often surprising ways.[1]

What struck me at the Jack Kerouac Centenary Conference was the energy in Kerouac studies, the real sense, palpable after two days of presentations and conversation, that there is much new to discover and appreciate about his work, even a hundred years after his birth and some fifty-three years after his death. Ann Charters, who had first met Kerouac in 1966, delivered the keynote address, about the shape of Kerouac's lifelong literary project, the Duluoz Legend, a multivolume portrait of his life and times named for his fictional alter ego, Jack Duluoz. Even today, casual readers may not realize that Kerouac intended various of his individual works to comprise "one vast book"; as he wrote in a headnote to *Visions of Cody*: "*On the Road, The Subterraneans, The Dharma Bums, Doctor Sax, Maggie Cassidy, Tristessa, Desolation Angels* and the others are just chapters in the whole work which I call *The Duluoz Legend.*" While in this instance Kerouac identified some particular books as forming "chapters" of the Duluoz Legend, as Charters observed in her keynote, he never made a definitive list of what was or was not to be considered part of the Legend, leaving a puzzle for fans and scholars alike. As someone who had been studying Kerouac for over sixty years, Charters naturally had some ideas about which of his works ought to be included as chapters in his "vast book," and yet the way her presentation proceeded was remarkable, at least to me. She explained in patient detail her latest thinking on the question, but then disclosed that her sense of the Legend was protean, that it never seemed finished, and she invited the audience of fellow Kerouac experts into a discussion. The spirited exchange that ensued indicated the degree to which Kerouac is a living author, by which I mean his work still retains its capacity to surprise and delight, to open up big, relevant questions – and, depending on the contexts one cares about or the formal or theoretical aspects one emphasizes – his life's work, the Duluoz Legend, can take on differing shapes, organically expanding or contracting.

I mention this anecdote because it speaks to the way that Kerouac's work is constantly changing and evolving – even after his death – because of the insights of readers and the efforts of researchers, who on the scholarly side build on existing theories, unearth archival discoveries, and address newly published work by Kerouac himself. In fact, just that same year as the conference, 2022, a new Kerouac book appeared: *Desolation Peak: Collected Writings*, edited by Charles Shuttlesworth. This book was published by Sal Paradise Press, which had recently been launched by Sylvia Cunha and Jim Sampas, Kerouac's nephew and current literary executor of the Jack Kerouac Estate. *Desolation Peak* contains previously unpublished writing by Kerouac, including detailed journals he kept while a fire lookout on Desolation Peak in the summer of 1956 (an experience he wrote about in *Desolation Angels*), but also stories, fragments of novels, poems, and even a transliteration of the Buddhist sutra "The Diamondcutter of Perfect Knowing." Certainly this material could change how we understand *Desolation Angels*, Kerouac's knowledge of Buddhism, the development of some of his other work, and indeed his state of mind in that crucial year of 1956 – but it could also perhaps change how we see the Duluoz Legend itself. For Kerouac aficionados, newly published primary material cannot help but to alter or enrich what we previously knew about him and his work, and the appearance of *Desolation Peak* invited even Ann Charters to reassess her ideas. The piece she wrote for this *Companion*, "Kerouac's Concept of His Duluoz Legend," forms Chapter 1, and grew from her keynote at the Kerouac Centenary Conference; interested readers can turn to it to discover the fullest expression of her latest thinking on the Duluoz Legend.

After this opening chapter, in Chapter 2, "Kerouac and the Profession of Authorship," Matt Theado explains how Kerouac broke into the publishing world with his first novel, *The Town and the City*. Offering a supplement to earlier accounts that emphasized how Kerouac's uncompromising artistic vision often put him at odds with the publishing industry, Theado shows how he was also interested in "commercial success," and that he was "an engaged, determined, and often savvy negotiator in the literary marketplace." Kerouac's eye on the literary marketplace notwithstanding, his artistic vision was resolute, informed by his deep reading in a range of literary, philosophical, and religious traditions. Nancy M. Grace had explored this vision in her book *Jack Kerouac and the Literary Imagination* (2007), and in Chapter 3, "Truth in Confession: The Foundation of Kerouac's Literary Experiment," she extends this work by showing how Kerouac drew on his eclectic reading "to seek and speak the truth." For Kerouac, truth-telling was often connected to Catholic notions of confession, and as Grace argues, "Kerouac consistently worked truth and confession together … twinning and twining them as he grappled with his spiritual and bodily identity as an American writer living in two conflicting Americas."

Chapter 4, Tim Hunt's "The Textuality of Performance: Kerouac's Spontaneous Prose," builds on his groundbreaking books *Kerouac's Crooked Road: The Development of a Fiction* (1981) and *The Textuality of Soulwork: Jack Kerouac's Quest for Spontaneous Prose* (2014), showing that Kerouac's signature innovation, Spontaneous Prose, transforms "writing from a medium for composing into a medium for performing." As Hunt argues, Spontaneous Prose recast "the mechanism of writing, the textuality of writing, by altering how alphabetic characters relate to sound and, thereby, altering how time and timing function within writing." Hunt's chapter accordingly offers new theories for appreciating Kerouac's complex – and often misunderstood – development of Spontaneous Prose. In this vein, Chapter 5, "The Spontaneous Aesthetic in *The Subterraneans*," by George Mouratidis, takes a deep dive into *The Subterraneans*, a novel Kerouac wrote over three days using the principles of Spontaneous Prose. Through a detailed reading of *The Subterraneans*, Mouratidis agrees with Hunt about the importance of this method to both Kerouac's vision and to twentieth-century letters, arguing that "with *The Subterraneans*, Kerouac let loose a hybridizing narrative form whose radical compositional and organizational logic demanded a reappraisal of the form and function of the narrative American novel in the mid-twentieth century."

Chapter 6, "Kerouac and the 1950s," by Douglas Field, adopts a wider-angle approach, examining the cultural and political contexts of a decade when Kerouac produced some of his most important work, including his most well-known novel, *On the Road*, but also *The Dharma Bums*, *The Subterraneans*, *Mexico City Blues*, *Visions of Gerard*, *Tristessa*, *Maggie Cassidy*, *Doctor Sax*, and *Visions of Cody*, among others. Sketching key cultural and political contexts largely cohering around the Cold War, Field shows how "Kerouac emerges in this period as both rebellious and at times conservative, as variously delinquent, but also patriotic." Kerouac's bona fides as a "rebellious" or countercultural writer are teased out in Chapter 7, "The Impact of *On the Road* on the 1960s Counterculture," by Kurt Hemmer. This chapter augments more familiar accounts of that novel as the paradigmatic "road" text of the 1950s – which it surely was – to investigate instead its profound and lingering effects on the 1960s counterculture, which married a rock ethos with an ethos borrowed from *On the Road*. An astute cultural chronicler, Hemmer uses *On the Road* to untie the knotty question of how the 1950s became the 1960s, an argument that likewise illustrates Kerouac's ongoing historical and cultural importance.

Chapter 8, "*Vanity of Duluoz* and the 1960s," by David Stephen Calonne, concentrates on Kerouac's last major novel, *Vanity of Duluoz*, a retrospective look at the period in his life from 1935–46 in the context of the 1960s, a tumultuous decade that seemed to have passed him by. As Calonne shows, *Vanity of Duluoz* "powerfully documents Kerouac's struggle with reconciling his traditional, 'conservative' upbringing with the nascent 'Beat' rebellious energies – born in the forties and continuing into the sixties." My own chapter, "Late Kerouac, or the Conflicted 'King of the Beatniks,'" continues the exploration of Kerouac's last decade by examining a cluster of "late works": *Big Sur*, *Desolation Angels*, *Satori in Paris*, and briefly, *Vanity of Duluoz*, to show how Kerouac's unwanted fame as a "spokesman" for his generation impacted his writing and worldview.

As most devoted readers of Kerouac are aware, despite the enduring popularity and cultural impact of *On the Road*, Kerouac was dissatisfied with the results, finding it still too conventional and not illustrative enough of his ideas regarding what modern prose should do or be. He therefore began to revise the material into a new book, eventually titled *Visions of Cody*, a far more formally complex novel that many observers see as his masterpiece. In Chapter 10, "*Visions of Cody* as Metafiction," Michael Hrebeniak explains in detail why *Visions of Cody* is the most "far-reaching" example of Kerouac's experimental form: "A compendium of nonlinear forms in the encyclopedic tradition of *Moby-Dick*, *Visions of Cody* comprises a synthesis of Kerouac's most far-reaching ideas over two decades of experimentation and, as such, is the key to understanding the radicalism of the Duluoz Legend." Erik Mortenson likewise analyzes Kerouac's more experimental work in Chapter 11, "Making the Past Present: Kerouac and Memory." That chapter focuses largely on Kerouac's strange, thrilling, unclassifiable novel of his Lowell childhood, *Doctor Sax*. The young Jack Kerouac was nicknamed "Memory Babe" for his prodigious powers of recall, and Mortenson plunges into the function of memory in his work, arguing that

"Kerouac's writing strives for nothing less than to create an experience of the past event in the present moment." Moving from fiction to poetry, in Chapter 12, "Spun Rhythms: Jack Kerouac as Poet," Regina Weinreich turns our attention to Kerouac's formal experimentations in poetry, focusing on two very different strains of this work: the jazz-inspired "choruses" found in his book-length volume of poetry, *Mexico City Blues*, and his efforts to develop an American form of haiku, found in *Book of Haikus* and elsewhere. Ultimately, Weinreich shows, Kerouac was a significant poetic innovator, and her chapter should encourage more scholarship on his work in that genre.

The *Companion*'s final six chapters look at some key issues in Kerouac's work and propose new contexts for understanding his writing. Ronna C. Johnson has spent her career working on both Kerouac and the women writers of the Beat movement, and in Chapter 13, "Kerouac's Representations of Women," she reckons with the fact that a consequential writer she admires can still often read as "sexist, misogynist, essentialist, racist." "The two assessments," she writes, "remain in unresolvable opposition," and her chapter moves across a range of Kerouac's work in the conviction that "there is no twentieth century writer of his measure, although his writing can disappoint and alienate." In Chapter 14, "Kerouac and Blackness," Amor Kohli is less sure of Kerouac's measure, marred as it was by problems in his engagement with Blackness. This chapter begins with the observation that Kerouac had been long fascinated by Blackness and certain modes of Black cultural production (namely bop) and is critical of Kerouac because "his often superficial readings ignore the reality of Black constraint, subsequently rendering Black life discrepant with the lived experience of Blackness in America. Problematically, his longing is ultimately predicated on Black silence and evasion of Black interiority." Far from being hagiographic or even celebratory, these chapters invite readers to contemplate a nexus of gendered and racialized social and cultural questions that suffuse Kerouac's work.

This is likewise the case in Chapter 15, "Kerouac, Multilingualism, and Global Culture," in which Hassan Melehy extends the important and pioneering work in his book *Kerouac: Language, Poetics, and Territory* (2016). For Melehy, understanding Kerouac means recognizing his "situation as a multilingual migrant of peasant heritage, displaced from the national metropole of France and the drifting colony of Québec by the global shifts of empire." Melehy shows not only how Kerouac aimed to "bring foreignness into his English prose by mixing it with his native language," but also how he "extends his explorations to the many languages and peoples of

North America and points to more remote geographies," resulting in "an appeal to a global literature that might not yet have existed in his time, that may still not yet exist, no less than a call to recognize and galvanize global culture."

Another aspect of global culture running through much of Kerouac's work is Buddhist scripture and philosophy, with which he engaged in varying degrees of depth throughout his life. In works such as *The Scripture of the Golden Eternity*, *Some of the Dharma*, *Wake Up: A Life of the Buddha*, *The Dharma Bums*, and *Mexico City Blues*, among others, Kerouac wrestled with Buddhist ideas; moving beyond even these published works, in Chapter 16, "The Two Phases of Jack Kerouac's American Buddhism," Sarah F. Haynes relies on over one hundred hours in the Kerouac archives to argue that his "Buddhist period should be separated into an Early Buddhist Period (1953–58) and a Later Buddhist Period (1959–mid-1960s)," revealing that Kerouac's "engagement with the religion was far longer than what has previously been delineated." Taking up some of the same texts as Chapter 16, in Chapter 17, "Jack Kerouac's Ambivalences as an Environmental Writer," Franca Bellarsi shows how the often "unorthodox East-West syncretism" found in these texts result also in particular kinds of ecological concerns. Bellarsi takes readers through Kerouac's complicated, "ambivalent" relationship with the natural environment, arguing that, following his Buddhist studies, "the embeddedness of the human mind in the nonhuman *combined with* a serene acceptance of the latter's elusiveness actually constitutes one of Kerouac's important, if paradoxical, contributions to an understanding of the web of environmental continuities." But she also notes how in several of his works, a darker fear of the natural is in evidence, and the chapter sketches these strains in his work.

Finally, a bookend to Chapter 1, in Chapter 18, "The Essentials of Archival Prose," Jean-Christophe Cloutier explores what we might call the archival era in Kerouac studies, perhaps inaugurated when Ann Charters published the first bibliography of Kerouac's work in 1967. Cloutier notes that Kerouac was meticulous about archiving his own work, and observes that in terms of sheer volume, the Jack Kerouac Papers now housed at the New York Public Library's Berg Collection stand "as one of the most imposing sets of literary papers of the twentieth century." Playfully revising the title of one of Kerouac's signature short pieces, "Essentials of Spontaneous Prose," Cloutier argues that "Kerouac's oeuvre must be reassessed as a unique case of the literary deployment of the archival," and explores a shared goal of Spontaneous Prose and Kerouac's archival impulses, "to record and preserve all experience for posterity." As Cloutier ultimately shows, "approaching Kerouac via the archive" changes our understanding of some of his most important books, and so his chapter presents another exciting development in Kerouac studies.

Taken together, the chapters in *The Cambridge Companion to Jack Kerouac* are a feast of critical engagements with the writer and his work, moving from wide-angled overviews to close textual analysis to theoretical frameworks that can help us understand his place in literary and cultural history by new lights. My hope is that this book will be of use to scholars, students, and fans alike, that those new to Kerouac will find rewarding avenues for further exploration, and old hands might discover a tidbit or two that they hadn't considered, perhaps seeing pieces of his work in fresh ways.

Hic calix!

Note

1. The conference program is available here: beatstudies.org/wp-content/uploads/Final-Kerouac-Conference-Program.pdf.

CHAPTER 1

Kerouac's Concept of His Duluoz Legend

Ann Charters

By the end of 1957, after the controversy stirred up by the publication of his best-known work, *On the Road*, Jack Kerouac had become a legend in his own lifetime as "the King of the Beats." In public he accepted his title. In private he had his own ideas about how he could achieve his cherished ambition of attaining the enduring literary status of his idols Marcel Proust, James Joyce, and William Faulkner. It was not obvious to the cultural gatekeepers of his time that this prize was within Kerouac's reach. As Joseph Lelyveld wrote in his *New York Times* obituary on October 22, 1969, Kerouac's "admirers regarded him as a major literary innovator and something of a religious seer, but this estimate of his achievement never gained wide acceptance among literary tastemakers." Lelyveld went on to note that Kerouac "painstakingly" documented the details of his life in his long series of autobiographical works, "which he intended to be read, ultimately, in sequence as one long novel."[1]

Kerouac's obituary made only a slight nod ("one long novel") toward his plan of creating what he called his Duluoz Legend. Why should we care that Kerouac's books – his "true-story" novels and dreams, his Buddhist studies and meditations – aren't read in sequence, the chronological order he intended, as chapters of his Legend? For starters, reading Kerouac's individual books in the context of the Duluoz Legend helps us to understand him better as an artist. It emphasizes the spiritual dimension in his writing, the deep feelings aroused by his exploration of his consciousness. It also allows us to appreciate the cultural significance of his work, his long struggle with language as the French-speaking child of French-Canadian immigrants, trying to find his own voice as an American writer. Reading his books in sequence deepens our pleasure at hearing Kerouac's unique voice on the page.

Sometimes Kerouac's grandiose plans for his Legend seem inconsistent or unclear, as when he wrote that "the Duluoz Legend [is] a river of writing unto the end, in which all tributary materials flow, unite, and go out."[2]

I confess that I'm not sure of all the titles that he considered to be part of his Legend. In 1963 he told an interviewer that it consisted of his novels, but in the previous decade he wrote in *Some of the Dharma* that this book was a section of his Duluoz Legend whose aim was "to penetrate into the mystery/myself without relying even on Buddha/or Jesus Christ."[3] To a certain extent, the total production of all writers becomes the way we think of them and their "legend" or career. Now that Kerouac's vast archive of manuscripts at the Berg Collection in the New York Public Library has become available to scholars, I'll try to clear away some of the mist around his concept of his Duluoz Legend.

Why is it that more of his readers are not aware that Kerouac intended his books to be read in a chronological sequence, depicting his life as a legend? The usual explanation is that Kerouac died of alcoholism at the age of forty-seven, before he had time to persuade his various publishers to change the different fictional names of the characters in his novels to their real names and publish them as a new series with photographic covers. These characters were modeled on actual people in Kerouac's life, such as Neal Cassady, named "Dean Moriarty" in *On the Road* and "Cody Pomeray" in *The Dharma Bums* (1958), *Big Sur* (1962), and *Desolation Angels* (1965).

In 1957 the publisher of *On the Road* insisted on using pseudonyms for the characters in the book to keep them from suing Kerouac. Kerouac gave himself the name "Sal Paradise."[4] When the other novels comprising the Duluoz Legend appeared over the years under the imprint of various publishers, he gave himself different names, adding to the confusion. These names included "Ray Smith" in *The Dharma Bums* (1958), "Leo Percepied" in *The Subterraneans* (1958), and "Jack Duluoz" in *Big Sur* (1963), *Desolation Angels* (1965), and *Vanity of Duluoz* (1968). Most readers encountering the different names didn't realize that Kerouac intended the novels to be read in sequence as chapters in his Duluoz Legend – as he wrote in the headnote to *Visions of Cody*, "In my old age I intend to collect all my work and reinsert my pantheon of uniform names."[5] Of course, he never made it to old age.

Kerouac chose the name of "Duluoz" for himself years before he conceived of writing the legend of his own life. He invented it as a teenager in 1941 after he dropped out of Columbia University to live at home in Lowell, Massachusetts, and work at the local newspaper while waiting to apply to the Navy College Training Program. Years later, in *Satori in Paris* (1966), he acknowledged that Duluoz "was a variation I invented for fun in my writerly youth (to use as my name in my novels)." He claimed that he based the name "Duluoz" on the "old Breton name Daoulas," to honor his French-Canadian ancestor who had left his noble family in Brittany when he emigrated to Québec in the New World nearly 200 years before Kerouac's birth.[6]

The real problem isn't with his fictional name Duluoz, though it is part of the confusion. His readers usually aren't aware of his larger intent to leave a record of his consciousness during his entire lifetime. Most of Kerouac's novels are read out of chronological order, perhaps because they weren't originally published that way. The majority of his readers start with his most famous books, *On the Road* or *The Dharma Bums*, rather than with the first novel that depicts the earliest chronological period of his life, *Visions of Gerard* (1963). Students interested in different aspects of Kerouac's life and work as an experimental writer often read the novels in order of their composition or their publication date. The various books can also be grouped according to their subject matter, as, for example, his Lowell novels or his "Road novels." That's how they are currently being merchandized in recent editions by the Library of America.[7]

Perhaps the most formidable barrier to the recognition of Kerouac's larger intent is that he didn't sufficiently clarify his intentions. He made countless references to his Legend, but he was vague about exactly which of his books belonged in the series. Although he meticulously organized his papers, journals, and manuscripts at home, at the end of his life he never drew up a definitive list of the titles he considered to be the different chapters in his Legend or even explained why he chose to name it the "Duluoz Legend" instead of, say, the "Kerouac Legend." Despite such ambiguity on Kerouac's part, we can begin to clarify the shape and substance of the Duluoz Legend by beginning to investigate its origins.

1.1 The Origins of the Duluoz Legend

When did Kerouac begin to think of creating his Duluoz Legend? In *Vanity of Duluoz* (1968), the last book published in his lifetime, he wrote that he first "devised the idea of 'The Duluoz Legend'" in Liverpool in 1944.[8] The concept evolved gradually over the next dozen years. It came into sharper focus in August 1951, during his treatment for thrombosis at the Kingsbridge Veterans Hospital in New York, after he'd written the scroll manuscript of *On the Road* and two months before he discovered sketching. More than a decade later he wrote his friend Hugo Weber that his stay in the hospital in 1951 was actually the turning point in his system of narrative art.[9]

In the hospital Kerouac read Herman Melville's novel *Pierre*, republished in 1949 by Hendricks House with an introduction by psychoanalyst Harry A. Murray. Kerouac was impressed by Murray's description of Melville's book as a depiction of his own self-image. He underlined the sentence "Melville was not writing autobiography in the usual sense, but from first to last, the biography of his self-image." Murray stated that Melville did not portray the characters in his novel objectively but rather presented their effect on "the hero's spiritual development."[10]

In 1951 Kerouac was so struck by the thought of an autobiographical novel projecting a spiritual self-image, rather than attempting a realistic self-portrait, that he made this idea his goal in creating the various books in the Duluoz Legend. On June 5, 1952, he wrote John Clellon Holmes, "Someday I'm going to write a huge Dostoevskyan novel about all of us .... What I am beginning to discover now is something beyond the novel."[11]

Six months later, on December 9, 1952, a specific reference to the Duluoz Legend appeared in a letter written in Mexico City to Holmes, when Kerouac told his friend, "Will keep you posted on the legend of Duluoz's life ... So that further books can be dense spates from this Duluoz World, such as *Dr Sax* already is, & *Road of Neal* visions" (*Selected Letters 1*, 388). This letter suggests that in the year after Kerouac's stay in the hospital, he gave considerable thought to creating books that would embellish his "self-image" in the Duluoz chronology. By the end of 1953 he had written two more novels – *Maggie Cassidy* and *The Subterraneans* – that he considered chapters of his Legend. On April 19, 1954, he began to write a story he titled "The Heart of the World: The Legend of Duluoz," about his earliest memories of his family in Lowell.[12]

Kerouac never abandoned his project of trying to create a complete record of his life. In his book *Some of the Dharma* (1997), we can trace the development of this idea in 1953–1956, the three years in which he thought most intensely about his Legend, culminating during the summer of 1956 in his two months of isolation on Desolation Peak. *Some of the Dharma* had its origins in October 1953, when, at the age of thirty-one, Kerouac embarked upon his study of Buddhism. Earlier that year, Allen Ginsberg had also begun reading about Buddhism in the New York Public Library, resulting in his poem "Sakyumuni Coming Out from the Mountain," but he hadn't substantively responded to most of the Buddhist texts he had encountered.[13] Kerouac began keeping notes about his reading in the first of the ten spiral notebooks that became the text of *Some of the Dharma*, intending them as a guide for Ginsberg, to whom he dedicated this work. He numbered his notebooks chronologically into ten chapters he called books. The first page of the "Book One" notebook begins with the "FOUR NOBLE TRUTHS" and "Eightfold Path," but by the third page he was already interspersing his own poems among his reading notes.

By Book Three, begun after moving with his mother back to his sister's home in North Carolina, Kerouac was often using his notebook to jot down his private thoughts (in both the third and the first person) as well as his reading notes. On October 8, 1954, he wrote, "If it had been ancient India, this 20th Century America in which Jean-Louis finds himself, I would have cut my hair a long time ago and put on the robe and gone with the begging bowl in the Eightfold Path" (*Some of the Dharma*, 138). Several days later he vowed to "make the 30-Volume DULUOZ LEGEND the greatest writing in America ever, on coffee, food, walks, faith" (*Some of the Dharma*, 139).

After the Second World War, many ambitious authors in the United States were obsessed with creating what was called "the Great American Novel," perhaps inspired by their awareness that the United States had become a world power. The idea of creating "the Great American novel" was a natural ambition of young writers coming after the Lost Generation, who longed to equal or surpass the achievements of the previous generation of novelists such as William Faulkner, Ernest Hemingway, and F. Scott Fitzgerald. In *Some of the Dharma,* Kerouac scoffed at himself for harboring his generation's lofty ambition despite his lowly French-Canadian background: "Who is this big writer Jean-Louis but a victim of his own imagination" (*Some of the Dharma*, 139).

Kerouac's route toward immortality as a great American writer was creating something beyond the novel in the various books that he envisioned as the chapters of his Duluoz Legend. As he wrote in *Some of the Dharma*, "I write the Duluoz Legend because of pride in my artistic stature, vanity in my name, & greed to lose nothing of my success-potential – As to deluding myself that the Duluoz Legend will be good for the world, it will only be additional blind detail" (*Some of the Dharma*, 145). A few pages later he concluded this third notebook by writing down for the second time the Eightfold Path, perhaps as a way reminding himself of his commitment to his Buddhist studies.

By Book Four, Kerouac had moved with his mother back to Richmond Hill, New York, where she found another job at a shoe factory. There he spent hours in his room retyping his already retyped novel *On the Road*, on the advice of his literary agent Sterling Lord, who sent the manuscript to Knopf. When it was rejected, Kerouac briefly gave up on the Duluoz Legend. He and his mother went back to North Carolina, where with bitterness he wrote in his notebook that he had learned two things: "1, there's no need to write like Proust / 2, No need to remember Lowell & the Duluoz Legend" (*Some of the Dharma*, 172). On December 19, 1954, he felt at the "lowest, beatest" point in his life (*Some of the Dharma*, 185).

On February 24, 1955, after starting Book Six, Kerouac somehow regained his confidence, although in the process he may have come close to suicide. In any case, within a month he felt a new commitment to the Duluoz Legend. "I wanta write the biggest book in the world," he declared (*Some of the Dharma*, 266). He had come to the realization that "No matter how sharp my visions of Neal or Proust or Baudelaire or Burroughs and no matter how wildly put down, it [Kerouac's work] will never be anything [without a spiritual component] but decay at some time or other" (*Some of the Dharma*, 278).

Kerouac told himself that discovering his method of Spontaneous Prose wasn't enough to achieve immortality; his practice of Buddhism would bring the necessary quality of spirituality to his writing. On May 23, 1955, he wrote in Book Seven, "I made my final writing decision – to write the Duluoz Legend like the Book of Dreams, either fresh or high, off selected tics belonging to chronological narrative sections.... First fruit of this decision, was TRISTESSA (Mexico City, August 1955)" (*Some of the Dharma*, 318). A few pages later in his notebook, he wrote down eight titles that comprised the Legend during the years 1922 to 1955. The first and the last books on his list were still unwritten (*Some of the Dharma*, 321):

SECTIONS OF THE DULUOZ LEGEND ALREADY WRITTEN *(Revised up to February 1956 ... ed. note)*

Time covered	Book
1922–1926	VISIONS OF GERARD
1932–1936	VISIONS OF DOCTOR SAX
1939	VISIONS OF MARY
1947–1950	VISIONS OF THE ROAD (Sal Paradise is Jack Duluoz, Dean Moriarty is Neal Pomeray) etc.
1947–1950	VISIONS OF NEAL
1952–1956	VISIONS OF OCTOBER IN THE RAILROAD EARTH (in progress)
1953	VISIONS OF THE SUBTERRANEANS
1955	VISIONS OF TRISTESSA

Thanks to his study of Buddhism, Kerouac had finally focused his ideas about how he could present the Legend of his life most coherently.

In Mexico during the summer of 1955, Kerouac wrote the first part of the new book he was calling "Visions of Tristessa." He also sent ecstatic letters to his friends and to the editor Malcolm Cowley, who had arranged for the grant that paid for his trip. Cowley was also reading the typescript of *On the Road*, still unpublished. On September 11, 1955, Kerouac was feeling so expansive that he went on to Cowley for two pages developing his comparison of his method of Spontaneous Prose to the sound of a jazz musician and the wisdom of a Buddhist sutra (*Selected Letters 1*, 514).

In the same letter, Kerouac explained that he was planning two other novels, one about the railroad and the other about the death of his brother, covering the first four years of the life of the character Duluoz in the Duluoz Legend. He told Cowley that currently the Legend included several volumes, but he was planning to write many more novels that would cover his entire lifetime, "like Proust, but done on the run, a Running Proust." He believed that "Everything from now on belongs to the *Duluoz Legend*" (*Selected Letters 1*, 515). Describing his work on his Legend as creating a "whole Cathedral of Form," Kerouac knew his writing was holy and "a well done thing" (*Selected Letters 1*, 515).

In Book Eight of *Some of the Dharma*, Kerouac left Mexico and made his way to Ginsberg's Berkeley cottage (*Some of the Dharma*, 338). In *The Dharma Bums*, he described his serendipitous meeting and adventures with two young students of Buddhism, the poets Gary Snyder and Philip Whalen, in Berkeley. Ginsberg was still an unbeliever. Two months later, in December 1955, after quarreling with his old friend over Buddhism, Kerouac moved out of the Berkeley cottage into a skid-row hotel in San Francisco, where he stayed until he took a train down to San Jose to live with Carolyn and Neal Cassady.

In Book Eight Jack and Neal weren't getting along, but Kerouac recorded his pleasure talking to the Cassady children. While spending time with them, he jotted down their words in his eighth notebook, for example, that God was Pooh Bear, a phrase he later quoted when he revised the ending of *On the Road*. He also began to plan *Visions of Gerard*, the earliest book in the Legend about his childhood. Just before he left the Cassady family to spend Christmas with his own family in North Carolina, he declared wryly in his notebook after being in the stimulating company of his writer friends for months in California, "MY FEAR WAS I'D NOT BE A BUDDHA THIS LIFETIME … I'll be a writer" (*Some of the Dharma*, 360).

He used his eighth notebook to write a long description of what he titled "EDITORIAL EXPLANATION OF VARIOUS TECHNIQUES

OF THE DULUOZ LEGEND," two pages of definitions and examples of the terms he invented to describe his new forms of writing. These included TIC, BLUES, MOVIE (formerly "bookmovie"), VISION, ROUTINE, and DHARMA – "Notes in any form about the Dharma. BOOK OF DHARMAS" (*Some of the Dharma*, 342). Since he considered these various techniques of the Duluoz Legend, he now felt that his book of dreams and his series of notebooks comprising his book of dharmas also belonged along with his novels as chapters in his Legend.

Kerouac began Book Nine in a new notebook with a long poem written on December 15, 1955, about trying to camp out overnight in Riverside, California (*Some of the Dharma*, 363). He hitchhiked to Rocky Mount by December 21, where he wrote his book about his brother Gerard on his sister's kitchen table in twelve nights with the help of Mexican Benzedrine. He completed his manuscript on January 16, 1956 (*Some of the Dharma*, 380). Kerouac's descriptions of his writing about Gerard are some of the most riveting pages in *Some of the Dharma*. Not only was the new book about the death of his cherished older brother, the major event of his childhood, but he also considered *Visions of Gerard* as the first chapter of his Legend, believing that it would set the spiritual tone for the "Cathedral of Form" created by all the volumes in his series.

Kerouac started his Book Ten notebook on February 17, 1956, a month after he completed *Gerard* and shortly before he began his trip back to the West Coast to work a summer job as a fire lookout in the Cascade Mountains in Washington state. In *Some of the Dharma*, this notebook seems incomplete, since it concludes abruptly on March 15, 1956, with Kerouac's comment in North Carolina, "All this BOOK OF DHARMAS since December 1953, hasnt it been mighty preparations for the Epic Novel THE TATHAGATA?" Three words follow in black ink – the word "NO" (underlined twice) and the two words "(next page):--" followed by a graceful line drawing in black ink of a flying dove (*Some of the Dharma*, 420). This is the last journal entry Kerouac included in the book he later typed up as *Some of the Dharma*.

Two weeks later, Kerouac's actual hymn of praise to "One that is what is, the golden eternity, or God, or, Tathagata – the name [of the Buddha]" found its form in California as *The Scripture of the Golden Eternity*. Kerouac began writing it in another, smaller, notebook on April 1, 1956, while living with Gary Snyder in Mill Valley.[14] With characteristic humor, he titled it a "scripture," like the sacred writings of the Bible, instead of a "sutra," a dialogue between the Buddha and his disciples. It summed up, in critic Eric Mottram's words, what Kerouac learned from Buddhism: "a joyful modesty as the condition of living in the universe without a restless urge to conquest, moral dogmatism and hierarchy."[15]

On June 18, 1956, before settling into his solitary life in a firewatcher's cabin on Desolation Peak, Kerouac began an eleventh notebook, his last Dharma notebook. He titled it "Desolation Journal," and it was published posthumously in *Desolation Peak* (2022). During his two months on the mountain, he thought obsessively about his Legend, unsure whether to continue writing spontaneous prose. Finally, during the first days of September, he convinced himself that his Legend "is illimitable, as it can go anywhere & do anything" (*Desolation Peak*, 117), because "From the point of view of Duluoz, everything marches forth in a pristine universe of literature" (*Desolation Peak*, 118).

Kerouac's letters continued to document his preoccupation with his lifelong literary project. On March 6, 1956, while still in North Carolina, he sent Whalen the titles of the unpublished novels in his Legend (*Selected Letters 1*, 565). He might have quarreled with Ginsberg about Buddhism, but their friendship had survived. In the summer of 1956, Ginsberg listed Kerouac's name and eleven unpublished books on the dedication page of *Howl*, soon to be published by City Lights. Ginsberg introduced him as the unrecognized genius who had "spit forth intelligence into eleven books written in half the number of years (1951–1956)." Though his poet-friend described Kerouac as a "new Buddha of American prose," Ginsberg's dedication didn't mention the Duluoz Legend.

Another lost opportunity for readers to learn about Kerouac's larger ambition for his writing occurred in early 1957, a few months after he signed a contract with the Viking Press for *On the Road.* On February 4, 1957, when he learned that Cowley planned to write an introduction to the book, he asked Cowley to include the information that as a "recording angel," he wrote his books with "a necessarily birds-eye personal-view of a legend, which is the DULUOZ LEGEND, to which all the books belong except first novel naturalistic fictional Town & City. 'Duluoz' is Kerouac, as you know, but might note."[16] After Cowley received this letter, he dropped his plan for an introduction.

It wasn't until 1959 that Kerouac was able for the first time to clarify for his readers what he was trying to achieve. After the success of *On the Road,* New Directions agreed to publish 120 pages of excerpts from *Visions of Cody,* and Kerouac wrote a special preface to this edition. This was where I learned for the first time about his larger literary ambition. There he explained that "My work comprises one vast book like Proust's *Remembrance of Things Past* except that my remembrances are written on the run instead of afterwards in a sick bed. Because of the objections of my early publishers I was not allowed to use the same personae names in each work" (*Visions of Cody*, np). As the critic Seymour Krim later understood, the reference to Proust's writing seemed "very much an afterthought with Kerouac rather than a plan that had been strategically worked out from the start."[17] As far as Kerouac was concerned, "The whole thing forms one enormous comedy, seen through the eyes of poor Ti Jean (me), otherwise known as Jack Duluoz, the world of raging action and folly and also of gentle sweetness seen through the keyhole of his eye" (*Visions of Cody*, np). This preface was important enough to Kerouac that it also appeared in *Big Sur* (1962) and was used nearly forty years later by his editors to introduce *Some of the Dharma* (1997).

Ironically, though by 1959 Kerouac had concluded his study of Buddhism, the publication of *The Dharma Bums* in October 1958 introduced millions of readers to Buddhism. On February 23, 1959, he complained to Snyder that "you've been silent and disappointed about me. I dont think the book was as bad as you think … you'll look back and appreciate the job I did on 'you' and on Dharma Bumism" (*Selected Letters 2*, 186). Snyder replied on March 10, 1959, "I told you I liked it, but that doesn't make it right. What concerns me is *your* mind.… Do you think you understand [Buddhism]?" Snyder thought that because Kerouac had put down women and sex in that novel, he was headed to "hell, where they pull out the writer's tongue with red hot pliers" (*Selected Letters 2*, 185).

Kerouac's life changed with the brief bestseller success of *On the* Road and the publication of *The Dharma Bums.* Though he no longer studied Buddhism, he never lost his ambition to continue writing books that filled the gaps in his life's story. In September 1960 he wrote Lawrence Ferlinghetti, whose City Lights Books was publishing his *Book of Dreams*, that it was important to include a "Table of Characters" as a way to help his readers link the people described in his three most popular books at that time – *On the Road*, *The Subterraneans*, and *The Dharma Bums* – to *Book of Dreams.*[18]

The poet Robert Creeley was sympathetic to Kerouac's larger intent and wrote a perceptive introduction to the later edition of *Book of Dreams* to explain its connection to the other volumes in the Legend. Creeley understood that as a writer Kerouac "was not working to understand or 'explain' the substance of dreams. Rather, he wanted the dream content, of presence and feeling, of place and its multiple resonances, to join with the narratives he had composed as 'novels,' 'visions' or 'poems.'" He was trying to show "the world to be all that he recognized as its defining experience, all places of mind, and so of dreams." Kerouac, like his friend William Burroughs, felt that he was "only a recording instrument." He wanted "to bear witness, to be in all the places of his life 'the great rememberer,' as Allen Ginsberg called him," and create "the intense and completing expression of a human life" rather than impose an imagined plot on his experience.[19]

In mid-June 1963, John Clellon Holmes sent Kerouac a letter describing his new book of essays, *Nothing More to Declare*, and asking for biographical information about his friend's life. On June 23, 1963, Kerouac replied with a poetic description of his Duluoz Legend. He told Holmes that he thought of creating the individual books the same way that Mozart thought of creating in various musical forms – some works as long as symphonies and others as short as sonatas. On December 8, 1964, Kerouac asked Holmes about the status of *Nothing More to Declare*. He was thinking of writing a new novel, adding "to that long shelf Duluoz Legend, fill in the gap between *Maggie Cassidy* and *On the Road* and don't think for one minute that I feel inferior to James Joyce because my life-work arrangement is in installments [of the Legend] that are eventually going to number in the twenties" (*Selected Letters 2*, 386).

Several months later, on July 21, 1965, Kerouac again wrote to Holmes, who had come up with the idea of creating a "Kerouac Reader." Earlier that month Kerouac had written a new novel, *Satori in Paris*, after his return from a trip to Paris and Brittany. He told Holmes that a reader with "the uniform pantheon names of the Duluoz Legend is the idea I thought would only be broached in my old age, and really brought a kind of tear to my mind's eye when I read your letter" (*Selected Letters 2*, 460).

When I visited Kerouac in 1966, I asked him questions about the creation of his individual books, not his larger ambitions as a writer. Later, in the twenty letters and postcards we exchanged, I questioned him about Proust in two letters as a preliminary to asking him about his Legend. On November 11, 1967, Kerouac wrote me that his "Proustness" was "just the idea of a whole lifetime, in sections coming as separate books, in personal first-person depiction and analysis." His tone became belligerent as he continued with "No analysis in me? What about *Subterraneans*, an analysis of the affair with Mardou more than a narration, after all." Then he growled, "What you call my 'thoughts' and what you call Proust's analysis tho not of the same consistency, are of same cornmeal, after all." On January 4, 1967, as an answer to an earlier question, he sent me a postcard with the words "And yes, Duluoz Legend is open ended."[20]

Earlier, atop Desolation Peak on July 18, 1956, Kerouac had written, "The Legend properly done contains all creation" (*Desolation Peak*, 71).

Here are the titles that comprise my concept of the Duluoz Legend. They include the books Kerouac listed when he wrote to his agent on May 5, 1961. Two unfinished books on that list were part of his chronology, including *Memory Babe* (a book describing his childhood before *Doctor Sax*) and *Visions of Julian* (about Lucien Carr, to be placed before *On the Road*). This letter ended with Kerouac's words "Now, more travel, more adventures, and future 'chapters' of the legend in novel form" (*Selected Letters* 2, 326–327).

1. VISIONS OF GERARD
2. DOCTOR SAX
3. MAGGIE CASSIDY
4. VANITY OF DULUOZ
5. ON THE ROAD [scroll version]
6. VISIONS OF CODY
7. LONESOME TRAVELER
8. THE SUBTERRANEANS [scroll version]
9. SOME OF THE DHARMA
10. TRISTESSA
11. MEXICO CITY BLUES
12. THE DHARMA BUMS [scroll version]
13. THE SCRIPTURE OF THE GOLDEN ETERNITY
14. DESOLATION PEAK
15. DESOLATION ANGELS
16. BOOK OF DREAMS
17. BIG SUR
18. SATORI IN PARIS

Since all readers bring their own concepts of Kerouac when they attempt to understand his Legend, the list of titles, as he wrote me, is "open ended." Someone else might add an early novel written in French to the list; another might include his unfinished novel *Memory Babe*, describing his life in Lowell when he was seven years old. Still other readers might add every manuscript in his literary archives. I'm not even sure that *Some of the Dharma* and *Scripture of the Golden Eternity* should be listed as two different titles, since Kerouac might have considered them to be one complete book – a Totem Press flyer from 1959 announced the fall publication of *Some of the Dharma*, though in 1960 what the Press actually issued was *The Scripture of the Golden Eternity.* In 1956, on Desolation Peak, when Kerouac wrote that "the Duluoz Legend [is] a river of writing," he meant that he considered all of his written words to be part of the Duluoz Legend, "thus uniting my life with my work, my work with my life" (*Desolation Peak*, 93).

Kerouac said it best in 1963 when he told his publisher that the final scope of the Legend would be "a completely written lifetime with all its hundreds of characters and events and levels interswirling and reappearing and becoming complete.... But each section, that is, each novel, has to stand by itself as an individual story.... Nevertheless they must all fit together on one shelf as a continuous tale."[21] The key word here is "tale." Kerouac wasn't writing his literal autobiography, true to fact; he was creating something larger than life, his Legend. His books were what he called "Beautiful lies – (which I'm good at)" (*Desolation Peak*, 117). After he turned his life into literature, he left each of his readers the task of envisioning his Legend in the shape of their own particular "Cathedral of Form." In the future, what development would I like to see for the Duluoz Legend? The titles I've listed here could be published the way Kerouac envisioned them as one long novel in a series of separate chapters placed in chronological order with uniform photographic book jackets. If they appeared this way, the sequence of the various books would be physically recognizable. Kerouac's wish to insert the real names of the people who appear in his published "true-story" novels could be achieved by listing the real versus fictional names before each book, as I did in *The Portable Jack Kerouac*.[22] Using the scroll version of some of his novels, if available, might help readers understand that he altered physical details as well as names for his publishers – *The Subterraneans* took place in New York City, not San Francisco, for example.

When I worked with Kerouac on his bibliography, he surprised me by saying casually – for fun? just to shock me? – that the name "Duluoz" also meant "the Louse." If the Duluoz Legend was intended to be the "biography of his self-image," was Kerouac hinting that Jack Duluoz (Jack the Louse), the name he invented for himself for his lowly status and his lofty ambition, was his self-image?[23] One of the characters in his novel *Vanity of Duluoz* actually calls him "the Louse" (*Desolation Peak*, 215). After his immersion in Buddhism, he was scrupulous about using only his own experiences as the basis for his autofiction. A generation later, this term was defined by Lydia Davis in her essay "The Story is the Thing" as "self-fiction," or "the narration of one's own life, lifted almost unchanged from the reality, selected and judiciously, artfully told."[24] Telling "beautiful lies" about his life, did Kerouac express his wry self-humor in creating his Legend as "one enormous comedy"? (*Selected Letters 2*, 240).

I'm not certain this republication of Kerouac's books would change his current status as an American writer, though it might encourage a broader perspective on his work. Kerouac's ambition, as biographer Joyce Johnson understood, was to capture "a life completely digested in spirit."[25] The enduring popularity of *On the Road* and *The Dharma Bums* attests to his solid literary achievement. His extraordinary life as a writer made Jack Kerouac a legend in his own lifetime, and to date this legend has inspired twenty-five biographies (at last count). If his titles in their matching jackets fail to find a publisher as one long novel, perhaps we should just let Jack Duluoz go his own way. Like Proust, Joyce, and Faulkner, Kerouac is a living presence in world literature, with his Legend secure in our hearts.

Notes

1. Joseph Lelyveld, "Jack Kerouac, Novelist, Dead; Father of the Beat Generation," *New York Times* (October 22, 1969), 47.
2. Jack Kerouac, *Desolation Peak: Collected Writings*, ed. Charles Shuttlesworth (Lowell, MA: Sal Paradise Press, 2022), 93.
3. "An Interview with Jack Kerouac," *Book News from Publicity Department* (New York: Farrar, Straus, and Cudahy, 1963), 1; Jack Kerouac, *Some of the Dharma* (New York: Viking, 1997), 178.
4. Although in this chapter I am focusing on the idea that Kerouac wanted to have a "pantheon of uniform names" throughout the Duluoz Legend, this should not be taken to mean he was simply writing down exactly what had happened in real life. He was writing a fictionalized version of his life, a legend, and many critics have attended to the ways Kerouac distances himself from his narrators as much as he seems close to them; see, for example, Steven Belletto, *The Beats: A Literary History* (New York: Cambridge University Press, 2022); Hassan Melehy, *Kerouac: Language, Poetics, and Territory* (New York: Bloomsbury, 2016); and Nancy M. Grace, *Jack Kerouac and the Literary Imagination* (New York: Palgrave Macmillan, 2007).
5. Jack Kerouac, *Visions of Cody* (New York: Penguin, 1993), np.
6. Jack Kerouac, *Satori in Paris & Pic* (New York: Grove Press, 1985), 89.
7. As in the Library of America volume, *Jack Kerouac: Road Novels 1957–1960*, that gathers *On the Road, The Dharma Bums, The Subterraneans, Tristessa*, and *Lonesome Traveler*.
8. Jack Kerouac, *Vanity of Duluoz* (New York: Penguin, 1994), 190.
9. Kerouac to Hugo Weber, *Selected Letters of Jack Kerouac, 1957–1969*, ed. Ann Charters (New York: Penguin, 1999), 384.
10. Henry A. Murray, "Introduction," in Herman Melville, *Pierre or, The Ambiguities* (New York: Hendricks House, 1962), xxxii.

11. Jack Kerouac, *Kerouac: Selected Letters 1, 1940–1956*, ed. Ann Charters (New York: Penguin, 1995) 449.
12. The thirty-page typescript of this story, still unpublished, is in the Kerouac Archive in the Berg Collection at the New York Public Library, listed as Berg 6.45. I am indebted to the Kerouac scholar Charles Shuttleworth for this information.
13. Bill Morgan, *I Celebrate Myself: The Somewhat Private Life of Allen Ginsberg* (New York: Viking, 2006), 157.
14. Ann Charters, "Notebooks in the Berg Collection." *Bulletin of Research in the Humanities* 84.4. New York Public Library (Winter 1981), 434.
15. Eric Mottram, "Introduction," Kerouac, *The Scripture of the Golden Eternity* (San Francisco: City Lights, 1994), 18.
16. Jack Kerouac, *Kerouac: Selected Letters 2, 1957–1969*, ed. Ann Charters (New York: Viking, 1999), 9.
17. Jack Kerouac, *Desolation Angels* (London: Mayflower, 1968), 20.
18. Jack Kerouac, *Book of Dreams* (San Francisco: City Lights Books, 1961), xix.
19. Robert Creeley, "Introduction," in Kerouac, *Book of Dreams* (2001), ix–x.
20. Kerouac's postcard to me dated January 4, 1967, never made it into *Selected Letters, 1957–1969*. All of my letters to him about his bibliography are published in the *Journal of Beat Studies* 5 (2017). The Kerouac Estate did not give permission to include his side of our correspondence, but I transcribed his letters to me in volume two of the catalog I prepared in 1994 of the Ann and Samuel Charters Beat Collection for the Berg Collection at the New York Public Library (195–211).
21. Michael White, ed. *Safe in Heaven Dead: Interviews with Jack Kerouac* (New York: Hanuman Books, 1990), 85.
22. Dave Moore has posted an exhaustive list of Kerouac's fictional versus real names on his website, *The Kerouac Companion: A Guide to the Duluoz Legend*: www.beatbookcovers.com/kercomp/intro.html
23. Murray, "Introduction," xxxii. In the unpublished fragment, "On the Path," written in Mexico City on August 19, 1955 (Berg 18.9 Holograph draft), Kerouac described how he began to study Buddhism in the Richmond Hill branch of the New York Public Library, and how he slipped out the library with a filched copy of Dwight Goddard's *The Buddhist Bible*. Charles Shuttleworth observed that this volume served as his primary Buddhist text over the next several years ("The Buddhist Years" [unpublished ms.], 219–220). Jack Duluoz *was* a louse for stealing a library book to begin his study of Buddhism, hardly what the Buddha would have considered one of the meritorious works necessary to become a Boddhisattva.
24. Lydia Davis, *Essays One* (New York: Farrar, Straus and Giroux, 2019), 94.
25. Joyce Johnson, *The Voice Is All: The Lonely Victory of Jack Kerouac* (New York: Viking, 2012), 370.

CHAPTER 2

Kerouac and the Profession of Authorship

Matt Theado

2.1 Getting Started in "the Racket"

The profession of authorship begins with the submission of a manuscript to a publisher. The work must be accepted, may be revised, and is usually edited, before being printed, packaged, advertised, reviewed, and if all goes well, sold. At this point, the author might receive compensation in the form of royalty payments. In 1946, twenty-four-year-old Jack Kerouac set out to be professional writer. Over the next two years, he produced a 1,180-page typewritten draft for his first novel, *The Town and the City*. The mass of Kerouac's typescript was not its only hindrance to publication. According to John Clellon Holmes, one of Kerouac's writing friends, "He didn't have any connections. He didn't have any editor. He didn't know anybody in the racket."[1] The process of publishing *The Town and City* (1950) provided Kerouac with experience he relied on in navigating the publication of his next novel, *On the Road* (1957). This chapter outlines Kerouac's negotiations with publishers as he balanced his desires for commercial success and literary recognition in *The Town and the City*, *On the Road*, and *Visions of Cody* (1972). Kerouac's biographers tend to emphasize his artistic drive, recounting his uncompromising commitment to his work combined with his resentment of critical responses; these led to what readers often see as his my-way-or-the-highway stance toward commercial publishing. This view is valid to a point but should be balanced with a nuanced account of Kerouac's aspiration for commercial success. The publication of his first two novels shows that he was an engaged, determined, and often savvy negotiator in the literary marketplace, willing to revise, reshape, and rewrite his work in order to gain publication.

Allen Ginsberg, who had been a fellow student at Columbia, played a significant role in promoting Kerouac's work, counseling him on strategies, and meeting on his behalf with publishers. When Kerouac finished *The Town and the City*, Ginsberg advised him to show it to Mark Van

Doren, one of their former professors, rather than submitting it directly to a publisher. Van Doren had served as literary editor and film critic for *The Nation* in the 1920s and 1930s, and in 1940 he won a Pulitzer Prize for his *Collected Poems*. Kerouac replied, "If [Van Doren] should happen to like my novel, I would get the same feeling that Wolfe must have gotten from old Perkins at Scribner's – a FILIAL feeling."[2]

Thomas Wolfe, Kerouac's chief literary model at the time, produced a famously massive typescript for his first novel, *Look Homeward, Angel* (1929), yet it contained 85,000 fewer words than Kerouac's. Even Kerouac's title *The Town and the City* echoes that of Wolfe's second novel, *Of Time and the River*. Naturally Kerouac thought he should have an editor like Maxwell Perkins, the Scriber's editor who discovered and worked closely with such prominent authors as Ernest Hemingway, F. Scott Fitzgerald, and Wolfe. In May 1948, Kerouac took two approaches toward publication; he showed his novel to Van Doren, and he submitted a selection from it to Scribner. Scribner quickly rejected the novel. Ginsberg consoled Kerouac, telling him that Scribner was the most difficult publisher to get into, and advising him to produce a clean, double-spaced typescript, and to get an agent.[3] Kerouac submitted his revised and retyped novel to Macmillan in August. They rejected it the following month. In early December, Little, Brown rejected his book.[4]

Despite these rejections, Kerouac was becoming known as a serious writer, and his manuscript was talked about on the New York literary scene. Again, Ginsberg was instrumental in promoting Kerouac's novel; he gave a few chapters to *Publishers Weekly* editor Ed Stringham, who passed it to composer Dave Diamond, who in turn gave it to Alfred Kazin, a well-known literary critic and teacher.[5] Kazin knew Kerouac as a student in his classes at The New School; he also served as a literary scout for Harcourt, Brace, where he brought the book to the attention of senior editor Robert Giroux. Van Doren was likewise impressed by the book and added his recommendation to Giroux. When Van Doren told Kerouac that Giroux wanted to see his book, Kerouac arrived at the Harcourt, Brace offices the following morning in a jacket and tie to deliver a box packed with his neatly typed pages.

On March 29, 1949, Harcourt, Brace accepted the novel and paid Kerouac an advance of $1,000 on signing, and $2,000 overall, the first money he earned as a novelist. This was big money in 1948, when the average family income was just under $3,000 per annum.[6] Still, such an advance from one of the big publishing houses was not unusual for a promising novel. A writer's "advance" is just what it sounds like: money the publisher provides to the writer in advance of royalty payments. Once the royalties exceed the amount of the advance, the writer receives additional payments. Advances are often paid in instalments. Kerouac's letters and journal entries indicate that he received $1,000 at signing, $250 during editing, and another $750 when the book was published.

2.2 Editing *The Town and the City*

Over the next two months, Kerouac and Giroux pared down the manuscript, which Giroux felt was too long. Holmes believed that in the first flush of professional acceptance, Kerouac agreed to cuts in the novel that he would otherwise have objected to. Ginsberg also worried that the excisions were excessive but concluded that Giroux was a trustworthy editor and Kerouac's novel would be well received.[7] The two men worked at the Harcourt, Brace offices in the evenings, after which Kerouac returned to his mother's house in Ozone Park in Queens to work until dawn on his next novel, one he was calling his "road book." Kerouac had met Neal Cassady in December 1946, and while he wrote *The Town and the City*, he was experiencing his on-the-road adventures and taking notes for his next book. For the first time in his life, Kerouac felt like a professional author.

Now that he was a working professional, Kerouac wanted to provide for his family. He dreamed of founding a "homestead" and taking the patriarchal place of his father, who had died in 1946. Kerouac moved to Denver in May, 1949, insisting not only that his mother but also his sister, her husband, and their child join him. He took a one-year lease on a house in Westwood, a Denver suburb, for $75 per month.[8] He estimated that the moving bill cost $300. The others joined Kerouac in his "homestead" on June 2. Kerouac planned to support himself and his mother by writing sports columns for the *Denver Post* until his royalties began arriving. By that time, he planned to have finished his road book, and he would repeat the publication process: acceptance, advance, royalties. His dream fell apart quickly. His mother was bored and wanted to earn her own living. She returned to New York on July 14. His sister and her husband lasted another month before packing up their son and returning east. Kerouac had spent his entire thousand-dollar advance on a plan that had come to nothing.

Back in New York that fall, Kerouac worked in the Harcourt, Brace offices through most of September. On September 28 the revisions were complete, and the manuscript was sent to the printer. The galley proofs were ready on November 1. From November 2 through November 13,

Kerouac and Giroux proofread the galleys. As Kerouac scrutinized the final version of the novel word by word, he conceded that his "Book of Sorrows … has been edited into a 'good work of fiction' now" (*Windblown World*, 246). In later years, Kerouac would complain that the deletions reduced his book to a "'saleable' ordinary novel."[9]

2.3 Marketing *The Town and the City*

Harcourt, Brace sent out review copies in January with a promotional letter announcing the novel as "our big novel for Spring, and we believe that no more absorbing or authentic picture of American life has emerged during the post-war years."

On March 2, 1950, 10,500 copies of *The Town and the City* were released to bookstores. The flap notes announced the new novelist:

> An exciting, fresh talent is introduced to American readers in *The Town and the City*.... Sweep of style combined with precision of language, an ear for dialogue, and an eye for dramatic detail are among the author's many gifts.

The back of the book jacket is taken up by a black-and-white portrait of Kerouac in a suit and tie, his face clean-shaven and his hair impeccably combed, looking every bit the young writer who embodied a combination of adventure and somber thoughtfulness.

Harcourt, Brace spent $7,500 on advertising and promotion, sending their new author on a round of autographing parties. Newspaper reviews appeared in *Boston Sunday Herald*, *New York Herald Tribune Review*, *New York Times*, *Chicago Sun*, *Chicago Tribune*, *San Francisco Chronicle*, *Washington Star*, and others. Magazine reviews included *Harper's*, *Newsweek*, *Catholic World*, and others. The placement of such high-profile reviews is one benefit of being published by a large, established firm such as Harcourt, Brace.

On March 5, *New York Times Book Review*'s John Brooks reached a wide readership, crediting Kerouac's "depth and breadth of vision" but comparing him negatively to Wolfe in that he "tends to overwrite." Brooks praised Kerouac's "Dostoevskian view of New York City life" as "powerful and disturbing."[10] *New York Times* reviewer Charles Poore identified Kerouac as a "brilliantly promising young novelist" with "a magnificent grasp of the disorderly splendor and squalor of existence."[11] Harcourt, Brace's ad ran adjacent to Poore's review, featuring a quotation from Van Doren: "John Kerouac is wiser than Thomas Wolfe, with whom he will be compared. He is serious, warm, rich, and mature." Not all reviewers were as ebullient. *Saturday Review* placed the book in the "category of the 'big' novel [with] general emotional appeals in the 'lost, lost, lost' cadence of Thomas Wolfe," while suggesting the book had "radical deficiencies in structure and style."[12] The *New Yorker* dismissed the book as "shambling" and "tiresome."[13] Overall, the reviews were reasonably positive; most reviewers admired Kerouac's accomplishment and pointed to his potential.

Initially, sales also showed promise. Kerouac's hometown paper, the Lowell *Sun*, bought excerpts for serialization. Eyre & Spottiswoode bought the rights to publish a British edition in the following year for which Kerouac received an additional advance and looked ahead to further royalties.[14] Nonetheless, sales fell off quickly. Ginsberg blamed Harcourt, Brace's lack of strategic support.[15] *The Town and the City* sold an estimated 5,000 copies at $3.50 retail. If his contract paid him 10 percent of retail, Kerouac's royalties would have come to less than $1,750.00, not enough to cover the $2,000 advanced to him.

Kerouac received a letter from Ellen Lucey, a reader who admired the novel, asking about his future; he replied that he was unable to make a living as a writer. He grumbled that because of *The Town and the City*'s low sales, he owed Harcourt, Brace $600. He concluded that publication transformed him from being merely poor to being poor and in debt.[16] It is unlikely that Kerouac was legally in debt to Harcourt, Brace. Publishers offer advance money at their own risk; authors typically are not required to return it if the book does not sell. The contract is not in Kerouac's papers; it is possible that Harcourt, Brace provided the second $1,000 with the stipulation Kerouac repay it out of royalties. In addition, Harcourt, Brace had sent Kerouac $100 in June 1950; this may have been a loan against future royalties.[17] In 1952, Lucey asked Giroux about Kerouac; he replied that to his disappointment he had had to reject Kerouac's second novel. When Lucey offered to repay Kerouac's unearned balance on his behalf if Harcourt, Brace would publish his second novel, Giroux explained that they would not reconsider the already rejected road book. Since he wanted the debt paid off, though, he admitted that if Kerouac should send them a third book, he would happily accept Lucey's terms.[18] This exchange indicates that Kerouac owed money to Harcourt, Brace, but the details are unclear.

There was nothing unusual about the publication of Kerouac's first novel, *The Town and the City*; it was rejected by several publishers, then accepted, edited, and published. Sales were lower than anticipated but not bad for a first novel. What was significant about Kerouac's first publishing experience, though, was that it introduced him to the machinations of the publishing industry. This glimpse opened a new world to him and influenced his writing. Even as he groused that his appearances at publicity promotions interrupted work on his road book, he found the experience beneficial: "One learns so much being published—about the cultural scene and the people of the world who are concerned with it."[19] Kerouac learned about completing a novel and working with an editor to prepare it for the market. Cutting sections from the lengthy story affected the work but made it publishable. Kerouac was not only willing to accept this compromise; he actively participated in it.

2.4 Producing *On the Road*

On the Road would present an entirely different set of challenges to publication because the characters were drawn from life and many scenes included marijuana and sex. In April, 1951, a year after Harcourt, Brace published *The Town and the City*, Kerouac typed the now legendary scroll typescript of *On the Road*, a 120-foot long unparagraphed typescript in which he used the real names of his friends in a thinly fictionalized version of their adventures. He unfurled the typescript for Giroux, who did not provide the celebratory reception Kerouac expected. Within a month, Kerouac had retyped the novel onto separate sheets, changing the names of his characters to partially fictionalize them, and formally submitted *On the Road*. Not long after, Harcourt, Brace rejected the novel. Explanations for its rejection vary. Kerouac complained that Harcourt, Brace wanted another novel in the style of his first one, while acknowledging that *On the Road*'s frank treatment of "hipsters, weed, fags, etc." made publication risky (*Selected Letters 1*, 320).

By July, Kerouac had enlisted the services of Rae Everitt at MCA Management, a literary agency. Everitt read his retyped draft of *On the Road*, finding parts of it to be "sheer magic poetry."[20] She also stressed that the book was too long and advised Kerouac to cut "ruthlessly" from the first two sections and reduce Dean's "repetitious" speeches. Everitt wanted to ascertain Harcourt, Brace's disposition on the book, and at the same time she sent the typescript to Farrar, Straus.

At least eleven publishers would reject the novel over the next five years. *On the Road* was not published until 1957, when it created a sensation and rose up the bestseller lists. Holmes claimed *On the Road*'s publication was delayed for so long "due to incomprehension, censorship, and plain stupidity."[21] Those possibilities notwithstanding, documentary evidence indicates that Kerouac could have published *On the Road* sooner if he had been willing to meet a publisher's terms. He had shepherded his first novel through the processes of publication, but neither big money nor literary accolades had come his way. He was determined that his next novel, one that he cared about in a more personally vital way as it portrayed his and his friends' actual experiences and was built on literary principles he more strongly valued than those in his first book, would meet a better fate. By summer 1951, Kerouac had labored day after day, night after night, for five years: writing, typing, revising, editing, and writing again. Now he wanted to make his labor pay in both cash and artistic appreciation.

2.5 *On the Road, Visions of Cody,* and Ace Books

After Harcourt, Brace rejected *On the Road,* Ace Books expressed interest in publishing it. Publishing with Ace represented a plummet in prestige from Harcourt, Brace, or other top-tier houses. Aaron A. Wyn organized Ace Books in 1952, so Ace was not an established name. Like most paperback publishers they relied on genre fiction; their first publications were mysteries and westerns, and by 1956, half of their ninety-nine titles would be science fiction and fantasy. Yet they also believed that literary writers could be published in paperback originals. While this practice was typical in France and other European countries – James Joyce's *Ulysses* was first published in 1922 as paperback – it was an innovative idea in the United States. Hardcover books rarely earned big returns unless they became bestsellers. Paperback reprints released a year after the hardcover publication usually sold in far greater numbers than their hardcover antecedents due to their lower price and greater availability. But when it came to paperback originals, there was a catch; first-edition paperbacks were typically disregarded as cheap pulp fiction and were seldom reviewed. In the 1950s many thousands of mysteries, westerns, and sci-fi yarns were sold in bus stations and drug stores based on their lurid cover art, to be read once and tossed aside. The cultural historian and literary critic Louis Menand summarizes their reputation:

> Editors at the old hardcover houses looked on paperbacks as a bottom-feeding commercial phenomenon, like the pulp magazines and comic books they were distributed with. Critics ignored them, or attacked them as a lowbrow and politically retrograde diversion.[22]

But in the 1950s, some independent publishers began to see the financial sense in publishing works first in inexpensive paperback editions. Ace also developed the idea of publishing two titles in one paperback book, back-to-back. Their most well-known double-book is William Burroughs's *Junkie: Confessions of an Unredeemed Drug Addict* backed with Maurice Helbrant's *Narcotic Agent* (1953). This publication came about because Ginsberg promoted Burroughs, as well as Kerouac, to an editor he knew at Ace Books.

Ginsberg met Carl Solomon in the Columbia Psychiatric Hospital in 1949; Ginsberg was undergoing analysis after he was implicated in a theft ring, and Solomon was institutionalized after a series of erratic behaviors. Solomon introduced Ginsberg to the works of Antonin Artaud and Jean Genet while Ginsberg spoke of his friends Kerouac and Burroughs. The full title of Ginsberg's most famous poem sometimes escapes notice: "Howl for Carl Solomon."

After his release from Columbia Psychiatric, Solomon was hired by his uncle, A. A. Wyn. Despite the unconventional format of the typescript scroll Kerouac submitted to Ace, Solomon convinced his uncle to accept it in December 1951. Solomon later claimed, "I had visions of myself being [Kerouac's] Maxwell Perkins and him being my Wolfe because his first novel had resembled Wolfe."[23] Rae Everitt requested a $1,000 advance. Kerouac signed the contract in February 1952; Ace paid $250 of the advance and agreed to pay installments of $100 a month while Kerouac worked on revisions.

Between completing the scroll typescript and signing Ace's contract, Kerouac had discovered a new way of writing, and his artistic innovation turned out to be his commercial undoing. Kerouac called his new method "sketching" – soon he would develop this method into "spontaneous prose" – and he would write an entirely new version of *On the Road* in this style. Although he referred to the new draft as *On the Road,* he would soon distinguish it from the earlier version by calling it *Visions of Neal* and finally *Visions of Cody*, which would not be published in full until 1972, three years after Kerouac's death.

Kerouac decided to substitute his new *On the Road* for the earlier one Ace had accepted, telling Solomon that he would not need a year to work on revisions since no revisions were necessary. Solomon fired back a letter insisting that Kerouac adhere to the terms of their agreement, reminding Kerouac that he was a risky investment since his royalties at Harcourt, Brace had not covered his advance.

Ginsberg stepped in as a referee between the two men. He instructed Kerouac to write a brief note to A. A. Wyn, saying that he was working on the novel and would need at least a year to complete it. This way, Kerouac would receive monthly payments of $100. Then, Ginsberg instructed, he should let Wyn know "in as *few* words as possible and in as *least* alarming manner as possible" that he had changed his writing method. Ginsberg wondered whether Kerouac, in relying on his don't-change-a-word-once-it's-written style was trying to avoid the hard work of composition and the painstaking revision he had undertaken in completing his first novel.[24]

Kerouac began typing up his new version of *On the Road* from handwritten drafts and sent the first twenty-three pages to Solomon. He suggested to Solomon a tactic for using his new version of *On the Road* to satisfy the contract he had signed. He recommended that Ace Books publish his new *On the Road* as a hardcover book; then they should publish a 160-page excerpt as a "sexy" twenty-five-cent paperback. Kerouac assured Solomon that this was a "real money idea." Kerouac was gaming the market, hoping to get his new prose published in a respectable edition while placating what he believed to be the publisher's desire for profit via the cheap paperback (*Selected Letters 1*, 342). This is the first time as a professional writer that Kerouac directed his own fate. He had earned neither cash nor literary recognition with *The Town and the City*. Now he was trying to engineer a strategy that he felt would ensure both.

But Solomon refused to be "mystified" or "cowed" by Kerouac's "mumbo-jumbo." Solomon admitted that Kerouac was a talented writer, but he would not get special treatment or be excused from the requirements of satisfying professional standards.[25] Solomon was in a precarious position, split between the literary world via his connections with Ginsberg, and the commercial world where profit-and-loss and marketability were vital concerns. He needed to demonstrate to his uncle that he possessed business acumen. Solomon insisted that Kerouac send the new version of the novel to him personally, not to the office, so he could prepare the more conservative board members for its reception.

By July Kerouac sent the complete 530-page typescript and, grateful for Ginsberg's help, insisted that the latter receive 10 percent of all earnings as his agent. After reading Kerouac's new road book, Solomon replied that the staff were "thoroughly bewildered" – it was "utterly unlike" the passages that had gotten him the contract. Solomon declared the manuscript "a thoroughly incoherent mess."[26] Kerouac doubled down, pointing out that novels by Ernest Hemingway and James Joyce were once considered unprintable but now were hailed as classics. He challenged Solomon to publish his new road book or return it. Solomon returned it. He urged Kerouac to send his manuscript of *Doctor Sax*, which he had recently completed, as a possible substitute. Solomon and the editorial staff rejected this novel, too.

One wonders about Kerouac's fate had Ace accepted his plan. The section Kerouac offered as a "sexy" paperback comprised the freshly composed narrative of his road travels with Neal, which was but one component of the vast collage of *Visions of Cody*'s text. If Kerouac were to build a literary reputation through Ace, it would rely on this paperback adventure tale and *Visions of Cody*. The paperback would get no promotion beyond a lurid cover; the hardcover book could hardly fare better. Ace was the new kid on the block, not a prestigious long-time publisher like Harcourt, Brace, so *Visions of Cody* would have had at best a lowkey promotion. Ginsberg was serving as Burroughs's agent at the same time, which means he was negotiating on behalf of two friends with a third friend, Solomon. A comparison with Burroughs's Ace publication helps chart the possibilities. Oliver Harris describes ways that Ace shaped the "form and content" of *Junkie* in ways that affected the book's reception and reputation. There were no literary reviews. While *Junkie* sold over a hundred thousand copies in its first year, author's royalties were based on the thirty-five-cent price, split two ways. Burroughs complained that he was not properly compensated.[27] It is likely that Kerouac would not have been satisfied, either.

2.6 Malcolm Cowley, Viking Press, and a Bestseller

Fortunately, Phyllis Jackson at MCA had been sending out Kerouac's first version of *On the Road*, for this is when the book came across Malcolm Cowley's desk at Viking Press. Had Cowley not seen this submission and subsequently sought out Kerouac, it is unlikely that *On the Road* would have been published by a major company. Born in 1898, Cowley had lived in Greenwich Village and then Paris in the 1920s, where he knew the writers of the Lost Generation. He describes these years in his best-known book, *Exile's Return* (1934). In 1951, Cowley was a literary advisor to Viking Press, and he thought *On the Road* should be published there. He was overruled at a Viking editors' meeting, but his interest in Kerouac continued. Meanwhile, Kerouac had grown disillusioned with MCA and, largely because no one – not even his friends – thought highly of his new writing style, he was disillusioned with publishing in general. When Cowley asked Jackson in May 1953 about Kerouac's whereabouts and his interest in finding a publisher, Jackson replied was that "he simply went away muttering that he didn't want to be published by anyone."[28]

Jackson told Ginsberg that Cowley hoped to place excerpts from *On the Road* in literary magazines. Cowley suggested *New World Writing*, edited by his friend Arabel Porter, and *Perspectives*, published by James Laughlin, as likely targets. Hardened by his disappointment at Ace Books, Kerouac now opposed excerpting his work, sensing that its strength lay in its accumulative effect. Ginsberg informed Cowley that Kerouac was working on "another version" of *On the Road* (*Visions of Cody*). After all, Viking had rejected *On the Road*, and Ginsberg had no way of knowing that Cowley alone had supported it. Ginsberg also suggested that he could obtain some "shorter pieces" from Kerouac, sidestepping for the moment the issue of excerpts.[29]

Helen K. Taylor was hired by Viking in 1953 as a senior editor, and her memo to Cowley corroborated his determination that the original version of the novel should be published. Taylor suggested that whole sections could be cut, but because Kerouac had "a bold writing talent" there would be little need for revising and editing. Despite her support, Viking did not accept *On the Road* for publication in the fall of 1953. Cowley pinned the reason on Viking's conservative bearing. Bookstores typically expected Viking books to be of a more stolid type, while *On the Road* featured drinking, smoking marijuana, reckless driving, and casual sex.

Viking's rejection did not stop Cowley from promoting Kerouac's book. In November he suggested three passages to Arabel Porter; he cautioned that the first, about the narrator's affair with a "Mexican girl," might be "a little dirty in spots, but could be censored"; the second featured San Francisco jazz scenes ("not so dirty"); and the third, a Mexican whorehouse ("very wild and dirty").[30] Porter chose the jazz scenes. *New World Writing* paid Kerouac $120 for "Jazz of the Beat Generation," which appeared in April 1955. Kerouac found an ingenious way to get a portion of his new spontaneous prose road book into print. As he typed up the excerpt, he blended in passages from *Visions of Cody*.[31] Some of Kerouac's mature work – from both versions of his road book – at last appeared in print. On the negative side, by using Jean-Louis as a pen name to avoid an ex-wife's pursuit of child support, Kerouac undercut Cowley's strategy for building his reputation.

Cowley also sent an excerpt to Peter Matthiessen at *The Paris Review*, a recently established English-language literary magazine. The managing editor of *The Paris Review* was Thomas Guinzburg, son of the president of Viking Press, Harold K. Guinzburg. *The Paris Review* published a section titled "The Mexican Girl" in 1955, paying Kerouac $50. "The Mexican Girl" was subsequently selected for publication in *The Best American Short*

Stories 1956, edited by Martha Foley, cofounder of *Story* magazine. Finally, Cowley asked James Laughlin to publish an excerpt in *New Directions*. Titled "A Billowy Trip in the World," the excerpt was published in 1957, shortly before the publication of *On the Road*.

Cowley's advice to Kerouac concerning the placement of excerpts and his influence with Arabel Porter, Peter Matthiessen, and James Laughlin resulted in a boost to Kerouac's literary reputation and paved the way for the book's publication. In addition, Cowley touted Kerouac in a *Saturday Review* article, "Invitation to Innovators."[32] Cowley identified John Kerouac as having invented the phrase "beat generation" as a label for a nonconformist group whose adventures he recounts in *On the Road* (*On the Road*, 39). Cowley included his references to Kerouac and the "beat generation" in his book *The Literary Situation*, published by Viking in 1954.

By this time, Kerouac had taken his business from MCA and retained the services of Sterling Lord of Lord & Colbert. Lord would remain Kerouac's agent for the rest of his life. On October 12, 1954, Lord took advantage of Cowley's plug in *Saturday Review* by sending the magazine to Blanche Knopf, who cofounded Knopf with her husband in 1915. Senior editor Joe Fox replied two days later that he had been seeking Kerouac and asked to see the novel, which Lord sent. Fox quickly returned the typescript, claiming that its physical condition was not up the expected standards. It is likely that the typescript, which Kerouac had typed on legal-size paper, had been edited by hand with deletions marked in black crayon. Kerouac retyped the whole book, an effort which occupied him most of the month of November.

On December 1, Lord reported that he was sending a "retyped version, 100 percent cleaner, of the BEAT GENERATION by Jean-Louis." The author's name and novel's title match the *New World Writing* publication. Knopf held the typescript until December 30. On January 4, 1955, Joe Fox wrote Lord conceding that Kerouac had "enormous talent of a very special kind," but the book was neither well-made nor likely to sell.[33]

On the other hand, support for *On the Road* was picking up steam at Viking. Thomas Guinzberg had returned from Paris to work for his father. He met Cowley, who told him, as Guinzberg later recalled, "I've got this manuscript, and I can't convince your old man, but maybe you'll like it.'"[34] Viking had added Keith Jennison to their editorial staff, who also valued the novel. When Cowley asked to see the novel again, Kerouac submitted the typescript he had prepared for Knopf. Now the support from Cowley, Taylor, and Jennison turned out to be sufficient for Viking to offer Kerouac a contract for *On the Road*. Viking offered a $1,000 advance plus 10 percent royalties on the first 10,000 sales, 12 and a half percent on the next 12,500, and 15 percent thereafter.

Taylor edited the novel, mainly providing house-styling in the form of punctuation and spelling. She also contended with the risk of the novel's real-life counterparts suing for libel since they could be recognized from their portrayals. Kerouac explained the changes he had already made: substituting made-up names and changing locations, occupations, and relationships. Viking's lawyers said these changes were insufficient to prevent readers from recognizing certain characters. This libel issue consumed months due to a line-by-line examination by lawyers and subsequent revisions. Major characters such as Dean Moriarty (Neal Cassady) could not be libel-proofed, so they would have to sign a release. Most scenes related to Denver D. Doll, whose real-life counterpart was a respectable and well-known Denver citizen, were deleted.

On the Road was published by Viking Press on Thursday, September 5, 1957. The text ran to 310 pages and sold for $3.95. The number of copies issued is unrecorded, but the book went through three printings in the first month and became a sensationalized topic in the media.

Kerouac's book was first mentioned in the *New York Times Book Review* on September 1, a promotion that featured photos of Ayn Rand (*Atlas Shrugged*), Isak Dinesen (*Last Tales*), and Kerouac. Kerouac's caption reads, "Jack Kerouac, roving author of 'The Town and the City,' tracks riotous members of the 'beat generation' across the country in 'On the Road.'" Gilbert Millstein's *New York Times* review on September 5 was extraordinary, calling *On the Road*'s publication a "historic occasion" and the book "an authentic work of art."[35] Millstein predicted that the novel would parallel Hemingway's *The Sun Also Rises* relationship with the Lost Generation and become the testament of the Beat Generation.

On the Road appeared on the *New York Times* bestseller list in fourteenth place on October 6, the same week as Ayn Rand's *Atlas Shrugged.* Kerouac's book rose to number eleven (October 27 and November 10) before dropping off the list. In the spring of 1958 Kerouac told Ginsberg that *On the Road* was selling two to four hundred copies per week.[36]

On the Road's greatest readership came with the paperback version. Keith Jennison contacted Truman "Mac" Talley at New American Library to arrange for the sale of paperback reprints for $4,000. Talley later recalled that "Viking's hardcover sale was 22,000. We sold a million copies within the first paperbound year."[37]

On the Road was the last Kerouac book to undergo publisher's editing and house styling. From that point, according to Sterling Lord, each contract included a clause preventing a publisher from changing words or altering punctuation.[38] In fact, after Helen Taylor edited *The Dharma Bums*, Kerouac paid to have his original wording and punctuation restored. By 1966, nine years after the publication of *On the Road,* Kerouac would publish twelve more full-length books with a variety of publishers. His insistence on adhering to artistic integrity in an inherently commercial enterprise brought him a reasonable income as well as an enduring literary reputation. Readers gain deeper appreciation of Kerouac's work by seeing it in the context of the midcentury publishing marketplace, which was necessary for a writer to gain an audience. Once he established himself as a writer whose books could be profitable, he earned greater freedom to direct his literary reputation.

Notes

1. Barry Gifford and Lawrence Lee, *Jack's Book: An Oral Biography of Jack Kerouac* (New York: Penguin, 1979), 77.
2. Jack Kerouac to Allen Ginsberg (April[?], 1948), *Jack Kerouac and Allen Ginsberg: The Letters*, ed. Bill Morgan and David Stanford (New York: Viking, 2010), 33.
3. Jack Kerouac, *Windblown World: The Journals of Jack Kerouac 1947–1954*, ed. Douglas Brinkley (New York: Viking, 2004), 85.
4. "On the Road Journal," holograph notebook, 1948; December 7, 1948. Jack Kerouac Papers, Harry Ransom Center, University of Texas at Austin.
5. Jack Kerouac to Allen Ginsberg (June 29, 1955), *The Letters*, 302.
6. "Income of Families and Persons in the United States: 1950," United States Census Bureau, March 25, 1952. www.census.gov/library/publications/1952/demo/p60-009.html.
7. "Correspondence" Allen Ginsberg Papers, Harry Ransom Center, University of Texas at Austin; AG to JK [n.d.] 1949.
8. Jack Kerouac to Allen Ginsberg (June 13, 1949), *The Letters*, 86.
9. Ted Berrigan, et al. "Paris Review Interview with Jack Kerouac," reprinted *Viking Critical Library On the Road* (New York: Viking/Penguin, 1979), 568.
10. John Brooks, "Of Growth and Decay," *New York Times Book Review* (March 5, 1950), 9.
11. Charles Poore, "Books of the Times," *New York Times* (March 2, 1950), 25.
12. Howard Mumford Jones, "Back to Merrimack," *Saturday Review* (March 11, 150), 18.
13. J.H. Jackson, "Review of *The Town and the City,*" *New Yorker* (March 25, 1950), 115.
14. Jack Kerouac to Frank Morley (June 27, 1951), in *Jack Kerouac: Selected Letters 1, 1940–1950,* ed. Ann Charters (New York: Viking, 1995), 226.

15. Jack Kerouac to Allen Ginsberg (March 30, 1950), *The Letters*, 123.
16. Jack Kerouac to Ellen Lucey, November 4, 1950(?) Jack Kerouac Papers, Columbia University.
17. Robert Giroux to Jack Kerouac, June 22, 1950, The Jack Kerouac Archive at the University of Massachusetts Lowell.
18. Robert Giroux to Ellen Lucey, July 14, 1952; July 21, 1952, The Jack Kerouac Archive at the University of Massachusetts Lowell.
19. Isaac Gewirtz, *Beatific Soul: Jack Kerouac on the Road* (New York: New York Public Library, 2008), 90.
20. Rae Everitt to John Kerouac, July 6, 1951, The Jack Kerouac Archive at the University of Massachusetts Lowell.
21. John Clellon Holmes, *Go* (New York: Scribners, 1952), xii.
22. Louis Menand, "Pulp's Big Moment: How Emily Brontë met Mickey Spillane," *New Yorker* (January 5, 2015): www.newyorker.com/magazine/2015/01/05/pulps-big-moment.
23. Carl Solomon, int. by John Tytell, "I'm with You in Rockland," *The Beat Interviews* (Beatdom Books, 2014), kindle edition.
24. Jack Kerouac to Allen Ginsberg (February 15, 1952), *The Letters*, 142.
25. Carl Solomon to John Kerouac, April 16, 1952. The Jack Kerouac Archive at the University of Massachusetts Lowell.
26. Carl Solomon to John Kerouac, July 30, 1952, The Jack Kerouac Archive at the University of Massachusetts Lowell.
27. Oliver Harris, "Editor's Introduction," William S. Burroughs, *Junky: The Definitive Text of 'Junk.'* (New York: Penguin, 2012), xxviii.
28. Phyllis Jackson to Malcolm Cowley, May 12, 1953. Malcolm Cowley Papers, Newberry Library.
29. Allen Ginsberg to Malcolm Cowley, July 3, 1953, Malcolm Cowley Papers, Newberry Library.
30. Malcolm Cowley to Arabel Porter (November 14, 1953), *The Long Voyage: Selected Letters of Malcolm Cowley, 1915–1987* (Cambridge: Harvard University Press, 2014), kindle edition (np).
31. Jack Kerouac to Allen Ginsberg (August 23, 1954), *The Letters*, 235.
32. Malcolm Cowley, "Invitation to Innovators," *Saturday Review* (August 21, 1954): 7–8, 38–41.
33. Knopf File, Ransom Research Center, University of Texas at Austin.
34. Al Silverman, *The Time of Their Lives: The Golden Age of Great American Publishers, Their Editors and Authors* (New York: St. Martin's Press, 2008), 154.
35. Gilbert Millstein, "Books of the Times," *New York Times* (September 5, 1957), 27.
36. Jack Kerouac to Allen Ginsberg (April 8, 1958), *The Letters*, 395.
37. Silverman, *The Time of Their Lives*, 434.
38. Sterling Lord, "The Kerouac I Knew," *Publishers Weekly*, (August 22, 2007): www.publishersweekly.com/pw/by-topic/authors/interviews/article/17340-the-jack-kerouac-i-knew.html.

CHAPTER 3

Truth in Confession

The Foundation of Kerouac's Literary Experiment

Nancy M. Grace

In the service of crafting a "New Form" of literature, Jack Kerouac drew on powerful writers and philosophical/literary/aesthetic traditions and innovations to craft a unique vision of mid-twentieth-century America and beyond. To say that he was a voracious reader and aficionado of popular and classical cultures is an understatement. So too is to say that the character of his mind was both voluminous and relentless in its capacity to absorb and synthesize. Kerouac's lifework, what he named the Duluoz Legend, blends American/Euro/Asian traditions and movements such as the Renaissance (e.g., Shakespeare, Donne), Romanticism (e.g., Thoreau, Blake, Melville), Realism (e.g., Twain, Galsworthy, Dostoyevsky), Naturalism (e.g., London), Modernism (e.g., Hemingway, Joyce, Faulkner, Stein, Celine), Surrealism (e.g., Lorca), philosophy (e.g., Spengler), Buddhism (e.g., the Diamond Sutra), Catholicism (e.g., The New Testament, St. Theresa), myth (e.g., Goethe's *Faust*), psychoanalysis (e.g., Freud), then-contemporary popular cartoon and comic figures (e.g., W. C. Fields and the Three Stooges), sports (e.g., horse racing, American baseball), jazz (e.g., Lee Konitz and Charlie Parker) along with travel narratives, populism, folk humor, journalism, burlesque, haiku, memoir, American film, and many others. It is truly what he called "an American poetic 'sprawl.'"[1] And a heady one at that. So heady that it perplexed him for much of his writerly life as he sought to become not simply a writer but a great writer of wisdom and humility. And it has confounded even the best of Kerouac readers seeking to wrap heads around the full confluence of materials undergirding his numerous publications.

However, the task, insurmountable it may seem, can become less unruly if one considers the primary mechanisms he most consistently employed as he moved away from his first published novel, *The Town and the City* (1950), and the traditional novel of social realism, rejecting what he deemed the "blight" of formal education in favor of an approach of "great beauty and mystic meaning."[2]

The first mechanism was his deep desire to seek and speak the truth, as he wrestled with his need to lead a godly life, a product of his Catholic upbringing, while simultaneously recognizing the almost requisite demand that a great novelist experience the darkness of the human soul. The second is the confession, which was not the legal confession of a court room or the spiritual confession of the church, but the broader truth of any human being who follows a path to forgiveness and wholeness by repeatedly purging themselves of sin, guilt, or embarrassment. Kerouac consistently worked truth and confession together – often to the dismay of some readers – twinning and twining them as he grappled with his spiritual and bodily identity as an American writer living in two conflicting Americas: (1) "the essential and everlasting America" of the above noted ethereal beauty and mysticism, and (2) the post–World War II, "V-for-Victory, America" of materialism and militarization (*Selected Letters 1*, 36–37). Both were of timely significance for Kerouac, but only the former for eternity.

3.1 Truth

Kerouac recognized in Thomas Wolfe, a well-acknowledged influence on *The Town and the City*, a classicist/Romantic/naturalist amalgamation seeking form and substance grounded in the autobiography of the soul and transcending the traditional novel, an achievement he saw in both Dostoyevsky's *Crime and Punishment* and Joyce's *Ulysses*.[3] By 1948, Kerouac had brought these two keywords, "soul" and "novel," together, declaring that "soulwork" would replace "novel" (although, as he self-corrected, the "name is too fancy, and laughable, but it does indicate someone's writing *all-out* for the sake of earnestness and *salvation*" (*Windblown World*, 95). He returned to and elaborated on the theme of "soulwork" throughout his career. For instance, in the unpublished "Dialogs in Introspection" from 1944, he self-debated creativity and morality with an opening salvo that spirituality is necessary for creation of cultural activities such as fiction writing, the latter incorporating aesthetic endeavors such as fiction writing.[4] Five years later, he repudiated science and pronounced the holiness of life the only truth – "it has been said so, a thousand million times" (*Windblown World*, 205). In early December 1949, he virtually shouted his belief that it is "NOT THE WORDS THAT COUNT BUT THE RUSH OF TRUTH WHICH USES WORDS FOR ITS PURPOSE" (*Windblown World*, 252).

It was the holiness of human life that led him to declare in that same entry that "[s]cholar's [sic] scholar, critic's [sic] critic, but the artist burns and beats and blows and jumps and rushes.... What the hell! Shit's not pink" (*Windblown World*, 205, 252). In more formal language, in an undated entry from his 1947–1948 journal titled "Forest of Arden," he expanded this colloquial portrait of feces with his belief that writing is *an act of surrender* (emphasis mine) requiring recognition of the self's "most personal secrets ... with humble understanding and perhaps chagrin" (*Windblown World*, 140). The entries, in effect, reflect his understanding of the American literary Romance, mirroring Hawthorne's belief that the Romance differs from the novel in that the author of a Romance must always address the "truth of the human heart," linking the past with the present with the right to do so "under circumstances ... of his own choosing or creation."[5] Kerouac recognized this link, writing to a childhood friend, Charles Sampas, on Dec. 27, 1949, that his own focus on their hometown of Lowell, Massachusetts, was no different from Sherwood Anderson's Winesburg, Ohio, Thomas Wolfe's Asheville, Carolina, or Hawthorne's Salem, all of which mystically augur their future through the human heart, specifically the heart of the authors themselves (*Selected Letters 1*, 221). This transcendental tradition elevating human emotion, the inward turning eye, and authorial freedom of choice became more accessible for Kerouac as he developed sketching as a narrative tool, instigated by his friend Ed White in 1951. But it was his earlier discovery of confessional writing – what would become spontaneous prose – that unlocked an even more significant human and artistic truth for him.

3.2 The Confession

For Kerouac, the combination of truth, soul, surrender, personal secrets, and the human heart created confession, the very foundation of his private act as a literary genre.[6] Kerouac himself at one point saw confession as the radical root for both writing and twentieth-century life in general. Perceiving a "dynamic philosophy behind the Progress of the 20th century," in a May 1949 journal entry, he called for a "Manifesto of Confessions" (*Windblown World*, 194). While he never composed such a manifesto, some of the tenets of his confessional method appear in his "Essential of Spontaneous Prose" ("the best writing is always the most painful personal wrung-out tossed from cradle warm protective mind-tap from yourself the song of yourself") and "Belief & Technique of Modern Prose" ("Telling the true story of the world in interior monolog"; "No shame or fear in the dignity of yr experience"; "Submissive to everything, open, listening"; and "Bookmovie is the movie in words").[7] In other words, truth-in-confession emerges through direct access from the working mind of one human being to that of another. Kerouac called the "Bookmovie" his "most ambitious invention," stating in a 1963 interview with John Clellon Holmes that people would be able "to see the movie going on in another man's mind, with headsets connected to encephalographic equipments"; a surprisingly bold prediction of today's Virtual Reality simulation devices.[8]

For Kerouac, the route to full confession began with his French-Canadian Catholic childhood in which the purging process was the obligatory aural practice of speaking of one's sins *privately with trust* to another, the ordained priest. A powerful example appears in *Visions of Gerard* (1963), crafted after he had developed spontaneous prose, which describes his nine-year-old brother, who died when Kerouac was four, confessing the sins of hitting a younger child out of anger, looking at another boy's penis, and lying about a reading assignment. Such scenes, to which Kerouac was obviously never privy, are based on his own experiences, and through the intermediary of Gerard he records the young child anxiously practicing what he will tell the priest, followed by the confession itself, and finally Gerard's release from the ordeal – "It's all over! It was nothing! He's pure again!" – possibly the most joyous passage in the entire Duluoz Legend.[9]

It's arguably his correspondence with Ginsberg and other friends, however, that propelled Kerouac away from the church and to his practice of confessional literary writing. Fortunately, readers now have access to Kerouac's earlier developmental texts, which illustrate how he transitioned from the privacy provided by the church and his own notebooks to a more precarious but productive relationship with correspondents, a relationship requiring a profound degree of both trust and the desire to confess facilitated by the safety of a contained space. Kerouac took this leap in a letter to Ginsberg dated September 6, 1945, describing his assault of an unconscious woman:

> Once I was in bed with a girl, down in Baltimore … When we got to bed, she fell asleep and couldn't be awakened … I spent the whole night wresting around with her limp rag of a body, as she snored. It is a horrible experience, that … You feel remorse the next day, ashamed of your desire; perhaps you feel like a necrophiliac, maybe there's a fear of necrophilia in all of us, and this business of wresting around with an unconscious woman is the closest thing there is to necrophilia … Well, that's the kind of remorse I felt, for exactly the same reasons … There was no one I could tell the story to who wouldn't in return blow a lot of hot air my way … I'm a son of Jehovah—I advance with trepidation towards the scowling elders, who seem to know about every one of my transgressions, and are going to punish me one way or the other.[10]

This passage should make any reader uncomfortable, and while Ginsberg did not directly address the confession in his reply, he did offer sweeping comments about wish fulfillment and Kerouac's artistic ego (*The Letters*, 26). Perhaps Ginsberg through analysand discourse signaled to Kerouac possibly greater flaws: the inability to admit remorse for the woman he had violated and, tragically, the inability to admit that failing – both perhaps functioning, even in veiled form, as the secular absolution Kerouac sought.

It's widely understood that Kerouac's next major move in developing his literary confession was ignited by his receipt of Neal Cassady's December 1950 "Joan Anderson and Mary Cherry" letter, which, as Ann Charters notes, Kerouac responded to the following day, December 28, 1950 (*Selected Letters 1*, 246). Kerouac specifically acknowledged his letter as a private confession to Cassady, who served as his literal intermediary to God: "This confession is for YOU, and through you to God," Kerouac wrote, "and God back to my life, and wife, whatever and whatall" (*Selected Letters 1*, 246). Like many confessors, he found that the process produced both relief and apprehension (*Selected Letters 1*, 248). But after a pledge to Cassady to "renounce all fiction," in effect, cleansing himself of the accusation that he was taking advantage of a friend in order to publish, he plunged forward, following the Hawthornean Romantic route away from standardized fiction to confess nothing as horrific as possible necrophilia but rather a lengthy personal account of the life, death, and burial of his brother Gerard, later rewritten as *Visions of Gerard*.

In some respects, Kerouac's personal epistolary confession replicates the conventional Catholic practice of confession: he tells his story to someone he knows (a parishioner will often know the priest who hears the confession, although he is typically hidden behind the confessional screen) and respects as better than himself. "No one is as great as you," he told Cassady, "nor humbler" (*Selected Letters 1*, 247). Kerouac replaced private confession to a priest with private confession to a bosom confidante, a distinct secularizing of the confessional relationship. With this change, Kerouac implies that when one tells the truth, whatever that may be at that moment, one can go back and retell the truth as one has come to know it, as he did in *Visions of Gerard* and in other works such as *On The Road* (1957), *Visions of Cody* (posthumously, 1972), *The Sea is My Brother* (posthumously, 2011), and *The Vanity of Duluoz* (1968). The confession becomes an open-ended, serial process; so too its literary construction.

As he told Cassady in that same letter, the epistolary confession also eradicated the disturbing need to write "with the mysterious outside reader, who is certainly not God, bending over [his] shoulder" (*Selected Letters 1*, 247), while paradoxically extending the privacy of the confessional into the greater public realm. Kerouac's fusion of spiritual and literary practices transitioned from Cassady as listener to an unknown/mysterious reader or "you" that remains linked to Cassady but is also the "you" to whom Kerouac addressed many of his journal entries. This "you" is another secular and presumably intimate auditor but simultaneously an enhanced version of the mysterious "you" that he tried to escape via confession to Cassady. Following this equation, the response to Kerouac's texts must be from not only readers/auditors (mysterious as in both the human and the divine), but also other writers. In other words, he yearned intensely not only for spiritual forgiveness from the Others to whom he confessed, but also for existential communication and artistic recognition. In the Legend, the self Duluoz offers is inextricably bound to what must have been in Kerouac's mind both greater *and lesser* Others, and the "I's" reality is nothing without them, God or human.

Here, Kerouac suggests a constructivist understanding that can be usefully illuminated through Judith Butler's philosophy of the speaking self. Butler argues that in the physical act of speaking to another, the self is not an isolated, unified reality but is instead "elaborated" in the relational discursive experience."[11] This reality is predicated upon a fundamental recognition that one's "persistence as an 'I'" depends upon "the sociality of norms that precede and exceed [one]" since one comes into this world "on the condition that the social world is already there" and immediately meets established norms by which one's reflexivity is both mediated and constituted. Or, Butler argues, "I am outside myself from the outset, and must be, in order to survive, and in order to enter into the realm of the possible."[12]

We see such negotiations foregrounded in, for example, *Tristessa* (1960), a slim but representative portion of the Legend, in which, while focused on the narrator's self, including his obsession with sex and death, the narrator is inextricably bound to other(s) – in this case, the Mexican prostitute Tristessa and the junkie Old Bull – who become part of his confession because he knows that he has somehow wronged them. In fact, a great deal of the narrative is devoted to describing their physical world in poverty-stricken Mexico City, a world to which Duluoz well knows he, unlike Tristessa and Old Bull, is *not* inextricably bound, and this guilt permeates his experience with and of them. It is Duluoz's recognition that he wants to, or believes he should, love and learn from Tristessa, but cannot, that drives his guilt. One finds the same situation in *The Subterraneans* (1958), in which the narrator, Leo Percepied, appears to desire redemption through his relationship with the African American–Native American Mardou Fox but cannot, and eventually leaves her and her bohemian world to write his novel about both. Kerouac's narrators become selves bound to the invisible recipients of the narrative who anchor it in the experiences and relationships about which he must confess. These mostly nameless readers are the ones who simultaneously pave the way to a better life for him, be it Christian heaven or Buddhist nirvana.

Duluoz's story becomes truthful only in its linguistic representation to the Others, who receive, reflect, and reify it in the act of reception. Kerouac declares this in *Tristessa*'s concluding sentence, "This part is my part of the movie, let's hear yours," a direct invitation to others to respond to the confession.[13] Duluoz, speaking from an autobiographical standpoint of epistemological truth that acknowledges the illusionary state of subjective existence, reconfigures the religious act of confession as a secular and literary two-way conversation. What this means is that Kerouac constituted a highly complex, if not contradictory, set of respondents, including friends, family ["wifey" in *Vanity of Duluoz*], anonymous readers, known critics, Tathāgata, and the Christian God, all expected to recognize the confessional method and respond appropriately.

Within this relational mode, the speaker may drop from the equation as the reader enters the confessor's space to become the one envisioning reality. In Kerouac's case, that reader was often a real life acquaintance who might see themselves as both the unwilling object of confession and an unwilling confessional actor, such as Alene Lee in *The Subterraneans*; Gary Snyder in *The Dharma Bums* (1958); Esperanza Zaregoza and Bill Garver in *Tristessa*,; Allen Ginsberg in *Desolation Angels* (1965); Stella Sampas Kerouac in *Vanity of Duluoz*; and Neal Cassady in *Visions of Cody*.[14] Public record provides evidence that some who received his confessions did not respond positively to seeing themselves through Duluoz's confessional eyes. For instance, Alene Lee, the African American–Native American upon whom Kerouac based the character of Mardou Fox in *The Subterraneans*, considered the book a cruel shock when Kerouac showed her the manuscript and threatened to sue him for libel.[15] Such reactions should not be surprising. Confessions are often ugly, subjective realities and never absolutely true. Kerouac's were never absolutely true and were often extremely ugly, as his necrophiliac confession to Ginsberg demonstrates. Neither are confessions easy to receive, even if one is simply sitting in silence knowingly letting the confessor unburden the soul. "Shit's not pink," as Kerouac had to remind himself – and as did publishers, some of whom required name changes in his manuscripts, since the confessional literary mode transgressed the line between fact and fiction, possibly triggering expensive libel suits.[16]

As a cognitive act of trading places, the relational mode that Kerouac calls for not only transforms the Others into confessor but also the narrator into responder, that is, one with the power to minister to others. Consequently, Kerouac's narratives spit forth in repentance often unsavory truths about himself and others, while conversely verbalizing the discourse of one who provides relief. In the role of comforter, Duluoz illustrates Butler's contention that "[i]mplicit within the Christian notion of the pastor … is that such a person has sure knowledge of the person to whom he ministers, and that application of this knowledge to the person is the means by which that person is administered and controlled."[17] The confessor, in turn, comes to speak about themselves through the same language of control used by the one who ministers, thus increasing his/her own power over others.

Such discourses permeate Kerouac's writing, especially his Buddhist notebooks published as *Some of the Dharma* (1997). Whether it be axioms such "All is well"; "You can't fall off a mountain"; "No more rebirth"; "I am God"; "Why travel if not like a child?"; "Life is a dream"; or "All is vanity" – the discourses of Buddhism, Christianity, British and American romanticism, psychoanalysis, and others of hegemonic power function throughout the Legend to tell others how to live. In *Tristessa*, for example, control gains traction via Duluoz's frequent use of Christian, Buddhist, and psychoanalytic discourses to shape his attempts at celibacy, his persistent objectification of females as evil yet pretty grave makers, his intense desire to save Tristessa through his touch and his love, and his obsession with the literal disappearance, or wasting-away, of her material body, which attracts yet terrifies him – he must have it, avoid it, save it, just as, in a more angelic Catholic form, he announces to readers that he is telling Gerard's story because the world "needs [Gerard's] soft and loving like."[18] Similarly, *The Dharma Bums* includes a lengthy passage in which the narrator, Ray Smith, tries to convince a mentally unstable woman named Rosie that she needn't fear police arrest because life is simply a dream. But she later kills herself. Ray, unable to understand her dilemma – just as Kerouac himself had been unable to empathize with the unconscious woman he violated – twists Buddhist beliefs to conclude that she is "in Heaven now, and she knows" that earth isn't real.[19] Interestingly, however,

Smith is haunted by Rosie's demise throughout the narrative, so much so that he confesses that he and Cody (Neal Cassady) should have realized the depths of her illness from the self-inflicted cuts on her arms: "I was just a dumb young kid and impractical fool who didn't understand the serious significance of this very important, very real world," he realizes in confessional retrospect, a significantly mature concession that he too eagerly, without true enlightenment, assumed spiritual knowledge that he didn't have (*The Dharma Bums*, 109–111).

Granted, Kerouac is speaking about his own beliefs and actions. However, the discourse of the minister, be it Christian or Buddhist, testifies to both the internalization of the Others' control over him and his subsequent verbalization to Others of those truths. Butler calls this process "desires muted by repressive rules" (163). As she explains, "[t]he role of the confessor within pastoral power is no longer understood primarily as governed by the desire to enhance his own power but to facilitate a transition or conversion through the process of verbalization, one that opens the self to interpretation and, in effect, to a different kind of self-making in the wake of sacrifice" (164). In the Catholic context, this sacrifice is the giving up of the body and desire through attachment to the nonhuman God. Butler sees the possibility of social control in this paradigm (164). In serial confessions, the confessor, then, transforms the self into a field of interpretation, an apt descriptor of the Legend. Kerouac in his various guises repeatedly confesses his personal story to many Others, including himself, who appear to dialogue with him upon that field of interpretation, where his persistent movement is toward a self, his and theirs, freed from the material world of sin and guilt.

Perhaps no greater example of this self-liberating process is Kerouac's handling of the American master narrative. In condensed form, it a tale of divinely inspired exceptionalism; manifest destiny; the open frontier; the primacy of youth; the supremacy of the individual; "equality" as a grounding principle; nature as both welcoming and wild; the right to own property; economic prosperity; the messianic importing of American values to improve lives elsewhere; and the assimilation of everyone into a unified whole.[20] These tropes began as patriarchal and racist, but, over 200-plus years, have proven sufficiently flexible to accommodate redemptive political and cultural changes. It's a narrative that Kerouac engaged with early on in his career, populating his journals with lists of American types, cowboy stories, American sports, and other such tropes, even including a brief explication of eight features separating America from Western Europe, an easily identifiable version of the points presented above (*Unknown Kerouac*, 7–8).

Later in life, the need remained with him, as he remembered that it was Wolfe who first awakened him to "America as a Poem instead of America as a place to struggle around and sweat in." Wolfe compelled him to "want to prowl, and roam, and see the real America … that 'had never been uttered'" (*Vanity of Duluoz*, 75), the America of *On the Road* with its introduction of Dean Moriarty (Cassady) as the archetypal American man whose story Kerouac could never abandon.

On the Road served as a public announcement of Kerouac's experiences as he roamed and wrote, which was also the realization that in the "V-for-Victory America" of post-World War II, the America of cowboy myths and white picket fences didn't exist, that the magical world of marijuana-infused Mexico offered no true redemption, and that even Cassady would never be his savior. In turn, the confessional mode forced him to confront his own Quebecois heritage and his efforts, like those of millions of other first-generation Americans, to become an American and repudiate his foreign roots (*Windblown World*, 259), which led him to see himself as not American, but as a half caste, "an Indian, A North American Exile in North America" (*Selected Letters 1*, 381). He was desperate to escape the humiliation he felt as both the metaphoric pipe-smoking writer in a Faulknerian body and the clumsy football player/lumberjack in a Canuck body. In turn, as a self-identified exile and a young writer intent on telling the true – complex, yet holy – tale of America, Kerouac looked to the mixed bag of "sandlot kids in uniform" whom he observed in his first trip to Denver, innocently and happily playing baseball for the pure love of the sport, the holy antithesis of himself with his "white ambitions," including being a professional football player (*Windblown World*, 216).

In the context of Kerouac's struggles to understand himself within the scope of the master American narrative, the confession signals his profound awareness of the betrayal that he and millions of others experienced. Whiteness was not the godliness of American exceptionalism, individualism, and unity, but a whitewash hiding class privilege and power that nonwhites and the poor could never fully achieve. These were hard truths for Kerouac to accept, but he dealt with them by attempting to reclaim his French heritage as he confessed to Yvonne Le Maître, who had reviewed *The Town and the City* for a local French language newspaper in 1950 (*Selected Letters 1*, 225–227) – and by refusing to present as downtrodden victims, whether African Americans, Native Americans, or Mexicans, the very individuals left out of the American dream, thereby robbing the American dream of some of its capacity to dehumanize.[21] In effect, the serial literary confession requires that readers seek out a more complete understanding of both the narrative self and America, since the human penitent lives and relives themselves not as static entities but as ever-changing in an ever-changing world with ever-changing narratives.

This Kerouacian act of self-construction foregrounds the very body from which he attempted to escape, which, as Butler contends, becomes again in the physical act of speaking or writing a confession, either "*before* another [or] obliquely *to* another," the physical body that did the deed, even in a diminished version of the prior act. Thereby it asserts its own capacities as a material, sexualized self. As Kerouac's confessions unfolded, this body took on a variety of forms. In the thirties, forties, and early fifties, his material reality encapsulated recognition that the young white American male must travel out into the world to seek fulfillment (*Unknown Kerouac*, 7), which emerged in his focus on the wealth provided by becoming a bestselling author. Yet his religious upbringing had ingrained in him so deeply the absolute duty of telling the story of his and others' miseries that he felt guilty for seeking worldly success. In turn, his own body became disgustingly vermin-like to him, and in response he used self-punishment to achieve a Christ-like existence. In *On the Road*, this duality is Sal Paradise's shambled male corpus, a deflated demasculinized survivor of a failed marriage, following the electrifying and hyper-masculinized brilliance of Dean Moriarty, reveling in moments of conventional romance with young women while also seeking corporal obliteration through mystical transformation.

Interestingly, however, Kerouac also played with more radical and gendered bodily possibilities. For example, in "Joan Rawshanks in the Fog," from *Visions of Cody*, the narrator subtly masks his confessional self in relationship to a female body, which the "I" describes via his observations of Joan Crawford filming a scene for the Hollywood movie *Sudden Fear* (1952). The "I" moves mysteriously in and out of the fog and the crowds of San Francisco onlookers, the body blurring and vanishing as the "I" smoothly morphs into a virtual third-person narration of others in the scene, only to reappear in clothing that deceptively reshapes his physical male identity as not only a masculine voyeur but also an invisible genderless presence/voice as the "I" takes on the persona of Rawshanks, the film crew, police officers, and neighborhood onlookers. These transformations mirror Rawshanks' heavily made-up face and illusionary facial expressions, confounding her physical female identity as empty object of the male gaze. Throughout, the "I" repeats the mantra "Joan Rawshanks in the fog," a virtual, although likely unintended, code for the twinning and false nature of the two bodies, both of which reside through partial erasure in a dissolute and foggy liminality.[22]

More unambiguously, in *Desolation Angels*, the sexualized male body is transformed into the female as the confessor ruminates upon his mother, Mémère. At times, she is simply his mother, a conventional physical body representing working-class immigrant experiences cleaning house and punching a timeclock, but as he saw her throughout his life, she more often existed as a site of fantasy and fear, of connections through time and cultures, and of wisdom and salvation – the Wise Old Woman who would teach him how to escape the conflicts of confession.[23] Appearing to him as a female representation of great suffering and endurance, a mop-headed Hecuba on Desolation Peak where he is serving as a fire watcher, Mémère leads him to imagine his own body as "*the last old woman on the earth* [emphasis mine] gnawing on the last bone in the final cave and I cackle my last prayer on the last night before I don't wake up no more."[24] Confessing his feelings for his mother transforms him into a body dramatically unlike the successful American male he had so desired to be but had failed to become. Of course, the confession returns him once again to his writing, that which he believes will have staying power beyond his own mortality, and yet again to despair in his physical reality. His repeated verbalization of the deeds reifying his body produce narrators perpetually guilty, unable to attach themselves to either the human or the nonhuman. Toward the end of his life, he faced this blunt conundrum: "[M]y body is so thick and carnal!," so much so that he couldn't understand the reality of fellow humans equally trapped – and was incapable of turning for redemption to his God (*Vanity of Duluoz*, 131).

What one sees in Kerouac is a reaction to the absence of a viable two-way conversation: the increasingly heightened sense of his own inadequacies, as if the louder and more truthful he speaks, the greater likelihood that Others will respond. But they do not. All too many responses to the romance of the American heart betrayed him. First, literary critics who often called for him to abandon the literary confession/spontaneous prose, as did Seymour Krim, who threaded an otherwise praise-filled introduction to *Desolation Angels* with candid pleas to Kerouac to change aesthetic direction, pronouncing the omniscient "I" overused and boring. "[D]uring the last ten years he taught us what he knows … and now we can … read him too transparently," Krim declared, erroneously stating, and implying that Kerouac knew as well, that the "[t]wo way communication" which had existed between Kerouac and readers of his published works had vanished.[25] Secondly, media outlets and Beatnik wannabees, both of whom transformed him into a shallow icon of American dissipation and consumerism. In his response to theirs, the sense of guilt increased exponentially – the "I" must be obliterated/sacrificed; God must be found; the "I" can never live up to Christ' s sacrifice or Buddha' s wisdom; the "I" has failed on many levels, even that of being a good son and good man attempting to extend love to others. The books he writes as confession and comfort, fall short. The penitent eventually becomes ensnared in a material and linguistic world that refuses to offer relief.

In a formal counseling setting, the listener could through language help to redirect and ameliorate this feedback loop syndrome. But Kerouac was not seeking a medical therapeutic relationship, and in an author/reader relationship, the chances of the confession being transformed through intersubjective discourse becomes almost moot. Most readers, whether lay or professional, don't dialogue in any productive way with authors, even in the current cyberworld of blogs and vlogs, Twitter/X, Facebook, Reddit, and TikTok. And once an author is deceased, the confession continues, but the listener has no one to whom to respond.

The average reader and average literary critic are even more poorly prepared – and, rightly so, don't see providing solace or therapy as their job, which it is not. No wonder Kerouac became progressively frustrated with his reception. Many Others, including some of those closest to him, publicly vented their opposition rather than providing the recognition and absolution that he sought and that confession, even as a literary genre, requires – but that which they legitimately could not offer. Kerouac, for whatever reasons, did not modify his chosen style for his American romance, which in his recasting as confession/spontaneous prose/mind movie, failed to appeal to the broader post–World War II readership he dreamed about, one likely more enamored with the speed of American life and the myth of its joyful stick-to-itiveness, lacking, like Krim, the patience necessary to recognize the pace and content of Kerouac's invention.

Consequently, Kerouac remained bound by the desires and norms of self and Others generated intersubjectively and marked with conflicting understandings of the nature and power of these realities. Fortunately, that world is now populated by readers more willing and now able to move beyond the published novels of the Duluoz Legend to Kerouac's published letters and journals to at least begin to understand and communicate the many layers of truth and confession that constitute his longsuffering – and beatific – contribution to American letters.

Notes

1. Jack Kerouac, *Windblown World: The Journals of Jack Kerouac 1947–1954*, ed. Douglas Brinkley (New York: Viking, 2004), 242.
2. Jack Kerouac, *Selected Letters 1, 1940–1956*, ed. Ann Charters (New York: Viking, 1995), 36. Ryan died in the South Pacific Jan. 10, 1943.
3. For Kerouac's essay on Wolfe, written while a student at the New School for Social Research in NYC, see Jack Kerouac and Elbert Lenrow, "The Minimization of Thomas Wolfe in His Own Time" in *Kerouac Ascending: Memorabilia of the Decade of On the Road*, ed. Katherine H. Burkman (Newcastle upon Tyne, UK: Cambridge Scholars, 2010).
4. Jack Kerouac, "Dialogs in Introspection, 1944," Jack Kerouac Papers, Henry W. and Albert A. Berg Collection of English and American Literature, The New York Public Library, box 43.
5. Nathaniel Hawthorne, *House of the Seven Gables* (New York: Bantam/ Random House, 1991), vii.
6. Tim Hunt's argument about Spontaneous Prose as performance in *Textuality of Soulwork* and my reading of Kerouac's focus on truth and confession are distinct yet complementary interpretations. See Chapter 4 of this volume.
7. Jack Kerouac, "Essentials of Spontaneous Prose," *Evergreen Review* (2:5 Summer 1958), 72–73 "Belief & Technique of Modern Prose," *Evergreen Review* (2:8 Spring 1959), 57.
8. Jack Kerouac, *The Unknown Kerouac*, ed. Todd Tietchen, trans. Jean-Christophe Cloutier (New York: The Library of America, 2016), 319.
9. Jack Kerouac, *Visions of Gerard* (New York: Farrar, Straus & Co., 1963), 38.
10. Jack Kerouac and Allen Ginsberg. *Jack Kerouac and Allen Ginsberg: The Letters*, eds. Bill Morgan and David Stamford (New York: Viking, 2010), 23–24.
11. Judith Butler, *Undoing Gender* (New York: Routledge, 2004), 173.
12. Butler, *Undoing*, 32.
13. Jack Kerouac. *Tristessa* (New York: Penguin Books, 1992), 9.
14. Esperanza Zaregoza, the person who inspired the character Tristessa, has been referred to in scholarship variously as Esperanza Villanueva and Esperanza Tercerero, but in letters to Kerouac, she signed her last name Zaregoza; see Esperanza Zaregoza ("Tristessa") to Jack Kerouac, 1955-1956. Jack Kerouac Papers, 65.11. Henry W. and Albert A. Berg Collection of English and American Literature, The New York Public Library. She also appears as "Esperanza Zaregoza" in Kerouac's address book.
15. Gerald Nicosia, *Memory Babe: A Critical Biography of Jack Kerouac* (Berkeley: University of California Press, 1994), 452, 541.
16. Matt Theado, *The Beats: A Literary Reference* (New York: Carroll & Graf, 2001), 162–164.
17. Butler, *Undoing*, 161.
18. Jack Kerouac, *Visions of Gerard* (New York: Penguin, 1991), 3.
19. Jack Kerouac, *The Dharma Bums* (New York: Penguin, 1984), 113.
20. The American master narrative can be traced back to Frederick Jackson Turner. See "The Significance of the American Frontier in American

History," billofrightsinstitute.org/activities/frederick-jackson-turner-the-significance-of-the-frontier-in-american-history-1893, accessed April 21, 2023. See also Ronald Takaki, *A Different Mirror: A Multicultural History of America* (Boston: Back Bay Books, 2008). The description provided here of the narrative comes from Daniel Hoffman, *Form and Fable in American Fiction* (Charlottesville: University of Virginia Press, 1994) and from a lecture that Manning Marable gave at The College of Wooster in September 2006.

21. The most significant turn in recent Kerouac scholarship has been research on his French-Canadian heritage and writing. See, for example, Hassan Melehy, *Kerouac: Language, Poetics, and Territory*. (New York: Bloomsbury Academic, 2016) and Tietchen and Cloutier's *Unknown Kerouac*. In *French Genealogy and the Beat Generation* (London: Bloomsbury, 2019), Véronique Lane also presents a valuable discussion of Celine's influence on Kerouac.
22. Jack Kerouac, *Visions of Cody* (New York: Penguin, 1993), 275–292.
23. A typical example is an August 29, 1951, journal entry in which he describes Mémère as a "conjurer, mystic, prophet, gravedigger, little girl, madwoman, pal."
24. Jack Kerouac, *Desolation Angels* (London: Andre Deutsch Ltd, 1966), 99–100.
25. Seymour Krim, "Introduction," in Kerouac, *Desolation Angels*, xxvii.

CHAPTER 4

The Textuality of Performance

Kerouac's Spontaneous Prose

Tim Hunt

In "Essentials of Spontaneous Prose" Jack Kerouac proposes a new method of writing in which the writer foregoes "'selectivity' of expression" and proceeds instead by

> free deviation (association) of mind into limitless blow-on-subject seas of thought, swimming in sea of English with no discipline other than rhythms of rhetorical exhalation and expostulated statement, like a fist coming down on a table with each complete utterance, bang![1]

Some have dismissed this as a rationale for ignoring craft and control – an excuse for careless writing. Others have hailed it as a clarion call to break free from arbitrary, restrictive conventions and thereby achieve what Kerouac elsewhere termed "wild form" in which the writer's confessional authenticity seems directly presented to the reader. Those who dismiss Spontaneous Prose typically do so in brief put downs such as Truman Capote's often quoted quip, "That's not writing, that's typewriting."[2] On the other hand, those who celebrate Spontaneous Prose, such as Allen Ginsberg, offer hymns of praise that are, in effect, the yin to Capote's yang.[3]

While Capote and Ginsberg differ over the value of what can be generated using Spontaneous Prose, both view it as a procedure.[4] For Capote, it's an excuse for not revising and, as such, can't yield artful writing, which is to say "literature." For Ginsberg, Spontaneous Prose is a visionary method – a self-evident Tao – that renews literature by freeing the writer from self-censoring revision so that writing can be simultaneously discovery and expression. And perhaps this is where we should leave things – as a matter of faith over the path to literary righteousness, with those observing the commandments of compositional control worshipping in the Church of Capote and those following the Tao of spontaneity praying in Temple Ginsberg.

But focusing on Spontaneous Prose as a procedure misses what is truly radical in Spontaneous Prose and its actual implications for understanding Kerouac's practice. For Kerouac, Spontaneous Prose was not just writing quickly or writing without self-censoring or writing without regard for his era's established conventions for fiction. Instead, it involved transforming writing from a medium for composing into a medium for performing. And this in turn led to recasting the mechanism of writing, the textuality of writing, by altering how alphabetic characters relate to sound and, thereby, altering how time and timing function within writing.[5] Both Capote and Ginsberg treat Spontaneous Prose a matter of how to write. But for Kerouac, Spontaneous Prose is also – and more fundamentally – an alternate conception of what writing *is* and can *also be*, as a mechanism and medium.

4.1 Style or Writing System: A Thought Experiment

Here are two sentences (each describing a Beat wannabe plying his coffeehouse bongos as the admiring girls in black look on) that illustrate the difference between how letters relate to sound in writing used as a medium for composing (the conventional textuality of writing as Capote practiced it) and how letters relate to sound in writing performed as Spontaneous Prose:

1. The coffeehouse cat with the scraggly goatee plays the bongos, while the kitty cats purr their cappuccinos, and the dimmed spots, like Eddie Poe on the nod, stain the smoky shadows.
2. Oowee! That bongo caaat is sooo hip the cap'cino sippin' kitties are lappin' up his bip'n' bop as he bloho*wo*ows his top. Ma*an*!

On the surface, the difference between these sentences is simply stylistic – a matter of using writing differently. But a closer look shows that how writing works differs in them.

In the first, words are predetermined combinations of letters sequenced in accord with syntactic norms.[6] In this sentence the structured interplay of its elements creates its tone and determines its inflections, and the artistry inheres in the writer's command of vocabulary and skill in manipulating syntactical patterns. Sentences of this sort typically result from a series revisions ("smoky shadows," might initially have been "shadowy smoke" or "acrid shadows") as the writer refines the composition in a process which, paradoxically, effaces the writer from the completed unit of writing even as the writing's carefully wrought artistry testifies to the writer's role as its maker – much as a ship in a bottle confronts us simultaneously with its having been made and the absence (erasure?) of its maker. In the first of these sentences, we can, that is, infer that there has been a writer (or as Roland Barthes would have it, an *author*), but we have no access to the writer's compositional process. Our focus is necessarily restricted to what has been written – the composed text. In the second of these faux-Beat sentences, the combinations of letters function as aural actions that can register variously as emotive sounds and gestures (which in writing à la Capote would be simply noise) as well as words. In this sentence each aural action impels the next, and word choice and syntax are secondary to pace and momentum. In this system, the writer performs the writing instead of composing it, and writing is simultaneously what is performed, the mechanism used to record the performing, and the product that results from the performance.

In one sense, the difference between these two sample sentences is procedural – the difference between using writing to compose and using it to perform, but this difference also entails a shift in how alphabetic characters function. It is both a matter of *how* writing is used and a matter of *what* writing is. The two extra *o*'s in "sooo hip" in the second sentence illustrate this difference in writing as a medium and how it matters for the performing of writing in Spontaneous Prose. In the writing system of the first sentence, the phrase would be written "so hip," and "so" would intensify the quality "hip." The word "so," that is, would function structurally, and how it might be spoken or heard, its possible aurality, would be irrelevant to its grammatical function and its role in the sentence. In the writing system of the second sentence, the extra letters in "sooo" convert the word into an aural action that we hear spoken with a specific inflection that functions dramatically within the speaking writer's performance. Where "so" (in the first sentence) is a unit in a syntactic system that governs its function and meaning, "sooo" in the second sentence is an action in a system in which spelling and syntactic patterns can be distorted and subverted for expressive purposes. In the writing system of the second sentence, "sooo" must be imagined/heard as different than the word ("so") it references in order for its performative function to register. In the writing system of the first sentence, by contrast, the sound of "so" is unrelated to meaning and function.

The way the writer in the second sentence plays "so" by adding the extra letters to create "sooo" resembles the way a performing musician (as opposed to a composer) extends or shortens or displaces a note so that it rushes the beat or lags behind it. In the writing system of the first sentence, the meaning of "so hip" is structural. In "sooo hip" (in the second sentence) meaning is performative. We register the writer playing, as it were, the word, and what matters is this aural (as if present) action in time and across time and how the enacted writing records this (that is, stores and transmits this) for the listening reader.[7] In Kerouac's Spontaneous Prose, the performing writer projects the writing and remains (sometimes implicitly, more often explicitly) a presence in it, unlike the composing writer who disappears from the writing the writer has composed.

4.2 Writing as System[s]

At minimum, these two sample sentences involve contrasting writing styles and fictional rhetorics.[8] But more fundamentally, they involve different writing systems. That is, the mechanism of writing, which is to say the medium of writing, differs in them, and this difference matters for understanding Spontaneous Prose. We typically understand the mechanism of writing (when we think of it at all) as a kind of linguistic erector set – a collection of elements and procedures that can be assembled in many ways. What matters are the products we make *by* writing and make *of* writing, which we also call *writing*. Writing itself – as a mechanism or medium – needn't be examined. In learning to tie knots, we don't care what twine is or bother learning how to make it; we focus on how to manipulate it into knots. But writing, the linguist Roy Harris has argued, is more complicated than this. Rather than a singular and constant medium, writing is, Harris proposes, an array of media, and this is because writing systems are composed of two elements:

- a notational set (for English the Latin-script alphabet that begins a-b-c)
- the procedures that govern how the notational set is deployed and how it functions.

For Harris, two writing systems could share the same notational set (alphabetic characters) but differ as systems if the logic and procedures for using the notational set differed.[9] This provides a basis for understanding the difference between the two sample sentences – between, that is, the conventional compositional textuality of the first and performative textuality of the second. The sentences use the same notational set but use the set differently and for different purposes.

In the first sample sentence, letter combinations designate words that have the same syntactic function within the sentence and the same meaning whether the reader registers them silently or imagines them as voiced. In this sentence words may derive from speech and speaking but needn't be spoken. This writing system supports using writing to compose structured verbal objects – the so-called *text* or *work*. And the text, the work in and of writing that results, is like that ship in a bottle, where the modeler's work fashioning the ship and placing it within the bottle is implicit but not visible. In the second sample sentence, letter combinations are aural actions that must be voiced or imagined as heard. They operate within a dramatic context, and spoken inflection is an aspect of meaning. In one sentence, writing is a medium for constructing (composing) a linguistic system/object in which the "written" is primary. In the other, writing is a medium for recording linguistic performing. Both systems use alphabetic characters but differ in how letters relate to syntax, sound, and time. In the system of the first sentence, syntax controls meaning, sound is secondary, and the composed text is an atemporal system/object. In the system for the second sentence, the enacting of the performative occasion controls meaning and can override syntax; sound is a primary and necessary feature; and the text is an action that occurs in and as time.

In both sentences alphabetic characters operate visually and aurally, but differently so. In the sentence that begins "The coffeehouse cat with the scraggly goatee," letters represent words; grammatical conventions control function and meaning; and whether we process the words silently by eye or imagine also hearing them, they have the same meaning and the same syntactical role.[10] In this sentence, words are aural units only secondarily. In the sentence that begins "Oowee! That bongo caaat is sooo hip," the letters convey sound. Words *mean* in being heard. In the textuality of this second system, the writing system implicit in Spontaneous Prose, letter sequences can be freely manipulated to distort or play against spelling conventions, so that words shift from being units within syntactic patterns (elements within a structure) into being aural actions arising from performance. In this writing system, momentum and dramatic inflection (as registered in sound and conveyed by sound) enact meaning.

4.3 How Spontaneous Prose Changes What We Mean by Writing

The difference between the two sample sentences underscores that Spontaneous Prose should not be dismissed as Kerouac's self-indulgent rationale for failing to compose writing but should, instead, be understood as his rationale (however idiosyncratically expressed) for performing in (and with) writing. Recognizing this clarifies both the textuality of

Spontaneous Prose as a writing system as well its implications for understanding Kerouac's mode of writing.

In "Essentials of Spontaneous Prose," Kerouac writes: "Time being of the essence in the purity of speech, sketching language is undisturbed flow from the mind of personal secret idea-words, *blowing* (as per jazz musician) on subject of image."[11] He then adds, "No periods separating sentence-structures already arbitrarily riddled by false colons and timid usually needless commas – but the vigorous space dash separating rhetorical breathing." For Kerouac, that is, writing is an action that occurs in time, and writing records the writer's performative action. The key to this is Kerouac's sense of the role of *time*. In the compositional textuality of Modernism as practiced by Ernest Hemingway and others (and continued by Capote), time can be a topic or a symbolic construct but it cannot be temporal action.[12] In Spontaneous Prose, writing cannot fully preserve and transmit time in the way that analogue sound recording can preserve and transmit the actual diachronic time of someone speaking, but Spontaneous Prose can convey that performed writing has a temporal dynamic and that this writing is a diachronic process that functions as an analogue to time in the performance. The distinction, that is, is between *compositional* textuality, in which "Time" is a symbolic construct or a topic, and *performative* textuality in which "Time" is a diachronic (as if actual) presence and is "of the essence."

The difference between writing representing Time and writing operating in time and as Time is evident in Kerouac's "Jazz of the Beat Generation," published January 1955 in the annual *New World Writing*.[13] The piece combines material drawn directly from *On the Road* as Kerouac first drafted it April 1951 in the three-week marathon of typing of the original scroll version, a few passages from *Visions of Cody* drafted spring 1952, and some additional passages that Kerouac apparently wrote (typed, performed) sometime in 1954 as he generated the typescript for *New World Writing*. In other words, as published, "Jazz of the Beat Generation" interweaves three distinct phases of writing:

- the scroll material written before Kerouac had fully developed to Spontaneous Prose
- the *Visions of Cody* material written as Kerouac was developing Spontaneous Prose
- the 1954 material unique to "Jazz of the Beat Generation" written after he had fully elaborated Spontaneous Prose and conceptualized it in "Essentials of Spontaneous Prose."

Comparing the April 1951 material to the 1954 material clarifies how Spontaneous Prose functions as a writing system and the role of performed time in it.

Here's an example of the 1951 material – a distinctly Kerouacian scene but not written in Spontaneous Prose:

> A bunch of colored men in Saturday night suits were whooping it up in front. It was a sawdust saloon, all wood, with a small bandstand near the john on which the fellows huddled with their hats on blowing over people's heads, a crazy place, not far from Market Street, in the dingy skid-row rear of it, near Harrison and the big bridge causeway[14]

And here's an example of the 1954 material written in Spontaneous Prose (not incorporated into *On the Road*):

> It was just a usual Saturday night goodtime, nothing else; the bebop winos were wailing away, the workingman tenors, the cats who worked and got their horns out of hock and blew and had their women troubles, and came on in their horns with a will, saying things, a lot to say, talkative horns, you could almost hear the words and better than that the harmony, made you hear the way to fill up blank spaces of time with the tune and very consequence of your hands and breath and dead soul; summer, August 1949, and Frisco blowing mad, the dew on the Muscat in the interior fields of Joaquin and down in Watsonville the lettuce blowing, the money flowing for Frisco so seasonal and mad, the railroads rolling, extraboards roaring, crates of melons on sidewalks, bananas coming off elevators, tarantulas suffocating in the new crazy air, chipped ice and the cool interior smells of grape tanks, cool bop hepcats standing slumped with horn and no lapels and blowing like Wardell, like Brew Moore softly … all of it insane, sad, sweeter than the love of mothers yet harsher than the murder of fathers. The clock on the wall quivered and shook; nobody cared about that thing.

In the 1951 example, Kerouac is composing a scene. The passage foregrounds *what* is observed more than the *act* of observing or the writer's *stake* in observing. The result is that we attend to what is described – not the writer reacting and interacting as he elaborates the description. The relatively conventional, compositional nature of the passage is also evident in the writing system for this pre-Spontaneous Prose material. While sound matters, sound (the word "whooping," for example) is a textural enhancement. The words are units of meaning, not aural actions, and the relatively conventional syntax of these relatively short sentences control their function.

Conversely, the 1954 passage is performative rather than compositional. The performing writer re-experiences the scene, participating in it as he generates it. Kerouac's memory initiates the passage, and his associational responses lead the writing, as he puts it in "Essentials of Spontaneous Prose," "outwards swimming in sea of language to peripheral release." In this passage, the sound of words can generate further performance and even become a kind of meaning. The phrase "the lettuce blowing," for instance, immediately elicits "the money flowing." Whether "blowing" is a typo for "growing" (as in "the lettuce growing") that Kerouac retains and plays from in generating the passage or a surreal treatment of the lettuce as a kind of jazz horn or is literal (in the sense of leaf lettuce rather than head lettuce blowing in the wind), the slang of "lettuce" for money leads associationally to "money flowing" and the "ing" of the string of participles is a further sonic weaving:

> and down in Watsonville the lettuce blowing, the money flowing for Frisco so seasonal and mad, the railroads rolling, extraboards roaring, crates of melons on sidewalks

In the Spontaneous Prose of the 1954 passage, performing the scene involves an associational energy that moves outward from the scene (even as it expresses it) and does so with a momentum that all but transcends time even as it unfolds in and as time.[15] Implicitly, that "clock on the wall" has been "quivering" and "shaking" all along, but "nobody," least of all the Spontaneous Prose performer, cares about the mechanical, arbitrary measure of clock time. What matters is the "mindflow" of associational performance in which time operates as the "time-race of work." In the 1954 passage we engage through and with the performing writer. As we *register* what is being described, we *attend* to, are *drawn* into, the performance of describing.

These two excerpts from "Jazz of the Beat Generation" illustrate the difference between treating writing as a medium for composing texts and using writing as a medium to perform texts. In reading the 1951 excerpt, it is sufficient to register the words *as* words and apprehend the scene they construct. In reading the 1954 excerpt, it is necessary to *hear* the words as the speaker's voiced actions and thus to treat the scene as the occasion for the speaker's performance. In the 1954 excerpt, the writing records the writer performing, and this results in time being present as a diachronic unfolding that replaces both Time as topic and Time as symbolic construction. In Spontaneous Prose, then, Time is experiential, and the writer's action in and as time aligns with the reader's action in and as time. The writing system is the medium that joins the two – a liminal space in which, from their different locations and temporalities, the projecting/performing writer and the engaging reader both participate.

4.4 Kerouac's Experimental Textualities

The 1951 excerpt from "Jazz of the Beat Generation" – and any number of other passages from Kerouac's early writing before the full development of Spontaneous Prose – demonstrate that he had the talent, like his contemporaries Capote, Norman Mailer, and others to compose conventional writing. Had he continued in this mode after *The Town and the City* he would probably have had an easier time publishing his work and perhaps be more generally recognized as a major literary figure. Conversely, had he dispensed with narrative altogether – as he did for much of *Visions of Cody*, the book he considered his masterpiece – his importance as an avant-garde writer (a peer to William Burroughs and other midcentury experimentalists) might be more widely recognized.

Exploring why Kerouac seems to have been compelled to explore experimental textualities yet remained committed to narrative would take us into the mysteries of biography and speculative *what ifs*, but this doubled ambition is evident, I'd suggest, in his multiple and evolving attempts at *On the Road* prior to the April 1951 scroll that became the spine of the novel as published, and then in the series of experiments that resolved into Spontaneous Prose and *Visions of Cody* as he worked to address what he felt was lacking in the scroll draft of *On the Road*. However we might understand his ongoing commitment to narrative, the developmental arc of these experiments shows Kerouac turning away from the conventional writing system that Capote presumes is the only possible writing system, and instead working out an alternative writing system in which sound becomes not only action but meaning.[16]

One explanation for Kerouac developing Spontaneous Prose was that he was searching for a style that would convey the speed and fluidity of his road experiences. Another is that he was drawn to the improvisational, elaborative freedom of jazz – especially Charlie Parker's bravura bop cadenzas and the lyricism of Lester Young. Both explanations have validity but neither seem sufficient. Mark Twain evoked the fluidity of the raft on the river in *Adventures of Huckleberry Finn*, and Kerouac tried to emulate Twain in an early, abandoned version of *Road* (eventually published as *Pic*). Similarly, Kerouac's work journals show him searching for a way to use his observations about jazz performance as the basis for a writing method instead of simply an aspirational analogy but uncertain about how to manage this.[17]

There is a third explanation to consider: analog sound recording. The developments of sound recording at the end of the nineteenth century and in the early decades of the twentieth, first on wax cylinders, then 78 rpm discs and then in conjunction with film as silent movies became "talkies," meant that language as spoken action could, for the first time, be recorded, stored, and transmitted without having to be converted into the visual code of alphabetic notation. Prior to analog sound recording, the aural dimensions of spoken language (pitch, pace, tone, texture, inflection) could be implied but not captured and preserved, and prior to analog sound recording the way spoken language operates in time and as time could only be implied (represented symbolically) but not captured and preserved.[18]

The German media theorist/historian Friedrich Kittler offers the most powerful analysis of this transition, and several factors are relevant to Kerouac and Spontaneous Prose. As an alternative procedure for storing language, analog (and subsequently digital) sound recording competes with writing, taking over some of its social and cultural functions and breaking its monopoly. One way to understand the experiments of such High Modernists as James Joyce in *Ulysses*, T.S. Eliot in *The Waste Land*, and Ezra Pound in *The Cantos* is to see them as defensive, even reactionary, moves against this competition and the mass pop culture discourse it was enabling in radio and film, where the audience interacts directly with voiced language rather than processing writing as visual code to infer an illusory presence from it. If we consider Modernist aesthetics in this context, the Modernist emphasis on compression, fragmentation, collage, and juxtaposition (what was once often celebrated as "spatial form") make perfect sense. These tactics utilize writing's distinctive capacities as a visual system (including the symbolic nature of time in writing) to create practices that do not derive from the embodied aural processes of speaking and therefore can't be fully replicated in speaking. The work of the High Modernists must be seen on the page and deciphered from the page to be fully experienced. Pound's emphasis on compression originates in his commitment to composing and writing, not speaking, even though he at times used spoken diction and even colloquial vocabulary in his poetry. And the specific writing system the modernists used – and brilliantly exploited – is what might be termed *the* textuality of print (while Spontaneous Prose might be termed *a* textuality of media).

Kerouac's relationship to sound recording was fundamentally different. The Modernists came of age (both personally and aesthetically) in an era where the textuality of print was coin of the realm and were then overtaken, challenged, even threatened by these new technologies and the cultural practices they made possible. Kerouac, however, grew up within this new mediascape of movies, radio, and sound recordings. He was deeply immersed not only in the masters and masterworks of the literary tradition but also in the popular culture of his era. And his responsiveness to the aural artistry of story tellers, and (as we'd now term them) spoken word artists such as Lord Buckley, and film personalities such as W. C. Fields, and jazz singers such as Billie Holiday led him, I'd suggest, to want to re-engineer writing so that it could convey the aural timing and expressive inflection of artful speaking, as these figures did in their recorded performances, while yet preserving the linguistic density and structural effects of the nineteenth and early twentieth century masters he revered.[19]

It is also noteworthy that Kerouac, unlike most writers of his era, had experience with sound recording technology in the 1940s. His friend Jerry Newman had a wire recorder, an early version of a tape recorder, that he hauled into the after-hours jazz clubs in 1941 and 1942 to record Art Tatum, Thelonious Monk, and other giants of jazz. And as early as 1944, Newman had a record store with a small recording studio that he let Kerouac use. The exposure to jazz recording sessions and access to recording equipment probably contributed to Kerouac believing for a time that he could bypass composing in writing by recording himself speaking, then transcribing the results. I've explored elsewhere how this failed to work, but the failure was one of the steps along the way as Kerouac came to reimagine how alphabetic notation could be used for an alternate system of writing that would support an alternate writing procedure – one governed by and conveying actual time rather than (as with the writing system of print literacy) constructing symbolic representations of time.[20]

4.5 Spontaneous Prose as a New Medium of Writing

Discussions of digitized writing practices typically label predigital writing practices as "old media" and digitized writing as "new media." In this mapping, Kerouac's Spontaneous Prose is either dismissed or celebrated – dismissed for failing to exploit the textuality of print or celebrated for pioneering an alternate way to practice the textuality of print. But what Kerouac achieved in Spontaneous Prose is something more fundamental than this and richer in implication: his development (or "discovery," if you like) that the medium of writing is neither singular nor permanent but can take a range of forms depending on the logic governing how the notational set functions within a specific writing system. As such, Spontaneous Prose, viewed as a writing system and as an innovation in textuality, mediates between the spatial logic of the "old media" of print and the temporal dynamic of digitized "new media."

When we read Kerouac well, we are adapting, I'd suggest, to his innovative textuality. Conversely, when we fail to read Kerouac well, we are failing to adapt to his innovative textuality. And if we want to understand how and why Kerouac's approach to writing (so derisively dismissed by Capote) could influence many of his contemporaries who have been celebrated for their experimental aesthetics, we need to start by acknowledging Kerouac's experimental textuality for what it actually was and is: a decisive break from the textuality of print and the creation of an alternative – a textuality responsive to, and building in dialogue with, such modern media as sound recording, film and radio.

Notes

1. Jack Kerouac, "Essentials of Spontaneous Prose," in *The Portable Beat Reader*, ed. Ann Charters (New York: Penguin, 1992), 57.
2. Emily Temple's March 12, 2019, blog post, "A Close Reading of Jack Kerouac's Advice to Writers," is a recent elaboration of Capote's critique of Spontaneous Prose: lithub.com/a-close-reading-of-jack-kerouacs-advice-to-writers/.
3. Ginsberg's enthusiasm for Spontaneous Prose is evident as early as his review of Kerouac's *The Dharma Bums* in the November 12, 1958, issue of The Village Voice, underscored in "The Great Rememberer," the introduction he wrote for *Visions of Cody*, and a primary tenet of The Jack Kerouac School of Disembodied Poetics that he established at what is now Naropa University.
4. In *Jack Kerouac: A Bibliography* (New York: Phoenix Bookshop, 1975), Ann Charters quotes Kerouac explaining the occasion for writing "Essentials of Spontaneous Prose": "Allen Ginsberg and Bill Burroughs said, 'Why don't you write a little brochure of instructions about how to write like you do?' I did it for them. We never knew it was going to get published" (81). Kerouac's decision to cast the piece as a series of (somewhat gnomic) instructions reflects this occasion.
5. For Kerouac experimenting with how to shift writing from composing to performing precedes (and leads to) his altered sense of the textuality of writing. See my *The Textuality of Soulwork: Jack Kerouac's Quest for Spontaneous Prose* (Ann Arbor: University of Michigan Press, 2014), an account of this process from the initial attempts at *On the Road* through the writing of *Visions of Cody*.
6. For a discussion of the role of spelling in the visual processing of words, see Josef Vachek's "Spelling as an Important Linguistic Concept," in *Written Language Revisited* (Amsterdam: John Benjamins Publishing Co. 1989), 167–174.
7. One might argue that reading is silent or that all writing has an aural dimension, but the interplay of silent (visual) and aural in these two sentences is qualitatively different. In the first, attending to the sound of the words may enhance the sentence aesthetically but is secondary to, or even extraneous to, its structure and meaning. In the second, the sound of the words and the non-words is fundamental to both the meaning and the aesthetic effect because the words are evoking the speaker's dramatic performance rather than registering the writer's compositional product.

8. The difference is akin to the difference between listening to Glenn Gould perform Bach's *The Well-Tempered Clavier* and listening to John Coltrane perform "Giant Steps." While Gould's brilliant musicality is important, how his artistry elaborates the intricate architecture of Bach's composition matters more. With Coltrane, the composition is a bare scaffolding from which the piece is created anew every time it is performed, and what matters is the emotional depth and creative energy of the performance itself. When we listen to Gould perform Bach, Gould is our channel to connect to Bach's composition. When we listen to Coltrane perform "Giant Steps" or "A Love Supreme" or "Crescent" or …, we listen to Coltrane and the occasioning composition disappears.
9. Harris, an integrational linguist, articulates this model in Part I of his study, *Signs of Writing* (New York: Routledge, 1995). Harris, it should be noted, sees his approach as an alternative to, and correction of, Saussure's analysis of writing as a system.
10. This first sentence illustrates the writing system we have been taught in school and take so much for granted that it seems the only writing system there has been, is, and could ever be. Writing systems, though, are historically and technologically contingent, as the contrasting norms for medieval manuscript culture and those for industrialized print as it emerged in the later part of the nineteenth century and continued through much of the twentieth century illustrate.
11. In Spontaneous Prose, it should be noted, that writing is not "speech" but resembles speaking in that the *writing* occurs in time, as time, and enacts time, and as such "rhetorical breathing" aligns with but differs from actual "breathing." Spontaneous Prose, as fully developed in *Visions of Cody*, involves the performing of writing rather than performing speaking. See Chapter 5 of *The Textuality of Soulwork*.
12. In composing writing, the written product does not preserve the temporal relationship between the units of writing; this labor is absorbed into the product. The writer can use writing to comment on time; but the written structure itself is an atemporal object, even though we process it in the temporal process of reading. To put it another way, the temporal action of composing and the temporal process of reading connect through the written object (text) but neither temporality is present to the other. How long it might have taken Hemingway to craft a sentence through multiple revisions and how long it takes to read the sentence have no relationship to each other. For an explanation of this, see Friedrich Kittler's "Gramophone, Film, Typewriter," trans. Dorthea Von Mücke, in *Literature, Media, Information Systems*, ed. John Johnston (Amsterdam: G+B Arts International, 1997). Kittler contrasts writing as a symbolic medium (what is meant in this article by writing as a compositional medium) with what he terms "mechanical media" such as analogue sound recording, which register the temporal dimension of performance and convey that temporal dimension. Kittler analyzes how the advent of mechanical media make apparent the symbolic nature of time and temporality in

symbolic media by preserving diachronic time so that the elapsing of time involved in playing a passage of music and the time it takes to listen to a recording of that passage being performed are synched and equivalent. The discussion of "Time" in Spontaneous Prose in this article is informed by Kittler's model for media, his view that media impinge on and alter each other, and his argument that media are not ahistorical structure/systems but historically, technologically, economically, and sociologically contingent and thus variable rather than static systems.

13. Malcolm Cowley, as part of his campaign to increase Kerouac's profile and thereby convince Viking Books, where he was a consultant, to publish *On the Road*, arranged for the publication of "Jazz of the Beat Generation" and two other pieces derived from the novel. See Gerald Howard, "The Kerouac–Cowley File," *Journal of Beat Studies* 10 (2022), 107–110.
14. Jack Kerouac, "Jazz of the Beat Generation," *New World Writing: Seventh Mentor Selection* (New York: New American Library, 1955), 7.
15. Here, again, it should be noted that it is writing itself, not speaking represented in writing, that is being performed.
16. See the Epilogue to *The Textuality of Soulwork*.
17. See Chapters 1 and 2 of *The Textuality of Soulwork*.
18. See Kittler's "Gramophone, Film, Typewriter."
19. See my *The Textuality of Soulwork* for a fuller treatment of this context and analysis of how it factors into the successive experiments that culminate in Spontaneous Prose.
20. See endnote 12.

CHAPTER 5

The Spontaneous Aesthetic in The Subterraneans

George Mouratidis

Jack Kerouac wrote *The Subterraneans* (1958) in October 1953 in a three-day marathon. From the outset, its "bop writer" narrator, Leo Percepied, is conscious of how difficult it is "to make a real confession and show what happened" as he begins recalling his love affair with biracial bohemian cognoscente Mardou Fox immediately upon its demise.[1] Recounting later an instance of his jealous paranoia, Leo interrupts himself in frustration, declaring "art is short, life is long" (*The Subterraneans*, 86). The maxim goes to the heart of Kerouac's spontaneous aesthetic and his project as a writer. For Leo, a preconceived art determined by codified forms, language, and practices is too abstract, too prescriptive to accommodate the organic dimensions and dynamics of his awareness of his own life and his ability to "let the truth seep out" as he initially hopes (*The Subterraneans*, 1). Through Leo's telling, Kerouac deliberately performs a writer's reaching towards form and language capable of engaging and transmitting the idiosyncrasy and nuance of his private consciousness and experience as it is taking place. Here, in what Hassan Melehy calls the author's "writing in real time," Kerouac also enacts his own effort towards the "undisturbed flow from the mind" described in "Essentials of Spontaneous Prose" (1957), an elucidation of his aesthetic written right after completing *The Subterraneans* at the request of Allen Ginsberg and William S. Burroughs, both astounded by the manuscript upon reading it.[2]

Liberated by the iconoclasm and improvisation of what he understood to be a bebop jazz aesthetic, Kerouac developed in *The Subterraneans* a "Modern Prose" he described to writer-critic Alfred Kazin in October 1954 as "jazzlike breathlessly swift spontaneous and unrevised floods," which "comes out wild" but "pure."[3] Kerouac thus privileges feeling over what he saw as the inauthenticity of compositional "craft" espoused by the reigning literary edicts of New Criticism. Kerouac proposes instead a poetics of the body, sensorium, imagination, and voice in concert: "tap from yourself the song of yourself, *blow! — now!* —[original emphasis]" he writes in

"Essentials," "*your* way is your only way — 'good' — or 'bad' — always honest. ('ludicrous') spontaneous, 'confessional' interesting, because not 'crafted' [original emphasis]" ("Essentials," 70). In such touchstone expositions as "Essentials" and "Belief & Technique for Modern Prose" (1959), as in *The Subterraneans*, Kerouac is not offering a methodology for writing but an individually adaptable way to engage and transmit consciousness, experience and circumstance to tell "what actually happened."[4]

The Subterraneans is a concentrated case study in how Kerouac composes, indeed rehearses and constructs a spontaneous prose text. The novel in this sense emphasizes "writing as writing," to borrow from critic Warren Tallman, making the writer's presence in the text as strong as that of the narrator.[5] This intense, nebulous and anarchic telling exemplifies how Kerouac deploys a vulnerable "pure" prose directly to his avowed reader, exploring the texture and kinesis of a consciousness-in-flux, the dynamic fluctuation of his interior and exterior worlds, and his immediate present and never too distant past. Most significantly, this fluidity points towards a sense of fusion between text and voice, writing and performance, and most significantly, prose and poetry. With *The Subterraneans*, Kerouac let loose a hybridizing narrative form whose radical compositional and organizational logic demanded a reappraisal of the form and function of the narrative American novel in the mid-twentieth century.

5.1 Telling "what actually happened"

The Subterraneans is Kerouac's fictionalized account of his short-but-intense romance with Alene Lee, a young, hip African American–Native American intellectual, editor, and bebop aficionado who was one of the luminaries of the postwar avant-garde centered in the bohemian enclave of Greenwich Village.[6] Along with Lee, Kerouac populates his novel with thinly veiled real-life "subterraneans," as well as his Beat compadres: Adam Moorad (modeled on Ginsberg), Frank Carmody (Burroughs), Yuri Gligoric (Gregory Corso), Sam Vedder (Lucien Carr), and Balliol Mac-Jones (John Clellon Holmes). However, Kerouac's portrayal of Lee, unlike others, is significantly complicated by the fact that the novel is not a straightforward roman à clef but one imbricated within Kerouac's intimately detailed "confession" of his own innermost private experience of their relationship. As Lee later recalled, Kerouac had given her the manuscript to read only days after completing it: "I started reading and I went into shock. A lot of it was still raw," adding, "These were not the times as I knew them and the people, with the exception of his friends, were not as I knew them."[7] Despite her fictionalization as Mardou Fox, *The Subterraneans* lent Lee an unwelcome notoriety and cult status, leading her to fiercely guard her anonymity for decades afterwards, especially from Beat biographers and historians. This only compounded Lee's subsequent occlusion as a significant figure within the Beat oeuvre. Though the novel wasn't published until mid-February, 1958, the fact that Kerouac composed it immediately upon the demise of his relationship with Lee distinguishes it as the spontaneous prose text of the Duluoz Legend written closest to the bone.

5.2 Developing "confessional madness"

The dynamic, improvisatory sensibility which drives the spontaneous aesthetic of *The Subterraneans* was itself part of an amalgam of writing modes Kerouac had honed over a number of years. Kerouac's voluminous correspondence, for instance, was crucial to his development of spontaneous prose, with the openness, vulnerability and intimacy of such a confessional mode directly informing the form, language, and affect of *The Subterraneans*. In a 1960 introduction to the novel, Kerouac writes: "Not a word of this book was changed after I had finished writing it in three sessions from dusk to dawn at the typewriter like a long letter to a friend."[8] Leo himself recognizes the incisive, affective impact of such intimacy and vulnerability as he works through his response to a letter from Mardou, declaring "And tonight this letter is my last hope" (*The Subterraneans*, 61).

Elsewhere in *The Subterraneans* Kerouac actually points readers to the inception of his spontaneous prose. Early in the novel Leo recalls "in 1951 cutting along with my sketchbook on a wild October evening when I was discovering my own writing soul at last" (*The Subterraneans*, 14–15). This brings the novel in dialogue with the author's "Journal 1951" in which he records the development of his aesthetic from late August to late November, including many of the phrases and maxims from "Essentials" and "Belief" almost verbatim. The journal also details both the catalytic revelation of seeing saxophonist Lee Konitz perform at Birdland and Kerouac's discovery of "sketching" with words (on October 8 and 16 respectively).[9] Like Leo who strove to capture the "history and hugeness" (*The Subterraneans*, 14) of his immediate experience, Kerouac subsequently developed these intensive bursts of feverish recording towards an interplay of his perception and imagination: He extends the "tranced fixation upon an object before [him]" he describes as "dreaming on it" to an interplay between sensorium and the unconscious (*Journal*, 161).

This improvisational sensibility of spontaneous prose asserts a fluid, regenerative aesthetic rather than a monolithic compositional methodology. As Kerouac explained, "the style has varied" across his oeuvre: From "The Railroad Earth" to *Big Sur*, with the "confessional madness" of *The Subterraneans* being but one iteration of the spontaneous aesthetic ("Interview," 288). That Kerouac formalized his aesthetic in this way right after writing *The Subterraneans* speaks to the dimensions and intention of the text, especially when compared to *Visions of Cody* and *Doctor Sax*, the two major spontaneous prose novels whose composition preceded it. Whereas *Cody*, for instance, was a painstakingly modular work inspired by Proust's "method of recollection and amazement" (*Journal*, 168), Kerouac wrote *The Subterraneans* in a three-day marathon, modeling it on the confessional form of Dostoevsky's *Notes from Underground* (1864), a similarly short, intense text whose "sick" narrator addresses the reader directly ("Interview," 288). *The Subterraneans*, while exhibiting clear aesthetic and compositional distinctions from *Cody*, engages uniquely with the "Essentials" Kerouac outlined after he wrote it, a consistently immediate, concentrated text not unlike that of a "sketch," whose subjectivization of narrative prose and its praxis demands from its outset the reconsideration of what a novel is.

5.3 "Speak now in own unalterable way"

Though as is well known Kerouac eschewed "craft" and the traditional editorial process of publishers, the text of *The Subterraneans* nevertheless necessitated construction and, indeed, revision, both in his own subsequent augmentation of the manuscript and, ironically, of his editor's interventions. When questioned about how he came to write *The Subterraneans* in three days, Kerouac clarified that a period of considered preparation and construction is necessary prior to the rush of writing:

> You think out what actually happened, you tell friends long stories about it, you mull it over in your mind, you connect it together at leisure, then … you force yourself to sit at the typewriter, or at the writing notebook, and get it over with as fast as you can … and there's no harm in that because you've got the whole story lined up. ("Interview," 307).

While Kerouac insists he had already worked out "what actually happened" in the story, what it will look and sound like is only fully realized at the moment of writing: "All of it is in my mind," he maintains, "except that language that is used at the time that it is used" ("Interview," 307).

At the same time, Kerouac makes clear the corporeality of the writing practice itself, drawing on the work of psychoanalyst Wilhelm Reich who theorized that physical and mental health is contingent upon harnessing the organic vitality of Nature ("orgones"), in part through sexual release. *The Subterraneans* is replete with references to Reich, both direct, such as Leo's discussion of Reich's book *The Function of the Orgasm* (1927) and "beclouding of the senses" (*The Subterraneans*, 72), and implicit, in his obsession with his sexual performance. Kerouac thus imbues the rush of spontaneous composition with an intensely physical, postcoital quality: "write excitedly, swiftly, with writing-or-typing cramps," he advises in "Essentials," "in accordance … with laws of orgasm, Reich's 'beclouding of consciousness.' *Come* from within, out — to relaxed and said [original emphasis]" ("Essentials," 71). The corporeal terms that describe the immediate practice of writing are made even more explicit in a later account of the novel: "Writing the Subs in three nights was really a fantastic athletic feat as well as mental, you shoulda seen me after I was done … I was pale as a sheet and had lost fifteen pounds and looked strange in the mirror" ("Interview," 307). The emphasis on energetic immediacy and temporality provides the structure for a confessing narrator's "dramatic need to speak now in own unalterable way," as he writes in "Essentials," "Nothing is muddy that *runs in time* and to laws of *time* [original emphasis]" ("Essentials," 70): How the story is told resides in and of the moment.

While maintaining the form and dynamics of the text in this moment is paramount, Kerouac's subsequent insistence in "Essentials" on "*no revisions* [original emphasis]" is not clearcut. Along with correcting "obvious rational mistakes" such as names, one key exception to this rule is what the author calls making "*calculated* insertions in act of not-writing but *inserting* [original emphasis]" ("Essentials," 70), referring to the writer augmenting an existing manuscript with additional text, an act of "not-writing" because it is separate to the immediate temporality and dynamics which for Kerouac define authentic writing.

One major example of such an "insertion" in *The Subterraneans* is the episode Kerouac subsequently referred to as the "Flipping Confessions of Mardou": Leo's account of Mardou telling her "story of spiritual suffering" (*The Subterraneans*, 36), a series of wanderings around the city while she was high (*The Subterraneans*, 21–36) is a sizable portion of the narrative. The section, as Kerouac told his editor at Grove Press, Donald Allen, was not in the original version of the novel but inserted later and which he was actually willing to cut.[10] Along with revealing *The Subterraneans* as being, to some extent, a constructed novel, Kerouac, in his preference for

Allen to excise "one large block" from the text rather than make piecemeal cuts, reinforces the characteristic importance of fluidity, prosody, and the rushing pileup of impressionistic detail which the close reading of traditional editing would undoubtedly compromise. As Leo insists, "the details are the life of it ... say everything on your mind, don't hold it back, don't analyze or anything as you go along, say it out" (*The Subterraneans*, 58). Hence Kerouac's subsequent need to revise, or rather restore the text of *The Subterraneans* to maintain such unencumbered, idiosyncratic detail of expression: "I labored days undoing the wreckage of Don Allen's commas and dumb changes," he told Ginsberg, "so it's now as original, shiny, rhythmic."[11] Such insertions and emphasis of detail point to Kerouac's practice of keeping close at hand material such as letters, sketching notebooks, or journals relevant to his text as he is writing it, using them as guides in shaping its content and language to ensure he transmits his experience of "what actually happened" as authentically as possible.

5.4 "Blowing (as per jazz musician)"

While Leo proclaims himself a "bop writer" (*The Subterraneans*, 98), *The Subterraneans* is not a "jazz novel" or "jazz writing"; rather, it is a text whose spontaneous prose was in part shaped by the tenets, techniques and sensibility of what Kerouac understood to be a modern jazz, specifically bebop aesthetic. His particular interpretation and engagement with bebop was not that of a musician or musicologist but of a writer and enthusiast entering the milieu of African American culture as an outsider. In bebop's studied spontaneity Kerouac found the catalytic equation which engendered the coalescence of various writing approaches and techniques such as sketching, automatic writing, and confession. Here he saw as bebop's key tenets energetic improvisation, prosody, and an emphasis on individualities-in-discourse.

It was bebop's iconoclasm and *newness* which excited Kerouac. Even at the early stage of his artistic development, what draws Kerouac most to bebop is the idea of what he can only explain as its "relaxation" of established structures, tensions and changes.[12] The sensibility towards progress and innovation of established forms, Kerouac felt, was inevitable, expressed in the novel with Leo's consistent appeals to the future: "the music of tomorrow" (*The Subterraneans*, 6); "the jargon of the future" (*The Subterraneans*, 42).

That the two pivotal moments in the early development of Kerouac's spontaneous aesthetic – seeing Konitz perform and discovering sketching –

occurred within a week of each other indelibly fused his transmission of his consciousness with improvisation. Upon seeing Konitz, Kerouac reports of "a great discovery of my life" while "listening to a fellow who's doing exactly what I am … but on alto" (*Journal*, 137). Thus, the author's explanation of his practice in "Essentials" as "sketching language is undisturbed flow from the mind of personal secret idea-words, *blowing* (as per jazz musician) on subject of image [original emphasis]" ("Essentials," 69).[13]

The interrelation of "infinitely new modes of rhythm, melody and counterpoint" Kerouac recognizes as bebop's "harmony" ("Contemporary," 20) is clarified by historian Daniel Belgrad as "prosody," which he explains in terms relating directly to language. For Belgrad, bop prosody is a "conversational dynamic" and an "intersubjectivity" of communication between individual musicians.[14] One way this dynamic translates for Kerouac is in the interrelation between the various subjective elements of his writing.

Inspired by bebop's conversational dynamic, both between performers and with the audience, Kerouac also creates a sense of intimacy and reciprocity with the reader in a more direct way. The composition of *The Subterraneans* is a crucial part of its artistic statement. The real story of the novel is Kerouac's transmission to the reader of his experience and sensibility of "what actually happened" via a self-narrator's written testament of confession. In this, Kerouac is ever conscious of his readers and generous towards them, inviting them inside moments of a becoming by way of a text which lays open his process of telling as it is taking place. The first of many examples in the novel of this metatextuality occurs at the outset of Leo's confession, in which jazz is central: "not a piece of my pain has showed yet—or suffering—Angels, bear with me—I'm not even looking at the page but straight ahead into the sadglint of my wallroom and at a Sarah Vaughan Gerry Mulligan Radio KROW show on the desk in the form of a radio" (2). The interaction between performer and audience which translated into that between music and text was, for Kerouac, crucial. He thus draws on what poet LeRoi Jones (later Amiri Baraka) identifies in African American music as antiphony – the reciprocity between individual and community – to create a similar dynamic with his reader in the belief that the intimate, idiosyncratic detail of his own improvisational yet rehearsed "confession" will create a mutual sensitivity and receptiveness in them, gaining their trust through his vulnerability.[15] The eight words Konitz first inspired the author to jot down, "Blow as deep as you want to blow," underpin "Essentials" and are crucial to this intimacy of mutual recognition: "write as deeply, fish as far down as you want," Kerouac insists, "satisfy yourself first, then reader cannot fail to receive telepathic shock and meaning-excitement by same laws operating in his own human mind" ("Essentials," 69) In blowing "Deep Form," the writer, like the bop soloist, leaves themselves wide open and vulnerable to the chance, affect, tragedy, and comedy of the moment. Kerouac is always in danger of losing the symbiosis between the anarchic kinetics of his consciousness and lightning-fast fingers on the typewriter (by most accounts he could type 100-plus words per minute): With what critic Ann Douglas calls the "anarchic simultaneity" and "mental and physical flux" of Kerouac's narrative, the author is on the verge of "unmooring the story."[16] This occurs at numerous points throughout *The Subterraneans*; in digressional sketches, parenthetical asides, "P.S." ("Essentials," 70) riffing, even the narrator interrupting or undermining his telling – "It's too much" (*The Subterraneans*, 76). In accepting the possibility his improvisational performance of a confessional text may be at points "ludicrous" ("Essentials," 70), Kerouac is in close step with Charlie Parker, "the king and founder of the bop generation" (*The Subterraneans*, 14), who advised fellow performers that if they "act just a little bit foolish, and let yourself go, better ideas will come [to you]."[17]

The freedom and vulnerability of bebop improvisation helped liberate Kerouac's own discursive subjectivity, which, for him, is embodied by the organic form and dynamic of his sentences. For Kerouac, sentences should emphasize what he calls individual "rhetorical breathing" ("Essentials," 69), correlating them with the unfettered expression and phrasing of a bop soloist. Thus, instead of the arbitrary "false colons and timid usually needless commas" demanded by "craft," he proposes the "vigorous space dash" in a similar way to a "jazz musician drawing breath between outblown phrases" ("Essentials," 69).[18] *The Subterraneans* is replete with such breath-statements, many of these connected in paragraph-long sentences, some continuing for several pages.

Leo's at times miasmic telling is simultaneously anchored and directed in part through a cycling of images, words, and phrases, even scenarios. These in sum carry the function of sound by punctuating the rhythm and musicality of Leo's telling, thus lending it a quality of synesthesia. It is within the dimensions of these sinewy, prosodic sentences Kerouac textualizes the interplay and exchange of his inner and outer worlds, his mind (sensorium, imagination, interior logic) and his body (breath, voice, speech). The simultaneities, divergences, variations, and repetitions of Leo's telling are anchored by the rush of his almost overwhelming urgency to transmit the full scope and complexity of his awareness and experience of losing Mardou's love – the organic dynamics of a sensorium and consciousness in perpetual crisis and flux.

5.5 "Submissive to everything, open"

Kerouac's advice that a writer of "modern" prose be "Submissive to everything, open, listening" and "Be crazy dumbsaint of the mind" ("Belief," 72) invokes an expansive, receptive psychedelic sensibility approaching what Aldous Huxley termed "Mind at Large."[19] In both the subject matter and material text of *The Subterraneans* Kerouac explores the texture of such a consciousness by enacting the transmission of his experience in the world of his relationship with Lee. He does this in the novel both as an observer, through Leo's account of Mardou's "madness," specifically her "Market Street reveries" (*The Subterraneans*, 69), and as the subject, in the transmission of "my eager impressionable ready-to-create construct destroy and die brain" (*The Subterraneans*, 45) through the dynamic interplay, indeed fusion of his interior and exterior awareness.

At one juncture in the "Flipping Confessions of Mardou" section of the novel (*The Subterraneans*, 21–36), Leo recounts Mardou's telling him of a transcendental moment while walking aimlessly through the city in an altered state, receptive to yet overwhelmed by the simultaneity of possible directions open to her:

> my mind kept turning into the several directions that I was thinking of going but my body kept walking straight along Columbus altho I felt the sensation of each of the directions I mentally and emotionally turned into, amazed at all the possible directions you can take with different motives that come in, like it can make you a different *person*— … —What's in store for me in the direction I *don't* take?— [original emphasis] (*The Subterraneans*, 21–22)

While this psychic conundrum appears at once liberating and debilitating for Mardou, the confluence of possibilities also speak to an atypical consciousness and sensibility, one outside the bounds of ontological reality or, in Mardou's terms, the "big abstract constructions" (*The Subterraneans*, 16) of the normative. Like an improvising soloist, Mardou resides purely in the moment of intersubjectivity in recognizing these possibilities.

As Mardou attempts to convey the idiosyncrasies and plenitudes of her "reveries," her movement is neither fixed nor linear. This functions as an analogy for Kerouac's own narrative dynamics in the novel: the confluence of myriad possible directions, a simultaneity of impressions both perceived and imagined, and the simultaneities of interior and exterior, past and present. The writer-narrator transcribes the awareness of his own experience in motion, where all elements of "what actually happened" are concurrent even if not immediately apparent.

Kerouac describes the site of significance as the "eye within the eye," advising writer's to "Work from pithy middle eye out" ("Belief," 72). This "eye" is the writer's inner world subsequently transposed onto his outer world, with his imagination, memory, and affect imbuing immediate perception and sensation. Not only do these dynamics of consciousness dismantle the "big abstract constructions" of narrative logic, they contort the modes of its representation. One way Kerouac recalibrates narrative logic to transmit a consciousness-in-flux is through an organic fluctuation of chronological time in the narrative. Most notably, these shifts – like cinematic jump-cuts – occur between the past and immediate present state of Leo's relationship with Mardou, but also the past and present of his life more broadly, creating a continuum along Kerouac's fluid sentence. Leo's loving impression of Mardou flows into his smalltown boyhood within a single "rhetorical breath":

> so beautifully her soul showing out radiant as an angel wandering in hell and the hell the selfsame streets I'd roamed in watching, watching for someone just like her and never dreaming the darkness and the mystery and eventuality of our meeting in eternity, the hugeness of her face now like the sudden vast Tiger head on a poster on the back of a woodfence in the smoky dumpyards Saturday no-school mornings, direct, beautiful, insane, in the rain.— (*The Subterraneans*, 36).

The simultaneity of impressions and points-of-view in Kerouac's rush to transmit the teller's consciousness-in-flux engenders a narrative sensibility completely at odds with the New Critical presuppositions of an objective, monolithic compositional logic.[20]

5.6 "Everything is poetry"

The Subterraneans is replete with examples of what critic George Dardess describes as Kerouac's "pedagogical injunctions."[21] As with Leo's furious reaction to young writer John Golz's avowal of the New Critics' "selectivity" (*The Subterraneans*, 75), Kerouac dramatizes the dynamic interaction between poetry and prose in *The Subterraneans* by staging another debate, this time between "bop writer" Leo and the poet Yuri:

> [Yuri] claimed everything was poetry, I tried to make the common old distinction between verse and prose, he said, "Listen Percepied do you believe in freedom?—then say what you want, its poetry, poetry, all of it is poetry, great prose is poetry, great verse is poetry."—"Yes" I said "but verse is verse and prose is prose."—"No no" he yelled "it's all poetry." (*The Subterraneans*, 83)

Leo subsequently takes on that value of "freedom" while regarding Yuri's approach as one closer to craft. Leo makes plain his (and Kerouac's) approach to writing upon hearing Yuri's "best line" of poetry: Leo, to whom the line sounds like "small magazine poetry" tells Yuri "I would say rather it was great if you'd written it suddenly on the spur of the moment." Yuri, despite Leo's skepticism, insists: "But I did—right out of my mind it flowed and I threw it down ... it was bang! just like you say, spontaneous vision!" Recalling the exchange, Leo doesn't change his mind about the line, only going so far as to concede that Yuri "saying [it] came to him spontaneously suddenly made me respect it more" (*The Subterraneans*, 83). While Leo and Yuri agree to disagree on the nature of the relationship between prose and poetry, Kerouac, by staging their dialogue, underscores the mutuality of their aesthetic preoccupations.

Kerouac himself enacted such a dialogue, both in his interactions with fellow writers as well as a natural progression of his artistic practice. For instance, echoing Leo's words, Kerouac assures his former editor Robert Giroux in the summer of 1954, "I agree with you, prose is prose, poetry poetry" (*Selected Letters 1*, 445), while three months prior to the novel's publication, Kerouac refers to *The Subterraneans* as "a real sweet poem of mine" (*The Letters*, 376).[22] In Kerouac's conception of writing as improvisation, Melehy argues, "the distinction between poetry and prose effectively breaks down."[23] This sense of fluidity and hybridity between narrative prose and poetry was par for the course in Kerouac's development of his spontaneous aesthetic from the outset. As he refashioned the prose sentence for his "lifework" (*Journal*, 140) Kerouac cites the Modern American and European novelists he considers his aesthetic antecedents, namely Proust, Louis-Ferdinand Cèline, Jean Genet, James Joyce, William Faulkner, and Henry Miller, but also a number of contemporary poets including e. e. cummings, Hart Crane, and William Carlos Williams. The latter was particularly influential on Kerouac's spontaneous aesthetic, the novelist telling Ginsberg in February 1952, "Williams is right: the original impulse of the mind is in the 'prose seed' or first wild draft of the poem, the 'formal ode' is a dull suit covering the great exciting nude body of reality" (*The Letters*, 135). Further, the maxims in "Belief" of "No time for poetry but exactly what is" and "don't think of words when you stop but to see picture better" ("Belief," 72) immediately recall Williams' statement in Book I of *Paterson*, "no ideas but in things—," approaching the impressionistic objectivism in his practice of sketching.[24]

Less explicit in Kerouac's stated rhetoric is the affinity of his aesthetic with Charles Olson's conception of "Projective Verse," specifically its measurement of the line through individual breath emphasizing the syllable, the movement and energy of the poem, and the poet's immediate engagement with their field of composition. Kerouac's maxim in "Belief" that "Something that you feel will find its own form" ("Belief," 72) – the synergy of content and form through feeling rather than craft – is not dissimilar to Olson's insistence that "Form is never more than an extension of content."[25] While Kerouac eschewed any outright affinity between Olson's poetics and his own unique "breath as measure" ("Interview," 301), his emphasis of the line hybridizes his narrative prose. The grouping of connected breath-units is for Kerouac no different to that in poetry: "Every paragraph," he insists, "is a poem" ("Interview," 300).

5.7 "Add alluvials"

One of the most uniquely *Kerouacian* manifestations in *The Subterraneans* are in the passages which feature what Kerouac referred to as "alluvials," essentially the author's transcription of particulate surplus or residue of the ebb and flow of his consciousness in Time – words, images, sounds, text. Such fragments of language Kerouac explains in "Essentials" as "the infantile pileup of scatological buildup words" ("Essentials," 69), which, he maintains, "will turn out to be a great appending rhythm to a thought" ("Essentials," 69–70), similarly in the "movement over subject, as river rock, so mindflow over jewel-center" until "what was dim formed 'beginning' becomes sharp-necessitating 'ending' and language shortens in race … to conclusion, last words, last trickle" ("Essentials," 70). The line's conclusion is not a definitive ending but an exhaustion, as an exhalation. It is in the appendix to Donald Allen's influential anthology *The New American Poetry 1945–1960* (1960) that Kerouac is more explicit in his explanation: "Add alluvials to the end of your line when all is exhausted but something has to be said for some specified irrational reason, since reason can never win out, because poetry is NOT a science."[26] He subsequently explains "alluvials" as "Sediment. Delta. Mud. It's where you start a poem" ("Interview," 299).

There are several outstanding examples of "alluvials" in *The Subterraneans*, such as when Leo recounts the aftermath of an argument with Mardou, their relationship already unraveling:

> [both of us] like happy unconcerned people you see in newsreels busy going down the street to their chores and where-go's and we're in the same rainy newsreel mystery sad but inside of us (as must then be so inside the puppet filmdolls of screen) the great tumescent turbulent turmoil alliterative as a

hammer on the brain bone bag and balls, bang I'm sorry I was ever born (*The Subterraneans*, 96–97).

In an earlier example, Kerouac allows a similarly alliterative alluvial to punctuate the sentence's flow as Leo reflects with regret upon his behavior towards Golz: "putting him down, [Mardou's] friend, was not nice—no, the world's no fit place for this kind of activity, and what we gonna do, and where? when? wha wha wha, the baby bawls in the midnight boom" (*The Subterraneans*, 75). In this metafictional moment, of which the novel has many, the reader is brought right into the narrator's experience of transmitting his reality: Leo's language shows his interior world coalescing organically with his immediate sensory environ, again uniting recent past and immediate present to rupture the narrative that rests on linear time. As poet Clark Coolidge observes, the increasing density of language in such passages, "turns the mind-ear away from impulse of remembered image towards sound as material for the making."[27] Such a move towards the aural and oral in transmitting the fluctuations of his consciousness underscores Kerouac's acuity for the performativity of language through the confluence of text with tongue, voice, and ear.

In the improvisation and prosody of bebop Kerouac learned to identify in his art the contour of his own mind and voice and write this to be heard. Thus, in the spontaneous prose of *The Subterraneans* the reader is listening to the writing of sound and voice, organic extensions of the author's interaction with his interior and exterior worlds all moving together through the body – his breathing and physically throwing down those sentences – in Time. Kerouac continued to develop spontaneous prose further towards the aurality of "alluvials" and what Coolidge termed "BabbleFlow"[28] with more experimental, form-defying texts such as *Old Angel Midnight* (1959; 1973), Kerouac's attempt to transcribe the sound of the universe outside his window, and "Sea," the sound poem at the conclusion of *Big Sur* (1962), the voice of the Pacific Ocean: "Shoo——Shaw——Shirsh——"[29]

Just like the subterraneans of the novel who sought "the music of the future," Kerouac felt that with the spontaneous prose of *The Subterraneans* he had found the future literature, that of speaking the unspeakable. As he told Allen in 1957, "I see it leading to a tremendously interesting literature everywhere with all kinds of confessions never made by man before, leading to a cool future" when, he believes, "it will be realized that everybody is an artist, naturally. And each good or bad according to his openness!" (*Selected Letters 2*, 18).

Notes

1. Jack Kerouac, *The Subterraneans* (New York: Grove Press, 1958), 3.
2. Hassan Melehy, *Kerouac: Language, Poetics, Territory* (New York: Bloomsbury, 2016), 83; Kerouac, "Essentials of Spontaneous Prose," in *Good Blonde & Others*, ed. Donald Allen (San Francisco: Grey Fox Press, 1993), 69.
3. Kerouac to Alfred Kazin (October 27, 1954), Jack Kerouac, *Selected Letters 1, 1940–1956*, ed. Ann Charters (New York: Penguin, 1995) 449.
4. "Interview with Jack Kerouac" in *Empty Phantoms: Interviews and Encounters with Jack Kerouac* (New York: Thunder's Mouth Press, 2005), 307.
5. Warren Tallman, "The Writing Life." *New American Story*, ed. Donald M. Allen and Robert Creeley (New York: Penguin, 1965) 20.
6. Lee, who is reported to have typed the manuscript of Burroughs' novel *Queer*, was herself a writer, albeit unpublished in her lifetime. See Alene Lee, "Sisters"; Christina Diamante, "Walking with the Barefoot Beat: Alene Lee," and "Finding Alene." *Beatdom* #6, February 17, 2010. www.beatdom.com [Accessed August 6, 2022].
7. Barry Gifford and Lawrence Lee, *Jack's Book: An Oral Biography of Jack Kerouac* (1978. New York: Thunder's Mouth Press, 1994), 176. Choosing to guard her identity, Lee appears here under the name "Irene May," her pseudonym in Kerouac's *Book of Dreams* (1960) and *Big Sur* (1962).
8. Quoted in Ann Charters, *A Bibliography of Works by Jack Kerouac* (New York: Phoenix Book Shop, 1967), 9.
9. Jack Kerouac, "Journal 1951," in *The Unknown Kerouac: Rare, Unpublished & Newly Translated Writings*, ed. Todd Tietchen (New York: The Library of America, 2016), 137–140, 145.
10. Kerouac to Donald Allen (March 19, 1957) Jack Kerouac, *Kerouac: Selected Letters 2, 1957–1969*, ed. Ann Charters (New York: Penguin, 1999), 16–17.
11. Kerouac to Ginsberg, Peter Orlovsky, and Gregory Corso (December 10, 1957), *Jack Kerouac and Allen Ginsberg: The Letters*, ed. Bill Morgan (New York: Penguin, 2010), 376.
12. Jack Kerouac, "On Contemporary Jazz—'Bebop,'" *The Unknown Kerouac*, 21.
13. See also Warren Tallman, "Kerouac's Sound," *The Tamarack Review* no. 11 (Spring, 1959), 58–74.
14. Daniel Belgrad, *The Culture of Spontaneity: Improvisation and the Arts in Postwar America* (Chicago: University of Chicago Press, 1998), 90; 91. See also LeRoi Jones, *Blues People: Negro Music in White America* (New York: Morrow, 1963), notably "African Slaves/American Slaves: Their Music," (17–32), and "The Modern Scene" (175–308); Regarding the influence of jazz prosody and "secondary orality" on "postliterary" writing, see Meta Du Ewa Jones, "Jazz Prosodies: Orality and Textuality" *Callaloo* vol. 25.1 (2002), 66–91; and Maria Damon, *Postliterary America: From Bagel Shop Jazz to Micropoetries* (Iowa City: University of Iowa Press, 2011).
15. Jones, *Blues*, xii. See also Belgrad, *Culture*, 191.
16. Ann Douglas, "'Telepathic Shock and Meaning Excitement': Kerouac's Poetics of Intimacy." *College Literature* 27.1 (Winter 2000), 16.

17. Charlie Parker quoted in Robert Reisner, ed. *Bird: The Legend of Charlie Parker* (New York: DaCapo Press, 1991), 187.
18. Kerouac details the function of the dash in *The Subterraneans* in a January 15, 1962 letter to Robert Giroux, in which he describes them as "visual separation signs" (*Selected Letters 2*, 371).
19. Aldous Huxley, *The Doors of Perception and Heaven and Hell* (1956; New York: Harper & Row, 1990), 23.
20. The New Critics dictated that a "good" writer set out one temporal, spatial, and impressionistic element at a time, in part through their practice of "selection" in their content and language. This was to ensure the "unity" and "coherence" of the narrative's form and "action." See Cleanth Brooks and Robert Penn Warren. *Understanding Fiction* (New York: Appleton-Century-Crofts, 1943); *Fundamentals of Good Writing: A Handbook of Modern Rhetoric* (New York: Harcourt, Brace, 1950). That Kerouac's Spontaneous Prose and *The Subterraneans* in particular garnered a largely negative critical response is therefore hardly surprising. See Douglas Malcolm, "Child's Play," *The New Yorker* (April 5, 1958), 137–138, 141–142; Norman Podhoretz, "The Know-Nothing Bohemians." *Partisan Review* 25. 2 (Spring, 1958), 305–318; John G. Roberts, "The 'Frisco Hepcats." *Mainstream* (July, 1958), 11–26; and Robert Brustein, "The Cult of Unthink." *Horizon: A Magazine of the Arts* 1.1 (September, 1958) 38–45; 134.
21. George Dardess, "The Logic of Spontaneity: A Reconsideration of Jack Kerouac's 'Spontaneous Prose Method'." *Boundary* 2, 3.3 (Spring 1975), 732.
22. Kerouac to Robert Giroux (late summer, 1954); Kerouac to Ginsberg, Peter Orlovsky, and Gregory Corso (December 10, 1957).
23. Melehy, *Language*, 94. See also Henry Miller, "Preface." *The Subterraneans* (New York: Avon Books, 1959), i–iii.
24. William Carlos Williams, *Paterson* (New York: New Directions, 1958), 6.
25. Charles Olson, "Projective Verse," *Selected Writings*, ed. Robert Creeley (New York: New Directions, 1966), 16.
26. Donald M. Allen, ed., *The New American Poetry 1945–1960* (1960. University of California Press, 1998), 414.
27. Clark Coolidge, *Now It's Jazz: Kerouac and the Sounds* (Albuquerque: Living Batch Press, 1999), 55.
28. Coolidge, *Jazz*, 56.
29. Jack Kerouac, *Big Sur* (1962; New York: Penguin, 1992), 219.

CHAPTER 6

Kerouac and the 1950s

Douglas Field

In June 1963, the writer John Clellon Holmes arranged an interview with his old friend, Jack Kerouac. Conducted by letter, the plan was to furnish material for a book that would be published as *Nothing More to Declare* four years later.[1] Holmes wanted to know: "How do you place yourself … in American literature? Whose son are you? What is your word to the world, in connection with such things as Cold War, Communism, Atom Bomb, twilight of Gods, human dilemmas of 20th century?" The Cold War had clearly been on Kerouac's mind, as two years earlier, he had denounced the ideology of American Cold War culture. Writing in *Book of Dreams*, he declared, "I feel sickened by the cowardice and hysteria of America become so blind as to misrecognize the freedom needs of imprisoned men 'Communists or not' – the great pileup of arms and pathological propaganda on them."[2] Kerouac's response to Holmes, however, moved from politics to ennui, from action to individualism, and from reverie to slumber: "I cant [sic] rank myself till I see what more I write, if any. – What is the world to *do*? Individuals should sleep more, really, and be alone more."[3]

Kerouac's response to Holmes jibes with his declaration elsewhere in the interview that "I have no time for politics, just Art," just as he described himself as "a solitary radical working on no platform."[4] By insisting that his interests lay with art, but not politics, Kerouac seemingly corroborates Irving Howe's assertion in *Politics and the Novel* (1955) that political fiction only thrives in periods of social and political upheaval, a theory elaborated by David Caute in *Politics and the Novel During the Cold War* (2010). For Caute, by the mid-century "the heyday of une littérature engagée was over," adding, in an echo of Kerouac, that "the dominant literary creed of the era was 'no politics.'"[5] While notable novels of the 1950s critiqued post–Second World War US society – among them J. D. Salinger's *The Catcher in the Rye* (1951), Ralph Ellison's *Invisible Man* (1952), and Kerouac's *On the Road* (1957) – literary critic Arthur Redding contends that these works "tended to culminate in existential and personal rather than political crises," a move from "social critique to self-critique."[6]

Ann Douglas has noted how "the Beats have attracted little attention from historians, even those who specialize in cultural and intellectual history." As she explains, "Part of the problem is the apparently congenital reluctance of historians to understand that cultural artifacts like novels, poems, songs, and movies are themselves primary sources."[7] This chapter considers Kerouac in the context of 1950s politics and culture, a period in which he came of age as a writer in step with the start of the Cold War. While the Cold War was, for Allen Ginsberg, "the imposition of a vast mental barrier on everybody, a vast anti-natural psyche," for Kerouac, this era was his most productive period.[8] His output during the 1950s includes *The Town and the City* (1950), *On the Road* (1957), *The Dharma Bums* (1958), *The Subterraneans* (1958), *Mexico City Blues* (1959), *Maggie Cassidy* (1959), *Doctor Sax* (1959), and *Visions of Cody*, written in the early 1950s, but not published until 1972.

Douglas's observation suggests the value in reading Kerouac's literary output of the 1950s as primary sources that reflect and refract Cold War culture, a period characterized by Manichean divisions between "us" and "them," good and bad, and American and Un-American. In fact, as Morris Dickstein put it, "nothing was more characteristic of the fifties than its weakness for hard-and-fast cultural distinctions, exclusions, hierarchies – between a poem and not-a-poem; between masscult and midcult, or highbrow, middlebrow, and lowbrow; between poetry and publicity; between culture and barbarism."[9] As I explore in this chapter, however, Kerouac, whose major work straddles the middle of the twentieth century, is understood productively in the context of 1950s culture. Scholars have noted how "Kerouac's development as a writer was connected to the rise of the Cold War," adding that "he fretted throughout his life about the threat posed by Communism," while one scholar claims that the author of *On the Road* "is the representative writer of the McCarthy era."[10]

As I explore through an overview of his prolific output during the 1950s, Kerouac emerges in this period as both rebellious and at times conservative, as variously delinquent, but also patriotic. He is both a writer, in his own words, "prophesying a new style for American culture," but also a writer whose work is rooted to the past; his novels are frequently steeped in nostalgia, including several accounts of his childhood in Lowell, Massachusetts.[11] Kerouac, whose first novel, *The Town and the City*, is published in 1950, occupies a mid-century position that is poised between looking back and moving forwards.

6.1 Containing Kerouac

In his infamous essay, "The Know-Nothing Bohemians," first published in *Partisan Review* (1958), Norman Podhoretz took the Beats to task, and Kerouac in particular. As part of the New York Intellectuals scene, which had moved from Trotskyism to a championing of Modernism and middle-class culture, Podhoretz's essay was one of the first sustained attacks on Kerouac from an intellectual peer, who was also a fellow Columbia University alumnus. Podhoretz contrasts Kerouac's prose with the "respectability and 'maturity' of post-war writing," a sleight of hand that leads to a critique of the Beats as juvenile, an accusation that the writer James Baldwin would make a few years later.[12] "It is not writing. It is self-indulgence," Baldwin told an interviewer in 1963, in a damning critique of Kerouac. "It is masturbation. It is not writing. I hate to say that, but it is true. I mean he's talented. So is everybody at the age of 5."[13]

For Baldwin and Podhoretz, the Beats, with Kerouac as ringleader, lacked intellectual maturity; as Podhoretz put it, in contrast to the "deep intellectual seriousness of the 1930s," the Beat writer "worships primitivism."[14] And if the Beats had any "intellectual interests at all," Podhoretz dismissed them as "mystical doctrines, irrationalist philosophies," – in other words, beyond the realm of rational and intellectual discourse.[15] "Their predilection for bop language," Podhoretz claims, "is a way of demonstrating solidarity with the primitive vitality and spontaneity they find in jazz and of expressing contempt for coherent, rational discourse which, being a product of the mind, is in their view a form of death."[16]

Although Podhoretz levels his attack at the Beats in general, his critical sniper rifle is aimed squarely at Kerouac's forehead, who is dismissed as "thoroughly unpolitical."[17] In his critique of Kerouac's writing style, Podhoretz lambastes the writer's "bob prosody" and ecstatic language, deriding his repeated use of "greatest," "tremendous," and "wild."[18] Podhoretz's attack on the Beats, and on Kerouac in particular, is driven by what the critic sees as a lack of intellectualism and immaturity, but above all, a lack of restraint. He views Kerouac's "spontaneous" prose as "a matter of saying whatever comes into your head," in contrast to the intellectualism to which Podhoretz subscribes, which is rational and considered.[19] In a comparable broadside in 1958, Robert Brustein, in his article "The Cult of Unthink," described *On the Road* as "energy misdirected," decrying his novels that are "stupefying in their unreadability."[20]

The early criticism of the "King of the Beats" is a useful way to consider Kerouac in relation to Cold War culture, and to the prevailing ideology of containment. Despite differing views on the genesis of the Cold War, the political and cultural period from about 1947 to the mid-1960s is characterized by a rhetoric of containment, a doctrine which sought to stem the "red flow" of Communism. In 1947, George Kennan, director of Secretary of State George Marshall's policy planning staff, drew attention to the rising geopolitical threat of the Soviet Union. In an article titled "The Sources of Soviet Conduct," written under the pseudonym "Mr. X" for the journal *Foreign Affairs*, Kennan argued that, unlike the clearly demarcated battles of the Second World War, Communism, "cannot be easily defeated or discouraged by a single victory on the part of its opponents." Instead, Kennan proposed that America must respond, not with "threats or blustering or superfluous gestures of outward 'toughness,'" but through a policy of "long-term, patient but firm and vigilant containment of Russian expansive tendencies."[21] Within three years, the National Security Council Report NSC 68, which was approved by President Truman in 1950, and which effectively became the blueprint for the militarization of the Cold War, became "the ultimate expression of U.S. containment policy."[22]

As Alan Nadel explains, "[a]lthough technically referring to U.S. foreign policy from 1948 until at least the mid-1960s," containment "also describes American life in numerous venues and under sundry rubrics during that period."[23] In *Homeward Bound: American Families in the Cold War Era* (1988), Elaine Tyler May tracks the ways in which the postwar ideology of domesticity was directly linked to the geopolitical ideology of the Cold War. As she explains, "Domestic containment was bolstered by a powerful political culture that rewarded its adherents and marginalized its detractors." Containment was "[m]ore than merely a metaphor for the cold war on the homefront," rather it "aptly describes the way in which public policy, personal behavior, and even political values were focused on the home."[24] And while May notes that "[r]ebellious youths and nonconforming Beats of the 1950s made it clear that not everyone or everything could be contained in the nuclear family ideal," these groups, however, were the exceptions.[25]

Containment, then, becomes a useful prism through which to explore the form and content of Kerouac's writing during the 1950s. While Dickstein singled out Ginsberg as the consummate outsider, Kerouac, as Douglas reminds us, was also "in multiple ways an outsider."[26] Although the author of *On the Road* is frequently depicted as quintessentially American, whose fascination with the West can be traced to Henry David Thoreau, his identity complicates what Dickstein refers to the as the Cold War's predilection for "hard-and-fast cultural distinctions." In a review of Joyce Johnson's *The Voice Is All: The Lonely Victory of Jack Kerouac* (2012),

Douglas points out that Kerouac was a "French-Canadian with some Iroquois blood raised in an immigrant working-class family in Lowell, Massachusetts," who did not speak English until around the age of five.[27]

Podhoretz's claim that Kerouac was "thoroughly non-political," does not mean, of course, that his writing did not engage with Cold War culture. In what follows, I track Kerouac's early attempts to define the Beat Generation during the 1950s, then moving onto a discussion of his writing in relation to travel and the confessional mode, both of which are in opposition to the prevailing Cold War discourse of containment.

6.2 Philosophies of the Beat Generation

During the late 1950s, Kerouac was frequently called upon to define the Beat Generation. A reluctant "King of the Beats," Kerouac nonetheless obliged, writing several explanations of them. In "Aftermath: the Philosophy of the Beat Generation," first published in *Esquire* in 1958, Kerouac explains how "Beat" emerged in the aftermath of the Second World War, just as the Cold War began. While postwar America is often characterized as an age of peace and economic prosperity, Kerouac identifies a menacing presence, claiming that "a sinister new kind of efficiency appeared in America" during the early-to-mid 1950s. And although Kerouac does not specify what he means, he speculates that "maybe it was the result of the universalization of television," a comment developed in *The Dharma Bums* ("Aftermath," 47). In his third novel, Kerouac writes of "colleges being nothing but grooming schools for the middle-class non-identity which usually finds its perfect expression on the outskirts of the campus in rows of well-to-do houses with lawns and television sets in each living room with everybody looking at the same thing."[28]

As historians have noted, "In 1949 television was a luxurious indulgence in one out of ten American homes; in 1959, television was essential furniture in nine out of ten American homes."[29] Television, as scholars including Alan Nadel and Thomas Doherty have demonstrated, was a technology that developed in step with the Cold War. It was, Nadel explains, "an external power—a mysterious science—that let invisible waves enter the home to produce images potentially both facilitating and controlling individual freedom."[30] For Kerouac in particular, television, unlike film, was associated with a growing belief, not only that 1950s US society was becoming increasingly homogenized, but that it threatened the fabric of individuality.[31]

Kerouac's concerns that individuality was being sublimated was played out across various cultural forms in the 1950s. In *Invasion of the Body Snatchers* (1956), the citizens of Santa Mira, California, lose their emotions and individuality in a sci-fi blockbuster that was at once farfetched – aliens who take over humans – but also a keen satire on the state of society. The following year, William Whyte's bestselling study of US society, *The Organization Man*, argued postwar US society was moving away from individualism in part due to the advancements of domestic technology, including the washing machine and coffee maker. And while Whyte made it clear that his book was "not a plea for non-conformity," his claim that "Man exists as a unit of society. Of himself, he is isolated, meaningless" would have struck a chord with Kerouac and the Beats in their rejections of white-collar work and domesticity.[32]

Notwithstanding William Burroughs's wry observation that *On the Road* "sold a trillion Levi's, a million espresso coffee machines," Kerouac's second novel has historically been read as a rejection of the "Organization Man" who gets his kicks from company loyalty and domestic harmony, and as a repudiation of postwar consumerism, underscored by the critique of characters in *The Dharma Bums*, who are "imprisoned in a system of work, produce, consume, work, produce, consume (*The Dharma Bums*, 83)."[33] In the second part of *On the Road*, Old Bull, a character based on Burroughs, remarks on the phenomenon of planned or strategic obsolescence. "They can make clothes that last forever," he explains, but "[t]hey prefer making cheap goods," a topical remark given the publication that year of Vance Packard's *The Hidden Persuaders*.[34]

Packard's influential study showed the extent to which advertising was a systematic way of persuading consumers to buy products, seemingly against their will, illustrated by "consumer trainees" (children), "who thanks to TV were learning to sing beer and other commercials before learning to sing "The Star-Spangled Banner."[35] In a description that bears similarities to *Invasion of the Body Snatchers*, Packard writes:

> Typically these efforts take place beneath our level of awareness; so that the appeals which move us are often, in a sense, "hidden." The result is that many of us are being influenced and manipulated, far more than we realize, in the patterns of our everyday lives.[36]

In fact, advertising was so pervasive during the mid-1950s, that Packard suggested that television was produced in order to increase advertising space: "Were some of the resolutely mediocre shows on television that way by design," he wondered, "to increase the impact of the commercials?"[37]

Given the exposure of the sinister aspects of technology in the early to mid-1950s, it is not surprising that Kerouac and his coterie critiqued and renounced the so-called advancements of society. For Ginsberg, there was "some kind of spiritual crisis in the west and the possibility of Decline instead of infinite American Century Progress."[38] As Holmes outlined in his essay, "The Philosophy of the Beat Generation" (1958), they were "the first generation for whom genocide, brainwashing, cybernetics, motivational research—and the resultant limitation of the concept of human volition which is inherent in them—have been as familiar as its own face." And crucially, they recognized that technology, was not only linked to consumerism, but to the eradication of civilization. As Holmes observed, "It is also the first generation that has grown up since the possibility of the nuclear destruction of the world has become the final answer to all questions."[39] Like Holmes, in "Aftermath" Kerouac pointed to the dangers associated with technology. He recalled "Western mankind before it went on its 'Civilization' Rationale and developed relativity, jets and superbombs had supercolassal, bureaucratic, totalitarian, benevolent, Big Brother structures" ("Aftermath," 49).

For Kerouac, then, technological advancements were inextricably bound to the domestic containment that May outlined, but also to the militarization of the Cold War. In "Aftermath," Kerouac refers to "this late stage of civilization when money is the only thing that really matters to everybody," and briefly mentions Oswald Spengler, whose two-volume study, *The Decline of the West* (1918/1922) claimed that the West, which sees the world through the epistemology of science, had reached its cultural zenith and was heading for decline. "What makes the man of the world-cities incapable of living on any but this artificial footing," Spengler posits, "is that the cosmic beat in his being is ever decreasing, while the tensions of his waking consciousness become more and more dangerous."[40] Kerouac's writing is littered with references to the "fellaheen," a term borrowed from Spengler, which roughly translates as peasant laborer, which becomes a shorthand for those untainted by consumerism and technology.[41]

While Kerouac was certainly suspicious of the ways that technology removed individuals from the "cosmic beat" of the world around, he was not a Luddite. Truman Capote's withering dismissal of *On the Road* as "that's not writing, it's typing," is a frequently cited but rarely analyzed comment that underscores the nuances of Cold War technology.[42] On the one hand, Capote's oft-cited line suggests that Kerouac's writing is mechanistic; a form of action writing, where the words are hurled at the page via a typewriter, as opposed to the measured craft of authors that Capote admired. Presumably Capote did not have in mind Charles Olson's connection between the act of poetic authorship and the operation of the typewriter in his famous essay, "Projective Verse" (1950). In his essay, Olson posited that, due "to its rigidity and its space precisions," the typewriter enabled the poet to "indicate exactly the breath, the pauses, the suspensions even of syllables, the juxtapositions even of parts of phrases, which he intends." In fact, Olson compared the typewriter to "the stave and the bar" of the musician, claiming that the device could accurately record the poet's "listening" and, in turn "how he would want any reader, silently or otherwise, to voice his work."[43] Reading Capote via "Projective Verse," brings *On the Road* closer to the importance of musicality in Kerouac's writing – and in jazz in particular – which early scholars, with the exception of Warren Tallman, were reluctant to take seriously.[44]

Capote's famous quotation unwittingly draws attention to the ways that Kerouac was alert to modes of transmission that enabled him to write, as he put it, "[s]traight from the mind to the voice with no hand intervening," a method which included experimentations with tape recorded conversations in *Visions of Cody*. In "Essentials of Spontaneous Prose," first published in 1957, Kerouac writes: "PROCEDURE: Time being of the essence in the purity of speech, sketching language is undisturbed flow from the mind of personal secret idea- words, blowing (as per jazz musician) on subject of image."[45]

Scholars have explored the ways that Kerouac used jazz a model for writing, but he was also attentive to other cultural forms in his pursuit of conveying the "undisturbed flow from the mind of secret idea-word." Much of Kerouac's writing draws attention to the influence of film on his work, including the claim in "Belief and Technique for Modern Prose" (1959) that "Bookmovie is the movie in words, the visual American form," an explanation that connects to early cultural analyses of televisual culture.[46] As one author put it as early as 1942, television was "destined to bring into the home total means for participation in the sights and sounds of the entire world," a description that aligns with Kerouac's writing during the 1950s, much of which restlessly captures the sounds, smells, and textures of his childhood in Lowell, Massachusetts.[47] Book Two of *Doctor Sax*, for example, is titled, "A Gloomy Bookmovie," in which Kerouac describes "the gloomy special brown Technicolor interior of my house."[48] As Kerouac told Holmes, with the "bookmovie" method, "people would be able to look at my page and become the camera themselves and even see unphotographable moviettes within the movie," adding, "this is my most ambitious invention."[49]

Kerouac's development of "bookmovie," underscores that he was far from resistant to all forms of early to mid-twentieth century technology, but also a reminder that he sought to innovate 1950s literature, illustrated by his experiments with spontaneous prose. As I explore in the final section of this chapter, the form and content of Kerouac's writing can be read productively through the prism of Cold War culture generally. Much of his work is resistant to notion of containment, either thematically – such as the theme of travel – or stylistically through the mode of spontaneous writing, which strives towards the creation of writing that is unmediated and unedited, a process closely linked to notions of censorship. And while the use of the first-person narrator in 1950s fiction was far from rare, Ann Douglas points out that "100% honesty," in Kerouac's words, "both psychic and social, makes little sense outside of its Cold War context and the drastic restrictions of civil liberties that war purportedly mandated." Kerouac's attempt to "declassify human experience," Douglas posits, needs to be understood in the context of the Cold War, an era in which information became increasing classified, just as the notion of spontaneity was at odds with government policies of caution and preparedness.[50]

6.3 Characteristics of Kerouac and the Cold War

The Town and the City ends with the protagonist, Peter Martin, "on the road again, traveling the continent westward …," a line which pre-empts Kerouac's most famous novel, *On the Road*, where mobility is a central theme, and which is extended in *The Dharma Bums*.[51] In each case, travel is not simply a matter of moving from A to B, but it is inextricably connected to individualism and experience, which in turn results in a questioning and repudiation of 1950s American values.

In *The Town and City*, the Martin siblings long to escape the parochialism of Galloway, Massachusetts, a thinly veiled portrait of Kerouac's hometown. When Peter travels to New York City, Times Square is described as a nexus that cannot be controlled or contained: "All the cats and characters … street drum and slain, crowded together, streaming back and forth, looking for something, waiting for something, forever moving around" (*The Town and the City*, 362). In sharp contrast to the stifling small town of Galloway, Times Square is described as a place of perpetual movement, populated by transient "drifters." There, he could "meet a Norwegian seaman he had drunk with in the alleys of Piccadilly, or a Filipino cook who had borrowed ten dollars from him in the Artic Sea, or a young wrangler-poolshark he had gambled with in some San Francisco poolroom" (*The Town and the City*, 362).

The emphasis on movement in *The Town and the City* foreshadows the theme of mobility in Kerouac's next two novels, which as one scholar points out, "is also a deeply threatening and transgressive form of behavior."[52] Travel in Kerouac's work is frequently associated with sexual adventure, as well as a rejection of the Cold War notion of the "Organization Man" in which the loyal individual is contained within a labor market. In the *Town and The City,* Peter recognizes three young men in Times Square, based on himself, Herbert Huncke, and Allen Ginsberg. Jack, the "hoodlum," is described "always looking around," his sense of movement underscored by claims he was born "on a barge in the East River" (*The Town and the City*, 364). Accompanying Jack is a drug addict known as "Junkey," and Leon Levinsky, a poet of Russian-Jewish heritage. In each case, the hoodlum, junkie, and poet are depicted as outsiders who reject the Cold War ideology of domestic containment.

In Kerouac's novels of the 1950s, travel, like much of his own work, is not concerned with linearity or pragmatism, but as a form of opposition to the dominant culture. The drifter, or vagabond, therefore, is a politically charged figure, one who rejects the conventions of the stable labor market. In *The Dharma Bums*, for example, there are over thirty references to the word "rucksack," an object is both a practical object, but also a symbolic rejection of consumer culture. The protagonist, Smith, observes that the free-spirited Japhy Ryder "doesn't need any money, all he needs is his rucksack with those little plastic bags of dried food and a good pair of shoes and off he goes and enjoys the privileges of a millionaire in surroundings like this" (*The Dharma Bums*, 66). Inspired, Smith vows to "learn all about how to pack rucksacks" when he is "sick of civilization" (*The Dharma Bums*, 49). And lest readers fail to make the connection between mobility, rucksacks, and a repudiation of consumer culture, Ryder extolls the notion of "a world full of rucksack wanderers, Dharma Bums refusing to subscribe to the general demand that they consume production and therefore have to work for the privilege of consuming, all that crap they didn't really want anyway such as refrigerators" (*The Dharma Bums*, 83).

Ryder's call for a "rucksack revolution," which is imbued with a rejection of 1950s consumer culture, is frequently couched in spiritual terms. Kerouac's writing of the 1950s, characterized by a first-person narration, draws on the Catholic practice of confession, but his insistence on honesty, sits at odds with the prevailing Cold War culture of subterfuge, including increased surveillance in the United States. The Central Intelligence Agency (CIA) was formed in 1947, the year the National Security Act was passed, followed by the creation of the National Security Agency (NSA) in 1952, who closely monitored activity deemed detrimental to the US government.

As Thomas Schaub has argued, first person narration was employed by many outsiders connected to subcultures as "the first person voice was the natural point of view to adopt in a politics of culture, because it gave voice to the communal impulses underlying the experience of alienation, and it was the idea by which many writers, like the critics with whom they quarreled, managed to retain a political relation to their society."[53] Compare, for example, the start of *On the Road*: "I first met Dean not long after my wife and I split up. I had just gotten over a serious illness that I won't bother to talk about ..." (*On the Road*, 3), with the opening of J.D. Salinger's coming-of-age story, *The Catcher in the Rye* (1951):

> If you really want to hear about it, the first thing you'll probably want to know is where I was born, and what my lousy childhood was like, and how my parents were occupied and all before they had me, and all that David Copperfield kind of crap, but I don't feel like going into it, if you want to know the truth.[54]

While the 1950s is remembered for the Confessional Poets, including Robert Lowell, Anne Sexton, and Sylvia Plath, scholars have pointed out that the Beats' confessional mode in fact took place earlier. As Fiona Paton observes, for example, not only was Lowell inspired by Ginsberg's "Howl," (1956) but, The Confessional Poets' "language was not the language of the streets; their poems did not threaten the very foundations of literary discourse."[55] "There is a dynamic philosophy behind the Progress of the twentieth Century," argued Kerouac in 1949, "but we need to reach the depths of a Static Metaphysical Admission—a Manifesto of Confessions—as well."[56] And as he noted in "The Origins of the Beat Generation," he hung around the drifters and hipsters in Times Square because "they kept talking about the same things I liked ... night long confessions full of hope that had become illicit and repressed by the War."[57]

As Kerouac's valorization of the confessional makes clear, it was a mode of writing and speaking that became repressed and "illicit" during the Cold War. Confession and spontaneity are connected to his claim that "every word I write is true," which sits at odds with the Cold War ideology of surveillance and subterfuge.[58] In Kerouac's writing of the 1950s, craft should not interfere with the transmission of experience. As one critic puts it, for Kerouac, "the contemporary emphasis upon technique meant subordinating experience to form, instead of allowing experience to develop its own form. Craft was thus a form of dishonesty ..."[59] Or, as Leo Percepied declares in *The Subterraneans* "[d]etails are the life of it, say everything on your mind, don't hold it back, don't analyze or anything as you go along."[60]

Kerouac's disregard for literary and social conventions, his *soi-disant* "wild form," ruffled the feathers of contemporary critics, who overlooked the writer's craft that he honed during the 1950s during the height of the Cold War.[61] During a period that was characterized by an ideology of containment, which extended beyond the realm of politics to the wider spheres of culture – including genre, race, sexuality, and style – Kerouac's profuse oeuvre not only challenges the dominant narratives of the era, but also continues to ignite debate. He remains an enigmatic figure: an innovator of form, whose sexual and racial politics seem outmoded; a writer who championed new modes of expression, even as his books remained preoccupied with the past. The "King of the Beats," who never voted, and whose later pronouncements, often fueled by alcohol, winked at Republican patriotism. But a writer, above all, who resists easy categorization, who refuses to be contained.[62]

Notes

1. The letters between Holmes and Kerouac were not, in the end, included in *Nothing to Declare*.
2. Jack Kerouac, *Book of Dreams* (San Francisco: City Lights, 2001), 148.
3. John Clellon Holmes, "Doing Literary Work: An Interview with Jack Kerouac," *The Unknown Kerouac: Rare, Unpublished & Newly Translated Writings*, ed. Todd Tietchen; trans Jean-Christophe Cloutier (New York: Library of America, 2016), 356.
4. Holmes, "Doing Literary Work," 355; Jack Kerouac, *Kerouac: Selected Letters 1, 1940–1956*, ed. Ann Charters (New York: Penguin, 1996), 52.
5. David Caute, *Politics and the Novel During the Cold War* (New Brunswick, NJ: Transaction Publishers 2010), 353.
6. Arthur Redding, "Cold War," *American Literature in Transition, 1950–1960*, ed. Steven Belletto (Cambridge: Cambridge University Press, 2017), 24.
7. Ann Douglas, "Holy Fools: the Beat Generation and the Cold War." *Reviews in American History, 41.* 3 (2013): 525–532 (526).
8. Cited by Fiona Paton, "The Beat Movement," *American Literature in Transition*, 1950–1960, 226.
9. Morris Dickstein, *Gates of Eden: American Culture in the Sixties* (New York: Basic Books, Inc., 1977), 4.
10. Robert Genter, "'Mad to Talk, Mad to Be Saved:' Jack Kerouac, Soviet Psychology, and the Cold War Confessional Self." *Studies in American Fiction* 40.1 (2013): 27–55 (36); Thomas Schaub, *American Fiction in the Cold War* (Madison.: University of Wisconsin Press, 1991), 83.
11. Jack Kerouac, "Aftermath: the Philosophy of the Beat Generation," *Good Blonde & Others*, ed. Donald Allen; preface by Robert Creeley (San Francisco: City Lights Books, 1993), 48.
12. Norman Podhoretz, "The Know-Nothing Bohemians," *The New York Intellectuals Reader*, ed. Neil Jumonville (New York and London: Routledge, 2007), 307.
13. Elsa Knight Thompson and John Leonard, "A Conversation with James Baldwin." First broadcast KPFA (Berkeley, CA) on June 6, 1963. Original transcription available online: americanarchive.org/catalog/cpb-aacip-28-8s4jm23q52.
14. Podhoretz, "Know-Nothing," 309, 315.
15. Podhoretz, "Know-Nothing," 309.
16. Podhoretz, "Know-Nothing," 309.
17. Podhoretz, "Know-Nothing," 309.
18. Podhoretz, "Know-Nothing," 313.
19. Podhoretz, "Know-Nothing," 314.

20. Robert Brustein, "The Cult of Unthink," *Beat Down Your Soul: What Was the Beat Generation?*, ed Ann Charters (New York and London: Penguin, 2001), 51, 53.
21. George F. Kennan, "The Sources of Soviet Conduct," *Foreign Affairs* (July 1947). Reprinted: wwnorton.com/college/history/archive/resources/documents/ch31_02.htm.
22. Andrea Friedman, *Citizenship in Cold War America: The National Security State and the Possibilities of Dissent* (Amherst: University of Massachusetts Press, 2014), 16.
23. Alan Nadel, *Containment Culture: American Narratives, Postmodernism, and the Atomic Age* (Durham: Duke University Press, 1995), 2–3.
24. Elaine Tyler May, *Homeward Bound: American Families in the Cold War Era* (New York: Basic Books, 2008), 16.
25. May, *Homeward Bound*, 16.
26. Douglas, "Holy Fools," 530.
27. Douglas, "Holy Fools," 530. In *Doctor Sax*, for example, a novel that draws heavily on his childhood, Kerouac writes numerous sentences in French.
28. Jack Kerouac, *The Dharma Bums* (London: Penguin Classics, 2007), 35.
29. Thomas Doherty, *Cold War, Cool Medium: Television, McCarthyism, and American Culture* (New York: Columbia University Press, 2003), 4.
30. Alan Nadel, "Cold War Television and the Technology of Brainwashing," *American Cold War Culture*, ed. Douglas Field (Edinburgh: Edinburgh University Press, 2005), 147.
31. See Steven Belletto, "A Sinister New Kind of Efficiency": Kerouac's Cold War, *Journal of Beat Studies* 10 (2022): 5–23. Belletto discusses Kerouac's short story "cityCityCITY," the writer's only foray into science fiction. Written in 1954, the dystopic tale captures Kerouac's distrust of Cold War technology.
32. William H. Whyte, *The Organization Man* (Harmondsworth: Penguin, 1963), 15, 12.
33. Sean O'Hagan, "America's First King of the Road," *Guardian* (August 5, 2007): www.theguardian.com/books/2007/aug/05/fiction.jackkerouac.
34. Jack Kerouac, *On the Road* (London: Penguin, 1991), 149. See Giles Slade, *Made to Break: Technology and Obsolescence in America* (Cambridge, MA: Harvard University Press, 2006).
35. Vance Packard, *The Hidden Persuaders*; introd. Mark Crispin Miller (Brooklyn: Ig Publishing, 2007), 153, 154.
36. Packard, *The Hidden Persuaders*, 31.
37. Packard, *The Hidden Persuaders*, 152.
38. Barry Gifford and Lawrence Lee, *Jack's Book* (New York: Penguin Books, 1979), 38.
39. John Clellon Holmes, "The Philosophy of the Beat Generation" *Esquire* (February 1, 1958): classic.esquire.com/article/1958/2/1/the-philosophy-of-the-beat-generation.
40. Oswald Spengler, "Oswald Spengler on Cosmopolis and Depopulation" in *The Decline of the West: Volume 2*, trans by C. F. Atkinson, *Population and Development Review* 28.4 (December 2002): 787–796 (792).

41. The word "fellaheen," for example, appears in *On the Road.* Chapter Two of *Lonesome Traveler* is titled, "Mexico Fellaheen."
42. Cited by David Barnette, "Jack Kerouac: still roadworthy after 100 years," (13 Mar 2022): www.theguardian.com/books/2022/mar/13/jack-kerouac-still-roadworthy-after-100-years.
43. Charles Olson, "Projective Verse," www.poetryfoundation.org/articles/69406/projective-verse. The essay can be found in Charles Olson, *Collected Prose*, eds. Donald Allen and Benjamin Friedlander (Berkeley: University of California Press, 1997), 239–250.
44. Warren Tallman, "Kerouac's Sound," *The Tamarack Review*, 11 (Spring 1959): 58–74.
45. Jack Kerouac, "Essentials of Spontaneous Prose," *Good Blonde*, 69.
46. See Tyler Keevil, "Writing Kerouac's bookmovie: cinematic influence and imagery in the modern road novel," *New Writing*, 14:2 (2017), 167–175; Jack Kerouac, "Belief & Technique for Modern Prose," *The Portable Jack Kerouac* (New York: Viking, 1995), 483.
47. Nadel, *Containment Culture*, 152.
48. Jack Kerouac, *Doctor Sax* (London: Penguin, 2012), 80.
49. Ann Charters, "Editor's Introduction," *The Portable Jack Kerouac* (New York: Viking, 1995), 13.
50. Douglas, "Holy Fools," 526.
51. Jack Kerouac, *The Town and the City* (London: Penguin, 2000), 498.
52. Tim Cresswell, "Mobility as Resistance: A Geographical Reading of Kerouac's *On the Road*," *Transactions of the Institute of British Geographers*, 18.2 (1993): 249–262 (250).
53. Schaub, *American Fiction in the Cold War*, 73.
54. J. D. Salinger, *The Catcher in the Rye* (Harmondsworth: Penguin, 1987), 5.
55. Paton, "The Beat Movement," 228.
56. Jack Kerouac, *Windblown World: The Journals of Jack Kerouac, 1947–1954*, ed. Douglas Brinkley (New York: Viking, 2004), 194.
57. Jack Kerouac, "The Origins of the Beat Generation," *Good Blonde*, 60.
58. Cited by Ellis Amburn, *The Subterranean Kerouac: The Hidden Life of Jack Kerouac* (New York: St. Martin's Griffin, 1998), 6.
59. Schaub, *American Fiction in the Cold War*, 54.
60. Jack Kerouac, *The Subterraneans* (London: Penguin, 2001), 58. As Paton observes in "The Beat Movement," Kerouac's novel "broke new ground in its depiction of an interracial relationship at a time when thirty states had laws in place banning miscegenation," a further example of the ways that Kerouac's subject matter resisted containment (230).
61. See Michael Hrebeniak, *Action Writing: Jack Kerouac's Wild Form* (Carbondale: Southern Illinois University Press, 2008).
62. See Robert Dean Lurie, "The Conservative Kerouac," *The American Conservative* (September 7, 2012): www.theamericanconservative.com/the-conservative-kerouac/ where Kerouac claimed that he and his family always voted Republican. See David S. Wills, "The Complicated Politics of the Beat Triumvirate," who claims that "Kerouac never actually voted." www.beatdom.com/complicated-politics-beat-triumvirate/.

CHAPTER 7

The Impact of On the Road *on the 1960s Counterculture*

Kurt Hemmer

7.1 *On the Road* – Jack Kerouac's Problem Child

A careful reading reveals that Jack Kerouac's *On the Road* is both a paean and a lament for a disappearing America in the 1940s, even though it was published in 1957. The novel's conservative ending, with narrator Sal Paradise getting off the road and heading toward a domestic life with his new girlfriend, is overshadowed by the romantic depiction of the hero, Dean Moriarty, bent to the magnetic pull of the road. *On the Road* made the *New York Times* bestseller list, rising to number eleven, and remaining on the list for five weeks. The novel's popularity helped identify it with the burgeoning youth culture of its time. Often Kerouac was linked with the tremendous enthusiasm over the actor James Dean and the singer Elvis Presley, and several times he was compared to these contemporary icons. Yet, one of the main phenomena that helped *On the Road* gain longevity as an important work of literature, and not just a pop-cultural artifact, was its influence on the 1960s counterculture. The epochal status of the novel was fueled by several artists and influencers, both cultural and political, that found inspiration in the book. Rock stars, hippie "dropouts," and activist "politicos" of the '60s counterculture, often not ideologically unified, recognized in the novel's pages elements of a common ethos.

Unwittingly, *On the Road* became an inspiration for the 1960s counterculture.[1] Plato is credited with the maxim, "Books are immortal sons defying their sires."[2] This was never more applicable than to *On the Road*'s relationship with its author. Fellow Beats viewed Kerouac's novel as a counterculture catalyst; as William S. Burroughs succinctly put it: "Woodstock rises from his pages."[3] Gregory Corso agrees with Burroughs, observing, "What was predicted by Kerouac, in *On the Road* particularly, of youth coming to the fore, of going on the road, of traveling with rucksacks through America, of finding themselves, or taking drugs … in the Sixties that came to fore and was expressed a lot through music."[4]

Lawrence Ferlinghetti claims, "[*On the Road*] just sort of kicked the sides out of everything and it was suddenly, overnight a whole new scene, just as when rock hit the music scene in this country in the '60s. It was very similar. In fact, it was the beginning of the same revolution."[5] The Beats, with the conspicuous exception of Kerouac, saw themselves, as Corso says, as "the Daddies of the Age."[6]

Whatever we believe was Kerouac's authorial intent, in the pages of *On the Road* the reader finds aspects of the counterculture's ethos. Damon R. Bach explains, "For the counterculture, spontaneity, individualism, and experience—untethered from security—represented the best kind of life."[7] If this is true, then *On the Road* is the countercultural novel par excellence. The narrator of Kerouac's novel, Sal Paradise, is attracted to the novel's hero, Dean Moriarty, because of his spontaneity, individualism, and experience – all untethered from security. Sal's desire to acquire, or try on, Dean's character traits himself while managing the pull of Sal's equally strong desire to integrate them with the conservative values of his upbringing is part of the book's tension. For many readers, it is Dean who is the focus of their fascination. As Sal says, the essence of Dean "was a wild yea-saying overburst of American joy; it was Western, the west wind, an ode from the Plains, something new, long prophesied, long a-coming."[8] Sal's enthusiasm for Dean is one of the reasons the book spoke to the 1960s counterculture, which was struggling to release itself from the mainstream culture's containment and conformity.

The 1960s started not too far removed from the 1950s. An easy demarcation for the shift is the assassination of President John F. Kennedy on November 22, 1963, which was quickly followed by The Beatles' first appearance on *The Ed Sullivan Show* on February 9, 1964. "Beginning in 1965, the alienated would attempt to create a new culture," writes Bach, "a new society—even a new civilization. ... valuing libertarianism over authoritarianism, liberation over repression, egalitarianism over inequality, cooperation over competition, the bizarre over the conventional, the precarious over the secure, community over isolation, love over hate, peace over war, life over death."[9] These new values are manifested in *On the Road*. One key aspect of the novel appreciated by the various groups of the counterculture was its resistance to the authoritarianism of the police. After being shaken down by the police, Sal writes, "The American police are involved in psychological warfare against those Americans who don't frighten them with imposing papers and threats. It's a Victorian police force; it peers out of musty windows and wants to inquire about everything, and can make crimes if the crimes don't exist to its satisfaction" (*On the Road*, 136). This attitude would appeal to the rock culture, dropouts, and politicos of the counterculture, that all wanted less police interference. The protagonists of *On the Road* seemed to defy authority righteously.

The sex and drugs of the book also spoke to the counterculture's desire for more liberation. For Dean "sex was the one and only holy and important thing in life" (*On the Road*, 4). Throughout the novel, in addition to describing promiscuous sex, Sal talks casually about the use of marijuana, amphetamine, barbiturates, and morphine. Sal and Dean share drugs and sexual experiences, while Dean reminds Sal of "some long-lost brother" (*On the Road*, 10). A big part of the appeal of the book to the counterculture is the brotherhood and lack of competition between the main characters. Sal's appreciation for Dean is partly because he is bizarre, calling him "the HOLY GOOF" (*On the Road*, 194). This spoke to the counterculture's rejection of conventional behavior. As far as being precarious, check out this description of Dean just before he takes Sal to Mexico:

> I saw his face huge over the plains with the mad, bony purpose and the gleaming eyes; I saw his wings; I saw his old jalopy chariot with thousands of sparking flames shooting out from it; I saw the path it burned over the road; it even made its own road and went over the corn, through cities, destroying bridges, drying rivers. It came like wrath to the West (*On the Road*, 259).

This romantic vision of Dean as a fallen angel resonated with the counterculture, which tended to see itself as the fallen children of an oppressive society.

At the same time, there is a sense of community that pervades the book, exemplified by Sal's famous revelation that there was "rising from the underground, the sordid hipsters of America, a new beat generation that I was slowly joining" (*On the Road*, 54). This sense of community spoke to the counterculture. Riding with Dean, Sal also has profound moments of spiritual love that meshed with the rejection of hate in the counterculture: "As we crossed the Colorado-Utah border I saw God in the sky in the form of huge gold sunburning clouds above the desert that seemed to point a finger at me and say, 'Pass here and go on, you're on the road to heaven'" (*On the Road*, 182). Sal and Dean's unorthodox Christianity, peppered with occasional Buddhist asides by Sal, foreshadowed the new spiritual explorations of the counterculture. This spirituality in *On the Road*, like the counterculture's rejections of the Cold War, valued peace over war. When encountering the indigenous of Mexico, Sal laments, "They didn't know that a bomb had come that could crack all our bridges and roads and reduce them to jumbles, and we would be as poor as they someday, and stretching out our hands in the same, same way" (*On the Road*, 199). Strikingly, Sal was tapping into the peace consciousness that led some members of the counterculture to reject "civilization" and embrace the innocence of what they perceived as "primitive." Even the politicos that believed violence was necessary to cause significant change in America did so with the intent of eventually undermining the violence they witnessed perpetrated by the American government during the Vietnam War. Former Students for a Democratic Society (SDS) president Todd Gitlin argues, "To guard against what they saw as the deathly pallor of middle-class culture, the beats followed a traditional romantic and bohemian route: they sought out noble savages."[10] A rejection of a civilization that created the atomic bomb and an embrace of life-affirming environmental concern associated with the "primitive" became a hallmark of the counterculture whether or not individuals in the movement believed it would take violence against the government to get to their desired new society.

7.2 *On the Road* Rocks

Unlike many of their contemporaries, Kerouac and the Beats had the advantage of being heavily publicized in the mainstream media in magazines such as *Time*, *Life*, and *Newsweek*. These often-derogatory depictions of the Beats had an inverse effect by intriguing some young readers, including Bob Dylan and Janis Joplin. Many of these readers participated in the new rock music scene in the '60s.[11] Bach tells us, "Promoters of 'rock revolution' contended that rock music contained within its power to change individuals and society."[12] Musicians influenced the 1960s counterculture more than any other social rebellion. Rock stars were seen as emissaries and shamans of the movement. *On the Road* resonated with many rock stars, and this helped make Kerouac a symbolic fellow traveler of the counterculture.[13]

The rock star most associated with the counterculture was Bob Dylan. The cover of the September 1965 issue of *Esquire* combined the faces of Dylan, Malcolm X, Fidel Castro, and John F. Kennedy, and inside listed Dylan as the number one icon for college rebels.[14] As Bach points out, "Dylan befriended members of SNCC [Student Nonviolent Coordinating Committee], sang for black farmers outside Greenwood, Mississippi, and performed at the March on Washington."[15] Former SDS president Tom Hayden remembers, "We studied the lyrics of Bob Dylan more than we did the texts of Marx and Lenin."[16] Those who knew and studied Dylan recognized the influence of Kerouac.[17] Fellow musician Dave Van Ronk believes, "Dylan really does belong in a rack with Kerouac."[18] Historian Sean Wilentz elaborates: "Dylan's involvement with the writings of Kerouac, Ginsberg, Burroughs, and the rest of the Beat Generation is nearly as essential to Dylan's biography as his immersion in rock and roll, rhythm and blues, and then Woody Guthrie."[19] Dylan considered *On the Road* one of the books with "street ideologies that were signaling a new type of human existence."[20] As a young man, Dylan recalls, "I suppose what I was looking for was what I read about in *On the Road*."[21] Before coming to New York, Dylan remembers, "[*On the Road*] had been like a bible for me":[22]

> I fell into that atmosphere of everything Kerouac was saying, about the world being completely mad, and the only people for him that were interesting were the mad people, the mad ones who were mad to live, mad to talk, mad to be saved, desirous of everything at the same time, the ones who never yawn, all of those mad ones, and I felt like I fit right into that bunch.[23]

Dylan's fascination with Kerouac inspired him to use phrases from Kerouac's novels in his songs and name several of his songs ("On the Road Again," "Visions of Johanna," "Desolation Row") based on the titles of Kerouac's novels. Timothy Hampton argues that "*Blood on the Tracks* [1975] is Dylan's rewriting of *On the Road*."[24] One could argue that had Dylan not read *On the Road* he would have been a very different lyricist.

Dylan was far from the only '60s rock musician to be influenced by *On the Road*. Jim Morrison, lead singer of The Doors, "read *On the Road* and plugged into its Beat Generation dreams, talking endlessly about the unimaginable joys of hitchhiking … and the endless highways of America illuminated by Zen flares of enlightenment."[25] Biographer Stephen Davis emphasizes that "[Morrison] fell in love with Dean Moriarty's ferocious American energy, and Kerouac's concept of Dean."[26] The Doors' keyboardist Ray Manzarek suspects, "I suppose if Jack Kerouac had never written *On the Road*, the Doors would never have existed."[27] Like Morrison, Janis Joplin gained confidence after reading Kerouac's *On the Road*. "For Janis," Holly George-Warren explains, "*On the Road* was 'a revelation'.... [T]his would inform everything going forward.... [Joplin] began calling herself a beatnik—which she would never stop doing."[28] Laura Joplin, Janis's sister, recalls, "Janis's gang saw Kerouac's character Dean Moriarty as a fanciful, modern-day outlaw."[29] Dean was the type of sympathetic outcast that they romanticized as a model for their own feelings of alienation from a hypocritical society. *On the Road* inspired Joplin to leave Port Arthur, Texas, and eventually make her way to San Francisco.

The 1960s countercultural band most closely tied to the Beats was the Grateful Dead, with whom Joplin performed. Grateful Dead aficionado Brian Hassett avows, "The Grateful Dead were Jack manifested as music."[30] Neal Cassady, the model for *On the Road*'s hero, became close with the band and even shared a room with the Dead's Bob Weir. "We're all siblings," said Weir, "we're all underlings to this guy Neal Cassady. He had a guiding hand."[31] For Jerry Garcia, the leader of the Dead, *On the Road* was "a book that changed his life forever. Kerouac's hymn to the world as an exploratory odyssey, and adventure outside conventional boundaries, would serve as a blueprint for the rest of Garcia's life."[32] According to Rock Scully, the Dead's manager, "Jerry was fifteen when *On the Road* came out, and it became his bible."[33] Garcia declares, "Kerouac became so much a part of me that it's hard to measure.... I can't separate who I am now from what I got from Kerouac."[34] No other band spread the spirit of Kerouac's *On the Road* to more people who would become part of the counterculture than the Grateful Dead.

7.3 *On the Road*, Dropouts, and Politicos

Many dropout hippies in the Haight-Ashbury neighborhood of San Francisco, their symbolic enclave, felt a kinship with *On the Road.* One of the dropout heroes was Ken Kesey, who asserts, "Everybody I knew had read *On the Road* and it opened up the doors to us just the same way drugs did."[35] Kesey's response to the Vietnam War was pure dropout: "*turn your backs and say ... Fuck it.*"[36] After reading Kesey's *One Flew Over the Cuckoo's Nest* (1962), Cassady found the author in Stanford's bohemian quarter and became part of the inner circle of the Merry Pranksters, Kesey's band of counterculture pioneers. Cassady drove the Pranksters' bus, sometimes purposely misspelled "Furthur," in their 1964 cross-country adventure from California to New York, where they had an unsuccessful party with Kerouac, who did not relate to their countercultural antics. The Warlocks, who became the Grateful Dead, was the house band for the acid tests, Kesey and the Pranksters' psychedelic parties. Dennis McNally explains, "The acid tests ... would serve as the template that permanently defined the Grateful Dead's view of its audience ... [as] companions in an odyssey."[37] Kesey and the Merry Pranksters became romantic heroes of the counterculture particularly after the publication of Tom Wolfe's *The Electric Kool-Aid Acid Test* (1968), which Gitlin sees as "still unsurpassed as a chronicle of the counterculture."[38] From the perspective of many in the counterculture, the baton had been handed by Kerouac and the Beats to Kesey and the Merry Pranksters.

Kesey was the West Coast's answer to Timothy Leary, who is known for his slogan "tune in, turn on, drop out." The big difference between them was Kesey's freewheeling attitude about acid and Leary's clinical and spiritual use of LSD. Few people represented the counterculture in the public imagination as much as Leary, the former Harvard professor who turned into the biggest, most recognized promoter of LSD in the world. When Leary gave Ginsberg psilocybin in late 1960, Ginsberg called the operator, said he was God, and wanted to be connected to Kerouac; feeling he was a messiah while high, Ginsberg wanted to start the peace and love movement with Kerouac as soon as he could.[39] After giving Kerouac psilocybin in January 1961, Leary writes, "Kerouac had propelled me into my first negative trip."[40] According to Leary, "Throughout the night Kerouac remained unmovably the Catholic carouser, an old-style Bohemian without a hippie bone in his body. Jack Kerouac opened the neural doors to the future, looked ahead, and didn't see his place in it."[41] Ginsberg remembers Kerouac's verdict: "Coach Leary, walking on water wasn't built in a day."[42] It was Kerouac's pithy way of saying that spiritual enlightenment did not come in pill form.

Nonetheless, several days later, Leary received a positive report on psilocybin from Kerouac: "It was a definite Satori. Full of Psychic clairvoyance.... There's no harm in Sacred Mushrooms and much good will come of it."[43] Kerouac wrote to Leary for more psilocybin to help him write and Leary sent Kerouac the pills, but Kerouac did not like the experience and stopped using them. Leary's biographer Robert Greenfield believes, "Kerouac's decision not to proceed any further down the path of psychedelic exploration effectively removed him from playing any significant personal role in the social and cultural revolution that his own writings helped create."[44] The psychedelic revolution would march on without Kerouac, but not without *On the Road*.

Many politicos on the campus at Berkeley, the symbolic home of the New Left, also admired *On the Road*. The New Left opposed the dropout hippies' escapism and wanted to change mainstream society with activism from within. Bach sees distinct differences among the rock culture, which thrived within the mainstream culture; the dropout hippies; and the New Left, which he does not count as part of the counterculture. Yet, many on the New Left did see themselves as part of the counterculture. As the '60s progressed, the New Left and the counterculture blurred into one another. Bach writes, "[I]t was an era of protest, especially against racism and the Vietnam War, and so more youths became hybrid counterculturalists, equally devoted to cultural and political radicalism."[45] When a peaceful resolution to the Vietnam War seemed unlikely with its escalation after the election of President Richard Nixon in 1968, various factions of the counterculture blended into one another causing many outsiders to see the various elements of the movement as indistinguishable. Members of the rock culture, which was influential on both the dropouts and the politicos, became more sympathetic with the idea of radical change in lifestyle (proposed by the dropouts) and/or activism (proposed by the politicos). Some dropouts began to see themselves as allies of the politicos, rather than antagonists. Many politicos began adopting the lifestyle (dress, physical characteristics, speech, musical tastes, and drug use) of the dropouts and rock culture.

One of the most famous politicos was Abbie Hoffman, who wanted to politicize the hippies. He was one of the founders of the Youth International Party, known as the Yippies. According to Hoffman's biographer Jonah Raskin, "On one occasion, he told Allen Ginsberg that his civil rights experience was an extension of the Beat adventure, and that on the road to Mississippi [as a Freedom Rider for the Student Nonviolent Coordinating Committee (SNCC)] he had read Jack Kerouac's *On the Road*."[46] At the 1968 Democratic National Convention in Chicago, where he mingled with Ginsberg and Burroughs, Hoffman pulled one of his more memorable stunts. "Most people thought the '*fuck*-on-my-forehead' was inspired by Lenny Bruce," recalls Hoffman, "but I had another incident in mind. Jack Kerouac, after once meditating on a mountaintop, descended to the press with a cross around his neck. The press took photos, but the cross got airbrushed in all the morning editions. I wanted to see if they'd airbrush my face."[47] Kerouac's photoshoot with other Beats for *Mademoiselle* in September 1956 produced the famous image of Kerouac used on the jacket of the first edition of *On the Road*. The cross was given to him by Corso, and it was cropped out, rather than airbrushed. Still, Kerouac was one of Hoffman's heroes and Abbie saw the Beats as the forbearers of the counterculture. Hoffman's fellow Yippie, Jerry Rubin, made a bid to become mayor of Berkeley in 1967 on a platform that called for legalizing marijuana, solidarity with the Black Power movement, and fighting for the end of the Vietnam War. Stew Albert, Rubin's campaign manager believed, "After the revolution, we'll be beats again."[48] This attitude suggested that the Beats had already found desirable communities removed from the strictures of mainstream society that could be emulated.

Hoffman was far from the only politico who found inspiration from Kerouac. Raskin writes, "When civil rights activists like Tom Hayden and Mario Savio went South to desegregate lunch counters and to register voters, they carried 'On the Road' with them as inspiration in backpacks and back pockets."[49] Savio was a leader of the Berkeley Free Speech Movement and delivered his influential "Operation of the Machine" speech on December 2, 1964. Hayden, one of the most well-known members of the New Left, was the author of the *Port Huron Statement* (1962) and became president of SDS in 1962. Reflecting in 2005 on the revision of the *Statement* by around sixty people during a five-day SDS convention, Hayden acknowledged that the "beat poets, such as Jack Kerouac and Allen Ginsberg, had stirred us."[50] Reading *On the Road* after graduating from high school, Hayden writes, "I too hitchhiked to every corner of America … embracing a spirit of the open road."[51] This experience helped lead Hayden to the political activism that would define his life.

In 1969, SDS was effectively dissolved by a splinter group, the Weathermen (later the Weather Underground), that took its name from Dylan's song "Subterranean Homesick Blues," which itself was named after Kerouac's novel *The Subterraneans* (1958). Weather Underground leader Mark Rudd, who had been an SDS leader at Columbia University, Kerouac's alma mater, writes that their goal was "the violent overthrow of the United States government."[52] Such a goal was, of course, anathema to Kerouac, but nevertheless, Bill Ayers, another leader of the Weather Underground, recalls that as a teen he had been inspired by many "tales of escape and reinvention," *On the Road* among them.[53] In this way, Kerouac's work can be seen as a stepping stone for some members of the counterculture toward more radical ideologies.

The counterculture was dominated by white males with at least some college education. Feminists, gay activists, and racial minorities, some of whom wanted their fair share of the economic privilege that the Beats were rejecting, often found it harder to identify with the ethos of *On the Road*. Yet there were some in these factions of the counterculture that were not averse to *On the Road*. Perhaps surprisingly, Eldridge Cleaver, later the Minister of Information for the Black Panthers, in *Soul on Ice* (1968), written in 1965, defended Kerouac's romanticization of Black culture in *On the Road*, against James Baldwin's dismissal of it, as an important stage in young whites' empathy for Black oppression.[54] Cleaver writes, "If many of these young people were content to lay up in their cool beat pads, smoking pot and listening to jazz in a perpetual orgy of esoteric bliss, there were others, less crushed by the system, who recognized the need for positive action."[55] For Cleaver, *On the Road* was a necessary step toward inspiring young countercultural whites to help Blacks fight for equality.

7.4 Coda: *Firing Line* – September 3, 1968

Kerouac's September 1968 appearance on *Firing Line* is a microcosm of Kerouac's exasperatingly ambiguous relationship with the counterculture. A year before he died, and at the height of the counterculture movement, Kerouac accepted an invitation by William F. Buckley to appear on his television show. The topic was "The Hippies." Kerouac, wearing the jacket he would be buried in, was on a panel with sociologist Lewis Yablonsky, author of *The Hippie Trip* (1968); and Ed Sanders, a Beat poet, publisher of *Fuck You/A Magazine of the Arts*, a founding member of the rock group The Fugs, and a Yippie. Kerouac was one of Sanders's heroes. Throughout the taping Kerouac was either falling asleep bored, playing the clown, or spouting his conservative views.

With some of his friends from his childhood home of Lowell, Massachusetts, where many of his values had been fostered, Kerouac traveled to New York for the taping of Buckley's show. At the Hotel Delmonico, Kerouac went to see Burroughs, who was working on his piece for *Esquire* about the recent Democratic National Convention in Chicago, which was already notorious in countercultural circles for the way the police had beaten protestors. Lucien Carr and Allen Ginsberg joined them. It was the first time the four friends had been together since 1953, and it would be the last.[56] Recognizing how drunk Kerouac was, Burroughs urged Kerouac not to go on television. Ginsberg, now a leader of the counterculture, went with Kerouac for moral support, but during the taping Kerouac put his thumbs down in a gesture to Ginsberg and told Sanders not to associate him with his old friend. After the show, Kerouac and Sanders would carouse in a Times Square bar like old friends – but during the taping Kerouac was alternately congenial and combative with the Yippie.

In his introduction of the panel, Buckley mentioned that Kerouac had become famous after the publication of *On the Road*; it was the only mention of the book during the show. When Buckley asked Sanders if he was a hippie, Sanders responded by saying that "hippie" was a limiting term imposed on people by the media. Sanders's solutions to social problems were more political. When asked about the relationship between the Beats and the hippies, Kerouac responds, "It's the same movement. It's apparently some kind of Dionysian movement, in late civilization, in which I did not intend, any more than I suppose Dionysus did."[57] After mispronouncing Dionysus as Dionysius, Kerouac says he should have been the Christian saint Dionysius the Areopagite. What is often overlooked is when Kerouac says, "The hippies are good kids. They're better than the Beats."[58] Kerouac both identifies with and praises the hippie dropouts, but dislikes the politicos, whom he sees as communists and proponents of violence, which he deplores. Kerouac explains that the Beat Generation was called in the press "the Beat Mutiny and Beat Insurrection, words I never used. Being a Catholic, I believe in order, tenderness, and piety."[59] The Beat movement was "pure," he says, in his heart.

Sanders, who had been on the streets of Chicago during the Democratic National Convention in August, recalls in brutal detail the violence perpetrated by the Chicago police. Buckley, who had also been in Chicago, but not on the streets, says that Sanders' description of events is unrecognizable to what he saw on television, which was the insurrection of the counterculture, an attempt to burn down the building where the convention was held, and a desire to assassinate Democrats they saw as promoting the war in Vietnam. Buckley says that everybody knows that Tom Hayden and Rennie Davis, members of the National Mobilization Committee to End the War in Vietnam, "are not sweet little old flower children."[60] From Buckley's perspective, the counterculture wanted a confrontation with police and benefitted from the sympathy they received after the convention. Sanders absolutely disagrees that most people were there to provoke the police. What they wanted, he tells Buckley, was a "Festival of Life with rock music."[61] Sanders remembers Ginsberg and Burroughs being driven out of Lincoln Park by tear gas set off by the police. At one point Kerouac interrupts to say that his mother calls presidential candidate Hubert Humphrey, "Flat Foot Floogie (with a Floy Floy)," the title of a 1938 jazz song by Slim Gaillard, one of the musicians idolized by Sal and Dean in *On the Road.* Kerouac cuts in on Sanders to tell him, "I was arrested two weeks ago. And the arresting policeman said, I'm arresting you for decay."[62] Everyone laughs.

The essential exchange, for our purposes, occurs in the middle of the taping. First Kerouac tells Buckley that he, his father, his mother, and his sister always voted Republican since Herbert Hoover. Of course, there is no record of Kerouac ever voting, and certainly not when he was six years old.

Then Kerouac tells Sanders, "I made myself famous by writing songs and lyrics about the beauty of the things I did, ugliness, too."[63] Sanders separates Kerouac's books from the drunk in front of him, and replies, "You're a great poet."[64] Decrying Sanders as a mere agitator, Kerouac tells him, "I cannot use your abuse; you can have it back."[65] And then, revealing what he truly feels about Kerouac's relationship with the counterculture, Sanders calmly replies, "You're a great poet, we admire you, in fact it's your fault."[66]

Notes

1. For a discussion of the Beats' influence on the counterculture, see Jonah Raskin's "Beatniks, Hippies, Yippies, Feminists, and the Ongoing American Counterculture," in *The Cambridge Companion to the Beats*, ed. Steven Belletto (New York: Cambridge University Press, 2017), 36–50.
2. This quotation is used by the character Ignatius J. Reilly in John Kennedy Toole's *A Confederacy of Dunces* (New York: Grove Press, 1987), 99, but, though it can be found all over the Internet, I could not determine its original source.
3. William S. Burroughs, "Remembering Jack Kerouac," *The Adding Machine: Selected Essays* (New York: Grove Press), 214.
4. Fred Misurella, "Interview: Gregory Corso," in *The Whole Shot: Collected Interviews with Gregory Corso* (Arlington, MA: Tough Poets Press, 2015), 126.
5. David Stewart, dir. *On the Road to Desolation* (BBC, 1997).
6. Gregory Corso, "Columbia U Poesy Reading – 1975," in *Herald of the Autochthonic Spirit* (New York: New Directions, 1981), 2.
7. Damon R. Bach, *The American Counterculture: A History of Hippies and Cultural Dissidents* (Lawrence: University Press of Kansas, 2020), 15.
8. Jack Kerouac, *On the Road* (New York: Viking Press, 1957), 10.
9. Bach, *The American Counterculture*, 15.
10. Todd Gitlin, *The Sixties: Years of Hope, Days of Rage* (New York: Bantom Books, 1993), 47.
11. For a discussion of the Beats' influence on rock, see Simon Warner's *Text and Drugs and Rock 'n' Roll: The Beats and Rock Culture* (New York: Bloomsbury, 2015) and Laurence Coupe's *Beat Sound, Beat Vision: The Beat Spirit and Popular Song* (New York: Manchester University Press, 2007).
12. Bach, *The American Counterculture*, xix.
13. For a discussion of Kerouac's influence on rock, see *Kerouac on Record: A Literary Soundtrack*, ed. Simon Warner and Jim Sampas (New York: Bloomsbury, 2018).
14. "28 People Who Count," *Esquire* 64, no. 3 (September 1965), 97.
15. Bach, *The American Counterculture*, 32.
16. Tom Hayden, "The Way We Were and the Future of the *Port Huron Statement*," in *The Port Huron Statement: The Visionary Call of the 1960s Revolution* (New York: Thunder's Mouth Press, 2005), 7.

17. For a discussion of Dylan and the Beats, see Steven Belletto's "The Beats" in *The World of Bob Dylan*, ed. Sean Latham (New York: Cambridge University Press, 2021), 169–180.
18. Robert Shelton, *No Direction Home: The Life and Music of Bob Dylan* (New York: Da Capo Press, 1997), 99.
19. Sean Wilentz, *Bob Dylan in America* (New York: Doubleday, 2010), 50.
20. Bob Dylan, *Chronicles: Volume One* (New York: Simon & Schuster Paperbacks, 2005), 34.
21. Dylan, *Chronicles*, 235.
22. Dylan, *Chronicles*, 57.
23. Martin Scorsese, dir. *No Direction Home: Bob Dylan* (PBS, 2005).
24. Timothy Hampton, *Bob Dylan: How the Songs Work* (New York: Zone Books, 2019), 122.
25. Stephen Davis, *Jim Morrison: Life, Death, Legend* (New York: Gotham Books, 2004), 18.
26. Davis, *Jim Morrison*, 18.
27. Ray Manzarek, *Light My Fire: My Life with The Doors* (New York: Berkley Boulevard Books, 1999), 68.
28. Holly George-Warren, *Janis: Her Life and Music* (New York: Simon & Schuster, 2019), 31.
29. Laura Joplin, *Love, Janis* (New York: Harper, 2005), 61.
30. Brian Hassett, "The Grateful Dead: Jack Manifested as Music," in *Kerouac on Record: A Literary Soundtrack*, ed. Simon Warner and Jim Sampas (New York: Bloomsbury, 2018), 169.
31. Dennis McNally, *A Long Strange Trip: The Inside History of the Grateful Dead* (New York: Broadway Books, 2002), 357.
32. McNally, *A Long Strange Trip*, 15.
33. Rock Scully with David Dalton, *Living with the Dead: Twenty Years on the Bus with Garcia and the Grateful Dead* (New York: Cooper Square Press, 2001), 23.
34. Tom Taylor, "Beats Entwined: How Jack Kerouac Influenced The Grateful Dead," *Far Out*, December 11, 2022, faroutmagazine.co.uk/jack-kerouac-influenced-the-grateful-dead/.
35. Alex Gibney and Alison Ellwood, dir. *Magic Trip* (Magnolia Pictures, 2011).
36. Wolfe, *The Electric Kool-Aid Acid Test*, 224.
37. McNally, *A Long Strange Trip*, 119.
38. Gitlin, *The Sixties*, 207.
39. Timothy Leary, *High Priest* (Oakland: Ronin Publishing, Inc., 1995), 122–123.
40. Timothy Leary, *Flashbacks: An Autobiography* (Los Angeles: J. P. Tarcher, Inc., 1983), 65.
41. Leary, *Flashbacks*, 67.
42. Robert Greenfield, *Timothy Leary: A Biography* (New York: A James H. Silberman Book, 2006), 135.
43. Greenfield, *Timothy Leary*, 136.
44. Greenfield, *Timothy Leary*, 137.
45. Bach, *The American Counterculture*, xxiv.

46. Jonah Raskin, *The Life and Times of Abbie Hoffman* (Berkeley: University of California Press, 1998), 57.
47. Abbie Hoffman, *The Autobiography of Abbie Hoffman* (New York: Four Walls Eight Windows, 2000), 125.
48. Gitlin, *The Sixties*, 211.
49. Jonah Raskin, "Jack Kerouac at 100: Honoring the 'King of the Beats' on His Centennial Birthday," *San Francisco Examiner* (May 7, 2022), www.sfexaminer.com/culture/jack-kerouac-at-100-honoring-the-king-of-the-beats-on-his-centennial-birthday/article_d9b5e6c5-8112-5a69-93f5-9eb72eb59559.html.
50. Hayden, "The Way We Were," 9.
51. Tom Hayden, *Reunion: A Memoir* (New York: Random House, 1988), 18.
52. Mark Rudd, *Underground: My Life with SDS and the Weathermen* (New York: Harper, 2010), viii.
53. Bill Ayers, *Fugitive Days: A Memoir* (New York: Penguin Books, 2003), 24–25.
54. Eldridge Cleaver, *Soul on Ice* (New York: A Ramparts Book, 1968), 71–72.
55. Cleaver, *Soul on Ice*, 72.
56. Dennis McNally, *Desolate Angel: Jack Kerouac, The Beat Generation, and America* (New York: Da Capo Press, 2003), 336.
57. Ed Sanders, *Fug You: An Informal History of the Peace Eye Bookstore, the Fuck You Press, The Fugs, and Counterculture in the Lower East Side* (New York: Da Capo Press, 2011), 337.
58. Sanders, *Fug You*, 337.
59. Sanders, *Fug You*, 338.
60. Sanders, *Fug You*, 344.
61. Sanders, *Fug You*, 344.
62. Sanders, *Fug You*, 349.
63. Sanders, *Fug You*, 347.
64. Sanders, *Fug You*, 347.
65. Sanders, *Fug You*, 347.
66. Sanders, *Fug You*, 347.

CHAPTER 8

Vanity of Duluoz *and the 1960s*

David Stephen Calonne

Vanity of Duluoz, published in February, 1968, was the final installment of five novels Kerouac published during the sixties: *Big Sur* (1962), *Visions of Gerard* (1963), *Desolation Angels* (1965) and *Satori in Paris* (1966). Kerouac revealed in Book Six, Chapter II of *Vanity of Duluoz* that his novel's title first came to him while working as a sportswriter for the Lowell *Sun*. discovering in an article there the name of a well-known Greek family – Daoulas – which he adapted to "Duluoz" to name his alter ego. He proceeded to compose a novel in imitation of the stream-of-consciousness style of James Joyce's *Ulysses* (1922). This places the novel's initial conception very early in Kerouac's career during his late adolescence, however he first started work on the manuscript in the early sixties, writing Allen Ginsberg on June 29, 1963: "Anyway my present job is to write 'Vanity of Duluoz' novel about 1939–1946, won't be easy, football, war, Edie, etc. Bronx jail, you, Columbia, etc. ouch. Come home soon."[1] *Vanity of Duluoz* was composed under fraught conditions. Kerouac labored under intense financial pressure to earn money to pay for his mother's debilitating illnesses: he hoped to settle her "in a proper home in the country outside Lowell Mass" (*Selected Letters* 2, 487). He typically drafted about 8,000 words at each sitting "in the middle of the night," and the same amount a week later, after "resting and sighing in between." He was also again drinking heavily – he wrote John Clellon Holmes on March 30, 1967 – "Have reached midway point in new novel, full of pep pills and booze" – and the gaps and odd quirks of the text suggest the prose was composed – it was finally completed in June, 1967 on a telex roll – under an extreme sense of exigency[2] Kerouac "confesses" his life to his wife Stella Sampas, several times addressing her directly, while engaging in an intense self-examination of his past against the backdrop of the contemporaneous tumult of the sixties. As Regina Weinreich has observed, the text is a kind of "dramatic monologue" and "Kerouac's Duluoz narrates the tale but acts also as an intrusive commentator on events."[3] Not only was it a struggle for Kerouac to complete *Vanity of Duluoz*, the novel also powerfully documents Kerouac's struggle with reconciling his traditional, "conservative" upbringing with the nascent "Beat" rebellious energies – born in the forties and continuing into the sixties – a conflict which this chapter seeks to explore.

Regarding the structure of *Vanity of Duluoz*, divided into thirteen "Books," it is likely that Kerouac was influenced by Homer's *Iliad* and *Odyssey* – required reading in the Great Books Program at his alma mater, Columbia University – each divided into twenty-four "Books" and Homer is mentioned several times in the novel. *Doctor Sax* (1959) features six "Books," while *Desolation Angels* (1965) is cast in the form of two "Books." After all, Kerouac – like Homer – is composing an "epic" featuring the battles and wanderings of his hero, Duluoz. For the novel's frequently brief episodes, Allen Ginsberg coined the quaint term "chapterettes": "Each chapterette is one section of writing, wherever the writing leads. That's how the book is composed. One day he'll write maybe a paragraph, and that's a chapter. The next day he'll get interested and idly write three pages, so that's a whole other chapterette."[4]

Vanity of Duluoz compresses in a brief space eleven years of Kerouac's life from ages thirteen to twenty-four – its subtitle promises "An Adventurous Education, 1935–46" – his accomplishments as a star athlete, his final years in high school and Horace Mann School before entering Columbia on a football scholarship, his time in the Merchant Marines and war years in Greenland, Ireland, his fateful meetings with Allen Ginsberg, William S. Burroughs as well as an extensive description of the events surrounding Lucien Carr's murder of David Kammerer in August 1944. However, the present several times "intrudes" in a somewhat jarring way into a narrative ostensibly concerned with the past. It is not only Kerouac's personal travails which the novel records and a re-examination of his past – one of Kerouac's favorite works was Marcel Proust's *À la recherche du temps perdu* (1913–1927) – but also his reactions to the seismic shifts in American culture during the 1960s. Kerouac told Ted Berrigan that he composed *Vanity of Duluoz* "in a more moderate style, so that, having been so esoteric all these years, some earlier readers would come back and see what ten years had done to my life and thinking."[5]

It is commonly believed that Kerouac himself was a wild-eyed "progressive"; however, a close analysis of *Vanity of Duluoz* indicates that his attitude towards the American counterculture was – or became with time – much more nuanced and ambivalent than is widely supposed. When Ken Kesey and his Merry Pranksters arrived in the summer of 1964 to meet Kerouac in New York City, for example, Kerouac was offended when he noticed a couch covered with an American flag. Kerouac was "uncomfortable" among the Pranksters and "walked over to the sofa, carefully folded the flag, and asked them if they were Communists. Conversation was impossible and Jack left abruptly."[6] In a move that may surprise some readers, according to Luc Sante Kerouac voted Republican in the 1960 presidential election.

Kerouac's "conservative" commentary on contemporary American political and social life in *Vanity of Duluoz* begins immediately as he places his tale in the present, informing Stella: "All right, wifey, maybe I'm a big pain in the you-know-what but after I've given you a recitation of the troubles I had to go through to make good in America between 1935 and more or less now, 1967." Kerouac informs the reader that he is writing the book *now*, in the present, in 1967, signaling that from the outset there will be no presumption or pretense of a distance between author/narrator and the temporally bound history he is writing. Indeed, Kerouac continues:

> Look, furthermore, my anguish as I call it arises from the fact that people have changed so much, not only in the past five years, for God's sake, or past ten years as McLuhan says, but in the past thirty to such an extent that I don't recognize them as people any more or recognize myself as a real member of something called the human race. (*Vanity of Duluoz*, 9)[7]

Kerouac mentions both the present date of 1967 as well as Marshall McLuhan in the second paragraph of the novel, immediately anchoring the book in a time when McLuhan had reached his greatest fame with the publication of *Understanding Media: The Extensions of Man* (1964) and *The Medium is the Message: An Inventory of Effects* (1967).

However, in a May 22, 1967, letter to John Clellon Holmes, Kerouac reveals little interest in McLuhan's groundbreaking theories of "the global village" or the role of media in shaping human consciousness:

> I've been reading MacLuhan [sic] … and came to the conclusion that he's the biggest 'communist conspirator' of them all, i.e., instead of mis-teaching literacy to children in public new-school methods, he simply dismisses the importance of literacy. How can anybody pay their bills and taxes ten years from now if they can't read or write anymore? I feel that those who advocate 'anarchy' are people who know very well how to manage their business affairs in a VERY NON-ANARCHISTIC way and only want everybody else to be stupid. Anyway, end of typing practice. (*Selected Letters 2*, 497)

This is a of course a laughable misreading of McLuhan's work. Kerouac finds evidence of nefarious plots where none exist; in language echoing Joseph McCarthy's Communist "witch hunts" of the fifties, McLuhan is transformed into "the biggest 'communist conspirator' of them all." The sentiment expressed in this letter is repeated in *Vanity of Duluoz* when Kerouac argues that "lying has become so prevalent in the world today (thanks to Marxian Dialectical propaganda and Comintern techniques among other causes)" (*Vanity of Duluoz*, 13). For Kerouac, these are "the original tricks of Bolshevist Communism."

For Kerouac, the changes he bemoans began to occur as far back as "the past thirty" years (*Vanity of Duluoz*, 9). Thus, he sets the date of American decline back to 1937 which gives the reader a clearer sense of the causes of Kerouac's disaffection for the contemporary state of affairs in his country. This is Kerouac's strategy throughout *Vanity of Duluoz* – linking what he sees as a variety of social ills with the fact that the United States has "changed so much" for the worse. Other cultural enthusiasms of the period beyond McLuhan also receive crotchety commentary in Kerouac's other books of the sixties. In *Big Sur*, for example, Kerouac attacks Hermann Hesse's novel *Steppenwolf* (1927) – a favorite text of the Beats and hippies – which Kerouac read while staying at Lawrence Ferlinghetti's Bixby Canyon retreat: "the stupid and senseless 'Steppenwolf' novel in the shack which I read with a shrug, this old fart reflecting the 'conformity' of today and all the while he thought he was a big Nietzsche, old imitator of Dostoyevsky, fifty years too late (he feels tormented in a 'personal hell' he calls it because he doesn't like what other people like!)."[8]

The world was changing around Kerouac, and he did not approve of the changes. Hitchhiking, for example, played a major role in *On the Road* and had been relatively common in the United States: hoboes and Beats alike sought this method of transportation. However, by the 1960s and early 1970s, coterminous with the slow fading of the counterculture, hitchhiking occurred less frequently and acquired a tinge of menace, likely due to the increasing levels of fear, distrust and violence that had come to characterize American social and political life during this volatile period: racism and frequent brutality by law enforcement, the assassinations of Martin Luther King, Jr. and Robert Kennedy, the overpolicing of the Democratic National Convention in August, 1968, the ongoing war in Vietnam, and the increasing polarization in the country. Even in his novel *Big Sur*, published in 1962, Kerouac already complained: "This is the first time I've hitch hiked in years and I soon began to see that things have changed in America, you can't get a ride any more." Instead of "people have changed" as in *Vanity of Duluoz*, here Kerouac bemoans that "things have changed." He goes on to portray the station wagons, "all colors of the rainbow and pastel at that, pink, blue white, the husband is in the driver's seat ... Beside him sits wifey, the boss of America, wearing dark glasses and sneering, even if he wanted to pick me up or anybody up she wouldn't let him." Kerouac describes children in the back seat "fighting and screaming over ice cream. There's no room anymore anyway for a hitchhiker tho conceivably the poor bastard might be allowed to ride like a meek gunman or silent murderer in the very back platform of the wagon" (*Big Sur*, 44–45). The whole passage serves as a rather fierce and comical satire on the notion put forward in a famous television commercial of the '60s – "See the USA, in a Chevrolet!" The gap between the late 1940s hitchhiking in *On the Road* and the sad early 1960s scene Kerouac paints in *Big Sur* is a large one indeed.

By 1967, the use of LSD had become more widespread, and Kerouac takes another of his many swipes against the counterculture which occur throughout *Vanity of Duluoz*. Kerouac veers from his narrative in Book One, Chapter III to contrast past with present in the first of several animadversions on LSD:

> And that today nobody walks hands-in-pockets whistling across fields or even down sidewalks. That long before I'll lose track of my beefs I'll go cracked and even get to believe, like those LSD heads in newspaper photographs who sit in parks gazing rapturously at the sky to show how high they are when they're only victims momentarily of a contraction of the blood vessels and nerves in the brain that causes the illusion of a closure (a closing-up) of outside necessities, get to thinking I'm not Jack Duluoz at all. (*Vanity of Duluoz*, 14)

On the sixth page, Kerouac already compares his concern that he could "go cracked" and lose his sense of personal identity as he claims has happened to LSD users. This is coupled with his nostalgia to return – a recurring theme as we shall see throughout *Vanity of Duluoz* – to an earlier time when he might see people walking about with "hands-in-pockets" or "whistling across fields or even down sidewalks." Kerouac couples the new drug culture with a deterioration in American life from a (presumed) prelapsarian state of innocence, casualness and mutual trust among citizens.

Later, while describing his time at sea with the Merchant Marines, Kerouac tells us: "As I was writing just now, I heard a hissing outside my porthole, the sea is heavy, the ship just rocks and rocks real deep, and I thought: 'Torpedo!' I waited for one long second. Death! Death!' (Think of your death scenes and death trips, LSD users!)" (*Vanity of Duluoz*, 121–122). This is a double temporal dislocation, for while recounting his past, he calls us back to the present, imagining his study as a room aboard ship – "As I was writing just now, I heard a hissing outside my porthole" – which then leads him to compare possible death during war with the "death scenes and death trips" which may occur to "LSD users!"

In the final physical, psychological and spiritual implosion at the end of the novel, when Kerouac is recovering from thrombophlebitis in the hospital, he extends his critique of modernity: "I began to get a new vision of my own of a truer darkness which just overshadowed all this overlaid mental garbage of 'existentialism' and 'hipsterism' and 'bourgeois decadence' and whatever names you want to give it … All the contemporary LSD acid heads (of 1967) see the cruel beauty of the brute creation just by closing their eyes: I've seen it too since: a maniacal Mandala circle all mosaic and dense with millions of cruel things and beautiful scenes goin on" (*Vanity of Duluoz*, 262). Kerouac will ultimately frame his quarrel with modernity within the context of a cosmic, spiritual battle.

In the passage cited above, Kerouac mounts a wholesale condemnation of several aspects of contemporary life which characterized the counterculture: left-wing politics in the form of Marxism (manifested in the Marxist phrase "bourgeois decadence"), already excoriated in *Vanity of Duluoz* as "Marxian Dialectical propaganda"; Jean-Paul Sartre's atheist philosophy of personal responsibility and free choice ("existentialism"); and "hipsterism," by which Kerouac appears to mock attempts at being "cool" and "fashionable" and "with it." Nearly ten years earlier, in a 1958 letter to Allen Ginsberg, Kerouac expressed similar sentiments – adding psychoanalysis to his anathematizing of modernity – explaining that he is "disassociating" himself from Kenneth Rexroth's

> sphere of influence because I DON'T WANT NOTHIN TO DO WITH POLITICS especially leftist West Coast future blood in the street malevolence. (There will be a revolution in California, it is seething with incredible hatred, led by bloodthirsty poets … I don't like it. I believe in Buddha kindness and nothing else, I believe in Heaven, in Angels, I eschew all Marxism and allied horseshit & psychoanalysis, an offshoot therefrom … beware of California.). (*Selected Letters 2*, 115–116)

One notes Kerouac cites Buddhism and the angels of Christianity as the things he "believes in," rather than the false gods of Karl Marx and Sigmund Freud's psychoanalysis, which he regards as an "offshoot" of Marxism.

It would perhaps be a salutary exercise for readers to peruse *Vanity of Duluoz* immediately after their first encounter with *On the Road*, because they may then well believe that the books had been written by two different authors – the "open-minded bohemian" and the "conservative" – and then struggle to decide Kerouac's true identity. However, William S. Burroughs argued that over the years, Kerouac never changed his social and political attitudes:

> It's generally construed that Jack underwent some sort of change and became conservative. But he was always conservative. Those ideas never changed. He was always the same. It was sort of a double-think. In one way he was a Buddhist with this expansionistic viewpoint, and on the other hand he always had the most conservative political opinions. He was an Eisenhower man and believed in the old-fashioned virtues, in America, and that Europeans were decadent, and he was violently opposed to communism and any sort of leftist ideologies. But that did not change. It wasn't something that came on in his later years. It was always there, and there was no change in the whole time that I knew him. It didn't really fit in with the rest of his way of life, but it was there.[9]

Richard S. Sorrell locates Kerouac's unchanging "conservatism" in his parents' French-Canadian roots, "the pure Catholic nationality which would expand the kingdom of God and expose the false material values of Protestantism. Religion thus became a way of life, rather than just a part of life, as Catholicism became increasingly associated with nationalism in Quebec, and with conservative and even reactionary theological and social views."[10] Michael Hrebeniak furthermore asserts that Kerouac "disintegrates into dependency and nostalgia for the hegemonies of Church and State. As the romantic aspiration toward literary fame fades, Kerouac reverts to the folksy proletarianism of his parents and unleashes the latent hostility toward liberal values upon which the New Republicanism preys."[11] Another possible interpretation is that the young Kerouac composing *On the Road* was expressing his Dionysian, spontaneous, open-to-all-experience, life-loving side which in any case may be seen as beyond politics. The young people in *On the Road* are immersed in travel, in sensation, in sexual pleasure, in transcendence, in the ecstasy of music, yet the book is also death-haunted and already features the Buddhist concept that all life is suffering – *dukkha*.

In one narrative digression in Book Six, Chapter I, Kerouac describes a trip back to Lowell, Massachusetts and a cold, November night sky "where Eve Star (some call it Venus, some call it Lucifer) stoppered up her drooling propensities and tried to contain itself in one delimited throb of boiling light." Kerouac then catches himself, interrupting his own lyrical aria:

> Ah poetic. I keep saying "ah poetic" because I didn't intend this to be a poetic paean of a book, in 1967 as I'm writing this what possible feeling can be left in me for an "America" that has become such a potboiler of

> broken convictions, messes of rioting and fighting in the streets, hoodlumism, cynical administration of cities and states, suits and neckties the only feasible subject, grandeur all gone into the mosaic mesh of Television (Mosaic indeed, with a capital *M*), where people screw their eyes at all those dots and pick out hallucinated images of their own contortion and are fed ACHTUNG! ATTENTION! ATENCION! (*Vanity of Duluoz*, 103–104)

Kerouac now extends his polemic to "hoodlumism." During his appearance on William F. Buckley's *Firing Line* on September 3, 1968, along with sociologist Lewis Yablonsky and co-founder of The Fugs Ed Sanders on the topic of "The Hippies," Kerouac – as he had in earlier essays – again drunkenly opined about "hoodlums": "The hippies are good kids, they're better than the Beats ... We're all in our forties, and we started this, and the kids took it up. A lot of hoodlums and communists jumped on our backs. Well, on my back, not his." And Kerouac then points to Allen Ginsberg who is in the audience as an example of the deleterious influence of "hoodlums and communists."[12] Likewise, during his boozy nights in 1965 at the Wild Boar Tavern in Tampa, Florida, Kerouac told Gerard Wagner, "I'm not a spokesman for a bunch of hoods. I'm a novelist in the great French narrative tradition."[13] Kerouac sometimes associated "communism" with "hoodlums" and in the passage from *Vanity of Duluoz* likely is referring to the anti-Vietnam protests and marches and perhaps the riots which erupted in pursuit of racial justice during this period.

The "doubleness" – or "double-think" in Burroughs' phrase – of Kerouac's perspective can be attributed at least in part to his French-Canadian ancestry. David G. Vermette has studied the role conservative newspaper editors and priests played in the shaping of attitudes among French-Canadian immigrants in the United States and argues that Kerouac's

> seminal work was utterly out of sync with the messages the conservative elite in the French-language newspapers was still preaching to Kerouac's generation. His books celebrating Franco-American Lowell, such as *Visions of Gerard* and *Vanity of Duluoz*, better works than *On the Road*, were misunderstood. The U.S. mainstream, least of all university-educated critics, had no context for the Franco-American mill town culture that inspired Kerouac's rhapsodies.[14]

Kerouac resembles a "rhapsodic" author whose "ethnic" roots and in many ways traditional sensibility is mentioned more frequently than any other in *Vanity of Duluoz* – the Armenian-American William Saroyan. One reason for Kerouac's enthusiasm for Saroyan – although Saroyan was untethered to any particular religion and his spiritual orientation might best be described as pantheistic – was Kerouac's nostalgia for a pre–Second World War America, a period Saroyan often joyously celebrated. In his *Paris Review* interview, Kerouac also revealed that Saroyan's free, Whitmanian, often jazz-inflected and humorous prose poetry was a major influence on his own writing: "As for Saroyan, yes I loved him as a teenager, he really got me out of the nineteenth century rut I was trying to study, mot only his funny tone but his neat Armenian poetic I don't know what … he just got me."[15]

Sebastian Sampas of Greek ancestry, "Sabbas Savakis" – the brother of Kerouac's wife Stella to whom he dedicated *Vanity of Duluoz* – appears in the novel as a dear friend who first told Kerouac about Saroyan. Sampas was wounded at age twenty-one during the battle of Anzio and later died of gangrene in Algiers. In *Visions of Gerard*, which concerns the death of Kerouac's much beloved brother, he recalled the influence of Sampas' poetic and spiritual sensibility: "It was only many years later when I met and understood Savas Savakis that I recalled the definite and immortal *idealism* which had been imparted me by my holy brother—And even later with the discovery … of Buddhism, Awakenhood."[16] *Vanity of Duluoz* bears the imprint Kerouac's friendship with Greek-Americans such as Sampas – as noted above, Kerouac took "Duluoz" from the Greek family name "Daoulas" – and through him the world of Armenian immigrants in Fresno, California, and the San Joaquin Valley during the Depression and its aftermath, memorialized by Saroyan in plays such as *My Heart's In the Highlands* (1939) and his story collections *The Daring Young Man on the Flying Trapeze* (1934) and *My Name Is Aram* (1940). Kerouac as a Franco-American felt – like Greek- and Armenian-Americans – a similar sense of estrangement which sometimes leads in turn to the hyper-American "patriotism" typical of those who wish to affirm the badge of belonging to the United States.

In *The Haunted Life*, for example, Kerouac portrays his father Leo as "Joe Martin" who espouses the far-right populism of Father Charles Coughlin, thus setting up the conflict between Kerouac's working-class Lowell background and his later entry to the world of *la jeunesse dorèe* at Columbia University, which informs the last sections of *Vanity of Duluoz*. We can see this mingling of patriotic fervor and allusions to Saroyan and Wolfe – 1930s writers who symbolized Kerouac's longing for an earlier, prewar, "innocent" United States – in "I Have to Pull Up my Stakes and Roll, Man." This is a text which Kerouac composed in August, 1941, at about the same time he began his Joycean first attempt at a narrative under the title *Vanity of Duluoz*:

> and I love Asheville, N.C. with the people sitting on the porches in the summer nights listening, seething to the trains shriek in the valleys, and little Tom Wolfe sitting on his porch steps, listening, seething, "a locomotive in his chest,"; yes I love Saroyan and Fresno (the ditches in the fields, the vines, the Assyrian barbers, yes I do. I love America, yes I do. I love the White Sox, the Dodgers, Ted Williams and Pete Reiser; I love America, I tell you I do.[17]

In this passage, Kerouac combines baseball as well as Wolfe and Saroyan, alluding to several Saroyan stories such as "Seventy Thousand Assyrians," a tender story from *The Daring Young Man on the Flying Trapeze* concerning an Assyrian barber with whom the Armenian narrator deeply identifies because the Assyrians – like the Armenians – had nearly vanished from history. Kerouac also evokes Saroyan's great fertile Californian vineyards and raisin – growing fields of Fresno and the San Joaquin Valley.

These connections to the immigrant Greek and Armenian communities on the part of a French-Canadian with working class roots offer us one clue to understanding the political and cultural conflicts which play themselves out in *Vanity of Duluoz.* In the final sections of the novel, Kerouac's "rampages" against modernity culminate in several vituperative passages. Book Thirteen, Chapter I begins with yet another fierce blast regarding the time Kerouac worked in Detroit factories where Edie Parker's father had arranged for him to obtain employment:

> Talk about "widening your consciousness" and all that crap they talk about nowadays, if I'da widened my consciousness enough to narrow down the piecework numbered on the counters of the piecework ballbearing laborers in Federal Mogul Factory in Detroit that September, where I went to earn and save that one hundred dollars I owed my new wife's aunt, they'da widened my arse and narrowed my head with a monkey wrench and not a left-handed one at that. (*Vanity of Duluoz*, 247)

The switch to "vulgar, working-class" language – not without its undeniable humor – from the sublime metaphysical and transcendental heights being scaled by Timothy Leary and the Beats during this period is Kerouac's way of deflating what he saw as the pretensions of many of the spoiled, "entitled" new youth of America who have the free time to "widen their consciousness" in ways that are forbidden to those who have to spend their time toiling for a living.

In the final sections of *Vanity of Duluoz*, Kerouac narrates the tale of his blossoming friendships with Allen Ginsberg and William S. Burroughs and describes in some detail Lucien Carr's murder of David Kammerer. Upon first encountering Carr ("Claude de Maubris") and Burroughs ("Will Hubbard"), Kerouac began

> to realize that this here New Orleans clique was the most evil and intelligent buncha bastards and shits in America but had to admire in my admiring youth. Their style was dry, new to me, mine had been the misty-nebulous New England Idealist style tho (as I say) my saving grace in their eyes (Will's, Claude's especially) was the materialistic Canuck taciturn cold skepticism all the picked-up Idealism in the world of books couldn't hide ... "Duluoz is a shit posing as an angel." (*Vanity of Duluoz*, 201)

Kerouac offers an acute self-analysis, revealing the twin sides of his own nature: the "Canuck skepticism" in opposition to his "New England Idealist style" in the tradition of his friend Sebastian Sampas, as well as Henry David Thoreau and Ralph Waldo Emerson. Kerouac in several passages also emphasizes the class differences he experienced leaving Lowell, Massachusetts, for the ivory towers of Columbia, and returns to the sarcastic tone of his earlier lambasting of '60s youth culture. He describes an evening when Claude, Will, and Franz Mueller (Kammerer) ruin Will's seersucker suit, ripping it up in a wild destructive act: "And of course to a 'Lowell boy' like me, destroying a coat was strange but to them ... they all came from well-to-do families" (*Vanity of Duluoz*, 215).

Kerouac does not fail to sharply criticize his new friends in several episodes in the final Books of *Vanity of Duluoz*, nailing Ginsberg as a bookish, neophyte publicity hound as well as a phony who lacks working-class street cred when he is questioned by the police following the murder of Kammerer: "the only honest lick of work he ever done in his life was when he was a bus boy in a California cafeteria" (*Vanity of Duluoz*, 230). If working at tough jobs and excelling at football and war define a "real American" – tasks and disciplines which test one's strength and self-sufficiency in competition and combat with other men – then Kerouac will dramatize the collision between this ideal of masculine toughness, patriotism, and Boy Scout values and the emerging Beat scene. In Book Thirteen, Chapter VIII, Kerouac reports a confrontation between the group of Beats with whom he was now associating and Harry Evans, a soldier returning from the Second World War:

> Still, there were guys coming home from the war and getting married and going to school on the GI Bill who had no taste for such negativism and who would have punched me on the nose if they knew about how low I'd fallen from the time, maybe, when they had a beer with me in 1940. But I had goofed throughout entire wartime and this is my confession. (*Vanity of Duluoz*, 261)

Vanity of Duluoz reveals the schism in Kerouac's soul which elucidates why the entire novel serves as his "confession" as he returns again in the closing sections to this key word of his text. In some part of his being, he felt he had been disloyal to the values of his working-class, immigrant, "conservative" Catholic parents. While young Americans were risking their lives in the fight against Fascism in Europe, Kerouac and his "skeptical" and "decadent" friends were lounging about in a drug-addled haze. These postwar "bohemians" were the ancestors of the '60s hippies who, as we have seen, serve as counterpoint throughout the novel to the values Kerouac seems to have at least partially believed he had betrayed.

Finally, *Vanity of Duluoz* veers into spiritual dark night of the soul in which the reader begins to view Kerouac's fierce critique of 1960s' counterculture – and indeed of his own creation of and participation in the Beat movement – within the context of a much larger spiritual withdrawal from "the things of this world" as Kerouac builds what D. H. Lawrence called in a late, great poem, his own "ship of death." Kerouac perhaps was aware that he was about to die – or indeed that he was involved in a conscious, slow act of suicide in his unstoppable alcoholism. Kerouac's dedication page of *Visions of Cody* (1960) reads: "Dedicated to America, whatever that is." One might say something similar about Kerouac himself – "whoever he is" – and his "belief system" as revealed in *Vanity of Duluoz.* Kerouac's dislike of modernity must be understood as the manifestation of the combat between the spiritual and material worlds which typified his Catholic/Buddhist/Gnostic philosophical orientation. *Vanity of Duluoz* illustrates the ways Kerouac juxtaposed an autobiographical survey of his past with commentary on the present, in particular the struggle between contemporary American life and the more traditional values which imbued the Franco-Canadian Catholic culture of his youth in Lowell, Massachusetts. What is clear from the evidence provided by *Vanity of Duluoz* is that the political, social, and cultural shifts of the '60s gave Kerouac the opportunity to review his experiences within the context of the radical changes which America was undergoing and that during the often-fraught composition of his final novel, Kerouac revealed the ambivalences, contradictions and furies within his own spiritually questing soul.

Notes

1. Jack Kerouac, *Vanity of Duluoz: An Adventurous Education, 1935–1946* (New York: Penguin Books, 1994), 105–106; Joyce Johnson, *The Voice is All: The Lonely Victory of Jack Kerouac* (New York: Viking, 2012), 112; Jack Kerouac, *Kerouac: Selected Letters 2, 1957–1969*, ed. Ann Charters (New York: Penguin, 1999), 420. Kerouac was at first uncertain what dates *Vanity of Duluoz* should cover, informing Sterling Lord on May 5, 1961 that the years would be "1939–43," *Selected Letters, 1957–1969*, 326.

2. Ted Berrigan, "Interview with Jack Kerouac," *Writers at Work: The Paris Review interviews: Fourth Series*, ed. George Plimpton (Harmondsworth: Penguin, 1977), 383.
3. Regina Weinrich, *The Spontaneous Poetics of Jack Kerouac; A Study of the Fiction* (Carbondale: Southern Illinois University Press, 1987), 152, 153.
4. Kerouac refers to Homer in relation to his University studies: "a college student pouring coffee and washing dishes and scrimmaging till dark and reading Homer's *Iliad* in three days all at the same time"; "homework: i.e., read Homer's *Iliad* in three days and then the *Odyssey* in three more." Kerouac, *Vanity of Duluoz*, 9, 66; Allen Ginsberg, *The Best Minds of My Generation: A Literary History of the Beats*, ed. Bill Morgan (New York: Grove Press, 2017), 75. In *Desolation Angels* (1965), Book One, "chapterette" 9 contains one sentence: "My eyes in my hand, welded to wheel to welded to whang." Jack Kerouac, *Desolation Angels* (New York: Riverhead Books, 1995), 14.
5. Berrigan, "Interview with Jack Kerouac," 366.
6. Dennis McNally, *Desolate Angel: Jack Kerouac, The Beat Generation, and America* (Cambridge, MA: Da Capo Press, 2003), 315.
7. See also Luc Sante, "Robert Frank and Jack Kerouac," in Sarah Greenough, *Looking In: Robert Frank's The Americans* (Washington, DC: The National Gallery of Art, 2009), 205.
8. Jack Kerouac, *Big Sur* (New York: Penguin, 1992), 31, 44.
9. Barry Gifford and Lawrence Lee, *Jack's Book: An Oral Biography of Jack Kerouac* (New York: St. Martin's Press, 1978), 303.
10. Richard S. Sorrell, qtd. in James Terence Fisher, *The Catholic Counterculture in America 1933–1962* (Chapel Hill and London, University of North Carolina Press, 1989), 207. Also see Richard S. Sorrell, "The Catholicism of Jack Kerouac," *Studies in Religion* 11 (Spring 1982), 190–200.
11. Michael Hrebeniak, *Action Writing: Jack Kerouac's Wild Form* (Carbondale: Southern Illinois Press, 2006), 127.
12. "Firing Line with William F. Buckley: The Hippies," www.youtube.com/watch?v=BYgv7ur8ipg.
13. McNally, *Desolate Angel*, 320.
14. David G. Vermette, *A Distinct Alien Race: The Untold Story of Franco-Americans: Industrialization, immigration, Religious Strife* (Montreal: Baraka Books, 2018), 309.
15. Berrigan, "Interview with Jack Kerouac," 378. On Saroyan and Kerouac, see David Stephen Calonne, *William Saroyan: My Real Work Is Being* (Chapel Hill and London: University of North Carolina Press, 1983), 32–33; Calonne, *Bebop Buddhist Ecstasy: Saroyan's Influence on Kerouac and the Beats with an Introduction by Lawrence Ferlinghetti* (San Francisco: Sore Dove Press, 2010); and Calonne, "On the Road with Saroyan" in *Critical Insights: On the Road*, ed. Robert C. Evans (Ipswich, MA: Salem Press, 2022), 246–262.
16. Jack Kerouac, *Visions of Gerard* (New York: Penguin, 1991), 6.
17. Jack Kerouac, *Atop an underwood: Early Stories and Other Writings*, ed. Paul Marion (New York: Penguin Books, 2000), 115.

CHAPTER 9

Late Kerouac, or the Conflicted "King of the Beatniks"

Steven Belletto

Jack Kerouac's late novel, *Satori in Paris* (1966), is about a trip he took to Paris and Brittany in 1965 to search for the origins of his family name. Unlike his other novels, in *Satori in Paris*, Kerouac insists on using "my real name here, full name in this case, Jean-Louis Lebris de Kérouac, because this story is about my search for this name in France."[1] This assertion, in the second paragraph of the novel, seems to portend quite a close connection between the implied author, Jack Kerouac, and the character of Jack Kerouac in the story – but in fact, there are numerous moments in the book that emphasize the distance between the two, moments when the implied author holds the narrator-character up for scrutiny and even derision.

By the time he wrote *Satori in Paris*, Kerouac was famous enough to get recognized around France, even in small provincial towns, and the book details a comic scene in the Brest train station in which a drunk-out-of-his-mind Kerouac struggles to open his suitcase:

> I realize I'm too drunk and mad to open the lock (I'm looking for my tranquilizers which you must admit I need by now), in the suitcase, the key is pinned as according to my mother's instructions to my clothes—For a full twenty minutes I kneel there in the baggage station of Brest Brittany trying to make the little key open the snaplock, cheap suitcase anyhow, finally in a Breton rage I yell "*O u v r e d o n c m a u d i t* !" (OPEN UP DAMN YOU!!) and break the lock—I hear laughter—I hear someone say: "Le roi Kerouac" (the king Kerouac). I'd heard that from the wrong mouths in America. (*Satori in Paris*, 107)

As he himself is looking for his tranquilizers, the scene presents the sloshed and bumbling character Kerouac being looked at and insulted, and there are at least three different categories of those doing the looking: the mocking travelers at the train station, the reader of *Satori in Paris* (the "you" of "you must admit"), and Kerouac the implied author. In this passage all three categories are simultaneously looking at – and likely judging – the drunken, sad sack behavior of Kerouac-the-character. A far cry from how one might expect a well-known writer to comport himself in public, in *Satori in Paris* the character "Jack Kerouac" is often hopelessly inept, a forty-three-year-old man-child whose mother still has to pin a suitcase key to his clothes so he doesn't lose it.

So what is going on? Why would Kerouac portray himself in this way? In my view, such a passage allegorizes Kerouac's experiences as a "famous author," when he was widely-known as an avatar of the "Beat Generation" while concurrently facing the fact that his writing itself was being just as widely misunderstood and maligned. As the train station scene details, in Brittany Kerouac did not exactly receive the warm ancestral welcome he had imagined, even though some people still recognized him as a notorious author from the States. When a voice in the crowd identifies him, it illustrates both Kerouac's relative celebrity and the general ridicule to which he was subjected as "Le roi Kerouac" – a reference to the title "King of the Beatniks," a sneering epithet bestowed upon him by the US media, or what he calls "the wrong mouths in America." This passage is thus illustrative of Kerouac's late preoccupations insofar as it explores his newfound – and largely unwanted – celebrity by staging situations where his first-person narrator is seen at removes by the implied author, held up as a kind of exhibition to be mocked. On the one hand, this gives readers what they want, as Kerouac was famous for his intimately confessional writing; and yet on the other hand, it creates a tension between Jack Kerouac the author and Jack Kerouac the character, playing as it does with the idea of intimacy packaged as celebrity spectacle, a damaging development for both versions of Kerouac. Broken under the impossible weight of being forced to speak for a generation, Kerouac lost himself in alcohol, both in real life and in his books, and his post-fame novels begin to depict an alcoholic narrator-character out of step with a society that has changed around him, while nonetheless being forced to confront and parry media-generated images of himself circulating through that society.

9.1 Writing in the Beat Spotlight

Kerouac's novels can be divided, broadly speaking, into pre- and post-fame works. In the pre-fame category, one would place the books he wrote before the publication of *On the Road* made him a literary and cultural celebrity in the fall of 1957. These books include *The Town and the City*, *On the Road* itself, *Visions of Cody*, *Doctor Sax*, *The Subterraneans*, *Tristessa*, *Maggie Cassidy*, and *Visions of Gerard*, among others. All these books but *The Town and the City* were published after *On the Road*, although Kerouac had written them earlier, as he recalled, "in poverty and some of them in self-imposed exile with no hope of ever seeing them published."[2]

But after *On the Road* became a cultural phenomenon, publishers were clamoring for his work, hoping to cash in on his name. In the last decade of his life, during which he felt a constant spotlight on him, Kerouac wrote and published *The Dharma Bums*, *Big Sur*, *Satori in Paris*, and *Vanity of Duluoz*, among others. Post-fame, Kerouac also resumed work on *Desolation Angels*, a book written, as Ronna C. Johnson puts it, in "two periods straddling his celebrity advent, [that] compare the writer-protagonist's condition before and after becoming famous."[3] With the arguable exception of *The Dharma Bums*, the novels Kerouac wrote post-fame respond in some way to that fame, exploring his feelings of what Johnson calls his "imprisonment by intrusive scrutiny," feelings which were inextricably linked to his worsening alcoholism – a connection illustrated with cringe-worthy, seriocomic precision in the Brest train station scene in *Satori in Paris*.[4]

In identifying features of what we might call Kerouac's "late style," I am following the lead of Edward Said, who memorably explored the qualities of later work by writers and musicians that did not seem to fit neatly in with their earlier efforts. Said focused in particular on late work characterized not by "harmony and resolution," but by "intransigence, difficulty and contradiction."[5] Certainly the latter notes can be found throughout Kerouac's post-fame novels, and so Said's thoughts are a useful entry into them. While Kerouac's late books do yearn for harmony and clarity – whether the calming communion with the sounds of the sea that ends *Big Sur*, or the insistence that he "received an illumination of some kind" in *Satori in Paris* (7) – they tend also to present a narrator at odds with his cultural environment. As Said writes, "There is therefore an inherent tension in late style that abjures mere bourgeois aging and that insists on the increasing sense of apartness and exile and anachronism, which late style expresses and, more important, uses to formally sustain itself."[6] In the case of Kerouac, it is surely not "mere bourgeois aging" that seems to exile him from his cultural environment, but his aging as a "famous author" in particular.

Big Sur (1962) illustrates this sense of disconnection early on by having the narrator, Jack Duluoz, attempt to hitchhike along the highway as he did when he was younger: "This is the first time I've hitch hiked in years," writes Duluoz, "and I soon begin to see that things have changed in America, you cant get a ride any more."[7] Reading *Big Sur* in the context of the Duluoz Legend, such a sentiment is a pointed contrast to an earlier book like *On the Road*, in which narrator Sal Paradise connects to various segments of American society via hitchhiking, as he catches rides across the country that inspire him to yell "for joy."[8] By *Big Sur*, dozens of cars just whizz by Duluoz without a second glance, until finally a truck driver takes pity, delivering him to the bus station: "The last time I ever hitch hiked—and NO RIDES a sign" (*Big Sur*, 39). This demoralizing experience suggests to Duluoz that he will need to find a new way of achieving joy in the world.[9]

Despite the fact that Duluoz's inability to catch a ride stems from his relative invisibility, the balance of *Big Sur* explores how his sense of estrangement from his social environment is exacerbated by or focalized through the lens of fame, by the way people are training *too much* attention on him. This idea is announced on the jacket copy for the Bantam paperback edition of *Big Sur*, which describes Duluoz as "The King of the Beatniks—tortured, broken idol of a whole generation; great, modern sex god who just wanted to be alone with his cat; all-time boozer of the century who was slowly drinking himself out of his mind."[10] This is as apt an encapsulation of the cultural position Kerouac found himself in after *On the Road* as one is likely to find – "Le roi Kerouac," idolized by the young, but for the wrong reasons, facing an unremitting attention that materially contributed to his "drinking himself out of his mind." And of course this alcoholism is only advertised here as a marker of dissolute authenticity, leveraged by the publisher to sell more paperbacks.

In the second half of *Desolation Angels* (1965), which chronicles the months just before Kerouac would be dubbed "King of the Beatniks," Duluoz offers a kind of oracular lamentation: "I foresaw a new dreariness in all this literary success. That night I called a cab to take me to the bus station and downed half a bottle of Jack Daniels while waiting."[11] Far from cause for celebration, with benefit of hindsight, "literary success" means misunderstandings and misreadings, and the author commodified right along with his books – a bleak future juxtaposed, as though there is no need for further explanation, with the bottom of a whiskey bottle.[12]

Elsewhere in *Desolation Angels*, Duluoz elaborates how fame seems to flatten out his nuances and complexities:

> Even I cant understand how to explain myself—When my books became notorious (*Beat Generation*) and interviewers tried to ask me questions, I just answered with everything I could think of—I had no guts to tell them

> to leave me alone, that, as Dave Wain later said (a great character at Big Sur) "Tell 'em you're busy interviewing yourself" … Nothing could stop me from writing big books of prose and poetry for nothing, that is, with no hope of ever having them published—I was simply writing them because I was an "Idealist" and I believed in "Life" and was going about justifying it with my earnest scribblings—Strangely enough, these scribblings were the first of their kind in the world, I was originating (without knowing it, you say?) a new way of writing about life, no fiction, no craft, no revising afterthoughts, … I wrote those manuscripts as I'm writing this one in cheap nickel notebooks by candlelight in poverty and fame—*Fame* of self—For I was Ti Jean, and the difficulty in explaining all this and "Ti Jean" too is that readers who havent read up to this point in the earlier works are not filled in on the background. (*Desolation Angels*, 229)

As in that train station scene in *Satori in Paris*, here we have Kerouac looking at himself (as Duluoz), conscious of the reader also looking at him (the "you" in "without knowing it, you say?"), this looking always impinged upon by the way he was packaged as a celebrity author. Although in one sense all of Kerouac's writing can be seen as his attempt to "explain" himself, once he became a cultural icon for writing intimately about his life – the "*Fame* of self" – a new kind of explanation was needed, one that both attended to and pushed back against the way "Jack Kerouac" was defined and circulated as the King of the Beatniks.

In the above passage, Kerouac has Duluoz sift out the writing itself from the fame attached to that writing. As a younger man, he was free to do his "scribblings" because when he first composed his work for free, pre-fame, this writing was for his own edification or moral growth. The mention of "scribblings" in "cheap nickel notebooks" recalls item one in Kerouac's well-known "list of essentials" in his short piece "Belief & Technique for Modern Prose": "scribbled secret notebooks, and wild typewritten pages, for yr own joy."[13] The secrecy here is protective, sheltering, a rough synonym of privacy, and accords Kerouac the freedom to write for his own "joy" without thought of molding this writing to fit the demands of publishers or the tastes of future critics – as he declares in *Book of Sketches*, "when I was / a boy poet & wrote / for myself—no / frantic fear of 'not / being published,' but / the joy."[14] And yet after his "books became notorious," Kerouac's anonymity vanished, secrecy became impossible, joy elusive, and these books were infamous not for the writing itself, but as justifications for his celebrity, evidence that he really was the spokesman of a generation.

But Duluoz laments that this is the wrong kind of justification and evidence. Notice that he specifies his fame is born of "readers who havent read up to this point in the earlier works," and so "are not filled in on the background" – otherwise put, the readers who "idolize" him are doing so with incomplete information. What Kerouac means is that anyone who sees *On the Road* as a standalone book (which would have been the vast majority of readers at the time, except for perhaps his close writer-friends) is only glimpsing a piece of the novel's achievement, since he considered it and most of his other books as "chapters in the whole work which I call *The Duluoz Legend*."[15] Thus those admirers who had not also read *Visions of Gerard* or *Doctor Sax* or *Maggie Cassidy* – all "chapters" of the Duluoz Legend that form the "background" for *On the Road* – could not in fact understand Kerouac's fictional alter egos in their complexity and contradiction over time. He signals as much in the above passage from *Desolation Angels* by referring to himself as Ti Jean, his real-life childhood nickname, a facet of Kerouac's authorial "self" not accessible at all via *On the Road*, whose narrator is the Italian-American Sal Paradise. What this passage is telling readers, then, is that if you open *On the Road* to gain better or more intimate access to "Jack Kerouac" the famous author, you are barking up the wrong tree.

In fact, in the above passage from *Desolation Angels*, Kerouac takes this suggestion a step further by swerving away from the notion that his books offer unmediated access to Kerouac the man, to insist instead that their true importance is found in their explorations with respect to representation and inventive language use. Kerouac has Duluoz maintain that his "scribblings were the first of their kind in the world, I was originating … a new way of writing about life, no fiction, no craft." This suggests that Kerouac's popular image had eclipsed what he might want to actually be remembered for: his innovations with language, an experimental, highly generative technique he called Spontaneous Prose (other chapters in this *Companion* explore Spontaneous Prose in more depth).

In January, 1962, just a few months after he had written both *Big Sur* and the second half of *Desolation Angels,* Kerouac published an essay in *Writer's Digest* titled "Are Writers Made or Born?" There he defines a literary "genius" as "a person who *originates* something never known before," a clear echo of the language Duluoz uses about his own writings, the "first of their kind in the world, I was originating … a new way of writing about life."[16] Although he doesn't have Duluoz announce it explicitly in *Desolation Angels*, by Kerouac's own parameters, he himself must be a literary genius, insofar as he has originated something "never known before." For the purposes of "Are Writers Made or Born?" Kerouac doesn't discuss himself directly, but he does use James Joyce (one of his literary heroes) as a case study: "people said he 'wasted' his 'talent' on the stream of consciousness style, when in fact he was simply *born* to originate it .... Joyce was insulted all his life by practically all of Ireland and the world for being a genius" ("Are Writers Made or Born?," 488–489). It's not hard to see Kerouac lingering in the shadows of this description, a self-styled "genius" insulted in both the Brest train station and in the wider literary world because his celebrity had ironically obscured and distorted how people understood his writing. Joyce's "stream of consciousness style" stands in for Kerouac's Spontaneous Prose, as many viewed him as a similarly sad case of wasted talent.

When *On the Road* first appeared, for example, *Time* magazine admitted the not-as-yet-famous Kerouac was "talented." But because even at that time he was seen as what *Time* called the "symbolic spokesman" of the Beat Generation, this judgment was qualified by the assurance that he had nowhere "near the talents of Fitzgerald, Hemingway or Nathanael West," comparable spokesmen of the Lost Generation.[17] Even before he became the King of the Beatniks, then, there was a kind of double-looking applied to Kerouac that measured the achievement of his books *and* their effectiveness as mouthpieces for a generation. In the case of *Time*, as in other venues, this sense only intensified as Kerouac's fame grew, as in this later review of *Desolation Angels*:

> For those who dropped out after, say, *On the Road*, *The Subterraneans* or *The Dharma Bums*, Jack Kerouac is remembered as a likable literary wild man, a frightener of librarians, a pie-eyed piper for young men with no socks. Perhaps because socklessness no longer seems the major menace (the young are activists now, not beatniks), Kerouac, at 43, appears mild and gentle.[18]

Desolation Angels is seen primarily in connection to the Beat Generation, and Kerouac most relevant as a chronicler of "the young." Because times have changed, both Kerouac and his writing are dismissed as embarrassingly passé. "What can a beat do when he is too old to go on the road?" *Time* asked in a review of *Big Sur*. "He can go on the sauce. In *Big Sur* Jack does."[19]

9.2 Jack Kerouac Takes a Fresh Look at Jack Kerouac

These examples from *Time* are broadly indicative of the critical judgment of Kerouac during his life, at least in the national media, and help explain why he likewise begins to introduce the double-looking in his own late books as both answer to and corrective of this judgment. The phenomenon of Kerouac looking at himself at some remove, or via some screen – as in the fractured funhouse mirror of Joyce as Kerouac – permeates his late work. The mirrors seem to multiply in another late essay he wrote: "Jack Kerouac Takes a Fresh Look at Jack Kerouac." This piece was published in *Escapade* in January, 1967, and revisits and reworks the first of the columns he wrote for that magazine, published back in June, 1959. Comparing these two meditations on his own place in the "current American literary scene" allows us to see how Kerouac was thinking about himself toward the beginning of his fame, and then again toward the end.

In the 1959 *Escapade* piece (which appeared under the column title, "The Last Word"), Kerouac opens by announcing: "My position in the current American literary scene is simply that I got sick and tired of the conventional English sentence which seemed to me so ironbound in its rules."[20] In this instance, certainly he is responding to his critics, and trying to account for himself by focusing on his techniques of writing, pointedly contrasting them to what passed for "good prose" at the time – prose he considers "childish." The balance of the article goes on to introduce *Escapade*'s readers to fellow writers in the Beat orbit, including Allen Ginsberg, Gregory Corso, William Burroughs, Philip Whalen, and Gary Snyder, writers Kerouac insists are "probably the most interesting things in American Lit today" (*Last Words*, 19). He also notes, with a whiff of optimism, that "my own best prose has yet to be published … when I want a friend to enjoy my style I hand him these unpublished things but the editors have been reluctant to go all out and print these" (*Last Words*, 19).

Eight years later, in 1967, Kerouac used the same opening paragraphs for "Jack Kerouac Takes a Fresh Look at Jack Kerouac," but rather than going on to champion his writer friends, he doubles down on the idea of "style" mentioned in the earlier column, elaborating the importance of Spontaneous Prose. While in those intervening eight years he did manage to get some of his "own best prose" into print, still he felt misunderstood, and was even more bitter that these published books remained critically dismissed: "And now my hand doesn't move as fast as it used to, and so many critics have laughed at me for those 16 originally-styled volumes of mine published in 16 languages in 42 countries, never for one moment calling me 'sensitive' or artistically dignified but an unlettered literary hoodlum with diarrhea of the mouth."[21] As in "Are Writers Made or Born?" Kerouac emphasizes both his "originally-styled volumes," and how this originality has been missed by those who focus on his pop cultural image as the "unlettered literary hoodlum."

9.3 I Want a Real Beatnik at My Annual Shindig Party

This circumstance is elaborated in *Big Sur*, which is framed by Kerouac's newfound life in the spotlight, and is largely about his struggle with both his alcoholism and his writing in the context of a relentless, unwanted celebrity.[22] Although unlike the later *Satori in Paris*, the narrator is still named Jack Duluoz, Kerouac purposively blurs the lines between author and narrator, and holds that narrator up for inspection and critique as he does in *Satori*. In *Big Sur*, the wider world is depicted as parasitical and threatening – as hoodlums, essentially – with Duluoz longing for the peaceful anonymity of his earlier life:

> since the publication of "Road" the book that "made me famous" and in fact so much so I've been driven mad for three years by endless telegrams, phonecalls, requests, mail, visitors, reporters, snoopers (a big voice saying in my basement window as I prepare to write a story:—ARE YOU BUSY?) or the time the reporter ran upstairs to my bedroom as I sat there in my pajamas trying to write down a dream—Teenagers jumping the six-foot fence I'd had built around my yard for privacy—Parties with bottles yelling at my study window "Come on out and get drunk, all work and no play makes Jack a dull boy!"—A woman coming to my door and saying "I'm not going to ask you if you're Jack Duluoz because I know he wears a beard, can you tell me where I can find him, I want a real beatnik at my annual Shindig party." (*Big Sur*, 2)

Despite trying literally to fence himself off from the world's prying eyes, Duluoz cannot escape the intense interest in his personal life caused by "the book that 'made me famous'" – a phrase set off in quotation marks, as if the truth of it can't quite be real. "I'd rather die than be famous," Kerouac writes in *Mexico City Blues*, and this passage from *Big Sur* starts to show why he seemed determined to drink himself to death, lost in his "old fatal double bourbons and gingerale" (*Big Sur*, 60).[23] In a perverse reversal of one of the most quoted lines in *On the Road*, that "the only people for me are the mad ones, the ones who are mad to live, mad to talk, mad to be saved," here Duluoz is being "driven mad" by those who want to consume him *as* a media image (*On the Road*, 8). There is no distinction in Duluoz's experience between "reporters" and "snoopers," or among fans, wide-eyed teenagers, and a disembodied "big voice" booming down through a basement window. What gets lost or sacrificed in all this superficial attention is not merely Kerouac himself (versus the character of Kerouac these people believe they know or want), but the writing, as Duluoz is assailed and interrupted just as he "prepare[d] to write a story" or when he was "trying to write down a dream."

The last line in this passage, about a woman who showed up wanting "a real beatnik at my annual Shindig party," seems a winking reference to the Rent-a-Beatnik scheme started by photographer Fred McDarrah in 1959. McDarrah had half-seriously placed ads in the *Village Voice* advertising "genuine" Beatniks one could rent for parties, a tongue-in-cheek acknowledgement of the general public confusion of Beat literature with the media-generated image of the "Beatnik" – a goatee sporting, beret-wearing, bongo-playing doper. McDarrah was surprised by the enthusiastic response to the ad, as people really were interested in renting Beatniks, and he enlisted the services of poet Ted Joans, among many others. Joans and Kerouac were friends, and Joans recalled that "Kerouac said to me about the Rent-A-Beat thing, that it was cool as long as we didn't leave the impression of the Beat Generation being crime, delinquency, and violence prone."[24] Clearly Kerouac was concerned about how the Beatnik had eclipsed his original vision of the Beat, and so the passage from *Big Sur* is quite deliberate in its use of the oxymoronic term "real beatnik," whose image had seemed even to erase his own existence: "I'm not going to ask you if you're Jack Duluoz," says the woman who shows up at his door, "because I know he wears a beard." A "real beatnik," after all, must have a goatee, and exists primarily to dazzle party guests.

In an indication of just how far the Beat phenomenon had traveled from the writing of *On the Road* to the writing of *Big Sur*, in April, 1960, Gilbert Millstein, the self-same critic and book reviewer who had launched Kerouac's celebrity by proclaiming the publication of *On the Road* "an historic occasion," turned his attention to the very sort of Beatnik parties Kerouac shudders at here: "If any further proof were needed that the beatnik has been lacquered into an interior-decorating vogue … it is that for some time now it has been possible for people to rent, inspect, sit at the feet of, listen to, harangue and generally be titillated by fully accredited members of the species."[25] In such an environment, even "Le roi Kerouac," aka the "King of the Beatniks," Jack Duluoz, isn't "real" enough for the woman in *Big Sur*, who demands an example of the Beatnik "species" or nothing, identifiable by obvious, cartoon accessories. Throughout *Big Sur*, this cultural schizophrenia is unyielding, inducing Duluoz into his own bouts of hallucinatory mania, binge-drinking in desperate attempts to reclaim a sense of self outside the gaze of endless streams of "snoopers" – and, as in *Satori in Paris*, the looking, the wrong kind of looking, is overwhelming and damaging, manageable only via drunken oblivion.

Versions of this situation abound in Kerouac's late work, where both his intimate confessions and his theories about writing are often filtered through what we might call his worsening fame. This is the case, for example, in the opening of his last major book, *Vanity of Duluoz* (1968). That book is dedicated and addressed to his wife, Stella, and purports to explain to her how he got to be "God help me, a WRITER whose very 'success,' far from being a happy triumph as of old, was the sign of doom Himself. (Insofar as nobody loves my dashes anyway, I'll use regular punctuation for the new illiterate generation)."[26] Although *Vanity of Duluoz* is framed as an intimate "recitation of the troubles I had to go through to make good in America" (*Vanity of Duluoz*, 9) addressed to his wife, the judgments of the wider literary and cultural landscape loom around the edges of this recitation, as the capitalized word "WRITER" does not so much seem to mean what Kerouac sees in this vocation, but what the culture does, an idea underscored again by setting "success" off in scare quotes, echoing the opening of *Big Sur*, in that "success" seems equated with being "famous" by everyone but Kerouac. He furthermore informs his wife – and the reader who is always eavesdropping – that the book she is about to read will not be written in the style he associated with his own "genius," Spontaneous Prose, "a new way of writing about life," but in a more conventional, and conventionally acceptable style; to repeat: since "nobody loves my dashes anyway," he writes, "I'll use regular punctuation for the new illiterate generation."As explained in "Essentials of Spontaneous Prose," the "vigorous space dash" was one key technique he used in said Prose, the kind of original writing he saw as marking his true "success" as a writer.[27] The alternative was "sentence-structures already arbitrarily riddled by false colons and timid usually needless commas" ("Essentials," 484) – in other words, the "regular punctuation" that he seems rather resignedly to be using in *Vanity of Duluoz* (a book that, perhaps not incidentally, William F. Buckley, that embodiment of 1960s pop cultural conservatism, said was "widely regarded as his best" when Kerouac made his infamous, drunken appearance on Buckley's show *Firing Line* in September, 1968).

But what if this statement about using "regular punctuation" is a kind of capitulation – or at least an acknowledgement of the ways that Kerouac's writing was becoming boxed in by the "new illiterate generation" and its expectations for him and his work? Ultimately, adjusting the sort of "vigorous" modern prose he had explored in his most innovative books – and championed in his articles for *Writer's Digest*, *Escapade*, and elsewhere – represents another way the spotlight of fame affected his late work; desperate for money, he wrote *Vanity of Duluoz* in what he called a "more moderate style," at least partly so it would be more palatable to publishers and book buyers.[28] In late Kerouac, then, the fact of publishing itself is depicted as hopelessly, tragically, tangled with his unwanted celebrity and his popular image: The desolation in *Desolation Angels* comes in no small part from his "published books and poems," and the conflicted sense of "success" named also in *Vanity of Duluoz*. The final paragraph of *Desolation Angels* in fact characterizes literary "success" as irrevocable horror, portraying fictionalized versions of Allen Ginsberg, Peter Orlovsky, and Gregory Corso – figures whom *Time* had called a "pack of oddballs" – "sitting around" with Duluoz:

> and now we're famous writers more or less, but they wonder why I'm so sunk now, so unexcited as we sit among all our published books and poems, tho at least, since I live with Memère in a house of her own miles from the city, it's a peaceful sorrow. A peaceful sorrow at home is the best I'll ever be able to offer the world, in the end, and so I told my Desolation Angels goodbye. A new life for me. (*Desolation Angels*, 366)[29]

Notes

1. Jack Kerouac, *Satori in Paris*, in *Satori in Paris & Pic* (1966. New York: Grove, 1985), 8.
2. Jack Kerouac, "Beat Spotlight," in *The Unknown Kerouac: Rare, Unpublished & Newly Translated Writings*, ed. Todd Tietchen and trans. Jean-Christophe Cloutier (New York: Library of America, 2016), 328.
3. Ronna C. Johnson, "'You're Putting Me On': Jack Kerouac and the Postmodern Emergence," *College Literature* 27.1 (2000), 23.
4. Johnson, "You're Putting Me On," 29.
5. Edward W. Said, *On Late Style: Music and Literature Against the Grain* (New York: Vintage, 2007), 7.
6. Said, *On Late Style*, 17.
7. Jack Kerouac, *Big Sur* (1962. New York: Bantam, 1963), 36.
8. Jack Kerouac, *On the Road* (1957. New York: Penguin, 1991), 27.
9. See Chapter 8 in this volume for a discussion of how this works in *Vanity of Duluoz*.
10. Jacket copy, Kerouac, *Big Sur*, np.
11. Jack Kerouac, *Desolation Angels* (1965. New York: Perigee Books, 1980), 281.
12. As Ronna C. Johnson notes, "These late novels specifically interrogate implications of representation by a media gaze and its impact on the living artist, figuring media such as television, and print and photographic journalism as agents of distorted representation." Johnson, "You're Putting Me On," 29.
13. Jack Kerouac, "Belief & Technique for Modern Prose," in *The Portable Jack Kerouac*, ed. Ann Charters (New York: Viking, 1995), 483.
14. Jack Kerouac, *Book of Sketches: 1952–57*, intro. George Condo (New York: Penguin, 2006), 76.

15. Jack Kerouac, *Visions of Cody* (New York: Penguin, 1993), np. In 1965, Suzanne Cane wrote an MA thesis at Brooklyn College titled "The Duluoz Legend: The Zen Influence on Jack Kerouac," but this focus on the Legend was an anomaly while Kerouac was living. Eight years later, Ann Charters observed that Kerouac's writing "can be read in order as the Legend he intended, even if most readers only encounter the books as separate novels, oblivious of the underlying loose chronology"; Charters, *Kerouac: A Biography* (1973. New York: St. Martin's, 1994), 358.
16. Jack Kerouac, "Are Writers Made or Born?," *Portable*, 488.
17. "The Ganser Syndrome," *Time* (September 16, 1957), 120.
18. "Bumbling Bunyan," *Time* (May 7, 1965), 110.
19. "Lions & Cubs," *Time* (September 14, 1962), 106.
20. "The Last Word," in Jack Kerouac, *Last Words & Other Writings* (no place of publication stated: Zeta Press, 1985), 18.
21. Jack Kerouac, "Jack Kerouac Takes a Fresh Look at Jack Kerouac," in *Last Words*, 50.
22. For a discussion of "what happens when an artist is overcome or threatened by his or her own popularity," see Timothy Hampton, "Tangled Generation: Dylan, Kerouac, Petrarch, and the Poetics of Escape," *Critical Inquiry* 39.4 (Summer 2013), 703–731; quotation on 703.
23. Jack Kerouac, *Mexico City Blues* (New York: Grove, 1959), 64.
24. Ted Joans, "I Went as Usual to the Desert," Ted Joans Papers, Bancroft Library, UC-Berkeley, box 18, folder 16.
25. Gilbert Millstein, "Rent-a-Beatnik and Swing," *New York Times* (April 17, 1960), 26.
26. Jack Kerouac, *Vanity of Duluoz* (1994. New York: Penguin, 1968), 9.
27. Jack Kerouac, "Essentials of Spontaneous Prose," *Portable*, 484.
28. Ted Berrigan, "The Art of Fiction: Jack Kerouac," *Paris Review* 11.43 (1968), 60–105, reprinted in *Conversations with Kerouac*, ed. Kevin J. Hayes (Jackson: University Press of Mississippi, 2005), 55. See also Kerouac to Ellis Amburn (June 1, 1967), in Jack Kerouac, *Kerouac: Selected Letters 2, 1957–1969*, ed. Ann Charters (New York: Viking, 1999), 439–440.
29. "The Cool, Cool Bards," *Time* (December 2, 1957), 1.

CHAPTER 10

Visions of Cody *as Metafiction*

Michael Hrebeniak

In a 1952 letter to John Clellon Holmes dispatched in the midst of writing *Doctor Sax*, Kerouac asserts that he has begun to discover

> something beyond the novel and beyond the arbitrary confines of the story ... into the realms of revealed picture ... *wild form*, man, *wild form*. Wild form's the only form holds what I have to say—my mind is exploding to say something about every image and every memory in—I have now an irrational lust to set down everything I know—[1]

Visions of Cody, published in part in 1960, and then posthumously as a whole in 1972, is the consummation of his search ("O my best prose there").[2] A compendium of nonlinear forms in the encyclopedic tradition of *Moby-Dick*, *Cody* comprises a synthesis of Kerouac's most far-reaching ideas over two decades of experimentation and, as such, is the key to understanding the radicalism of the Duluoz Legend. Referring throughout to its own construction and using techniques introduced into the novel by Laurence Sterne and Denis Diderot and advanced across Modernism, Kerouac's novel freely deploys metacommentary; abrupt switches of subject, dialect and tone; movements between narrative logic and sound structure; and incursions of nonverbal forms, at times turning page into canvas and drawing attention to the book's materiality. *Cody* thus qualifies as a work of "fabulation" according to Robert Scholes' definition, which confers freedom upon fiction as its paramount condition and pronounces orthodoxy a bore:

> With its wheels within wheels, rhythms and counterpoints, this shape is partly to be admired for its own sake ... Delight in design, and its concurrent emphasis on the art of the designer, will serve in part to distinguish the art of the fabulator from the work of the novelist or the satirist. Of all narrative forms, fabulation puts the highest premium on art and joy.[3]

10.1 Narrating a Shape-Shifter

Kerouac had quickly determined after working through the "novel-type novel" of *The Town and the City* that the Wolfian Naturalism that "anticipat[es] the organic confusion and variety of life with a strict iron-clad 'concept,'" might, in itself, be repressive. "I began to think," Kerouac tells Cassady of his own revolution of the word, "who's laid down the laws of 'literary' form? Who says that a work must be chronological; that the reader wants to know what happened anyhow … Let's tear time up. Let's rip the guts out of reality" (*Selected Letters 1*, 162; 274). Dismissing his publisher's entrenched conservatism – "Giroux isn't fond of my idea, he insists on 'narrative' and 'narrative styles'" – the ensuing works pull free from a logic of imitation to shed the mundane literalism upon which social realist writers habitually rely: namely, a consensus grounded in thematic metamorphosis, totality of coverage, omniscient narration, full-bodied characterization, and fixed denouement from the laying bare of relationships and motives (*Selected Letters 1*, 449). While the subject of Kerouac's books may be the author's own life in retrospect, his concentration on the supplementarity of writing confers an independence upon the texts, something that consistently eludes his biographers. As Ronald Sukenick suggests, "Rather than serving as a mirror or redoubling on itself, fiction adds itself to the world, creating a meaningful 'reality' that did not previously exist. Fiction is artifice but not artificial. It seems as pointless to call the creative powers of the mind 'fraudulent' as it would to call the procreative powers of the body such."[4]

By *Cody*, the textual focus has swerved from the instrumentality of final meaning to an attitude of uncertainty underpinning the interrogation of memory and event. Fluctuating patterns and recesses between nonnarrative sections encourage agility in the act of reading. Kerouac accordingly celebrates the "fabulous artificer," Dædalus, in *Cody* and punning allusions to *Ulysses* abound: "Bloom let the soap melt in his back-pocket he was so hot"; "JACK. Yes – fit for desert nights, I'd say it was fit for rugs in loverooms."[5] Recalling, too, the circularity of *Finnegans Wake* and *On the Road*'s adventures, the novel's final unnumbered, untitled section doubles as a preamble to "VISIONS OF CODY," the section even invoking the traditional start of an American quest narrative, Duluoz setting "out West to find" his alter ego "in the Summer of 1949" (*Visions of Cody*, 398) Again, at another point Kerouac asserts, "It began in Denver" (*Visions of Cody*, 396). With the nation cast into disturbance through perpetual warfare, the imperative for the genre is to refuse any representation of security.

Documenting the same period, *Cody* expands *Road*'s linear elegy of deprivation into a generative metafiction dependent on intensity of experience rather than chronological ordering. Kerouac's hero is invoked once more, but this time on the level of form itself: "a muscular rush of your own narrative style and excitement" (*Selected Letters 1*, 247). The narratological position is thus marked by the nonlinear thrusts, associations, interruptions and reversals characterizing his behavior. The earlier text's charge into exhaustion is transformed, eclipsing Kerouac's self-deprecating sense of his role as "jolly storyteller" of the limitless speed and multiplicity of Cassady's "hurricane of energy."[6] *Cody* circulates references within the Legend's continual recreation of events, being composed of labyrinthine tales within tales with different points of genesis, completion, and abandonment. In so doing Kerouac invokes the recognition common to all accomplished improvisers: namely, that other modes of experience – and versions of history – are possible. Writing becomes commentary for both techniques and subject matter, reflecting Raymond Federman's insistence that to create fiction is "to abolish reality, and ... the notion that reality is truth."[7] Accordingly, *Cody*'s unstable authorial voice is liable to continuous and random self-scrutiny, a comparable orientation to the Bop soloist, who jettisons linear development and adopts a critically reflexive stance towards performance. When traditional syntax is adequate to convey his observations, Kerouac works comfortably within it; but when the situation demands a projective stance he pivots, risking fragmentation. It is this perpetual movement between poles of recognition and experiment that gives the book its unique energy.

The channeling of desire of two lives held in tension – as text, as myth – breaks the novel into five discrete sections. These are rewritten in multiple styles over many separate sittings, a key difference from the circumstances of *Road*'s three-week burst. A fiction emerges that cannot be subsumed into a single interpretation or skeleton paraphrase. Rather than asserting an authoritative reading of the past, Kerouac reflects the jazz musician's use of cross-references traced in memory to generate measures of fervor, offering a variety of directions beyond causality. "I began sketching everything in sight," he told Ginsberg in 1952, implying that *Cody* is the earlier version of *Road*, "so that *On the Road* took its turn from conventional narrative survey of road trips etc. into a big multi-dimensional conscious and subconscious invocation of Neal in his whirlwinds" (*Selected Letters 1*, 356). The motive is no longer to contain Cassady, but to register his Dionysian energies inside an open field, the novel dynamically balancing events within a heterogeneity of times, methods, and speeds. With confessional remembrances of both author and hero continually dismantled and reassembled, the book of Cassady outstrips private chronicle to become an exploration of the prose-poem as vessel for wildness.

Kerouac designates a number of alternative paths through principles of improvisation and overlay that his configuration of Cody Pomeroy might take. Because his reminiscences proceed from personal associations with an originating experience replayed variously throughout the Legend, questions of veracity are superseded. To remember is to create and vice versa with the text its own end, regardless of external style to which it might point. *Cody* advances a fast current where an effective reading does not position a static image of Cassady as icon, but rather seeks to experience flashes of intensity, of moments great and minor, none of which are privileged over one another. For Eric Mottram, *Cody*'s text

> does not require passive-consumption and acts of writing recognition. At the moment we read reminiscences of style, the text subverts. One of Kerouac's strategies is to make us find out how to read at different points of entry … Nor are we invited to interpret the text into *a priori* meaning at every point, the fallacious basis of academic literary criticism. *Visions of Cody* draws us to an experience of language in itself and to speculations on the foundations of material presences rather than to poke around for prior subject.[8]

Kerouac narrates a mid-century rhizomic complexity at full tilt, a would-be documentarian who enters, as Henry Adams did four decades earlier, "a far vaster universe, where all the old roads ran about in every direction, overrunning, dividing, subdividing, stopping abruptly, vanishing slowly, with side-paths that led nowhere, and sequences that could not be proved."[9] *Cody*'s sense of American rhythm and energy shifts thematically from the centripetal image of "thousands of young men of Denver hurrying from their homes with arrogant clack and tie-adjustments towards the brilliant center in an invasion haunted by sorrow because no guy whether he was a big drinker, big fighter or big cocksman could ever find the center of Saturday night in America" (*Visions of Cody*, 78).

10.2 *Bricolage* and the "field of empirical discovery"

Part One's tableau of semi-dereliction apprehends the nation through industrial images and technologized locations, evoking intense revelations of solitude within public spaces.[10] The story of Cassady's early life in Denver is dramatized through an inexhaustible litany of urban minutiae without developmental logic, a bleak carnival of lunch counters, body parts, and journeys connecting mimesis and catalogue via rough interjections of meta-commentary:

> the backplaces of what we call downtown, the nameless tunnels, alleys, sidings, platforms, ramps, ash heaps, miniature dumps, unofficial parking lots fit for murders, the filthy covered-with-rags plazas that you can see at

the foot of great redbrick chimneys—the same chimney that had bemused Cody on many a dreaming afternoon when he looked at it toppling forward as clouds upswept the air in readiness for the big disaster—it was as though these things had been the—(and of course many more, why list any further, and besides we shall come back on other levels and more exhaustively)—these things had been the necessary parts of his first universe, its furniture. (*Visions of Cody*, 103)

The spatial field makes no reference to given schemata and prescribes no connection between signs. These indeterminate prose chains, which continue into Part Two, are notated in all their disjunctive plurality without fixed reading order or thumping final cadence. The third section consists of "Frisco: The Tape," a transcription of recorded conversations between "Jack" and "Cody" adapted from the historical versions Kerouac made with Cassady at the turn of the 1950s. This section ditches literary convention and is bereft of the editorial comment typically used to guide elucidation. Here the transition from what Kerouac describes as "just a horizontal study of travels on the road," to the nomadic principles of his "vertical, metaphysical study" of Cassady, is inextricably linked to technologies of memory retrieval (*Selected Letters 1*, 327). "We also did so much fast talking between the two of us, on tape recorders, way back in 1952," reports Kerouac, "and listened to them so much, we both got the secret of LINGO in telling a tale and figured that was the only way to express the speed and tension and ecstatic tomfoolery of the age."[11]

Portable tape machines thus complement his use of nonaddictive narcotics to break linguistic habit and extend what J. D. Bernal defines as "the human sensory motor arrangement."[12] As Walter Ong notes:

> Many of the features we have taken for granted in thought and expression in literature, philosophy and science, and even in oral discourse among literates, are not directly native to human existence as such but have come into being because of the resources which the technology of writing makes available to human consciousness. We have to revise our understanding of human identity.[13]

Kerouac's devotion to radio as recorded in *Doctor Sax* testifies to his awareness of speech-body transactions from an early age. *Cody*'s shift to orality gears the narrative into a condensed sense of time, bearing out Ong's contention that the "electronic age" builds on writing and print while still remaining "an age of 'secondary orality,' the orality of the telephone, radio and television, which depends on writing and print for its existence."[14]

Moving beyond *On the Road*'s exchanges between colloquial American hip and approximated dictation, *Cody*'s mapping of the two voices exceeds transcription and prepares Kerouac for his delineation of the nonhuman sound world of *Big Sur*. Cody's speech, frequently edging into mania, dramatically challenges the rhetoric of print technology that ironically controls language. Kerouac emphatically defies given platitudinous illustrations of the spoken word, a consensus which, in referring to an individual version, is always ideological. The contesting of restriction fuels Federman's contention that to write "is to *produce* meaning, and not to *reproduce* a preexisting meaning. To write is to progress, and not *remain* subjected (by habit or reflexes) to the meaning that supposedly precedes the words." His term for this is "surfiction," the revelation of life as fiction:

> [The purpose of fiction is] to unmask its own fictionality, to expose the metaphor of its own fraudulence, and not to pretend any longer to pass for reality, for truth, or for beauty. Consequently, fiction will no longer be regarded as a mirror of life, as a pseudorealistic document that informs us about life, nor will it be judged on the basis of its social, moral, psychological, metaphysical, commercial value, or whatever, but on the basis of what it is and what it does as an autonomous art form in its own right.[15]

By the time of *Cody*, a stable subjectivity has been superseded narratologically by the process of language itself, and by the reconstruction of materials, utterances and texts emerging elsewhere in the Legend. Kerouac introduces a spoken hermeneutics: a tape of talking about talking about writing. As John Tytell suggests, *Cody* is "the grand register of how Cassady affected the Beats with the kinesis of being and an appreciation of the cataclysmic import of the here and now." Yet Tytell's contention that Cassady was "the model of the common urge to communicate ordinary experience in a natural, unpretentious voice," overlooks not only Kerouac's declaration of his textual status as fabulator, and his openness to a range of demotic and hieratic discourses, but also Cody's attention to the phrase and "get[ting] it down."[16] For here, as Michael Davidson notes, Duluoz is both interlocutor and editor, self-consciously constructing his hero by shaping the tone and context of the conversation through stage directions ("CODY. [*laughs*] That tea'll overcome anything. [*pause*] … Why don't you let me read John's letter? [*playing whiny little boy*]") (*Visions of Cody*, 155).[17] The metadiscourse extends into Cody's concern with Duluoz's parenthetical description of his "*demurely downward look*" in the previous transcript, recounting details of his visit to Old Bull Lee:

> And, so – that's what I say when I say "I can't get it down," and then … "two minutes" – but you picked up on that, of all the different things I was sayin, and so you said, "But you don't *have* to get it down," you know, that's what you said … and so the demure downward look … was simply in

> the same tone and the same fashion … as my reaction and feeling was when I said the words "but you can't get it down" you know. (*Visions of Cody*, 133)

The rhythm of Cassady's speech thus qualifies as an apprenticeship in the phenomenology of writing. "Consider, too," Kerouac told him in 1955, "that our friendship and brotherhood has really been a literary association, djever think that?" (*Selected Letters 1*, 474). Cassady's own body of work as a published writer, *The First Third* and a few surviving letters, is small and largely unexceptional – "There is something in me that wants to come out," he discloses to Kerouac in 1947, "something of my own that must be said. Yet, perhaps, words are not the way for me"[18] – but the "speaking man" fully materializes inside *Cody*'s polymorphism: a textual performance of Robert Jay Lifton's idea of "Protean Man" without permanent shape or identity. Activating previous experience in perpetual variation, terms such as character, role, and narrator receive evolving definitions, reinforcing Lifton's sense of a "continuous psychic recreation of self as the person's symbol of his own organism," which "takes place in the social constellation."[19] Accordingly, Kerouac's book continually criticizes, disintegrates and reshapes itself, the memory of Cassady recurring as a generative core rather than fixed presence. The first-person narrative dissolves into tapescripts and their imitations, and third-person modulations: a speech act canceling the distance between observer and observed, author and subject. This theme is announced at the beginning of "Frisco: The Tape:"

> CODY .... I've just spent the last minute thinking and I had a complete block.
>
> JACK. Well speaking of that, look at this sentence (*flute*). Now. Concerning … THE TAPE RECORDER IS TURNING, THE TYPEWRITER IS WAITING, AND I SIT HERE WITH A FLUTE IN MY MOUTH. And so you're just sittin there thinking while it's playing (*plays flitty flute*)
>
> CODY. That's just what I've been doin but I couldn't think of the thought. And I guess the reason I can't think of it and why I'm blocked is because I didn't formalize it or I didn't think about it long enough, soon as the thought hit me, why, I didn't think it out, because I was gonna blurt it out. Damn, if I'd have just spoken—(*Cody running water at sink, flute blowing, watery flute*) Your coffee's gettin cold. *I'll* bring it over but I don't know which one it is (really meant, he says, he didn't know whether I wanted cream or sugar or what) … (*Visions of Cody*, 187–188)

The act of talking spurs the multidirectional imprint through which the postwar Beat experience can be remembered. Kerouac admits the outside world into his performance, which synchronizes with dialogue to lend the impression of thinking, feeling and writing at once. The book's constant reminder of the transactions between speech and language, body and typography is voiced by Cody in Part Three:

> I go on talking *about* these things, thinking about things, and memory, 'cause we're both concerned about, ah, memory, and just relax like Proust and everything. So I talk on about that as the mind and remembers and thinks. (*Visions of Cody*, 179)

Through the decade of *Cody*, *Sax*, and *October in the Railroad Earth*, a pattern develops whereby Kerouac's written idiolect moves closer to spoken forms, pitched uniquely between literary and sonic composition. Outlining his intention in a 1950 journal entry to create an "American Times series to be narrated in the voices of the Americans themselves," Kerouac admits to Cassady that "For a long time [my voice] sounded false":

> I labored on several other variations … one an outright voice for "the boys" … and a [LITERARY] voice for the critics … My important recent discovery and revelation is that the voice is all …. What I'm going to do is let the voices speak for themselves.

That "enormous rushing noise of a great voice muted in the silence of books," will arise from an act of cultural negative capability (*Selected Letters I*, 230–233). In *Tristessa*, for example, the delineation of voices crosses race, class, and national boundaries with a Mexican prostitute junkie appointed as speech catalyst. Kerouac omits articles, prepositions and connectives to notate the rhythms of her broken-English: "I breeng you back the moany."[20] As is the case with Mardou Fox in *The Subterraneans*, Kerouac synchronizes asides and thoughts eddying above the level of consciousness via urban measures in both monologue and conversation.[21] Kerouac's reflexive position in *Cody* similarly resolves the dilemma of how to transform dialogue (the "first-happening") into prose without retreat into linear maxim or single voice. Jack and Cody's compulsion to arrest the elusive quality of spontaneity in their metatalk is clear. Prompted by his study of the transcript of the previous night's tape, which has become "a telling" and therefore a narrative, Cody remarks:

> what it actually was, was a recalling right now on my part … all I did now was re-go to that memory and bring up a little rehash … a little structure line, a little skeletonized thing of the—what I thought earlier, and that's what one does you know, you know when you go back and remember about a thing that you clearly thought out and went around before, you know what I'm sayin' the second or third or fourth time you tell about it or say anything like that why it comes out different … the effort to go back

and remember in detail all those things that I've thought about earlier, is such a task, and unworthy. (*Visions of Cody*, 145)

This is, of course, thematic. The Duluoz Legend's leitmotif of permanent loss, both personal and national, is locked into the memory of Cassady, impelling Kerouac to retrieve by language the "orgiastic future that year by year recedes before us": Fitzgerald's words qualify as a subtext to *Cody*. Recurrent pairings of "night" and "time" alongside "rainy," "gloomy," "sad," and "tragic" amplify the struggle to regain the early equilibrium of exhilaration and dissipation. Speeding erratically between confidence and despair, the novel's episteme emerges from what Mottram locates as an

> urgent desire to counter imminent loss of vitality – that the Dionysian form of Cody will leave, as the gods used to leave men in ancient Mediterranean societies, and as Shakespeare says the gods left Antony. But the gain is language which produces a text to recover both the presence of energy and its absence. Kerouac is here a master of those urgent gestures to recover what escapes all too easily into the unconscious, to regain by techniques of memory at the transmission point of language in discourse.[22]

Visions of Cody's textual surface does not advocate nostalgia; rather, it eschews re-presentation for a leap into ceaseless new form. Charged with hermeneutic pressure, minute decisions made within the confessional dialogue echo the jazz improviser's split-second interactions with an ensemble. Observations collapse into one another without break or explanation to precludes chronometric frame: "the moment is ungraspable," notes the narrator, "is already gone and if we sleep we can call it up again mixing it with unlimited other beautiful combinations – shuffle the old file cards of the soul in demented hallucinated sleep" (*Visions of Cody*, 31).

10.3 Visuality and Unconcealment

This test of perception extends into the fourth section of the book, the "Imitation of the Tape" an imagined recreation of a recorded dialogue or Duluoz's "movie house of mine in the dream." Deliberately redolent of *Finnegans Wake*, the interior monologue of merging personalities and voices offers a world trajectory transmitted through a solitary speaker. Again, the text assumes an analytical stance towards language, as demonstrated by "Lady Godiva's" dissertation on composition and memory:

> Let us ascertain, in the morning, if there is a way of abstracting the interesting paragraphs of material in all this running consciousness stream that can be used as the progressing lightning chapters of a great essay

> about the wonders of the world as it continually flashes up in retrospect. (*Visions of Cody*, 258)

Godiva's sentence stands as a commentary on Kerouac's fictive processes, the reworking of past experience being the foundation of the Legend. Before closing with continuing "imitations," and a recreation of *Road*'s adventures, Kerouac introduces "Joan Rawshanks in the Fog," an observation of the film, *Sudden Fear*, made in the streets of San Francisco. This "American scene" joins disparate frames in cinematic montage, a panoramic technique removed from *Road*'s unitary perspective and eponymous structural device of linear advancement, that he calls "Bookmovies, or Mindmovies, prose concentration camera-eye visions of a definite movie of the mind with fade-ins, pans, close-ups, and fade-outs."[23] As Ellis points out, the symbolic meaning and position of the passage within the text forms a contrast to the Detroit Cinema episode in *On the Road*, where Paradise is constrained by the mythic patterning of the plot:[24]

> The people who were in that all-night movie were the end ... if you sifted all Detroit ... the beaten solid core of dregs couldn't be better gathered. The picture was Singing Cowboy Eddie Dean and his gallant white horse Bloop, that was number one; number two ... was George Raft, Sidney Greenstreet and Peter Lorre in a picture about Istanbul. We saw both of these things six times each during the night. We saw them waking, we heard them sleeping, we sensed them dreaming, we were permeated completely with the strange Gray Myth of the West and the weird dark Myth of the East when morning came. All my actions since then have been dictated automatically to my subconscious by this horrible osmotic experience. (*Visions of Cody*, 201)

Here Kerouac dramatizes through its Hollywood simulation the supremacist Western myth of boundless expansion and entrapment. In *Road* this code prescribes a constant reversion to the culture of "rubbish America," within which the narrator's desire for freedom is given, to paraphrase Baudrillard, endless, timeless, discursive replication.[25] Paradise awakes to the stench of trash collected by the cinema's attendants, before 'they almost swept me away too:'

> Had they taken me with it, Dean ... would have had to roam the entire United States and look in every garbage pail from coast to coast before he found me embryonically convoluted among the rubbishes of my life, his life and the life of everybody concerned. (*On the Road*, 202)

Whereas *Road*'s narrator twice compares his authoritarian dumbshow as a reluctant uniformed guard to "a Western Movie," (62) in *Cody* he follows his own advice in "Belief & Technique for Modern Prose," to become

"Writer-Director of Earthly movies, Sponsored & Angeled in Heaven."[26] From within the text, and perhaps drawing on his short-lived role as a synopsis writer for Twentieth Century Fox, Kerouac recognizes the hypnotic design of commercial media which, for those contained within the "narrow milieu" of the city, creates "a psuedo-world beyond, and a psuedo-world within themselves as well" – C. Wright Mills' observation from 1956.[27] Unlike Paradise in Detroit, Duluoz is a producer, not consumer of meaning – "In the movies but not at all At them," as F. Scott Fitzgerald has it – as is consistent with his own changed narrative bearings.[28]

Using the cinematic plasticity of light thematically in "Rawshanks," Kerouac recoils from complicity in the proletarian rhetoric of the production called "America," a commodification that Guy Debord defines as an "immense accumulation of *spectacles*" replacing "all that was directly lived" with "mere representation."[29] Distanced from Hollywood's confounding of illusion, news and history, he fastens instead upon a narrative principle of inclusiveness – voices, moods, speeds, points of view, modes of lighting – to confront the problem of presentation. The containment and ranking of observations shift into collage, an architectural method rendering the events of perception flush with language, the density and rapidity of Kerouac's writing being part of the process:

> Joan Rawshanks stands alone in the fog. Her name is Joan Rawshanks and she knows it, just as anybody knows his name, and she knows who she is, same way, Joan Rawshanks stands alone in the fog and a thousand eyes are fixed on her in all kinds of ways … the angry technicians muster and make gestures in the blowing fog that rushes past klieg lights and ordinary lights in infinitesimal cold showers, to make everything seem miserable and storm-hounded, as though we were all on a mountain top saving the brave skiers in the howl of the elements, but also just like the lights and the way the night mist blows by them at the scene of great airplane disasters or train wrecks or even just construction jobs that have reached such a crucial point that there's overtime in muddy midnight Alaskan conditions. (*Visions of Cody*, 318–319)

The metatheme of visual depiction is introduced in Part One, where city sketches integrate references to the film industry. The second textual block opens with a description of the run-down "capricio B-movie," its broken marquee lighting and misplaced lettering "spelled out by crazy dumb kids who earn eighteen dollars a week," symbolizing the broken fabric of representational illusion and the commodity code alike. Surrounded by the detritus of "banana peels," "old splashmarks of puke," "broken milk-bottles," and "an old beat gas station – diner on the other corner …

with a big scarred Coca-Cola sign at base of an open counter topped by a marble now so old that it has turned gray and chipped," this, realizes the narrator, "is the bottom of the world" (*Visions of Cody*, 18). The mythic commercial signs no longer invigorate the mass story incessantly rehearsed by Hollywood. Even the word "America" corrodes into a signifier of degradation:

> America is being wanted by the police, pursued across Kentucky and Ohio, sleeping with the stockyard rats and howling tin shingles of gloomy hide-away silos … America is what's laid on Cody Pomeroy's soul the onus and the stigma – that in the form of a big plainclothesman beat the shit out of him in a backroom till he talked about something which isn't even important anymore – America (TEENAGE DOPE SEX CAR RING!!) is also the red neon and the thighs in the cheap motel – it's where at night the staggering drunks began to appear like cockroaches when the bars close … America's a lonely crockashit. (*Visions of Cody*, 118)

The interrogation continues in the "Rawshanks" passage, which stresses the affectation behind "the general materialism of Hollywood"; the manipulation of the "surrounded," "cooped up" onlookers; the tears concocted to order; and the Director's "cruel" manipulation of Joan's head in a "scarf noose." The actress "stands alone" in a variation on the B-movie stunt hero who evokes suspicion in Part One, and who "wouldn't act like that in real unreality" (*Visions of Cody*, 68). The fluid masks endemic to her profession seed new identities, as her name resonates through the circular structure of the prose as "jewel center," to use Kerouac's term from his manifesto. The passage winds down into broken syllables of alliterative sound freed from literal analogy ("bay goes b-o, as a buoy in the bag goes b-o"), taking with it the vitality of the myth that her performance supposedly conveys.

Kerouac thereby gives himself license to relinquish the compromised vision and reproduction of the official stories of America that limited the possibilities of *Road* ("our B-movie again") (*On the Road*, 202). The realization that "little raggedy Codys dream, as rich men plan" follows, along with the exposure of Hollywood's pressure to homogenize experience into a simulacrum of "all the movies we've ever been in" (*Visions of Cody*, 116)[30] "Wise repose" and "independence from all false education, propaganda, and organized entertainment" (*Some of the Dharma*, 111) therefore starts with refusing consumer instructions of shock and sentiment:

> This movie house of mine in the dream has got a golden light to it though it is deeply shaded brown, or misty gray too inside, with thousands not

> hundreds but all squeezed together children in there diggin the perfect cowboy B-movie which is not shown in Technicolor but dream golden. (*Visions of Cody*, 251)

Kerouac's celebration of the dynamics of fabulation extends to the admission of quotations and parodies from exterior sources: sonic and filmic, as well as literary. Following the "Rawshanks" episode, Kerouac plants a metafictional homage to a previous *bricoleur* into his text, complete with bibliographic protocols, to supply an exegesis on his own prose: "'Obviously an image which is immediately and unintentionally ridiculous is merely a fancy.' – T.S. Eliot, Selected Essays, 1917–1932, Harcourt, Brace and Company" (*Visions of Cody*, 355).

Moreover, the emphasis on the Rawshanks film as something made, a series of retakes leading to a final "TAKE," which in itself might not be authoritative, suggests a further meta-analogy with Kerouac's strategies. The meanings of *Cody* accrue through comparing its events with those in *Road*; hence Ginsberg's sense of *Cody* as its "in-depth … historical sequel."[31] The emphasis on self-referentiality informs the novel's closing sections, where the speaker cranks himself up with a mock entreaty to muse and patron that characterizes the traditional Medieval quest, and launches into a further rewrite of his great picaresque narrative of 1940s America:

> The thing to do is put the quietus on the road—give it the final furbishoos and finishes, or is that diddling? Kind King and Sir, my Lord, God, please direct me in this—The telling of the voyages again, for the very beginning; that is, immediately after this. The Voyages are told each in one breath, as is your own, to foreshadow that or this rearshadows *that, one!*
>
> I first met Cody in 1947 but I didn't travel on the road with him till 1948 … (*Visions of Cody*, 381)

The sense of time regained and lost in *Road* now allies personal and mythic planes and is articulated through a phantasmagoria of re-evocation and revision, blurring life and dream. Duluoz becomes a cipher in his own book and recomposes the beginning of Cody's story. This includes the story of his own story, seemingly infinite and circular, the ramifications of the central tale being dizzyingly redoubled into digressing tales with no attempt made to grade their verisimilitude. Laboring now to perpetuate Cody's image by setting down each experience to the present instant, the life of "a great rememberer redeeming life from darkness" inevitably hits the juncture of composition. The fabulation must terminate and the hero be released:

Goodbye Cody—your lips in your moments of self-possessed thought and new found responsible goodness are as silent, make at least a noise, and mystify with sense in nature, like the light of an automobile reflecting from the shiny silverpath of a sidewalk tank this very instant, as silent and all this, as a bird crossing the dawn in search of the mountain cross and the sea beyond the city at the end of the land.

Adios, you who watched the sun go down, at the rail, by my side, smiling—Adios, King. (*Visions of Cody*, 462–463)

Notes

1. Jack Kerouac, *Selected Letters 1, 1940–1956*, ed. Ann Charters (New York: Viking, 1995), 371.
2. Jack Kerouac, *Selected Letters 2, 1957–1969*, ed. Ann Charters (New York: Viking, 1999), 189.
3. Robert Scholes, *Fabulation and Metafiction* (Chicago: University of Illinois, 1979), 2–3.
4. Raymond Federman, *Surfiction: Fiction Now and Tomorrow* (Chicago: Swallow, 1975), 24.
5. Jack Kerouac, *Visions of Cody* (New York: McGraw-Hill, 1973; reprinted London: Flamingo, 1992), 290.
6. Jack Kerouac, *On the Road* (New York: Viking, 1957; reprinted London: Penguin, 1988), 165.
7. Federman, *Surfiction*, 8.
8. Eric Mottram, "A Preface to Visions of Cody," *The Review of Contemporary Fiction*, III: 2, Summer 1983, 50.
9. Henry Adams, *The Education of Henry Adams* (1918; London: Penguin, 1995), 400.
10. Jacques Derrida, *Writing and Difference*, trans. Alan Bass (London: Routledge, 1990), 284.
11. Ted Berrigan, "The Art of Fiction XLI: Jack Kerouac," *The Paris Review,* No. 43, Summer 1968; reprinted in George Plimpton, ed., *Writers at Work: The Paris Review Interviews, Fourth Series* (New York: Penguin, 1976), 103.
12. J. D. Bernal, *The Extension of Man: A History of Physics before 1900* (London: Weidenfeld & Nicolson, 1972), 11.
13. Walter J. Ong *Orality and Literacy: The Technologizing of the Word* (London and New York: Methuen, 1982), 5.
14. Ong, *Orality and Literacy*, 9.
15. Federman, *Surfiction*, 7–8.
16. John Tytell, *Naked Angels: The Lives and Literature of the Beat Generation* (New York: McGraw-Hill, 1976), 175.
17. Michael Davidson, *The San Francisco Renaissance* (Cambridge: Cambridge University Press, 1989), 74.

18. Carolyn Cassady, *Off the Road: My Years with Cassady, Kerouac, and Ginsberg* (New York: Morrow, 1990), 49.
19. Robert Jay Lifton, *Boundaries: Psychological Man in Revolution* (New York: Vintage, 1970), xi–xii.
20. Jack Kerouac, *Tristessa* (New York: Avon, 1960; reprinted London: Paladin, 1992), 43.
21. Regina Weinreich, *The Spontaneous Poetics of Jack Kerouac: A Study of the Fiction* (Carbondale: Southern Illinois University, 1987), 115.
22. Mottram, "A Preface to Visions of Cody," 50.
23. Jack Kerouac, *Some of the Dharma* (New York: Viking, 1997), 342.
24. R.J. Ellis, "'I am only a jolly storyteller:' Jack Kerouac's *On the Road* and *Visions of Cody*," in Lee, A. Robert, ed., *The Beat Generation Writers* (London: Pluto, 1996), 53.
25. Ellis, "I am only a jolly storyteller," 49.
26. Jack Kerouac, *Good Blonde & Others* (San Francisco: Grey Fox, 1993), 73.
27. C. Wright Mills, *The Power Elite* (New York and Oxford: Oxford University, 1956), 321.
28. F. Scott Fitzgerald, *Tender is the Night* (1934; reprinted London: Penguin, 1997), 101.
29. Guy Debord, *The Society of the Spectacle*, trans. Donald Nicholson-Smith (New York: Zone Books, 1995), 12.
30. See also Ellis, "I am only a jolly storyteller," 53.
31. Ginsberg, *My Years*, 353.

CHAPTER 11

Making the Past Present
Kerouac and Memory

Erik Mortenson

This chapter examines Jack Kerouac's attempts to make sense of memory. As we shall see, Kerouac was obsessed with recalling the past events of his life, crafting them into a series of works meant to protect his memories from the ravages of time. But for him, it was not enough to simply record memory – instead, he sought nothing less than preserving his remembrances in a form that allowed not just their content to be accessed, but their intensity as well. While he was not always successful in his attempts, at his best, Kerouac's memory writing animates the past, bringing it back alive in the present as a force that allows for an opening to occur. Focusing primarily on works like *Doctor Sax* that attempt to represent his childhood to his readers, this chapter argues that Kerouac's writing strives for nothing less than to create an experience of the past event in the present moment.

11.1 The Reasons for Looking Back

Kerouac was blessed (or perhaps cursed) with an amazing ability to recall the past details of his life. According to Ann Charters, Kerouac's childhood friends called him "Memory Babe" in tribute to his "possession of a very accurate, very detailed memory."[1] The phrase stuck. Gerald Nicosia borrowed it for the title of his biography and Kerouac himself used it for a then-unpublished novel on his Lowell childhood. He was clearly proud of his prodigious memory, and while many of Kerouac's works chronicle recent adventures on the road, wandering through cities, or meditating in nature, an equal number look back even further, obsessively returning to the same childhood memories for inspiration. Kerouac conceived his corpus, or at least a majority of it, as his "Duluoz Legend" meant to chronicle "what I'd seen with my own eyes, told in my own words, according to the style I decided on at whether twenty-one years old or thirty or forty or whatever later age, and put it all together as a contemporary history record for future times to see what really happened and what people really thought."[2] Explicitly comparing his project to Honoré de Balzac's novel sequence *La Comédie humaine* (*The Human Comedy*), Kerouac sought to write memory in an effort to salvage the moments of his life from oblivion.[3] But the driving reason for this continual return is open to debate.

Early in *Doctor Sax*, Kerouac gives us a visual representation of his fascination with memory. Looking back onto scenes from his childhood, the narrator passes a doorway where he used to linger with friends, ruminating "passed the holy doorway where G.J. and Lousy and I hung sitting in the mystery which I now see hugens, huger, into something beyond my Grook, beyond my Art & Pale, into the secret of what God has done with my Time."[4] That "mystery," which increases with each passing year, drives Kerouac to find a means of reclaiming it, even if it might ultimately reside "beyond Art & Pale." Memory needs redemption. Why? Because for Kerouac the passing moment is "holy" and must be saved from the loss that time brings. In *Visions of Cody*, Kerouac explains that he struggled "in the dark with the enormity of my soul, trying desperately to be a great rememberer redeeming life from darkness."[5] This theme of writing as the preserver of the sanctity of the passing moment stays with Kerouac throughout his life. In a late piece, "Beat Spotlight," he reiterates this idea of writing as a spiritual or even religious practice, claiming that "life was holy" and that he should "write about it pointing out the holiness throughout the squalor and commonplaceness, that the very streets of life were holy."[6] Part of this impetus resides in Kerouac's desire to do justice to those like his father and older brother who passed before him (the novel *Visions of Gerard* is devoted to a brother lost in childhood), but it becomes clear that Kerouac is interested in preserving *all* the events of his life as sacred occurrences. Kerouac believes in the "holiness" of each moment and laments the loss that occurs as time rushes inextricably onwards, setting himself the task of transcribing not just the lives of those he cares about, but of the constantly changing material world itself.

Of course, it is also possible Kerouac is simply getting "high" off the past. Kerouac was certainly no stranger to intoxicants, and memory was yet another mode of getting outside ordinary experience. In *Visions of Cody*, the narrator relates a memory about his father's friend, then, musing, concludes: "the (as Proust says God bless him) 'inexpressibly delicious' sensation of this memory – for as memories are older they're like wine rarer, till if you find a real old memory, one of infancy, not an established often tasted one but a *brand new one!*, it would taste better than the Napoleon brandy Stendhal himself must have stared at" (*Visions of Cody*, 26). The inexpressible joy of the undiscovered memory is related directly to alcohol. The moment is so "rare" that Kerouac goes on to declare that he's only experienced about five such memories of "*complete inspiration*" (*Visions of Cody*, 27). In his "Belief & Technique for Modern Prose," Kerouac admonishes, "Like Proust be an old teahead of time," in this case linking memory and its reclamation to the high he enjoys experiencing with marijuana.[7] Marcel Proust is an important touchstone not simply because of his attempt to record his life in the colossal *À la recherche du temps perdu* (*Remembrance of Things Past*), but more importantly due to Proust's idea of involuntary memory. As Proust scholar Roger Shattuck explains, "This heightened stage of perception builds on earlier impressions. When one reencounters some part of the sensation that provoked the original impression, the new sensation may … trigger a *moment bienheureux*, a reminiscence, a twinge of pleasure."[8] Later, in *Visions of Cody*, Kerouac experiences another epiphany, this time occasioned while getting a cold drink of water from the faucet (while high) that sends his mind racing back to "the cool exact waters of Pine Brook on a summer afternoon" (*Visions of Cody*, 258). Like Proust's famous bite of madeleine, Kerouac is immediately abstracted out of present time, and his corpus is in fact replete with celebrations of such ecstatic states. Here memory becomes another means, like visions and dreams, of attaining the transcendent moment.

Despite this almost exalted sense of himself as a chronicler of a fading world, a lone savior preserving the present from an ever-encroaching future, there is also a feeling of hauntedness in Kerouac's attempts at writing memory. In his *Book of Sketches*, Kerouac explains how he chooses the scenes he focuses on in his work: "A scene / should be selected by / the writer, for haunted- / ness-of-mind interest. / If you're not haunted / by something, as by a / dream, a vision, or / a memory, which are / involuntary, you're not / interested or even involved" (*Book of Sketches*, 65). Kerouac's idea of memory as a continual return gives his work a sense of compulsion, as if writing is more exorcism than exhumation. As Todd F. Tietchen comments in his introduction to the collection *The Haunted Life*, "much of Kerouac's work continues to revolve around its originating sense of loss, as if the act of recalling or commemorating can never fully liberate him from the thing being recalled."[9] Despite a professed joy in the past moments of his life, Kerouac's memories are often overlaid with nostalgia, loss, and an almost uncanny desire to repeat.

Ultimately, what pushes Kerouac's reclamation of memory continuously forward is an unease about what will happen to the moment if he is not there to record it. Writing of his boyhood friends in *Doctor Sax*, Kerouac's narrator muses

> that gray's forgotten too, as I say Cy and Bert were dreadfully young in a long-ago of moving Time that is so remote it for the first time assumes that rigid post of posture deathlike denoting the cessation of its operation in my memory and therefore the world's—a time about to become extinct—except that now it can never be, because it happened, it—which led to further levels—as time unveiled her ugly old cold mouth of death to the worst hopes—fears—Bert Desjardins and Cy Ladeau like any prescience of a dream are unerasable. (*Doctor Sax*, 72–73)

The uncertainty is palpable. What's to become of Kerouac's boyhood friends Cy and Bert? They existed, so will always have existed. Yet that is not enough. They exist in Kerouac's mind, in his memory, which seems to save them from the loss time brings, but a problem obviously arises – what happens when Kerouac's memory ceases? Kerouac will posit some extra-temporal zone where this event is collected regardless of whether it stays in memory, but such a solution is uneasy. Though he will insist Cy and Bert are "unerasable," a hesitancy remains. How will they be redeemed, if not by Kerouac's mind? Through his prose.

11.2 Preserving Time on the Page

But not just any prose. What Kerouac was searching for was a type of writing that could capture the sort of intense feelings and sensations his memory produced. He found such a technique in the Spontaneous Prose style he developed in the early 1950s. In his manifesto "Essentials of Spontaneous Prose," Kerouac explains that one should "Begin not from preconceived idea of what to say about image but from jewel center of interest in subject of image at *moment* of writing, and write outwards swimming in sea of language to peripheral release and exhaustion."[10] As its title suggests, Kerouac's poetic theory stresses the spontaneous nature of composition. His solution to the problem of representing memory is to focus on the *act* of remembering as it occurs in the present. Rather than trying to make the past event adhere to the "preconceived idea" of what occurred, the memory instead becomes resurrected in the act of telling.

Kerouac's spontaneous reclamation of memory is powerful. Rather than rendering the past moment as an expired event, it instead re-enters the present as actual force. To see how this works, we can look at a key early passage of *Doctor Sax*, where Kerouac relates one of the first memories of his life. Describing what he calls the "Great Bathrobe Vision," where he remembers being held in his mother's arms while looking up at her brown bathrobe, he writes:

> I'm in my mother's arms but somehow the chair is not on the floor, it's up in the air suspended in the voids of saw-dust smelling mist blowing from Lajoie's wood yard, suspended over yard of grass at corner of West Sixth and Boisvert—that daguerreotype gray is all over, but my mother's robe sends auras of warm brown (the brown of my family)—so now when I bundle my chin in a warm scarf in a wet gale—I think on that comfort in the brown bathrobe—or as when a kitchen door is opened to winter allowing fresh ices of air to interfere with the warm billowy curtain of fragrant heat of cooking stove ... say a vanilla pudding ... I am the pudding, winter is the gray mist. (*Doctor Sax*, 20–21)

Kerouac could simply have related the memory of being in his mother's arms by describing the details of the memory and how the experience felt. But in seeking to present the import of the past event, he eschews pure description, opting instead to allow the associations he experiences in connection with this memory to unfold. Kerouac is attempting to capture the feeling he has of the bathrobe in the present moment, and to do that he envelops it in a series of sensory phenomena that seek to recreate the affect he experiences when thinking of the memory.

The passage is anything but static: "mist" is "blowing," colors "send auras," and a "saw-dust smell" permeates the air. The goal here is to reignite the memory in the mind of the reader, and even though Kerouac has recourse to simile, comparing the bathrobe vision to the intrusion of cold winter air into a warm kitchen, he again does so in terms that evoke affect. The reader almost shudders at the physicality of "fresh ices" of air interfering with the warm, rich, cloying fragrances of a dessert cooking on the stove. Thus, the declaration "I am the pudding, the winter is the gray mist" should not be read as a simple analogy, but rather as the reenactment of the memory itself designed to cause an actual shift in the consciousness of the rememberer. This is precisely why Kerouac keeps the passage in present tense. The memory is not an extinguished event to be recalled – it is happening to Kerouac, and thus the reader, in the present time of narration.

Kerouac's ability to bring memories to life is even more pronounced in a passage from *Maggie Cassidy*, his novel of high-school love. Describing a memory of looking at baseball cards at a friend's house, Kerouac relates:

> He took me to his house and showed me his scrapbook full of pasted pictures of baseball stars of 1920's and 1930's with incredibly old stars whose bones are long interred in crumbling files in the archives of red sun sinking in the

> Ninth Inning with Nobody On .... Lost forever the still figure in right center with a tanned taut expression on solid legs waiting for the crack of the bat as a little shrill creamy whistle splits the atmosphere stadium hush.[11]

The reference to baseball cards here is apt. A keepsake meant to memorialize a player through visual depiction and statistical record, for Kerouac, the cards are nevertheless only the starting point, defining his project by contrast. Not content with such static depictions, Kerouac moves from a memory of the baseball cards to an imagination of the "bones" of the physical players themselves now "long interred," to a reanimated present where the "crack of the bat" sends a "creamy whistle" that reinvigorates both an imagined past as well as a contemporary present. Through the present tense of writing, Kerouac makes this memory an actual occurrence, breathing new life into photographs of baseball stars long since gone.

Kerouac's reliance on the visual image raises an obvious question – why not just take a photograph?[12] Kerouac's corpus is replete with references to the visual. In *Visions of Cody*, he spends an entire section describing Joan Crawford filming a scene in San Francisco, and in *Doctor Sax* he labels one section "A Gloomy Bookmovie" and then proceeds to relate a series of film scenes. Kerouac references films and photographs throughout his work, but continually rejects their efficacy as mnemonic devices – while in *Visions of Cody* Duluoz stands enthralled to Joan Crawford about to open a door, marveling at "the actual moment, the central kill, the riddled middle idea, the thing, the Take, the actual juice suction of the camera catching a vastly planned action," the description quickly extends beyond the camera's shutter to include the movement of the crowd, the lights, the police officers standing guard, even the director's "red lollipop" (*Visions of Cody*, 281–282), And throughout *Doctor Sax*, Kerouac constantly describes scenes as "unphotographable," then goes on to provide thick visual descriptions instead. The implication here is that memory cannot be fully expressed by the visual. In *Remembrance of Things Past*, one of Kerouac's primary inspirations for his depictions of memory, Proust explains why the image falls short: "What we call reality is a certain relationship between these sensations and the memories which surround us at the same time (a relationship that is destroyed by a bare cinematographic presentation, which gets further away from the truth the more closely it claims to adhere to it)."[13] For Proust as for Kerouac, the photographic image is ironically too precise, its mimetic efficacy destroying the delicate interplay between memory and sensation. The photographic image is ultimately incapable of capturing the multitude of nuances that lend memory power and force in the mind; writing does a better job.

11.3 Difficulties with the Method

Kerouac's spontaneous reclamation of memory can be extremely powerful, but it is also very difficult to effectively achieve. The books of Kerouac's middle period, written shortly after he "discovered" his spontaneous technique, are widely considered his most successful. But as his career unfolded, it often became difficult for Kerouac to maintain his vaunted style. *Vanity of Duluoz* was written in 1968, a year before his death; bitter and disillusioned, he gives the book a feeling of nostalgic looking back by drawing attention to the difference between the occurrence of the memory and the time of writing. Consider the beginning of the novel, where Kerouac opines that "my anguish as I call it arises from the fact that people have changed so much, not only in the past five years … or past ten years … but in the past thirty years to such an extent that I don't recognize them as people any more or recognize myself as a real member of something called the human race" (*Vanity of Duluoz*, 9). Despite the novel being ostensibly about the years 1935–1946, many of *Vanity*'s passages are prefaced with such statements, clearly made from the vantage of the present, alerting readers to a value judgment implicit in the text – things were better back then. This reminiscent style displays a longing for the past that serves to extract the reader out of the narrative's present. Memories are not set in motion but are rather presented straightforwardly as rigid depictions of past events.

Kerouac calls many of these moments "cameos" and presents them in list form throughout his novel: "Weekends at Ray Olmsted's apartment with his parents and kid brother, in Yonkers, the affair with Betty there, skating on the Yonkers pond and a few kisses here and there. Sharpy Gimbel yelling 'Hi' from his convertible at the dance" (*Vanity of Duluoz*, 51). Events are often rendered as mere visual occurrences devoid of affect. In *Visions of Cody*, Kerouac's friend and muse Neal Cassady warned of the "skeletonization" of memory that denuded the past event of its import. In a tape recording of one of their marijuana-fueled discussions, Cassady explains that once a memory becomes discussed, subsequent returns to that past are forced to proceed along demarcated lines. Memory in *Vanity of Duluoz* does not reenter the space of present time but is forced to remain as an already-taken-place that reads as expired force rather than current intensity.

But even when Kerouac is at his best, there are necessarily limits to the reclamation of memory through writing. Some things simply cannot be recalled, or at least not in the sort of detail that Kerouac would desire.

Here he is on the obviously unrecoverable moment of his birth in *Doctor Sax*: "Golden birds hovered over her and me as she hugged me to her breast; angels and cherubs made a dance, and floated from the ceiling with upsidedown assholes and thick folds of fat, and there was a mist of butterflies, birds, moths and brownnesses hanging dull and stupid over pouting births" (*Doctor Sax*, 19). This passage allows us to glimpse the scope of Kerouac's ambitions: he wants to record everything, but while he was of course present at all moments of his life, not everything can possibly be remembered. Yet this does not stop him from attempting a complete recall, and inspiration stands in when memory must stand down. This is true of all of Kerouac's memory writing to some extent, as past event becomes imbued with present thoughts, feelings, and associations. As Kerouac relates in *Doctor Sax*, "memory and dream are intermixed in this mad universe" (*Doctor Sax*, 14). However, the ratio of "dream" to "memory" is often fluid, allowing Kerouac to supplement his remembrances when necessary or desirable.

The urge to augment memory is even more noticeable in *Visions of Gerard*. Kerouac seeks to memorialize his older brother, Gerard, whose death was the central traumatic event of Kerouac's youth, and one he returns to again and again. Taken as a whole, the book is a moving tribute, but at times does strain credulity. Kerouac was, after all, only four years old when Gerard died, and it's hard to believe that even the great Memory Babe is able to recall such detailed events, many with dialogue, from before kindergarten. Kerouac himself admits these limitations when describing a scene in which Gerard tends to an injured mouse: "I don't remember rationally but in my soul and mind Yes there's a mouse, peeping, and Gerard, and the basket, and the kitchen the scene of this heart-tender little hospital."[14] Kerouac's admission helps explain his use of "Visions" in this title and others. The term gives Kerouac the license to go beyond recalled memory when recording his subjects. This desire to push beyond the constraints imposed by standard conceptions of memory is certainly in keeping with an overall tendency in Beat literature for boundary pushing, and like other Beat attempts, demonstrates both the possibilities and limitations of the desire for transcendence. Drawing on "dream" and "vision" when capturing memory helps push Kerouac's writing in new and invigorating directions, but ceding fidelity to imagination also raises important ethical questions when applied to other characters in the novel.

The Beats have come under scrutiny for the ways in which they represent others, both in terms of gender and race. Kerouac's desire to capture memory exemplifies this difficulty. Kerouac's project pushes against the physical constraint of what he can himself remember, but it also strives to capture the thoughts, feelings, and words of those around him, even when unknowable. Despite isolated successes, Kerouac is generally not considered a master of dialogue; the bulk of his writing is an attempt to write himself. The trouble starts when he begins to project his thinking onto others. In *Maggie Cassidy*, for instance, he is willing to put words into others' mouths that he could not possibly have remembered and that they very likely never spoke. Consider the following passage, where his high-school sweetheart sounds much like the author himself in her attempts to woo her "Jacky" back:

> "The fog'll fall all over you, Jacky, you'll wait in fields—You'll let me die—you wont come save me—I dont even know where your grave is—remember what you were like, where your house, what your life—you'll die without knowing what happened to my face—my love—my youth—You'll burn yourself out like a moth jumping in a locomotive boiler looking for light." (*Maggie Cassidy*, 184)

Here Maggie "speaks," but speaks Kerouac. Why Kerouac decided to render this memory as direct quotation is an open question, as he could as easily have expressed his reaction to Maggie's words instead. But bidding her memory speak illustrates the problem of putting his spontaneous method in the mouths of others – it risks ventriloquism.

Seemingly aware of this problem, Kerouac often instead opts for a concept known as "digging."[15] Drawn from both the underground world of conmen, where it pejoratively means to "size up" a mark, as well as more positively from a Black jazz milieu that defines it in terms of understanding and appreciation, this observational technique lets the thoughts of others become "available" in hypothesized form through the creation of narratives drawn from first-hand observation of speech, appearance, and demeanor. In *Tristessa*, Kerouac becomes fascinated with a Mexican prostitute addicted to morphine. While he does record many of her words, the bulk of this recollection is given to his own attempts to understand or "dig" her. Digging often has recourse to the simile – his narrator repeatedly celebrates Tristessa's "dark Aztecan instinctual belief," but translates it into his own Catholicism, describing her in religious terms, "with her lidded eyes and clasped hands, a Madonna," and at other moments, drawing on American culture, as looking "like a Black Ava Gardner" with "lidded Billie Holiday eyes" and a voice "like Luise Rainer."[16] While he wants to believe in Tristessa's universal comprehensibility, claiming "She knows, I know, you know," he immediately describes how she hunches down at the table, "understanding herself in a way that I cannot" (*Tristessa*, 23). In the end, it is Tristessa herself who highlights the failure of digging when she explains why she does not mind when she gives a friend a shot of morphine and they fail to repay her: "'Eees when, *cuando*, my friend does not pay me back, don I don't care. Because' pointing up with a straight expression into my eyes, finger aloft, 'my Lord pay me—and he pay me *more*—M-o-r-e'" (*Tristessa*, 21). Kerouac cannot possibly access Tristessa's relationship with her "Lord," troubling him to the extent that he uncharacteristically ends the section with her own words, not his.

When memory reaches its limit, Kerouac's prose often stops, but this blockage can also be productive, forcing him, or at least his readers, to question what exactly is at stake in his recording of memory. Just as scenes from Kerouac's mind's eye are often termed "unphotographable," many passages contain writing in his boyhood French that Kerouac claims are untranslatable.[17] During an argument in *Maggie Cassidy*, Duluoz's father ends his response with the exclamation "*Comprends?*" which Duluoz explains "loud, in French, like an uncle calling the idiot from the corner making clear to me meanings that can never be recorded in the English language" (*Maggie Cassidy*, 97). Later, when describing his thoughts after a win at a track meet, he writes in parenthesis "(These thoughts were all in French, almost untranslatable)" (*Maggie Cassidy*, 97). But given that Kerouac does attempt a translation, why is he so hesitant about transcribing them into English? It is not that the words or even that the content cannot be rendered, but rather that the effect produced when Kerouac speaks his native dialect cannot be fully communicated.

Spontaneous composition demands attentiveness to the conditions of the passing moment. It is not just the memory being transcribed, but the state (mental, physical, and emotional) of being in which the moment manifests that Kerouac is trying to capture. Kerouac writing memory in French is not Kerouac writing memory in English, and thus one is not fully translatable into the other. Kerouac's transcription of memory is highly idiosyncratic since each return is governed by the present in which it emerges, influencing both how the memory itself will be told as well as providing everchanging contexts for its relation. Thus, the irony of Kerouac's memory writing project is that it is both extremely productive and simultaneously incapable of offering a final memorialization of the past – Kerouac can repeatedly return to an event and get different results, but this means that the past can never stabilize into one final telling since every new present that time brings offers Kerouac the possibility for more rewriting. While Kerouac claims to be turning the past events of his life into "legend," he is simultaneously chronicling his contemporary life in novels that capture his current preoccupations.

11.4 Universalizing Personal Memory in *Doctor Sax*

While any attempt to write memory is going to necessarily be highly personal, Kerouac's memory writing nevertheless strives to remain accessible and even inspirational to his readers. Despite the fact that contemporary critics tended to label his work solipsistic, Kerouac himself viewed his spontaneous method as intensely intersubjective.[18] Kerouac claimed that the spontaneous style he pioneered gave every reader access to "telepathic shock and meaning-excitement" because everyone has the "same laws operating in his own human mind" ("Essentials," 69). But writing memory as it arises in the mind also inevitably leads to intrusions and slippages, as his method runs "in time" and is thus subject to his moods, feelings, and stimuli at the time of writing. Often these asides capture a wistful sense of nostalgia as the spontaneous reclamation of memory meets present-moment contingencies and frustrations. Thus, when an older author complains about a cartoon about storing coal in the winter in a parenthesis in *Doctor Sax*, "(Depression Themes, now it's atom-bomb bins in the cellar communist dope ring)" (*Doctor Sax*, 74–75) we are immediately reminded of historical, rather than narrative, time. The Cold War 1950s replaces the Depression 1930s as the historical condition of the text's making. As we've seen with *Vanity of Duluoz*, these authorial intrusions often disrupt the affect that Kerouac's spontaneous method strives to create.

But not always. Kerouac also found a means of employing these diversions in meaningful ways. In *Doctor Sax* in particular, Kerouac harnesses a Gothic subplot that, while much different than his spontaneous reclamation of memory, nevertheless serves to heighten the book's impact by creating universals that allow the reader to enter the narrative productively.[19] While its nominal aim is to describe the coming-of-age Kerouac experienced as an adolescent, the present, in the form of shadows like Doctor Sax, are always seeping through, sending their own specters to haunt Kerouac's Depression-era remembrance. When Doctor Sax enumerates the future to his young charge, it feels like an older Kerouac lecturing his younger self, and thus the audience, and we have caught up to the current Kerouac, in 1952, huddled in Mexico City in his friend William S. Burroughs's dank hall toilet:[20]

> You'll roll your feet together in the tense befuddles of ten thousand evenings in company in the parlor, in the pad—that is known as, ah, socializing.

> You'll grow numb all over from inner paralytic thoughts, and bad chairs,--that is known as Solitude. You'll inch along the ground on the day of your death and be pursued by the Editorial Cartoon Russian Bear with a knife, and in his bear hug he will poignard you in the reddy blood back to gleam in the pale Siberian sun—that is known as nightmares. (*Doctor Sax*, 186–187)

Here Kerouac is parodying Jacques's speech in Shakespeare's *As You Like It* in which he discusses the seven ages of man, updated to include his own personal frustrations along with broader cultural fears of Communist infiltration. While the imagined character of Doctor Sax initially represents childhood fears of the dark, as the novel progresses, he increasingly comes to be seen as a teacher of worldly knowledge, and the novel's climax involves nothing less than a battle between good and evil for the fate of humankind. Readers are thus invited to see Doctor Sax in mythic, rather than strictly personal, terms.[21]

The novel, while chronicling the specific childhood of a French-Canadian boy growing up in Lowell Massachusetts during the 1930s, actually speaks to a wider audience. The character of Doctor Sax, modeled primarily on the comic book figure "The Shadow" which haunted Kerouac's own youth (and subsequent works), stands for an unknown that is nevertheless desirable, an undefined possibility that both attracts and disturbs the narrator and represents the sort of entry into adulthood that every human being must inevitably experience. While little Ti Jean's world might seem circumscribed by his French-Canadian upbringing, the Gothic subplot of *Sax* serves a universalizing function. Jackie Duluoz frequents his local French-Canadian store throughout the novel, but that store also sells the *Shadow* comic books that inspired Kerouac's titular figure and get read and traded across French-Canadian, Irish, and Greek neighborhoods alike. The radio, which plays his favorite hits and airs his beloved *Shadow* program, is accessed by all, and for contemporary readers calls to mind the leveling effect of American media in general. Even his local sandlot baseball team is comprised of kids living across a variety of ethnic neighborhoods, demonstrating in nostalgic terms the allure of baseball as the "great American pastime." The universal themes Kerouac captures in works like *Doctor Sax* (and in others like *Maggie Cassidy* which addresses the perennial difficulties of teenage love) make Kerouac's reclamation of childhood memory at once personal hymn, cultural study, and inspiration for readers to ponder the relationship to their own adolescences that can be understood as simultaneously individual and common.

While Kerouac might not have solved the "secret of what God has done with my time," he nevertheless found a method to restage that secret with as much force as possible. These deep dives into discrete moments of past time are powerful, but as effective as they are in presenting the past as intensity, they also simultaneously remind the reader of the present tense of the telling. Ironically, Kerouac's desire to refashion memory in the present is in fact in keeping with modern scientific notions that see memory as a reworking of the past rather than as the accessing of a recording. This has important implications for how we understand Kerouac's corpus, especially given his desire to craft a "legend" of his life. Kerouac may feel, like John Locke, that his memories are providing stability to his life, an archive of events that it is his job to maintain. But in fact, Kerouac's real genius lies in his ability to continually revisit the past through prose that allows his readers to reside in the affects he creates for as long as possible. This explains his recourse to the dash, to the portmanteau, to the lack of period – don't stop the magic for fear the spell might be broken. But we must come up for air sometime, and when we do, there is always the possibility waiting for us to make sense of the unique experience Kerouac's writing provides. And what is that lesson? Surely the goal is not to simply take inventory of Kerouac's memories. Those who focus exclusively on the lore and legend of the Beats miss the mark – the point isn't to immerse oneself in Kerouac's life, however well-told his tales, but rather to use his excursions into his past as jumping off points for a journey into our own untamed land of feeling, sensation, and memory. For our futures rely, paradoxically enough, on how we access, conceive, and reshape the memories of our past.

Notes

1. Ann Charters, *Kerouac: A Biography* (New York: St. Martin's, 1994), 63.
2. Jack Kerouac, *Vanity of Duluoz* (New York: Penguin Books, 1994), 190.
3. In *Book of Sketches*, Kerouac proclaims, "Ah / James Joyce, Proust, / Wolfe, Balzac—I'll / combine you in my forge—" (New York: Penguin, 2006), 170. While Joyce's influence was mainly stylistic, it was Proust who exerted perhaps the greatest influence. See Véronique Lane's *The French Genealogy of the Beat Generation: Burroughs, Ginsberg and Kerouac's Appropriations of Modern Literature, from Rimbaud to Michaux* (New York: Bloomsbury, 2017) for an extended discussion of Kerouac's reading and use of Proust. For a discussion of the importance of Thomas Wolfe to Kerouac, see the second chapter of Regina Weinreich's *Kerouac's Spontaneous Poetics: A Study of the Fiction* (New York: Thunder's Mouth, 1987).
4. Jack Kerouac, *Doctor Sax: Faust Part Three* (New York: Penguin, 1987), 5.
5. Jack Kerouac, *Visions of Cody* (New York: Penguin, 1993), 103.

6. Jack Kerouac, "Beat Spotlight," *The Unknown Kerouac: Rare, Unpublished & Newly Translated Writings* (New York: Library of America, 2016), 328.
7. Jack Kerouac, "Belief & Technique for Modern Prose," *Good Blonde & Others*, Ed. Donald Allen (San Francisco: Grey Fox Press, 1994), 72.
8. Roger Shattuck, *Proust's Way: A Field Guide to In Search of Lost Time* (New York: W.W. Norton, 2000), 111. Kerouac does draw a distinction, however, claiming in his introduction to *Visions of Cody* that "My work comprises one vast book like Proust's *Remembrance of Things Past* except that my remembrances are written on the run instead of afterwards in a sick bed" (*Visions of Cody*, unpaginated).
9. Jack Kerouac, *The Haunted Life and Other Writings* (Boston: Da Capo Press, 2014), 20.
10. Jack Kerouac, "Essentials of Spontaneous Prose," *Good Blonde & Others*, 70.
11. Jack Kerouac, *Maggie Cassidy* (New York: Penguin, 1993), 90.
12. For an extended discussion of how Kerouac attempts to write memory as well as the role photography plays in Beat writing, see the fourth chapter of my book *Capturing the Beat Moment: Cultural Politics and the Poetics of Presence* (Carbondale: Southern Illinois University Press, 2011).
13. Marcel Proust, *Remembrance of Things Past*, trans. Frederick A. Blossom (New York: Random, 1932), 2:1008. See also Martin Jay's *Downcast Eyes: The Denigration of Vision in Twentieth-Century French Thought* (Berkeley: University of California Press, 1994).
14. Jack Kerouac, *Visions of Gerard* (New York: Penguin, 1991), 8. In *Desolation Angels*, Kerouac is even more open about his inability to recall his brother, admitting "my brother Gerard who said things to me before he died, though I don't remember a word, or maybe I do remember a few (I was only four)." Later in the book, Kerouac goes even further, announcing that "I actually remember the dark swarming bliss of 1917 altho I was born in 1922!" (New York: Riverhead Books, 1995), 256, 316.
15. This concept deserves further exploration. See John Clellon Holmes's article "The Philosophy of the Beat Generation" (1958) as well as Norman Mailer's "The White Negro" (1957) for critical discussions, as well as Kerouac's novels *Tristessa*, *Visions of Cody*, and *On the Road* for further literary examples.
16. Jack Kerouac, *Tristessa* (New York: Penguin, 1992), 22; 23; 8.
17. For an extended discussion of Kerouac's bilingualism, see Hassan Melehy's *Kerouac: Language, Poetics, and Territory* (New York: Bloomsbury, 2016), and his chapter in this volume.
18. This charge of solipsism was leveled at Kerouac most famously by Norman Podhoretz in his *Partisan Review* article "The Know-Nothing Bohemians."
19. Kerouac himself always believed in the novel, telling his friend Lucien Carr in a letter a few years after *Doctor Sax* was published that it was the "greatest book I ever wrote, or that I will write" (Gerald Nicosia, *Memory Babe: A Critical Biography of Jack Kerouac*, New York: Grove, 1983), 410.

20. As biographer Tom Clark explains, he sat on the toilet, "smoked his joints, and as he 'hallucinated,' scribbled away in pencil on children's notebooks held in his lap" (*Jack Kerouac: A Biography*, New York: Marlowe & Company, 1984), 109.
21. For an elaboration of this argument see the second chapter of my book *Ambiguous Borderlands: Shadow Imagery in Cold War American Culture* (Carbondale: Southern Illinois University Press, 2016).

CHAPTER 12

Spun Rhythms
Jack Kerouac as Poet

Regina Weinreich

The little worm
  Lowers itself from the roof
By a self shat thread

This three-line triolet, or haiku, comes from a slim Kerouac volume, *Heaven & Other Poems,* from 1959. A resonant year for Kerouac and poetry, 1959 was also the year his important book of poetry, *Mexico City Blues,* was published, and the year he recorded his album *Blues and Haikus* with Al Cohn and Zoot Sims, bringing together his jazz and Buddhist preoccupations. In 1959, Kerouac would also publish pieces of his relentlessly experimental prose-poem, *Old Angel Midnight* in the little magazine *Big Table*, a poem only published in full in 1993. Other posthumously published volumes of poetry include *Pomes All Sizes* (1992), *Book of Blues* (1995), and *Book of Haikus* (2003). As suggested by the fact that much of Kerouac's substantial body of poetic work was only published after his death and canonization as a major countercultural novelist of the twentieth century, he was not in his lifetime generally considered an important postwar American poet, at least by the academy, although certainly a case can – and has – been made for such a claim. Even though Kerouac made his own specific distinctions between his prose and poetry in essays and interviews, the distinction for readers of his poetic prose remains difficult to discern, which may, in turn, make it harder to see him as a significant poet.

Allen Ginsberg, for one, always insisted on Kerouac's importance and influence as a poet; in his introduction to *Pomes All Sizes*, for example, he declares: "His influence is worldwide, not only in spirit, with beat planetary Youth Culture, but poetic, technical."[1] As evidence Ginsberg cites a range of poets influenced by Kerouac, from Philip Whalen, whose "Big Baby Buddha Golden 65 feet high" was inspired by *Mexico City Blues*, to Bob Dylan, who, according to Ginsberg, said *Mexico City Blues* was "the first poetry that spoke his own language" (*Pomes,* ii). Gary Snyder was "taken by the ease" of *Mexico City Blues*, "the effortless way it moved on—apparently effortless—at the same time there was some constant surprise arising in the words, always something happening with the words. You can see the mind at work, see the mind in it."[2] And, Michael McClure thought *Mexico City Blues* Kerouac's masterpiece, declaring it "the surpassing religious visionary poetic statement of the twentieth century."[3] This is extravagant praise from those who would seem to know best: other poets in Kerouac's circle. And yet the fact remains that Kerouac has not been widely recognized for his poetic achievement.

When *Mexico City Blues* appeared, it was generally dismissed or outright savaged. Perhaps the most scathing review came from the poet Kenneth Rexroth who had been present at the historic Six Gallery reading when Allen Ginsberg read his "Howl" while Kerouac passed around a jug of wine. Reviewing *Mexico City Blues* in the *New York Times*, Rexroth faulted Kerouac for what he saw as a shoddy interpretation of Buddhism, as if Kerouac were "a dime store incense burner."[4] Correctly assessing the damage of so scathing a review in the *Times*, Ginsberg understood this was condemning the work to obscurity.[5] More generous – though still broadly negative – reviews came from others: Herbert Feinstein in *Prairie Schooner* found Kerouac's verse too guarded, and adolescent.[6] The poet Anthony Hecht in *The Hudson Review* thought it best to read *Mexico City Blues* in one sitting: "This is the voice of a man who has a lot of knick-knacks and hocus-pocus to get rid of, but it is the voice of a man."[7]

The contemporary responses to *Mexico City Blues* are indicative of the ways that Kerouac has been dismissed as a poet. Although the farsighted editor Donald Allen did include Kerouac's work in his landmark anthology *The New American Poetry* in 1960, that was something of an anomaly, and Kerouac's poetry tends to be absent from non-Beat anthologies of postwar American poetry. This is still the case even a century after Kerouac's birth, and in March 2022, City Lights Books in San Francisco hosted a panel framed by Kerouac's status as "literary outsider." This description of Kerouac still does hold, despite the legs of *On the Road*, *The Dharma Bums* and other novels that continue to sell well, particularly with respect to his poetic achievement.

Observers of the cultural ethos out of which Kerouac emerged offer partial explanations. Morris Dickstein identifies the hostility of critics to the Beats' "incipient experimentalism," which, "like most such 'experiments,' had a rich but neglected literary ancestry."[8] Seymour Krim goes farther by explaining the revolt of the avant-garde of the late 1940s and early 1950s as one against a prevailing "cerebral-formalist" temper that was shutting new writers out of literary existence because both their personal experience and their literary language had been suppressed by the critical straight-jacket of post-T. S. Eliot letters.[9] It could also be that Kerouac's poetry has been underrecognized both because his prose itself was widely considered poetic, and because he himself often eschewed hard distinctions among poetry and prose.[10]

As Kerouac once remarked to Ginsberg, "You guys call yourselves poets, write little short lines, I'm a poet but I write lines paragraphs and pages and many pages long."[11] Little wonder, then, that many a reader has been struck by the poetic lyricism of Kerouac's prose. As many have observed, for instance, Kerouac's masterwork *Visions of Cody* is filled with lyrical passages; Ginsberg even called the descriptions of food in the "Hector's Cafeteria" section of the novel a "Homeric poem."[12] Framed by the image of Cody coming to brilliant New York from drab, downtown Denver, Kerouac's cafeteria, recreated in poetic repetition, becomes a cathedral of neon glitz, an ode to both Cody's and Duluoz's immigrant hungers. Likewise, *Visions of Cody*'s "Joan Rawshanks in the Fog" segment is filled with slant rhymes, alliteration and assonance: the description of the real-life actress Joan Crawford filming a movie in San Francisco pans as if Kerouac's writerly eye were a movie camera detailing the background onlookers watching the spectacle below with Joan Rawshanks in the foreground. The passage has its own sound system, devolving into the music of a buoy in the bay going b-o, bab-o, and if you cut off the section in the precise place where all words are made-up, they all sound onomatopoeic. One of the more famous examples of this onomatopoeic technique occurs at the end of *Big Sur*, to which Kerouac appends the poem, "Sea," which mimics the sounds of the waves crashing on the rocks: "Ker plotsch— / Shore—shoe— / god—brash—."[13] Our ears swim in his sound – no matter what the influence, as in bebop, or Frank Sinatra, or the instantaneous flash of what Ginsberg called "snapshot poetics."[14]

Despite the endless instances of poetic prose one can locate in Kerouac's writing, he still clearly saw his poetry as distinct from his prose when he explained his poetic practice to his *Paris Review* interviewers, poet Ted Berrigan and novelist Aram Saroyan:

> For my regular English verse, I knocked it off fast like the prose, using, get this, the size of the notebook page for the form and length of the poem, just as a musician has to get out, a jazz musician, his statement within a certain number of bars, within one chorus, which spills over into the next, but he has to stop where the chorus page *stops*. And finally, too, in poetry you can be completely free to say anything you want, you don't have to tell a story, you can use secret puns.[15]

Kerouac's note on the title page of *Mexico City Blues* corroborates: "I want to be considered a jazz poet blowing a long blues in an afternoon jam session on Sunday. I take 242 choruses; my ideas vary and sometimes roll from chorus to chorus or from halfway through a chorus to halfway into the next" (*Mexico City Blues*, title page). His explanations illuminate the poetic aspects of his prose phrasing, and then extends to the sequential *Mexico City Blues* with connecting tissue between each chorus not necessarily evident on first read.

In *Mexico City Blues*, Kerouac's choruses, constructed in the space of a notebook page, offer memory-laden portraits of everything from his parents and his hometown of Lowell, Massachusetts, to his friends Gregory Corso and Allen Ginsberg; his explorations of Buddhist concepts; and recordings of apparently throwaway images, and more – the panoply of his existence. The book's composition came at the time of his experimentation with spontaneity, connected to his idea of documenting unrevised thought – or, in other words, his "mind." As Michael McClure observed, "He was writing voices he had overheard into the bodies of the choruses and he was writing the structure of his passing thoughts."[16] Thus the concept of "true-life" as is often applied to Kerouac's prose fiction extends as well to his poetry, which also fits into his idea of his work as comprising "One Vast Book," the Duluoz Legend. Indeed, in a handwritten note on a manuscript page of "Daydreams for Ginsberg," (dated February 10, 1955), he called his vast book "The Divine Comedy of the Buddha": "I am beginning to see a vast Divine Comedy of my own based on Buddha—on a dream I had that people are racing up and down the Buddha Mountain, is all, and inside is the Cave of Reality."[17]

Evoking Dante's epic work is hardly casual, but rather reflective of the larger conception, the poetic structure, of both his poetry and prose, a cathedral that is also satirical of the worldly realm and housing a quest for Beatitude. Dante's *Divine Comedy* provides a grand design that may serve as a scaffolding for a view of Kerouac as poet. A profoundly religious poem, the *Divine Comedy* was structurally unified via an interlocking rhyme scheme, *terza rima*, which was – to use a modern term – sequential.

Thinking of his entire opus taken together, Kerouac likewise imagined disparate elements fitting into a whole – his novels and poems hang together like jazz riffs insofar as he breaks down traditional language, phrasing with no end stop, no periods, just dashes indicating breath pauses. Paragraphs or units flow in rhythms of breath, words alliterating, sounds connected through assonance. Units of writing spiral, featuring his signature oscillating tropes of immense sadness juxtaposed with great joy, often in the same image.

12.1 The Bones of *Mexico City Blues*

In Kerouac's poetic masterpiece, *Mexico City Blues*, a sequential poem nodding not only to Dante but also evoking both Walt Whitman and Ezra Pound's *Cantos*, the substance and subject is memory and language, an uncensored portrait of the poet's mind moving. McClure says that in the early 1950s, when Kerouac was writing *Mexico City Blues*, he had just studied and been impressed by Pound's *Cantos* and wanted to emulate the experience and create his own "equivalent work."[18] The very rules of the chorus' composition, rooted in spontaneous thought, make the biographical component explicit in image and texture.

For example, the 89th chorus serves as an origin myth:

> Remembering my birth in infancy, the coughs,
> The swallows, the tear-trees growing
> From your eyeballs of shame; the gray
> Immense morning I was conceived i [*sic*] the womb,
> And the red gory afternoon delivered therefrom.[19]

The imagery of "tear-trees," "eyeballs of shame," "gray immense morning," "red gory afternoon" may reference Catholicism and the inherent shame of sex, preceding conception, all tempering the usual joyful aspects of birth, providing a murky "gray" tone to the images of being alive: the "coughs, the swallows" of "my birth in infancy." As in much of *Mexico City Blues*, there is a preoccupation both with life, living, and its inevitable inverse, death.

On this point, consider Chorus #211, in which Kerouac sings his blues in a dark revision of God's creation:

> The wheel of the quivering meat conception
> Turns in the void expelling human beings,
> Pigs, turtles, frogs, insects, nits,
> Mice, lice, lizards, rats, roan
> Racinghorses, poxy bucolic pigtics,
> Horrible unnamable lice of vultures,
> Murderous attacking dog-armies
> Of Africa, Rhinos roaming in the jungle,
> Vast boars and huge gigantic bull
> Elephants, rams, eagles, condors,
> Pones and Porcupines and Pills—
> All the endless conception of living beings
> Gnashing everywhere in Consciousness
> Throughout the ten directions of space
> Occupying all the quarters of in & out,
> From supermicroscopic no-bug
> To huge Galaxy Lightyear Bowell

Illuminating the sky of one Mind—
Poor! I wish I was free
of that slaving meat wheel
and safe in heaven dead. (*Mexico City Blues*, 211)

This poem illustrates Kerouac's studies of Buddhism during this period with the controlling image of the Wheel of Life and phrases like "all … living beings" and "the ten directions of space," the latter of which alludes to Buddhist cosmology.[20] But there is also the infusion of Christian conceptions of suffering (as in the word "Gnashing," echoing the Biblical phrase "gnashing of teeth," which appears several times throughout the New Testament). Kerouac places himself in a kind of fusion of Buddhist and Christian cosmologies, so that he wishes he "was free" of Buddhist Samsara, the "slaving meat wheel," not by achieving nirvana, but by being "safe in heaven," which seems a squarely Christian wish.

Death is of course a major Kerouacean preoccupation, and attention to the "Mind" is a way of freeing up the soul from the exigencies of the flesh, consciousness remaining alive in all its components. Chorus #176 is an especially important exploration and illustration of Kerouac's conception of the mind:

The reason why there are so many things
Is because the mind breaks it up,
The shapes are empty
That sprung into come
But the mind wont know this
Till a Buddha with golden
Lighted finger, hath pointed
  To the thumb, & made an aphorism
  In a robe on the street,
  That you'll know what it means
  For there to be too many things
  In a world of no-thing.

    One no-thing
    Equals
    All things

When sad sick women
Sing their sex blues
In yr ear, have no fear—
  have no fear—
the moon is true, enough,
but, but, but, but, but,
it keeps adding up. (*Mexico City Blues*, 176)

This chorus explains "Mind" as a shapely grab-bag of consciousness and energy. Kerouac's perception in this chorus, informed by Buddhist thought and language, gives him a way of rearticulating the oscillating tropes in *On the Road*; as Sal Paradise says in that book: "Everything seemed to be collapsing."[21] In Chorus #176, as in much of *Mexico City Blues*, the solidity of, say, red brick against the illusion of neon imagined in *On the Road*, the solidity of Western values and institutions, are in fact coming apart in time. As Kerouac illustrates in this chorus, Buddhism teaches us that the mind forms arbitrary discriminations, that the "shapes are empty" because they contain no meaning.[22]

Insofar as the choruses in *Mexico City Blues* offer snapshots of Kerouac's mind, they are of a piece with another poetic form that he came to master: haiku. Indeed, when he was praising the "epic-length" *Mexico City Blues*, McClure also took care to draw attention to the book's smaller components, arguing that "each line becomes a complete, and whole, independent image."[23] Such a description sounds like the basis for haiku, and as Kerouac discovered, this form offered him a more concise poetic structure for articulating how his mind moved – and along the way, he would reinvent haiku in an American image.

12.2 Inventing American Haiku

The little worm
  Lowers itself from the roof
By a self shat thread

"Worm" was not part of a collection of haiku Kerouac put together in a black folder to be published by Lawrence Ferlinghetti at City Lights, but as mentioned above, he did record it in a 1959 album with Al Cohn's and Zoot Sims' jazzy backup. Hundreds more haiku, embedded in blocks of prose, in his pocket notebooks, in letters, and other unpublished writings awaited me when I was asked to edit his *Book of Haikus*. I mined these writings for three days at the turn of the millennium in Kerouac executor John Sampas' cat-filled sitting room in Lowell, Massachusetts. Most challenging were the pocket notebooks themselves, covered with Kerouac's distinct tiny scrawl in pencil, the paper now aged, translucent, making it harder to discern his words in the shadows and silhouettes of others on the flip side of the page. Composed from 1956 to 1966, rather than a sideshow to his already infamous career, these haiku are a substantial addition to it, an important facet of his dynamic art.

Although the positive reception was hardly uniform, when *Book of Haikus* appeared, some observers noted Kerouac's innovations. Writing in the *New York Times*, for instance, Verlyn Klinkenborg offered an appreciation:

> To read these poems is to hear how raucously Kerouac reinvents the genre. Haiku is a poetry of exclusion. Just think, after all, of everything that can't be said in three short lines. And yet Kerouac turns his pops into strange miracles of inclusion.... His haiku remain fundamentally American. "The windmills / of Oklahoma look / in every direction."[24]

Likewise, writing for a specialty journal, *Modern Haiku*, Cor van den Heuvel, declared that, "If we judge him by the poems he chose for his original "Book of Haikus," we find enough outstanding haiku to place Kerouac not only among the pioneers of American haiku, but to give him an honored place as the creator of some of the best American haiku to have been written in the first half-century of its existence."[25]

During his lifetime, Kerouac may have been criticized for his ragged ungrammatical prose style, but now he is slowly being appreciated for his haiku practice, for which I believe he should be considered a master poet. He eschewed the seventeen-syllable rule. Kerouac understood, after studying the Japanese masters of the form – Basho, Issa, Shiki, and Buson – that this rule was untenable in English. He studied the form under Gary Snyder's expert tutelage, and reading D. T. Suzuki, he made a discovery, actually more of a declaration: in English, haiku required fewer syllables. "I'll invent / The American Haiku type," he wrote, "The simple rhyming triolet:-- / Seventeen syllables? No, ... / Simple, 3-line poems."[26]

Kerouac labored over crafting his haiku, as he told his *Paris Review* interviewers, unlike his "first thought, best thought" prose policies. Kerouac made a key distinction, in explaining his poetic practices to *The Paris Review*, that his methods for writing regular verse were quite different for the crafting of haiku, and quite different from his Japanese models. Haiku practice was, for Kerouac, much more than a syllable count. Observing nature and human nature, infusing his highly honed visions, his discipline incorporated the complexity and panorama of his sweeping bop prosody with a new kind of depth. Looking for ways to express eternity in language, haiku gave him a tool, for poetry and for prose. He was going for haiku spirit, the expression of life to death, all of it in a single "pop":

> Evening coming—
> The office girl
> Unloosing her scarf (*Book of Haikus*, 32)

The office girl in this senryu, a form of haiku focused on human nature, is you and me in the continuous repetition, all those "-ings" of eternal human activity. How many times in a single lifetime, Kerouac asks without stating it directly, is the same action, any action, any routine repeated?

Kerouac practiced well enough that he had fun with key haiku principles, such as the mandate to reference the seasons:

In my medicine cabinet
the winter fly
Has died of old age (*Book of Haikus*, 12)

The summer chair
rocking by itself
In the blizzard (*Book of Haikus*, 36)

So that winter fly has died in his medicine cabinet, but in what season? What is a summer chair doing rocking by itself in a winter blizzard?

Kerouac certainly practiced well enough to break the Japanese masters' rules, mocking Basho and his most famous haiku:

An old pond:
a frog jumps in
—the sound of water.[27]

Here is Kerouac's response:

Run over by my lawnmower,
waiting for me to leave,
The frog (*Book of Haikus*, 33)

Kerouac was not always known for laughs, but he was amusing in haiku, especially to himself. Here is an inside joke, as he wants to know what Basho would make of his running over a frog with his lawnmower!

Kerouac further recognized the "cut" of haiku as liberating for language – a "jump" he dubbed what others call the "cut," two images set side by side that make a flash in the mind – similar to eliding time, or to the juxtapositions of William S. Burroughs's cutups.[28] To illustrate how a Kerouac haiku reads, note the following poem:

Straining at the padlock,
the garage doors
At noon (*Book of Haikus*, 9)

The jump occurs between the first two lines with the juxtaposing images of "the padlock" with "the garage doors." Visually, Kerouac focuses on one part of the overall picture and then cuts to the larger image, perhaps framing the padlock. As haiku reference the seasons, the last line suggests summer, the padlock "straining" when the heat is most intense.[29]

While Kerouac understood haiku form from his studies of the Japanese translations, his development of the American haiku allowed for the signature Kerouacean tropes, infused with Western thought; for example, Catholicism, the preoccupation of the non-Buddhist world he knew best. Indeed, one thing Kerouac contributed to haiku was Catholicism, the preoccupations of the non-Buddhist world he knew best. Struggle. Drama. Suffering. Guilt. Martyrdom. Death. In his more Catholic moods, Kerouac gave haiku the anguish it needed least:

> Useless! useless!
> —heavy rain driving
> Into the sea (*Book of Haikus*, 8)

This haiku expresses more than the simple description of the driving rain, judging its action useless, even repeating the word for emphasis, and for the sound of it. Unlike his Japanese forebears in the craft, he allows for this particular kind of subjectivity: his anguish reflected in the pointlessness or futility of rain driving into the sea. He used haiku to illustrate a pervasive Kerouacean type: a sole, fragile individual in a harsh expanse or Void:

> One flower
> on the cliffside
> Nodding at the canyon (*Book of Haikus*, 167)

Here is one flower, much like Kerouac himself, facing the Void. Or perhaps a sometimes hostile literary atmosphere; the next poem in *Book of Haikus* is:

> A long way from
> The Beat Generation
> In the rain forest (*Book of Haikus*, 167)

As a haiku poet, the designation of "literary outsider" is particularly apt, as many Westerners regard haiku as a kind of trivial gimmick poem on the order of limericks. Kerouac was dubbed the King of the Beats – or, worse, "King of the Beatniks" (see Chapter 9) – and to some he wears another crown as King of American Haiku. Like the King of the Beats, that title hardly acknowledges Kerouac's exceptional and original contribution to American letters.

In his novel *Big Sur*, Kerouac's narrator Jack Duluoz converses with an experimental poet, Pat McLear (based on Michael McClure), who says: "When I read your poems Mexico City Blues I immediately turned around and started writing a brand new way, you enlightened me with that book." Duluoz replies: "But it's nothing like what you do, in fact it's miles away, I am a language spinner and you're an idea man" (*Big Sur*, 123–124). Kerouac's idea of himself as a "language spinner" goes far to explain both his prose and poetry, spinning filament: "The little worm / Lowers itself from the roof / By a self shat thread." The worm like Kerouac is a spinner, descended from another spinner, Walt Whitman's "Noiseless Patient Spider," who spreads filament over expanses of space, connecting. Far from a "literary outsider," Kerouac as poet goes back to the grand tradition of American letters, to Whitman's sequential epic, *Song of Myself.* It's the mainline American thread.

Notes

1. Allen Ginsberg, "Introduction," in Jack Kerouac, *Pomes All Sizes* (San Francisco: City Lights, 1992), ii.
2. Gary Snyder quoted in Ginsberg, "Introduction," iii.
3. Michael McClure, *Scratching the Beat Surface* (San Francisco: Northpoint Press, 1982), 75.
4. Kenneth Rexroth, "Discordant and Cool," *New York Times* (November 29, 1959).
5. See Barry Gifford and Lawrence Lee, *Jack's Book: An Oral Biography of Jack Kerouac* (New York: St. Martin's Press, 1978), 222.
6. Herbert Feinstein, "A Free Poet?" *Prairie Schooner* 34. 2 (Summer 1960), 100–101.
7. Anthony Hecht, "The Agony of the Spirit and the Letter," *The Hudson Review* 12. 4 (Winter, 1959–1960), 593–603.
8. Morris Dickstein, *Gates of Eden: American Culture in the Sixties* (New York: Basic Books, 1977), 12. This study goes far to show how serious critics were hostile to both *Howl* and *On the Road* and excluded beat poetry altogether from the anthology *New Poets of England and America* (1957).
9. Seymour Krim, "The Kerouac Legacy," *Shake It for the World, Smartass* (New York: Dial, 1970), 195. This essay was first published as the Introduction to Kerouac's *Desolation Angels* (New York: Putnam's, 1965), ix–xxviii.
10. A newer generation of Kerouac critics more ably assess his achievement as poet and writer of poetic prose. See, for example, James T. Jones, *A Map of Mexico City Blues: Jack Kerouac as Poet* (Carbondale: Southern Illinois University Press, 1992).
11. Ginsberg, "Introduction," i.
12. Allen Ginsberg, "The Visions of the Great Remember," in Jack Kerouac, *Visions of Cody* (New York: Penguin, 1972), 404.
13. Jack Kerouac, *Big Sur* (New York: Bantam, 1963), 182.
14. Kerouac's work in his native French opens up new avenues for discovering his poetic output. The French-Canadian cadences of poems like "On Waking from a Dream of Robert Fournier," composed in the mid-1950s in both French and English, about a real-life person from Lowell, the father of one of his childhood friends, suggest further possibilities. First published in *City Lights Journal* in 1978, and later in *Pomes All Sizes* (1993), the poem illustrates

Kerouac's ability to compose in French, and his talents as a translator, recomposing in English. Lawrence Ferlinghetti brought the manuscript of this City Lights publication to Québec City, to the Rencontre Internationale Jack Kerouac conference in 1987, so that he could hear it read in proper language.

15. Ted Berrigan, "The Art of Fiction LXI: Jack Kerouac," *The Paris Review*. 43 (Summer 1968), reprinted in *Conversations with Jack Kerouac,* ed. Kevin J. Hayes (Jackson: University Press of Mississippi, 2005), 56.
16. McClure, *Scratching*, 72.
17. Jack Kerouac, "Daydreams for Ginsberg," (February 10, 1955); Allen Ginsberg Papers; box 19, folder 20; Rare Book and Manuscript Library, Columbia University Library.
18. McClure, *Scratching*, 72.
19. Jack Kerouac, *Mexico City Blues* (New York: Grove, 1959), 89.
20. See, for example: www.nichirenlibrary.org/en/dic/Content/T/45.
21. Jack Kerouac, *On the Road* (1957. New York: Penguin, 1991), 56.
22. For more on this point, see Regina Weinreich, *Kerouac's Poetics: A Study of the Fiction* (Carbondale: Southern Illinois University Press, 1983).
23. McClure, *Scratching*, 71.
24. Verlyn Klinkenborg, "Appreciations: Jack Kerouac's Haiku," *New York Times* (April 13, 2003), section 4, 12.
25. Cor van den Heuvel, review of *Book of Haikus*, *Modern Haiku* 43:2 (Summer 2003). modernhaiku.org/bookreviews/Kerouac2003.html.
26. Kerouac quoted in Regina Weinreich, "Introduction: The Haiku Poetics of Jack Kerouac," in Kerouac, *Book of Haikus* (New York: Penguin, 2003), ix. For a more detailed discussion of Kerouac's thoughts on haiku craft, see my introduction to *Book of Haikus*.
27. This poem has been translated countless ways into English; this version comes from Hiroaki Sato, *One Hundred Frogs: From Renga to Haiku to English* (New York: Weatherhill, 1983), 149, but note that Sato includes over a hundred translations and versions of this poem by later poets (including Allen Ginsberg [164] and Kenneth Rexroth [155], but not Kerouac).
28. See my introduction to Kerouac's *Book of Haikus*.
29. Kerouac had selected this haiku for publication; a prior version from a notebook indicated that he originally had the last line read, "At noon in May." Understanding haiku's concision, he edited to allow for fewer syllables.

CHAPTER 13

Kerouac's Representations of Women

Ronna C. Johnson

Appraising Jack Kerouac's literary representations of women – or "girls," as he often designated them – in the twenty-first century is complicated. His sweeping oeuvre encompasses novels, short stories, poetry, and non-traditional and experimental genres including science fiction; almost all delineate, display, feature, women, a panopticon of human textual portrayals. Recent critical attention to his depictions of postwar life, however, show that these portrayals of women, white and of color, are problematic for some readers.[1] The work is read variously as savory or offensive depending on the perspective taken and the values brought to it, vacillating from literary appreciations to feminist dismay. As a premier innovator of the famously misogynistic Beat Generation literary movement, Kerouac is a master whose work, on one hand, expresses a muscular patriarchal attitude, but, on the other, a tender iconoclasm that resists and revises that perspective with voluptuous descriptions and spontaneous tellings. Assessing delineations of the female and the feminine in male-authored literary and visual art is hardly novel, given the persistence of late mid-twentieth-century feminist attentions to representation.[2] However, Kerouac's work, contradictory and inconsistent, is especially challenging. It is both more innovative – artistically experimental – and more atavistic – conventionally patriarchal – than his Beat Generation repute indicates. His writing may be more controversial now than it was in the 1950s, since while the literature remains unchanged, its reception faces shifting perspectives. Kerouac's representations of women were early overlooked or dismissed, or celebrated and glamorized, but nearly seventy years after the publication in 1957 of *On the Road*, those same figures raise objection, resentment, repudiation on the verge of cancellation, particularly among recent literary consumers, culture commentators, and academic critics aligned with second-wave feminism and Generation Z sensitivities. Kerouac's works stay in print and sustain a mythic status in popular culture, but his reception and assessment founder on the more discerning, and adverse, views of his depictions of women, as well as those of racial minorities. So, how do we read him today in light of these manifold reservations?

Kerouac's controversial representations of women are disconcerting in so admired a writer, for, though they are mesmerizing literature, they are, just so, sexist, misogynist, essentialist, racist. The two assessments remain in unresolvable opposition. Women in Kerouac's works, even at their most indelible and dramatic, are, as the Beat writer Joyce Johnson termed them, "minor characters"; they catalyze or support action, struggle for recognition, then disappear from the story.[3] Even when the female characters are presumptive protagonists, as in *Maggie Cassidy* or *Tristessa* or "Good Blonde," they are still not much more than objects of narrative delectation or vehicles for emotional expression. As film theorist Laura Mulvey observes of traditional cinematic narratives, woman "stands in patriarchal culture as a signifier for the male other … [who] can live out his fantasies and obsessions by imposing them on the silent image of woman still tied to her place as bearer, not maker, of meaning."[4] Women in Kerouac's works carry others' but not their own meanings. And while individually distinctive, women in Kerouac ultimately become indistinguishable; they are always in the rooms, the clubs, the bars, the fields, the homes, the body of the world itself, themselves the othered bodies of the writer's vision and visions. They comprise an international, cross- and multi-cultural, multilingual caste of humans transversing classes, races, and ethnicities, religions and belief practices; they are a generic population. In contrast, male characters in Kerouac, such as Dean Moriarty or Sal Paradise or Carlo Marx, are distinct and unlike each other: identifiable individuals, they are not types.

Race, class, and ethnicity are intersectional in gender identity formation and materially affect representations of women and "girls" in Kerouac. Tropes and stereotypes, they form a class of sexually accessible and sometimes "mad" females that signify the work's Beat Generation entitlements. In his 1959 essay "The Origins of the Beat Generation" Kerouac observed a postwar "revival" of "wild self-believing individuality" that, waning "around the end of World War II with so many great guys dead," was now channeled into a "certain new gesture, or attitude … a new *more*" embodied by "hipsters … glid[ing] around saying 'Crazy, man.'"[5] However, this resurgence of American esprit, this "revolution in manners" ("The Origins of the Beat Generation," 363), did not extend to women; the "cool" hipster "girls" "say nothing and wear black" ("The Origins of the Beat Generation," 362), neither expressing nor advancing the "new *more*" in their supporting roles.[6] As Mulvey notes, "[i]n a world ordered by sexual imbalance, pleasure in looking has been split between active/male and passive/female."[7] Kerouac's iconoclasm is contradicted and challenged by this existential divergence between the sexes; unlike the riotous male figures of his stories who embody the radical enfranchisement of anti-establishment subjectivity, female characters, subordinated or passively figured in narrative, are often types rendered as objects of "[t]he determining male gaze [that] projects its fantasy onto the female figure, which is styled accordingly" (Mulvey 19). Kerouac's female characters rebuke the hipsters' radical enfranchisement, the "new bohemianism of the Beats," as in Galatea Dunkel's chastisement of Dean Moriarty in *On the Road*, "You have absolutely no regard for anybody but yourself and your damned kicks. All you think about is what's hanging between your legs."[8] Kerouac writes this irate dismissal, but his iconoclasm – in content and formal modes – is conditional, excluding women as subjects from postwar bohemian freedoms while exploiting women as objects to construct those freedoms as in Galatea's put down. We now have a retrospective opportunity to revise assessments of Kerouac's representations of women, and there is much to reconsider. Kerouac is a brilliant mid-twentieth-century literary originator of undimmed impact that derives, in part, from his works' intriguing contradictory embrace and reversal of radical (non)conformity, specifically here on the stage of sexual politics.

Kerouac's representations of women date to the mid-twentieth century, the zenith of his literary output. Entangled in Kerouac's road, women in his works are themselves paradoxically usually not mobile and mostly found sheltered in place in urban and rural areas; mountain towns and agriculture fields and migrant camps; northeastern, west coast, western, middle western, and southwestern US states; Mexico and the borderlands – a panoply of the Americas. These representations are drawn from heart's preserves, memory, dreams, and field notebooks in which Kerouac recorded events daily on the road and in domesticity, the stasis that women in his stories – and in canonical US male-authored literature more broadly – virtually denote.[9] The diversity of their contexts serves Kerouac's literary experimentalism, its restless search for a geographic or spiritual end, or an end that is literally a book (*On the Road*, *The Subterraneans*). Female characters map a body politic, a territory of the desired and the desirable who demarcate the road and its motivations. *On the Road*'s iconic credo – "along the line … there'd be girls, visions, everything" (*On the Road*, 11) – is both fulfilled and contradicted by women as goal of movement and its *telos* or ending, as in the way Dean Moriarty's soul is said to be "wrapped up in a fast car, a coast to reach, and a woman at the end of the road" (*On the*

Road, 230) – a woman waiting where movement stops.[10] The literature's material depictions of women and their narrative uses constitute a poetics of the feminine, a discourse that serves Kerouac's literary composition.

Women abound in the human panopticon of *On the Road*; the roster of American and Mexican beauties is long and visually repetitive. Here is a partial survey of the objectified figures who occur in the narrative as signs of rising male desire liberated by the road's avoidance of domestic social obligation. This list collects typical depictions of the descriptive process by which females are tropified in Kerouac – that is, employed in a way not consonant with usual usage, as when "blonde" signifies for other than hair.

Marylou is a "beautiful little sharp chick … a pretty blonde with immense ringlets of hair like a sea of golden tresses … a longbodied emaciated Modigliani surrealist woman in a serious room. But, outside of being a sweet little girl, she was awfully dumb and capable of doing horrible things …. – 'the whore!'" (*On the Road*, 5,6) – the "dumb little box" (*On the Road*, 184); a waitress is "Mexican and beautiful" (*On the Road*, 34); "a pretty young blonde … [is] dumb and sullen" with a "curl of her lips" (*On the Road*, 34–35); Babe Rawlins is a "beautiful blonde … tennis-playing, surf-riding doll of the West" (*On the Road*, 41); Camille is a "brunette on the bed, one beautiful creamy thigh covered with black lace" (*On the Road*, 43); Rita Bettencourt is "a nice little girl, simple and true, and tremendously frightened of sex" (*On the Road*, 57); Lee Ann is a "fetching hunk, a honey-colored creature, … [with] … hate in her eyes" (*On the Road*, 62); Terry is "the cutest little Mexican girl in slacks … Her breasts stuck out straight and true; her little flanks looked delicious; her hair was long and lustrous black; and her eyes were great big blue things" (*On the Road*, 81); "a pretty little blonde [is] called Dorothy … [whose] nose was too long" (*On the Road*, 191); a "furious" Galatea Dunkel "looked like the daughter of the Greeks … her long hair streaming" (*On the Road*, 192); thirteen-year-old Janet is "the prettiest girl in the world … about to grow into a gone woman" (*On the Road*, 218); a sixteen-year-old farmer's daughter is "absolutely and finally the most beautiful girl Dean and I ever saw … Plains complexion like wild roses, and the bluest eyes, the most lovely hair, and the modesty and quickness of a wild antelope. At every look from us she flinched … and blushed" (*On the Road*, 226–227); Walter's African American wife is "a *real* woman"; she "smiled and smiled as we repeated the insane thing all over again. She never said a word" (*On the Road*, 203; italics in original); there's a "gorgeous country girl wearing a low-cut cotton blouse that displayed the beautiful sun-tan on her breast tops" (*On the Road*, 242); a prostitute, "only eighteen … [of] tender cheek and fair aspect," while another, fifteen, has "almond colored skin and a dress that was buttoned … halfway down," while a third is a "little dark girl … a queen … [a] dusky darling" (*On the Road*, 287–291); and Laura, Sal's final love in *On the Road*, is "a pretty girl … with the pure and innocent dear eyes that I had always searched for and for so long. We agreed to love each other madly" (*On the Road*, 306).[11]

Halting narrative movement, "girls" galvanize male desire, which is whetted by being on the road; they are essential to *On the Road*'s narrative continuity and momentum even as they impede and obstruct it, the gendered double bind of desire in Kerouac. They are all beautiful, young, barely known, otherwise there's no point in putting up with their disruptions of the road's homosociality and narrative momentum. Sal "rued the way I had broken up the purity of my entire trip, not saving every dime, and dawdling and not really making time, fooling around with this sullen girl and spending all my money" (*On the Road*, 35). Women violate the sacramental road, the radical enfranchisement of the hipster, and their claims deflate pleasure.

These obsessed-upon and ubiquitous women in just one Kerouac novel, *On the Road*, are the "second sex" Simone de Beauvoir described in her 1949 classic feminist testamentary. Beauvoir's critical history and theoretical analysis of "the second sex" arrived in and derived from precisely the same western mid-twentieth-century postwar moment of Kerouac's literary visions of women. In Beauvoir's famous maxim, "One is not born, but rather becomes, woman," just as writers "make" or write females in narrative.[12] While there is a certain homogeneity to representations of women in *On the Road* in their superficial sameness of mien even across race and class lines, as the medley of "beauties" above suggests, individual works after that sprawling linear road tale provide more focused contexts to review and assess heterogeneous representations of women in Kerouac's oeuvre, his own canon of women and "girls."

Kerouac composed *Visions of Cody*, widely regarded as his masterpiece, in 1952, right after the 1951 scroll manuscript of *On the Road*, but it was not published in full until 1972, after his death in 1969. Although Kerouac prepared the book for publication – and it was published exactly as he had prepared it – he feared it might trigger an obscenity trial, not least for its exposed and frank depictions of women's bodies and male sexual desire. One lengthy passage set in Times Square, New York, depicts Duluoz and Cody gazing at a black and white photograph of Ruth Maytime, "famous Hollywood actress," and Ella Wynn simulating striptease; both are white women posed for shared male delectation – and masturbation: "Cody used to say 'Have this picture, I've used it.'"[13] The description of this photograph occupying two dense pages is rendered in a granular and voluptuous narration, no detail too minor to omit:

> – what tremendous lovely tits Ruth has, one shoulder strap of her suit is down, the other is flimsy, they reach very low because her breasts are low, heavy and way out thus stretching strap even further ... – her left breast occupies me for five nameless unconscious minutes on the sidewalk of Times Square and not her breast, just a pix of it, it is so vast, heavy, three-fifths concealed which is better than any other percentage, the nipple is in no danger of showing, what's in danger is the point at which the soft yearning bulge might plop up, almost out – Ella's is conventionally concealed, you can see the rich delicious soft living valley and then the bulge of the cloth following the holy contours we all know – but Ruth's is as if Ella was a stripteaser who started the act and Ruth went next step – (*Visions of Cody*, 76)

The passage proceeds graphically and more assiduously with every further detail, body parts cited as sources of narrative revelation: "the exact nipple will tell us more than Ruth's entire life story" (*Visions of Cody*, 76). Beauvoir's dispute with patriarchy's essentializing of woman and her correction that cultural forces and systems of patriarchy and capitalism create woman are exemplified by the neoromanticism of this passage, the unconventionality of Kerouac's unedited and uncensored composition mode, Spontaneous Prose. It has a poetics, a narrative method of telling by tantalizing slo-mo focus on the females' bodies. This is Kerouac's literary resistance to patriarchal encomiums or self-silencing editing, a circumvention of the genre Millett termed "misogynist literature,"[14] by an appreciative detailing of the female body, however gritty. In *Visions of Cody* women's representations range from in the home to fields of miscarriage remains to brothel to Bible to altar, and here, to the "adult" magazine precincts of Times Square.

Every instance of Kerouac's depictions of women, Joyce Johnson's "minor characters" of Beat bohemia, is a projection of the writer's import, not an instrument of independent meaning that the depiction serves. *Lonesome Traveler*, published in 1960, provides female "objects" for narrative account, one mininarrative set in Mexico and the other in Southern California.[15] The two images of Mexican females – one a child, the other a teenager – are cameos of innocence and sexuality, respectively. In the story "Mexico Fellaheen" (*Lonesome*, 21–36) Kerouac's portrayal of a little girl is at its most sincere and unexploitative, but at the same time, born of a categorical racism. He defines "fellaheen," a trope taken from his Burroughs-guided study of Oswald Spengler, as embodying a "fellaheen feeling about life, that timeless gayety of people not involved in great cultural and civilization issues" (*Lonesome*, 22).[16] That tautological definition notwithstanding, Kerouac, who is explicitly the narrator of these stories, celebrates the world's poor and powerless, more visible "the further you go away from the [US/Mexico] border … as though the influence of civilizations hung over the border like a cloud" (*Lonesome*, 22); he believes that the nonwhite, non-Anglo fellaheen are laudably *un*civilized. And so their living is a pure experience of sentiment and performance. Kerouac recounts that in the "little church near Redondas in Mexico City" (*Lonesome*, 33), "I see a little tiny girl one foot or and-a-half high, two years old, or one-and-a-half, waddling tinily lowly" between her brothers who are holding "a shawl over her head, [and] … under the canopy marched Princessa Sweetheart examining the church with her big brown eyes, her little heels clacking" (*Lonesome*, 36). This charming image mixes with worldly elements. The "clack of heels" sound pulls Kerouac out of his reverie; surely it is the sound of civilization that the tiny girl performs, her body a percussive motor of walking shoes. This little girl is innocence personified, uncompromised by Kerouacian sexism although darkened by the racism ascribed to fellaheen indigeneity. A set piece about a young Mexican woman in a small section of "The Railroad Earth" also published in *Lonesome Traveler* is of another order of depiction. In "The Railroad Earth," Kerouac announces "Now it's 1952 October" (*Lonesome*, 65); he imagines

> beautiful little Carmelita O' Jose will be gomezing along the road with her brown breasts inside cashmere sweater bouncing ever so slightly even with maidenform bra … and her dark eyes with pools in em of you wonder what mad meaning … soft neck like swan, little voice, little femininity and doesn't know it – her little voice is little-tinkled. (*Lonesome*, 78–79)

Here is the fantasy of "little" innocence, a young brown woman with a neck like a swan – a young brown woman whitened by comparison to a swan – and, for Kerouac, a young brown woman unaware of her body's presence and effect. The perfect tabula rasa for the narrator's projections, the young woman is the bearer of his meanings but not the maker of hers, as in Mulvey's lexicon. The innocence of that depiction is dispelled by an erotic fantasy of sex with her and, failing that, "watching" Jose have sex with her. Carmelita becomes her private body:

> the brown knees of Carmelity, the dark spltot between her thighs where creation hides its majesty and all the boys … want the whole the hole the works the hair the seekme membrane the lovey sucky ducky workjohn … he presses her little behind down … lunging her downthru and into the

> portals of her sweetness … and she softly pants with parted brownly lips and with little pear teeth showing and sticking out just far and just so gently almost biting, burning in the burn of his own, lips – he drives and thrives to pound (*Lonesome*, 79).

Kerouac finishes his narration with "out there Carmelity is coming, Jose is making her electricities mix and interrun with his and the whole earth charged with juices" (*Lonesome*, 83), and with this evocation of the earth's electrification by Carmelita and Jose's intimacies, "The Railroad Earth," one of Kerouac's most stylistically accomplished narratives, ends. The rhythm and rhyming riff of "whole"/ "hole" and the portmanteau words "seekme," and "workjohn" leading to the "biting" "burning" lips charges the kisses of intercourse with sensuality; this poetry of desire conveys an appeal that repudiates its potential misogyny.

In the next year, 1953, Kerouac wrote *Maggie Cassidy*, a short novel about teenage romance set in Lowell, Massachusetts, and its environs. The protagonist Jackie Duluoz is a high school athlete who earns a football scholarship to a New York prep school. His love story for Maggie begins in "the New Year 1939, before the war, before anyone knew the intention of the world toward America."[17] *Maggie Cassidy* presents another young woman as the object of the "determining male gaze" of the enraptured narrator Duluoz "project[ing] its fantasy onto the female figure, which is styled accordingly"[18]; as he wants to see her. Unlike Carmelita, whom Kerouac never actually looks at as he invents her, Maggie and Duluoz directly interact; the two are in fantasy teenage love and lust, with Maggie, an Irish American flirt often playing hard to get. She is one year older than Jackie who is too young to know what to do with his desire for her. He wants to "eat her, bring her home, hide her in the heart of my life the rest of my days" (*Maggie Cassidy*, 38), but his passion for her stymies him: "we'd hold a kiss for 35 minutes until the muscles of our lips would get cramps and it was painful to go on" (*Maggie Cassidy*, 37). No objectifying eroticism here, but several nearly chaste and painful clinches; this love hurts so good. Maggie is white, not whitened by metaphor and fantasy; she is a destination of whiteness itself, for "in her neck I hid myself like a lost snow goose of Australia" (*Maggie Cassidy*, 38). White, virginal, pure but naughty Maggie whose body "just ripened, the flesh bulged and was firm," is inaccessible, while her face is available for delectation:

> her mouth pouted soft, rich, red, her black curls adorned sometimes the snow-smooth brow; up from her lips came rosy auras hinting all her health and merriness, seventeen years old … her chin had a little doublechin of

> beauty ... that unnamed dimple chin, to perfection, and Spanish – her lip curled, slightly parted teeth charmed and enhanced sensuous, drowning lips, devourous lips. (*Maggie Cassidy*, 28–29).

Overcome by lust Jackie supposes that her last name "in its time must have been Casa d'Oro – sweet, dark, rich as peaches" (*Maggie Cassidy*, 28). A nearly divine foodstuff, she is the pure gold piece of Sylvia Plath's rage poem "Lady Lazarus,"[19] but in this narrative, Duluoz styles Maggie the unattained beauty, her facial features lingeringly enumerated as in a blazon poem cataloguing the physical attributes of the beloved, not erotic but not sexually indifferent. Duluoz styles Maggie, her visage feels "like drowning in a witches' brew, Keltic, sorcerous, starlike" (*Maggie Cassidy*, 29), with words invented for his desire. But in their later reunion, she resists his conquest with an impenetrable girdle, her flesh prevented from taking its free shape even as Jackie's words take limitless linguistic freedoms in this ethereal tribute to the enchantress of his adolescence.

Kerouac wrote *The Subterraneans* also in 1953, a story of bohemia set in San Francisco, not the New York of its autobiographical origins. This brilliant masterpiece of spontaneous prose narrated by writer Leo Percepied, the "hot" Beat Generation artist, is also deeply offensive regarding gender and race. "[C]rudely malely sexual and cannot help myself and have lecherous and so on propensities,"[20] Leo desires Mardou Fox, the mixed-race female hipster or "girl"– a coveted, fetishized human prize. He cannot manage the competition she poses to his writing life and arranges for her to betray him with a poet-rival, *The Subterraneans* ending with Leo choosing writing: "And I go home, having lost her love. And write this book" (*The Subterraneans*, 152). Its misogyny and racism mar the book, which is also, dismayingly, the purest instance of spontaneous prose Kerouac would publish. It is so exceptional that he wrote "Essentials of Spontaneous Prose," his manifesto of composition, in 1953 at the request of Ginsberg and Burroughs who'd asked how he'd composed this impressive hipster novel. The manifesto and the novel are inextricable, as its jarring woman-hatred and race fears are inextricable. Which is one way "wild self-believing individuality" played out in Kerouac's representations of women, with his vaunted high avant-garde art passages built on what can only be termed misogyny.

The Subterraneans, however, is also an expression of Kerouac's bivalent representations of the female in his work, a literary and compositional contradiction that in this novel exposes the deleterious impact of unchecked, unexamined racism in his depictions of women; their subordination to the masculine provides an apparent permission for race-baiting. First, in an astute aesthetic description of the 1950s bohemian heirs of Henry David Thoreau, the narrative hovers over the subterraneans, who are "hip without being slick ... intelligent without being corny ... intellectual as hell ... without being pretentious or talking too much about it, they are very quiet" (*The Subterraneans*, 2). In this poetics of the new postwar bohemia, a striking representation of a hipster woman – not Mardou – exemplifies Kerouac's composing genius at its apex, rightly touted for its exalted composition.

> (a woman of 25 prophesying the future style of America with short almost crewcut but with curls black snaky hair, snaky walk, pale pale junkey anemic face and we say junkey ... if not ascetic or saintly? ... But the cold pale booster face of the cold blue girl and wearing a man's white shirt but with the cuffs undone untied at the buttons so I remember her leaning over talking to someone after having slinked across the floor with flowing propelled shoulders, bending to talk with her hand holding a short butt ... with long long fingernails an inch long and also orient and snake-like) (*The Subterraneans*, 18).

This rendering of Roxanne, the disinterested object of Leo's reportorial gaze, is a many-layered representation. Built on syncopated repetitions and imagistic description it is contained in and set off in parentheses that emphasize the marginality of the figure even as she is said to represent the "future style of America": she is a dangerous desire, a white woman wearing a man's white shirt with the "orient" in her long "snake-like" fingernails, blue-skinned, cold, as if she is the slinking, walking dead presented through living literary language. The eroticism of this passage offers an aesthetic – but improbable – specularized attraction to corpses; this woman is too cool to touch. The true subterranean of this story, Mardou Fox, is also subject to exoticizing representation, but focused instead on her genitalia.

Almost every way that Leo specularizes Mardou – holds her in his gaze – fetishizes her parts. First her feet in sandals, then her face and feet, "her special cool lips and Indian-like hard high soft cheekbones ... dark, sweet, with little eyes honest glittering and intense" (*The Subterraneans*, 3) in a blazon-style enumeration of features, to which is added the "thongs of sandals of such sexuality-looking greatness I wanted to kiss her, them" (*The Subterraneans*, 4), culminating in a repetition, "her dark feet, thongs of sandals, dark eyes, little soft brown face, ... cheeks and lips ... softly snake-like charm as befits a little thin brown woman disposed to wearing ... poor beat subterranean clothes" (*The Subterraneans*, 15). Mardou is also "snakelike," but lauded for her hip way of speaking that invokes African

American speech codes only to be ceded, as in the depiction of Carmelita's "swan-like neck," to whiteness: Mardou's "cultured funny tones of part [North] Beach, part I. Magnin model, part Berkeley, part Negro high-class, something, a mixture of *langue* and style of talking and use of words I'd never heard before except in certain rare girls of course *white*" (*The Subterraneans*, 10; italics in original). This whitewashing of her multiethnic language does not prevail; race-fear breaks through in subsequent passages that enumerate Mardou's genitalia in ways that are unquotable and undermine her as lover, poet, muse. In one instance, a microscopic investigation of Mardou's genitalia, the interior of a black female body, is casually incorporated into the narrative (*The Subterraneans*, 63), and in a second case, an inspection of Mardou's "stubble-like quality of the pubic [hair], which was Negroid and therefore a little rougher" (*The Subterraneans*, 104) – rougher than white? – that culminates in a graphic image of the aftereffects for a man having intercourse with Mardou as if she possessed the *vagina dentata* of myth, preposterously causing him "piercing unsupportable screamingsudden pain so he had to … have himself bandaged and all"; Leo "wonder[s] and suspect[s] if our little chick didn't really intend to bust us in half" (*The Subterraneans*, 104). Here, Mardou is a Beat Medusa, too beautiful and too dangerous to resist as writing object even under the cover of "unsupportable" gynophobia. This misogynist literary gynophobia – fear of femaleness – coerces collaboration in its contempt; its unacceptable assumption of the peril and power of the female.

In the story "Good Blonde," first published in *Playboy* in 1965 but derived from a 1958 incident, gynophobia is soothed by the beauty and inferred gentility of "pure" whiteness. The woman whose embodiment in this story has no other name is not a literary vision but a realistically rendered person.[21] The titular subject of the piece is also its exponent, and the unnamed narrator – presumably Kerouac – is a supplicant; she is the driver and he needs a ride.[22] The narrator sees "a brand new cinnamon colored Lincoln driven by a beautiful young blonde in a bathingsuit that flashed by and swerved to the right and put to a stop in the side of the road for me. I couldn't believe it" ("Good Blonde," 5). The female driver is not determined by the narrator's inventing gaze but simply presented in her car. This relative objectivity of presentation is the sign of privileged whiteness. Not working class, like Maggie Cassidy or a burlesque dancer like Ella Wynn, but rich, confident, savvy to the ways of the road, the blonde takes Benzedrine to keep awake while driving. This story departs from Kerouac's objectifying and eroticizing depictions of women and presents a plain text of the case. She is described almost neutrally:

> She was a gorgeous young blonde girl of about 22 in a pure white bathingsuit, barefooted with a little ankle bracelet around her right ankle. Her bathingsuit was shoulderless and low cut. She sat there in the luxurious cinnamon sea [of her car] in that white suit like a model. In fact she was a model. Green eyes, from Texas, on her way back to the City [San Francisco] ("Good Blonde," 5).

She has a costume change but the representation remains relatively neutral: she "came out … clad in tightfitting black slacks and a neat keen throwover of some kind, and sandals, in which she padded like a little tightfit Indian. I felt humble and foolish with two men staring at her and me waiting by the car for my poor world ride" ("Good Blonde," 14). Here, the blonde, in slinky black, is raced not-white but Native American and the narrator is now held in the onlookers' gaze. Agency obtains to both, but both are conditionally diminished; he is a "foolish and humble" man though still the storyteller, while she displays the "tightfit" glamour of a desirable woman though still the driver. The story "Good Blonde" is as balanced in gender representation, though nevertheless askew in sexual politics, as might be found in Kerouac's texts that depict women who are not the protagonist's lovers, or potential or actual wives (e.g., Laura in *On the Road*; "wifey" in *Vanity of Duluoz*); unadulterated whiteness and apparent upper-class status as exemplified by this tale's "bathingsuit blonde," rare in Kerouac to be sure, seem to assuage gendered fears and envies felt in the oeuvre's unviable, unpalatable depictions of women as noted in this discussion. In this and in his representations of women at large, Kerouac partakes of and perpetuates the patriarchy of his era and of the "classic" American literary canon which he aimed to join, bringing Beat movement writing into the mainstream literary fold, albeit on his own Beat bohemian terms.

An alternative response to this post-50s, post–Beat Generation, feminist-influenced reading of Kerouac's representations of women – representations often found insulting and offensive, belittling, to female anatomy and existential integrity – was articulated by the writer and editor Joyce Johnson. At a conference in 1995 Johnson protested a presenter's negative analyses of representations of women in *On the Road* and defended Kerouac's apparent misogyny, insisting that what he offered, even if only for his male characters, was the only role model for personal freedom and individuality available to postwar Silent Generation iconoclasts. Taking a divergent approach, Johnson sees in Kerouac a way out of conformity that women could adapt: his was a rough road map, a passage to a liberated American life for the very women his stories consume, paradoxically showing women the self-realization for which his celebrated novels are coded For (White) Men Only.[23] Women of the 1950s Silent Generation like Johnson could still appreciate Kerouac if they would identify against themselves and with the bohemian male model of iconoclasm in Kerouac's stories and styles.[24]

That is Joyce Johnson's assessment of the fraught subject of Kerouac's representations of women in his work. While Kerouac's writing poses challenges for feminist readers, female and male, the grace and ebullience of its rhythms and poetic movements take reading attention in often transcendent directions, away from the censure of content to admiration of form and celebration of art. There is no twentieth-century writer of his measure, although his writing can disappoint and alienate. Rereading Kerouac always repays the effort to wrangle with his deficits for the literary high it can give, even against better sense. Let's let Kerouac have the final word, the narrator's prerogative, since he has been rather roughly treated here: "I'll write long sad tales about people in the legend of my life – This part is my part of the movie, let's hear yours" (*Tristessa*, 96).

Notes

1. See Nancy McCampbell Grace, "A White Man in Love: A Study of Race, Gender, Class and Ethnicity in Jack Kerouac's *Maggie Cassidy, The Subterraneans,* and *Tristessa,*" in *College Literature* Special Issue 27. 1: Teaching Beat Literature, ed. Jennie Skerl, Winter 2002. 39–73; Mary Paniccia Carden, *Women Writers of the Beat Era: Autobiography and Intertextuality* (Charlottesville: University of Virginia Press, 2018); Joyce Johnson, *Minor Characters: A Memoir* (New York: Washington Square Press, 1983); Ronna C. Johnson, "Gender, Race, and Narrative in *On the Road,*" in *The Beats: A Teaching Companion*, ed. Nancy McCampbell Grace (Clemson: Clemson University Press, 2021), 87–102; Ronna C. Johnson and Nancy M. Grace, "Visions and Revisions of the Beat Generation," in *Girls Who Wore Black*, ed. Ronna C. Johnson and Nancy M. Grace (New Brunswick: Rutgers University Press, 2002), 1–24. See also Ronna C. Johnson, "The Beats and Gender," in *The Cambridge Companion to The Beats*, ed. Steven Belletto (New York: Cambridge University Press, 2017), 162–178, for a survey of the gender binarism characteristic of the Beat generation subculture.
2. Starting with Kate Millett, *Sexual Politics* (New York: Avon Books, 1970), which contains some of the earliest feminist literary criticism of male-authored texts in groundbreaking chapters on D.H. Lawrence, Henry Miller, and Norman Mailer. In this study Millett also introduced the genre "misogynist literature," 57.
3. Joyce Johnson, *Minor Characters*.
4. Laura Mulvey, "Visual Pleasure and Narrative Cinema" (1975) in Mulvey (ed.) *Visual and Other Pleasures* (Bloomington: Indiana University Press, 1989), 15.

5. Jack Kerouac, "The Origins of the Beat Generation," in *On the Road: Text and Criticism*, ed. Scott Donaldson (New York: Penguin, 1979), 357–367; 361.
6. See Johnson and Grace, Girls *Who Wore Black*; Joyce Johnson, *Minor Characters*, and John Clellon Holmes, *Go* (New York: New American Library, 1952); rpt. NAL 1980, for books or writing about hipster "women in black."
7. Mulvey, "Visual Pleasure and Narrative Cinema," 19.
8. Barbara Ehrenreich, "The Beat Rebellion: Beyond Work and Marriage," in *The Hearts of Men: American Dreams and the Flight from Commitment* (New York: Anchor Press, 1983), 52–67; see 55; Jack Kerouac, *On the Road* (1957. New York: Viking, 1990), 193–194.
9. See Jack Kerouac, *Windblown World: The Journals of Jack Kerouac, 1947–1954*, ed. Douglas Brinkley (New York: Viking, 2004).
10. Teresa de Lauretis, *Alice Doesn't: Feminism, Semiotics, Cinema* (Bloomington: Indiana University Press, 1984), 142. See also Ronna C. Johnson. "Gender, Race, and Narrative in *On the Road*," in *The Beats: A Teaching Companion*, ed. Nancy McCampbell Grace (Clemson: Clemson University Press, 2021), 87–102.
11. See Steven Belletto, *The Beats: A Literary History* (New York: Cambridge University Press, 2020), 92–97, for analysis of Kerouac's rendition of the Sal–Terry romantic interplay with regard to race, class and gender.
12. Simone de Beauvoir, *The Second Sex* (Vintage Books Edition), Introduction by Judith Thurman, trans. Constance Borde and Sheila Malovany-Chevallier, (New York: Vintage, 2011).
13. Jack Kerouac, *Visions of Cody* (New York: McGraw-Hill, 1972), 76.
14. Millett, *Sexual Politics*, 57.
15. Jack Kerouac, *Lonesome Traveler* (New York: Grove, 1960).
16. See Oswald Spengler, *The Decline of the West, Vols. 1 and 2*, 1918; both volumes 1923; published in English 1926.
17. Jack Kerouac, *Maggie Cassidy* (New York: McGraw-Hill, 1959), 5.
18. Mulvey, "Visual Pleasure and Narrative Cinema", 19.
19. Sylvia Plath, "Lady Lazarus" in *Ariel* (New York: Harper Colophon, 1965), 5–9.
20. Jack Kerouac, *The Subterraneans* (New York: Ballantine, 1958), 5.
21. Ann Charters, *Kerouac: A Biography* (San Fransisco: Straight Arrow Books, 1973), 360.
22. Jack Kerouac, "Good Blonde," in *Good Blonde & Others*, ed. Donald Allen (San Francisco: Grey Fox Press, 1993), 3–18.
23. Joyce Johnson to the author, at the Beat Literature Symposium at the University of Massachusetts-Lowell on October 5, 1995, in response to my talk "'girls, visions, everything': Masculine Narrative Spaces in *On the Road*."
24. This theory was developed at length by the feminist critic Janice Radway in her book, *Reading the Romance: Women, Patriarchy, and Popular Literature* (Chapel Hill: University of North Carolina Press, 1982), reprint 1991; reprint with Introduction by the Author, 2009.

CHAPTER 14

Kerouac and Blackness

Amor Kohli

Examine the indices of the critical studies on Jack Kerouac's work, and one finds entries for "Buddhism" certainly, "Catholicism" often, but rarely an entry dedicated to another guiding spiritual force for Kerouac: Blackness. Anne Waldman observes Allen Ginsberg's "assessment and insistence on the influence of Black culture and jazz on the Beats, which is also a 'spiritual' thing."[1] Blackness is usually subsumed under "race," but Kerouac's worshipful relationship to Blackness arguably had as significant an impact on Kerouac's aesthetic as did the others.

Kerouac referred to the Black American as "the essential American" and "the salvation of America," phrases that, while never adequately explored in Kerouac's writing, signal at least recognition of the centrality of Black Americans and Black American culture to the broader American society.[2] Consumption of Black culture and Blackness as a catalytic theme weaves throughout Kerouac's work and is key to his broader aesthetic philosophy. A longing exists within Kerouac's work for the liberated energy he perceived in Black American experience. However, his often superficial readings ignore the reality of Black constraint, subsequently rendering Black life discrepant with the lived experience of Blackness in America. Problematically, his longing is ultimately predicated on Black silence and evasion of Black interiority.

What are the political and ethical – together, racial – implications of Kerouac's aesthetic alongside his approach to Blackness? How willing is he to acknowledge the racial dynamics and inherent tensions in his participation in the troika of Blackness, Black culture, and portrayals of Black people? Critics have argued that Kerouac's identification with Black people is linked to his identity as the child of French-Canadian immigrants who did not speak English at home. Kerouac's conflicted relationship with his identity as an American purportedly allowed him an empathetic sense of outsiderness with Black Americans and other minority groups. Any identification with Black people, however, is transitory and does not ameliorate his uses of Blackness. Kerouac's engagement with Blackness shows a desire to, as Frederick Douglass would put it, have "the ocean without the awful roar of its many waters."[3] Yet, as Black expressions of discontent got louder, Kerouac moved inland.

On a warm Denver night, a man called Sal Paradise walked, spiritually adrift, in search of meaning and meaningful experience. He announces his desire to be someone and, ultimately, somewhere else:

> At lilac evening I walked with every muscle aching among the lights of 27th and Welton in the Denver colored section, wishing I were a Negro, feeling that the best the white world had offered was not enough ecstasy for me, not enough life, joy, kicks, darkness, music, not enough night.... I wished I were a Denver Mexican, or even a poor overworked Jap, anything but what I was so drearily, a "white man" disillusioned. All my life I'd had white ambitions.... I was only myself, Sal Paradise, sad, strolling in this violet dark, this unbelievably sweet night, wishing I could exchange worlds with the happy, true-hearted, ecstatic Negroes of America.[4]

This passage (which I'll refer to as the Denver Statement), arguably the most contested in Kerouac's writing, has become an indelible part of the story of Kerouac's most famous novel, *On the Road*, and, ultimately, of his career. Naturally, this passage does not occur in a vacuum, nor can its sentiments or criticisms thereof be restricted to only what critics have called the "political" or "sociological." Nor is it particularly easy to leave these in the mouth of Sal Paradise. Kerouac appears cognizant of how this might read, as in his journal he writes he "walked on Welton Street wishing I was a 'nigger,'" which he attempts to soften in the novel with the more socially acceptable "Negro."[5] A version of this passage appears almost verbatim in Kerouac's journals, an echo of it appears in Kerouac's third novel, *The Subterraneans*, and Kerouac defends these sentiments later in his career.[6]

The Denver Statement is particularly troubling in its conformation to damaging racial myths about Black Americans and other nonwhite people. While these messages derive from a longitudinal tradition in Western culture, *On the Road* dates from a period of increasingly contentious discourse around the position of Black Americans. This passage has been criticized for its allegiance to primitivist beliefs about Black people, its implicit denial of Black historical struggle, and its misrepresentation of the contemporary situation of Black Americans. Conversely, it has been defended for celebrating nonwhite peoples and for Kerouac's willingness to explicitly name whiteness and the psychic pressure it inflicts on white people. Kerouac's novel acknowledges instances of racial violence and does not present the lives of Black people as free from toil; its white characters, in their transitory marginality, sometimes participate alongside them.

Other than the primitivism echoing through this passage, the reference to "happy … Negroes of America" most rankles many readers. For all of Norman Podhoretz's dismissive rhetoric about Beat writers, he is not wrong to connect the Denver Statement and "certain Southern ideologues [who] tried to convince the world that things were just as fine as fine could be for the slaves on the old plantation."[7] Not only was *On the Road* published during a period when Black voices were gaining strength, but its conception and publication occurred amid resurgent Southern Lost Cause ideologies in politics, historiography, and popular culture, a fantasy to which Kerouac himself was drawn. "Happy" reads as denying and whitewashing Black dissatisfaction increasingly evident in national discourses. Kerouac adds a comment that "Negro families" filled "the air with the vibration of really joyous life that knows nothing of disappointment and 'white' sorrows" (*On the Road*, 181).

Paradise, Kerouac's narrator, appears to bemoan his whiteness, its imposition, and "ambitions." But does Kerouac's/Paradise's wistful move away from "white ambitions" represent an opposition to white supremacy in principle or action? At best, he only wishes "to be a Negro" because "his" world – and it is notable that Kerouac/Sal positions himself as white, not French-Canadian or Italian-American – does not offer him "enough," a word redolent with the expectations of a whiteness that demands total freedom and cognizance of a racial due. A rapaciousness underlies these expectations, resulting in disenchantment when those demands are unmet.

If Kerouac so thoroughly misreads nonwhite existence as the locus of "ecstasy … life, joy, kicks," how can we trust his apprehension of "white ambitions" as any kind of broader intervention? To his credit, Kerouac nominally recognizes a distinction between white and nonwhite existence. However, it is not that he wants something more just, moral, or fair. It is that he wants more ("the best the white world had offered was *not enough* … for me"; emphasis mine), imagining such unfettered excess and access in the Black world. In a twist from the credo of American materialism, the more here is not material but sensual. It is, then, not especially what whiteness is or the power it wields that he wishes to relinquish but the paucity of its sensory rewards, given its societal demands and expectations ("white ambitions").

Even though he is unusual among white writers by even engaging whiteness, it is significant that Kerouac's whiteness is cited primarily for the impact it has on *whites*. While it is meaningful that a white male author at mid-century explicitly states awareness of whiteness, he repeatedly fails to ask the basic questions essential for understanding and self-reflection.

His guiding ethos does not seem to be "why" (why, even, is there a "colored section" for him to walk in?) but "I want." The passage does not primarily reflect Kerouac's acknowledging what Linda Martin Alcoff calls "the arbitrariness of his dominant status"[8] as much as he senses that others have what he wants. Note the quick move from "wishing [he] was a Negro" to "exchang[ing] worlds" with Black people. What world Black people will then inhabit is conveniently murky. Black people have something; this white person wants it but doesn't know how to achieve it on his own terms. However disillusioned the writer or his creation, this is not a plea for harmony or a broader justice but for white transformative consumption.

In a 1963 conversation, John Clellon Holmes offers Kerouac the opportunity to address the controversy around the Denver Statement: "Baldwin and most other [N]egroes, have complained about your 'wishing to be a [N]egro, etc.' Denver night in O.T.R. … Answer them through me. Indeed, tell me about what [N]egroes have meant to you…." Kerouac responds:

> I *was* romantic when I wrote that line and I meant it when I wrote it. I was a kid and I wanted to have more fun in Denver that night in 1949. James Baldwin wants to stir up as much interest in his Civil Rights fight as he can, get everybody involved, all the writers probably, but I have no time for politics, just Art.[9]

In Kerouac's narrow formulation, "politics," and by association "Civil Rights," refers not to the pursuit of justice, a fully realized America, or the freedom Kerouac valued and desired, but a distraction from "Art." Notwithstanding Holmes' slick questioning and Kerouac's defensive reaction, it usually goes unmentioned that Baldwin acknowledged pain in Kerouac's passage. Even in Baldwin's critique, he recognized the kind of damage that people like Kerouac were working through, an empathic position that Kerouac did not reciprocate.

At once deflecting, defensive, and disingenuous, Kerouac uncharacteristically avoids taking advantage of Holmes' invitation to "expatiate" and defend or at least develop his romantic primitivism. As has been a timeworn tactic of authors held to task for their statements, Kerouac hides behind "Art." In so doing, he asserts an unequivocal politics – the inviolability of his authoritative position. Doubling down with "I meant it when I wrote it," Kerouac sidesteps the request to reinforce or clarify the importance of Blackness and Black culture, however misguided and misinformed, to his larger project.

Kerouac, over the years, increasingly downplayed any Black influence. His retreat under the erroneous protection of Art lies in a refusal to fully reckon with the implications of his whiteness and its inseparability from his broader ideas of freedom. Indeed, for Kerouac, Blacks are already free in the most meaningful ways and, crucially, freer than him, which can release him from the need to worry about it – a need that we may also call "politics." Black critiques and Black creative assertiveness ultimately force examination of his and his society's racial presumptions, highlighting the failure of his aesthetic to live up to its arrogated ethic.

Nowhere is the intersection of Blackness, aesthetics, and societal expression more evident and fraught than in the realm of popular music. In this case, that music was jazz, particularly the stylistically audacious form known as bebop. There is no contradicting Kerouac and other Beats' enthusiasm for the music. Their energetic response to jazz is often translated into evidence of white Beat writers' receptivity to Black people and aspects of Black expressive culture. While Kerouac attempts to imitate bebop's approach to sound and structure as a basis for his own writing method, such a usage has stakes, the kind that allowed "bop" the dubious privilege of shedding the Black associations that historically kept jazz from mainstream acceptance. In a classic American culture sleight-of-hand, when the music was feared and derided, jazz was "Black." As more aesthetic and commercial value was ascribed to jazz, its status as "American" and thereby purportedly raceless developed, albeit not without resistance. Moreover, jazz's "Blackness" would come to signal a singularly political stance that, as critics would argue, was elevated to the detriment of purely musical considerations. Discussions of jazz's Blackness were contrived as political, but discussions of jazz as faithful expressions of America and American-style democracy were not so. The latter view expresses a utopic ideal wherein people of all races can come together and contribute on a horizontal axis; the former also forecasts a utopic ideal but additionally reckons with the decidedly less utopic realities of Black history and social existence.

In a later reflection on Kerouac's relationship to Black music and Black speech, Allen Ginsberg names something that Kerouac usually avoided explicitly acknowledging: his debt to Black culture. Kerouac's work is, according to Ginsberg, resonant of "Black musicians … imitating [Black] speech cadences and Kerouac was imitating the Black musicians' breath cadences on their horns and brought it back to speech. It always was speech rhythms or cadences as far as the ear that Kerouac was developing. All passed through Black music."[10] This form that Kerouac embraced as a model of aesthetic and personal discovery is product of a shared social language honed under historically specific circumstances. The attraction to Blackness and Black culture, in part due to a promise of release from the burdens and expectations of whiteness, suggests a recognition that, on some fundamental level, there is a Black way of doing and being in the world. We shouldn't discount the existence, then, of a Black aesthetic that attracts nonblack listeners, viewers, and consumers. The attraction is not only visual but manifest in the sounds, rhythms, structures, and style – the very building blocks – of expressive practices in Black life. Separating Kerouac's vision of jazz from Blackness is difficult, yet as he continued to theorize his method in poetically informed language, a debt to Black culture was all but disappeared.

An important but often-misread essay by LeRoi Jones (later Amiri Baraka; hereafter cited as Jones) addresses the fundamental gaps in the ways that white critics engage Black music, in this case jazz, as a reflection of historically determined Black expression. First published in *Down Beat*, "Jazz and the White Critic" begins with a direct and unassailable statement: "Most jazz critics have been white Americans, but most important jazz musicians have not been."[11] Jones's essay asserts that white critics have misguidedly focused on their appreciation of jazz at the expense of understanding. For Jones, central to understanding is seeking to parse the attitudes – social, historical, philosophical, aesthetic – that compelled the musicians to change the music as dramatically as they did, particularly with bebop.

Jones makes a countercultural argument wherein Black musical innovations derive from and express the attitudes of Black Americans. White jazz critics misunderstood Black musical expressions due to a failure or unwillingness to soberly consider the experiential attitudes that produced them. No one, as Jones wryly observes, questions Mozart's sociocultural philosophy; it is an a priori presumption. That a historically inflected sociocultural philosophy exists in jazz is too often rejected as irrelevant or as an expression of mere politics. According to Jones, these critics fail because their energies focus on appreciating the sound of bebop without considering why it was made in the first place. He formulates a pithy, essential question: "People made bebop. The question is why?"[12] Jones asks for consideration of how the music functions as collective memory and social language, comprising a desire to commune and insist upon being seen. The inability to even conceptualize this question results, from Jones's perspective, in the woeful state of jazz criticism, damaging broader jazz discourses.

Kerouac's dismissal of "politics" for an "Art" requiring no further definition is possible because of his imbrication and participation in whiteness as a falsely universalized identity. It may be that enjoying the music transcends the identities of the creators and consumers, but the development of that creative output is informed by a specific, shared historical experience. When the creative group had long been excluded from the mainstream and developed a powerful and ultimately influential counterculture, that historical experience matters. Hassan Melehy approvingly cites Scott DeVeaux's point that the "bebop pioneers seemed unmotivated by racial exclusivity,"[13] that is, uninvested in blanket prohibitions of white musicians playing bebop. Nevertheless, it is as much that bebop innovators were motivated by racial exclusion, particularly the exclusion of Blacks from the means of control, distribution, and remuneration. Numerous musicians have recounted bebop's early days and the conscious attempts to create sonic structures that couldn't be easily copied. Mary Lou Williams encapsulates this dynamic:

> When the thing started, Thelonious Monk and others had a little band going. They were afraid to come out because they were afraid that the commercial world would steal what they had created.... And in no time, the commercial world from downtown was coming in on it, and they tried to learn it. I heard some of the guys speak about not wanting to play downtown or play in the open so everybody could take it from them. Because you know the Black creators of the music have never gotten recognition for creating anything.... After a while, you get kinda really disgusted and tired out because everything you create is taken from you, and somebody else is given recognition for it.[14]

Copying, borrowing, echoing, and sharing have long had a place in jazz and other Black expressive forms. The opposition is not simply to white musicians playing what Black musicians developed but to their copying and profiting from it in such a way that diminishes Black innovation and valorization of Black aesthetic production.

Jones's essay has been accused of wholesale rejection of white participation in jazz in response to an improper "appropriation" of jazz by white musicians and critics. In fact, Baraka recognizes the participation of fully engaged white musicians:

> The white musician's commitment to jazz, the ultimate concern, proposed that the sub-cultural attitudes that produced the music as a profound expression of human feelings, could be learned and need not be passed on as a secret blood rite. And Negro music is essentially the expression of an attitude, or a collection of attitudes, about the world.... The white jazz musician came to understand this attitude as a way of making music, and

> the intensity of his understanding produced the "great" white jazz musicians and is producing them now.[15]

The music, then, is not biologically established but historically and culturally situated. Black music's historical integrativeness and hybridity invite and celebrate immersive participation, but that does not render it historically or culturally acousmatic. Nonetheless, for writers like Kerouac, the music certainly said something and, especially, something of Blackness and (an imagined) Black life. Where, after all, did he hear the "happiness," the "true-heartedness," and the "ecstasy" in the Black social group but in and mediated through Black cultural productions, particularly the music?

Black thinkers have long commented on whites' inability, often accompanied by a willful deafness, to adequately hear the Black histories, desires, and stances expressed in Black music, what Ralph Ellison considers "the most authoritative rendering of America in music."[16] Douglass hears a philosophy in which "every tone was a testimony against slavery, and a prayer to God for deliverance from chains," expressing astonishment "to find persons who could speak of the singing among slaves as evidence of their contentment and happiness."[17] Sterling A. Brown writes about whites in 1920s Harlem who "found what they believed to be the Negro, *au naturel* … synchronized to a savage rhythm, living a life of ecstasy superinduced by jazz.… Few were the observers who saw in the Negroes' abandon a release from the troubles of this world similar to that afforded in slavery by their singing." Like Kerouac, many "urged that the Harlem Negro's state was that of an inexhaustible joie de vivre."[18] In 1964's *Dutchman*, LeRoi Jones more antagonistically targets miscomprehension of sublimated desires:

> They say, "I love Bessie Smith" and don't even understand that Bessie Smith is saying, "Kiss my ass, kiss my Black unruly ass".… All the hip white boys scream for Bird. And Bird saying, "Up your ass, feeble-minded ofay! Up your ass".… Bird would've played not a note of music if he just walked up to East Sixty-seventh Street and killed the first ten white people he saw.[19]

Black music as a faithful reader of the nation that many white Americans faithfully misread remains a potent undercurrent in discussions of Black music.

Daniel Belgrad surmises that the Beats "seem to have remained willfully innocent of the racial power dynamics structuring their reception of the music – dynamics that allowed them to move more freely between African American and white social spaces than many Black jazz musicians themselves."[20] "Innocent" does not quite hit the mark; willfully ignorant is a better characterization. Kerouac was no political naïf. His reading was indeed expansive, and his historical sense is evident throughout his journals and letters. Kerouac kept "meticulous and extensive records … of his career and his times," invested in being read within "the larger life of his times."[21] Despite his 1963 dismissal of "politics," he was certainly aware of racial power dynamics in society, including in jazz.

In a 1959 essay, "The Beginning of Bop," Kerouac stakes a position sympathetic to "Jazz and the White Critic."[22] Kerouac here exhibits his bardic jazz listening while acknowledging historical impetuses of the music: "Bop is the language from America's inevitable Africa … Africa is the name of the flue and kick beat, off to one side." Kerouac not only recognizes a legacy extending to the African continent but, even as he falls back into an idealized and mythic history, acknowledges Black Americans: "you can't believe that bop is here to stay – that it is real, Negroes in America are just like us, we must look at them understanding the exact racial counterpart of what the man is."[23] He recognizes the growth of Black Islam in New York, particularly among jazz musicians, and expresses knowledge of the Black press through a subsequent mention of the *Amsterdam News*. The significance of these references lies in their particularity, showing that he knows something of the specificity of Black (jazz) existence in 1950s New York. Although Kerouac doesn't explicitly trace the music's debt to African American traditions, he does obliquely posit the presence of Black life in the heart of the music. These references demonstrate a recognition, however fleeting, of the need to confront others' social realities.

Kerouac's concentration on whiteness reasserts itself, again occluding Blackness. Presuming his audience, centering whites as his readers and intellectual engagers in jazz, he argues that "Negroes" are "just like us," thereby reinforcing the normative positioning of listeners and thinkers about jazz as white. "Us" here is white, unlike the Black musicians who are "mis-placed in a white nation" and "mis-noticed for what they really were." The "us" squarely places him as identifying with and being part of this "white nation" while also presumably separating him from those who "mis-notice" what the musicians really are. And "like us" in what way? American? Human? Transcending racial, historical, or cultural distinctions?

In a 1962 interview, Miles Davis recounts pushback after hiring the white saxophonist Lee Konitz: "I said if a cat could play like Lee, I would hire him, I didn't give a damn if he was green and had red breath."[24] Davis' statement has been cited many times in the service of celebrating jazz as a color-blind meritocracy and model of interracial exchange. Regularly elided is the fact that in most of the interview, Davis directly discusses race and the racial discrimination afflicting Blacks in jazz and the larger society.

A similar pitfall is evident in Kerouac's vision of jazz as a basis for his literary aesthetic. His journals detail a pivotal experience from 1951 in which he hears Konitz interpret "I'll Remember April" at Birdland. In that moment he hears an approach that he characterizes as "doing exactly what I am … but on alto," which gives him courage to continue elaborating his "Spontaneous Prose" style (*Unknown Kerouac*, 137). Kerouac, after listening to Konitz, records "a great discovery in my life" that gives him permission to begin understanding writing as performance. As Tim Hunt shows, this brings Kerouac to the position that "writing should be a recording medium rather than a compositional medium."[25] It is unclear what he heard in Konitz's playing that night that he hadn't in all the years of listening to jazz musicians, but the inspirational flash is what Kerouac wishes to focus on. And yet, it is not quite the case that we don't know what he heard. He posits hearing "ideas" in Konitz's playing that he characterizes as "more white … more metaphysical" than what he hears from Charlie Parker (*Unknown Kerouac*, 137). While the specifics are slippery, it is meaningful that Kerouac hears a racialized thought process in the music. Whether Kerouac's use of the comparative "more" suggests that he is not completely excising Black people or Black "ideas" from metaphysical concerns or capability, his comment nonetheless encapsulates centuries of presuppositions of white hegemonic philosophy regarding the cerebral and spiritual/soulful capacities of Black people. As Mark Sanders argues, "As ametaphysical, 'the Black' (or, better yet, Blackness) must exist beyond the aesthetic, beyond the redemptive possibilities central to the humanistic tradition of arts and letters."[26] Curiously, Hunt does not address the racial descriptor of Konitz's musical "ideas," perhaps seeing it as separate from an aesthetic discussion. Yet, given the role of bebop's spontaneity and sound in his developing aesthetic – Kerouac had long been listening to saxophonists demonstrate the aesthetic he sought to emulate – surely "more white" means something in aesthetic terms for Kerouac. While what it is precisely, past "more metaphysical," is unclear here, it is plainly juxtaposed against Blackness, particularly in reference to jazz. Kerouac addresses aesthetics through an explicitly racial lens. It is through the white metaphysics of a white musician "who inspired me in 1951 'to write the way he plays'" that he finally recognizes his aesthetic.[27]

Kerouac makes no overt claims to being a historian, journalist, or sociologist, but he is clearly positioned through his writings as someone with expertise, understanding, and a position, that is, a critic whose knowledge and insight into jazz qualifies him to publish columns and essays on the music in mainstream publications. Nonetheless, Kerouac's inability to fully reckon with jazz as a product of Black historical culture is of a piece with the shallowness with which he addresses Black interiority and lived experience. Critics arguing that he doesn't need to know much about jazz to incorporate its aesthetic lessons fail to note this as a key stopping point in his quest for a universal humanism. Mere outsiderness did not create bebop; there were quite evidently several historical and artistic stimuli. Kerouac's celebration of Black Americans as "the essential American" or "the salvation of America," sits uneasily with his ultimate approach to Black existence, Black thought, and, certainly, Black writing. Kerouac's work, in fact, betrays a lack of interest in excavating Black interiority. What, then, is his responsibility as a novelist, humanist, and lover of Black culture?

While reviewing Kerouac's 1958 novel *The Subterraneans*, Kenneth Rexroth writes, "The story is all about jazz and Negroes. Now there are two things Jack knows nothing about—jazz and Negroes."[28] Despite the generally positive review, Rexroth's caustic comment has been seized upon by some, including Kerouac himself, as an untoward and unfair attack. While Kerouac's jazz writings are riddled with errors and vague assessments, his corpus contains signposts indicating that even if relatively unlearned about jazz's structure or history, he had extensive knowledge of musicians and recordings, and spent substantial energy trying to harness his enjoyment as a model for his writing. A more pointed issue arises when we seek evidence that Kerouac knew or cared to know much about Black people, Black history, or Black experience – except, of course, for that experiential model of ecstatic spontaneity central to his misreading.

The Subterraneans offers hope that he might engage not only Blackness, but Black and white relations, with depth, sensitivity, and honesty. The novel recounts a relationship between Kerouac and a Black girlfriend, Alene Lee ("Mardou Fox" in this roman à clef). *The Subterraneans* courts controversy and incisive social commentary through its depiction of an interracial love affair in mid-1950s San Francisco. While, formally, the novel successfully evokes bebop jazz solos at points, it fails to reach its potential of a clear-eyed engagement of racial relations, due largely to the novelist's own racial presumptions, mirrored in the protagonist, Leo Percepied. As Rexroth aptly states in his review, "Kerouac *is* the subject" of the novel, and Kerouac's portrait of Leo reveals the author's conflicted views on Blackness.

At times, *The Subterraneans* appears to acknowledge the dilemma presented by its larger goal and the power of its narrator's racial fantasies. The novel depicts the powerful hold of American racist fantasies on Leo, imaginings that whiplash between romantic and fear-based descriptions of Mardou, at once seeing in her Blackness that "somehow [she is] the first, the essential woman," then in a flash his "hurt hate turning the other way … every time I see a Mexican gal or Negress I say to myself 'hustlers,' they're all the same, always trying to cheat and rob you."[29] Interracial love as a potential blow against an oppressive social order is subdued by Leo's racial fantasies.

At one point, Leo's discussion of Mardou's genitalia references seeing "some kind of black thing I've never seen before, hanging" that "*scared* him" (*The Subterraneans*, 45). This, as critics have noted, reflects a hermaphroditic image, but also potentially refers to an image of the body of a lynched Black person. The "some kind of black thing … hanging" conjures the conjoining of sexuality and violence, linked as they are in the Southern, and broader American, racist mythos. It scares Leo as Mardou's psychoanalysis, reflecting a complex consciousness, does, as they point to a reckoning with truth and history on personal and societal levels.

During sexual intercourse, Leo is overwhelmed by what he experiences as the clenching force of Mardou's vagina, calling it her "greatstrength of womb" (*The Subterraneans*, 45). This ultimately leads Leo, in a bout of retrospective revisionism, to "now wonder and suspect if our little chick didn't really intend to bust us in half" (*The Subterraneans*, 76), reflecting another dubious product of misogynist, racist mythologies that circumscribe Black women. After Leo admits his fear and revulsion of Mardou's body, he and Mardou examine her body together. Leo's beliefs are slightly tempered after this examination, momentarily assuaging his horrified misapprehension of the "pernicious and pizen juices" (*The Subterraneans*, 46) he imagined accompanying intercourse with her. These descriptions echo enslavers' and colonizers' use of physical and medical research on non-white peoples, leading to erroneous but nonetheless powerfully authoritative "knowledge." A. Robert Lee notes two "opposing turns" criticism on *The Subterraneans* takes, as "a novel of persuasive confessional verve or a novel loaded in race-cliché and chauvinism."[30] *The Subterraneans* sits at the intersection of both but is finally content to continue in its damaging racial fantasies.

Leo's willingness to be momentarily guided through his racist "phantasies" about her body is not extended to Mardou's interior life. The novel avoids entering Mardou's consciousness or taking it and her feelings seriously. In one instance, Leo wants to go into a bar filled with white men, but "she was afraid of all the behatted men ranged at the bar, now I saw her Negro fear of American society she was always talking about," which Leo reads as "her little girl-like fear so cute, so edible" (*The Subterraneans*, 68).

This fear that she is "always talking about" is never represented by the novel. There is little sense that her emotional struggles might have anything to do with racial fears or being a Black woman desired and pursued as a sexual object by groups of white men. Conversely, Leo's fears of Mardou's Black body, of being with her, of what her Blackness might signify outside of his intentionally narrow comprehension, and that signification's reflection on him repeat throughout the novel. When Mardou discusses her life and her feelings, Leo loses interest and retreats into his mythologizing of her Black and Cherokee ancestry, often using "Negro" and "Indian" as adjectives to write his erroneous, often fantastic beliefs onto her. He repeatedly casts her into racial metonymies ("you are the child of bop" (99); calling her "Eve" (109) as "Eden's in Africa" (94); "you are the essential woman" (94, all *The Subterraneans*) that she resists, unsuccessfully.

Leo collects Mardou as literary material, claiming but not fully acknowledging her, laying his fantasy of Black and Indigenous people over her attempts to articulate her own experiences and their meaning for her. Her suffering is fuel only as it fits his agenda, informed as it is by the racist myths that he perpetuates. Mardou is a mere instrument, and her Blackness makes her – and also makes her Blackness – a potent instrument indeed. His appropriation of her story, over her own recounting, coincides with Kerouac's tendency to occlude Black voices and interior life. Consumption of Blackness, for Kerouac and many young white men of his generation, is a path to their holistic fulfillment: sensual, emotional, spiritual, and sexual.

It is fair to wonder how Kerouac gained a sense of the "essential American's" thinking or lived experience. As James Campbell notes, there is little evidence in Kerouac's writings, letters, or journals that he read literature written by Black authors, either prior or contemporary to him.[31] Black writing disrupts, through its unfolding of Black interiority, the racial myths to which Kerouac subscribed. Ralph Ellison's *Invisible Man* won the National Book Award in 1953, a selection that made national news. Perhaps Kerouac didn't read Richard Wright's *Native Son*, a controversial Book of the Month Club selection, but a journal entry indicates that he attended the stage adaptation of Wright's novel. While Kerouac might recoil from Wright's naturalism, certainly Ellison's jazz-evocative novel could provide insight into a Black experience, even from its first few paragraphs. Langston Hughes appeared in Beat circles, and Kerouac probably knew of Hughes' 1958 jazz-poetry collaboration with Charles Mingus, *Weary Blues*, since Kerouac admired Mingus and it was one of the few jazz-poetry recordings available. Further, Kerouac was likely aware of the buzz around figures like Lorraine Hansberry and the bestselling and prizewinning works of Ann Petry and Gwendolyn Brooks. However, he does not contend with any of these authors' works in his writings.

While Kerouac does not discuss Black writing, references to Black writers dot his works. He addresses Baldwin on a few occasions, but only as antagonist, not writer (how much could Kerouac have learned had he really engaged with Baldwin's "Sonny's Blues"?). More strangely, despite fond references to LeRoi Jones as a compatriot, Beat scene fixture, and editor, there is no recorded engagement with Jones's actual writing. This disinterest in Black writers writing about Black life – but not white writers writing about Black life, however faultily construed – is more than curious. Despite Kerouac's obvious debt to Black life as expressed in Black speech, especially as modulated through Black musicians' horns, Black silence is central to Kerouac's aesthetic approach to Blackness.[32]

Notes

1. Anne Waldman, Foreword, in Allen Ginsberg, *The Best Minds of My Generation: A Literary History of the Beats* (New York: Grove, 2017), xiv.
2. Jack Kerouac, *Lonesome Traveler*, 1960 (New York: Grove, 1988), 39; Jack Kerouac, *Desolation Angels*, 1965 (New York: Riverhead, 1995), 136. While Kerouac usually subsumed minority identities under a broader category of "Fellahin," after Oswald Spengler, "Blackness," needs examination on its own, especially given the symbolic power of the Black/white dyad in American culture.
3. Frederick Douglass, *Selected Speeches and Writings* (Chicago: Lawrence Hill, 1999), 367.
4. Jack Kerouac, *On the Road* (New York: Penguin, 1991), 180.
5. Jack Kerouac, *Windblown World: The Journals of Jack Kerouac, 1947–1954* (New York: Viking, 2004), 215.
6. I am sympathetic to recent criticism that resists reading Kerouac's work purely as "memoir," yet it remains that Kerouac referred to his novels as interviews, and consciously mined his journals for material, some of which, like the Denver Statement, he incorporates into his novels.
7. Norman Podhoretz, "The Know-Nothing Bohemians," in *Casebook on the Beat*, ed. Thomas Parkinson (New York: T.Y. Crowell, 1961), 207.
8. Linda Martin Alcoff, "Towards a Phenomenology of Racial Embodiment," *Radical Philosophy* 95 (May/June 1999), 19.
9. John Clellon Holmes, "Doing Literary Work: A Conversation with Jack Kerouac," in *The Unknown Kerouac: Rare, Unpublished & Newly Translated Writings*, ed. Todd Teitchen (New York: Library of America, 2016), 320. Italics in original.

10. Ginsberg, *Best Minds*, 8.
11. LeRoi Jones, *Black Music* (1967. New York: Da Capo, 1998), 11.
12. Jones, *Black Music*, 16.
13. Hassan Melehy, *Kerouac: Language, Poetics, and Territory* (New York: Bloomsbury Academic, 2016), 93.
14. Dizzy Gillespie, with Al Fraser, *To Be or Not … to Bop*, (Minneapolis: University Press Minnesota, 2009), 149–150.
15. Jones, *Black Music*, 13.
16. Ralph Ellison, *Shadow and Act* (New York: Quality Paperback Book, 1994), 255.
17. Frederick Douglass, *Narrative of the Life of Frederick Douglass, an American Slave* (New York: Penguin Books, 1982), 58.
18. Sterling A. Brown, "Negro Character as Seen by White Authors," *Callaloo*, 14/15 (Feb-May 1982), 80.
19. LeRoi Jones, *Dutchman and The Slave* (New York: Morrow, 1964), 35.
20. Daniel Belgrad, *The Culture of Spontaneity: Improvisation and the Arts in Postwar America* (Chicago: University of Chicago Press, 1999), 210.
21. Ann Douglas, "'Telepathic Shock and Meaning Excitement': Kerouac's Poetics of Intimacy," *College Literature*, 27 no.1 (Winter, 2000), 12.
22. Earlier in his journals Kerouac approximates Jones's position, writing "that the music of a generation whether it is swing, jazz or bop … is a keypoint of mood, an identification, and a seeking-out." (*Windblown*, 194).
23. Jack Kerouac, "The Beginning of Bop" in *Good Blonde & Others* (San Francisco: Grey Fox, 1994), 114.
24. Alex Haley, *The Playboy Interviews* (New York: Ballantine, 1993), 13.
25. Tim Hunt, "'Blow As Deep As You Want To Blow': Time, Textuality, and Jack Kerouac's Development of Spontaneous Prose," *Journal of Beat Studies* 1 (2012), 66.
26. Mark A. Sanders, "Sterling A. Brown and the Afro-Modern Moment," *African American Review*, 31, no. 3 (Autumn, 1997), 393.
27. Jack Kerouac, "The Last Word 10" (December 1960), in *Good Blonde & Others* (San Francisco: Grey Fox, 1994), 170.
28. Kenneth Rexroth, "*The Subterraneans* by Jack Kerouac," *San Francisco Chronicle* (February 16, 1958).
29. Jack Kerouac, *The Subterraneans*, (New York: Grove, 1981), 94.
30. A. Robert Lee, "The Beats and Race," in *The Cambridge Companion to the Beats*, ed. Steven Belletto (New York: Cambridge University Press, 2017), 198.
31. James Campbell, "Kerouac's Blues," *The Antioch Review* 59, no. 2 (Spring 2001), 456.
32. This chapter received support from DePaul University's URC Paid Leave Program. Additionally, it bears noting that in 1950 Kerouac began a novella narrated by an African American child, a version of which was eventually published in 1971 as *Pic*. While *Pic*, in revisiting of some of Kerouac's early 1950s work, showcases his attempt to stretch his narratorial voice, it is also limited by the myopia addressed throughout this chapter. Regrettably, due to space limitations, this relatively minor work could not be fully analyzed in this chapter, but I plan to address it elsewhere.

CHAPTER 15

Kerouac, Multilingualism, and Global Culture

Hassan Melehy

Often in his writings, Kerouac makes clear that he is aware of not being a native speaker of English, that he regards his native French as basic to his relationship to language. Given the name Jean-Louis Kerouac at birth, he grew up in the large French-Canadian immigrant community in Lowell, Massachusetts. From their first arrival in the mid-nineteenth century through most of the twentieth, French-Canadian communities throughout the United States, especially the northeast, maintained a strong awareness of their displacement from Québec. For Kerouac, this awareness is a major source of his fascination with travel: the road that is central to his best-known work is a place where peoples of different cultures and who speak different languages encounter each other. In the explorations across the United States and into other countries that fill most of his novels, he builds a vast image of an emerging global culture in which a variety of peoples mix together. An important part of conveying this image is his distinctive writing style: one of his aims is to bring foreignness into his English prose by mixing it with his native language.

In a letter he wrote in September, 1950, at age twenty-eight, to Lowell journalist Yvonne Le Maître, he explains: "All my knowledge rests in my 'French-Canadianness' and nowhere else. The English language is a tool lately found ... so late (I never spoke English before I was six or seven). At 21 I was still awkward and illiterate-sounding in my speech and writing. What a mixup."[1] He wrote to Le Maître in response to her review of his first novel, *The Town and the City* (1950), in *Le Travailleur* [*The Laborer*], the French-language weekly in Worcester, Massachusetts. Not only does he state that his immigrant heritage makes him at least partly foreign in America, but he also expresses concern about his relationship to the French-Canadian community. This community's commitment to maintaining linguistic fluency is attested by the very existence of French-language newspapers: beginning in the late nineteenth century there had been more than 400 in the United States, and in the 1950s close to thirty remained, most in New England; *Le Travailleur* was the last holdout, closing in 1978.[2] Because Kerouac began writing in English well before the age of twenty-one, his words also suggest that part of his motivation for doing so is to bring himself closer to the language he experienced as foreign. He continues the letter with a brief description of his approach to writing: "The reason I handle English words so well is because it is not my own language. I refashion it to fit French images."

One of Le Maître's criticisms of *The Town and the City*, a novel in which she otherwise finds superb writing – "he knows how to populate a place with an active, quivering, trembling, dense life [*il sait peupler un milieu d'une vie agissante, trépidante, frémissante et drue*]"[3] – is that Kerouac omits the pre-immigration past of the peoples of Galloway, the town of the title, his fictional version of Lowell. He does so despite painting it as a New England mill town, typical for its many immigrant communities, with no shortage of French Canadians in the background. Le Maître takes him to task especially for including nothing substantial about the language and culture of his and her community, the connections to the past that its members carry with them. She quips caustically: "Imagine *Hamlet* without the ghost of the *father* [*Pensez à un* Hamlet *où manquerait le spectre du père*]."

The Town and the City has only one sentence in French, a brief exclamation by a pretentious out-of-town character.[4] The main characters, the large Martin family, are all clearly natives of the United States; the mother, Marguerite Martin, is of French-Canadian heritage but originally from New Hampshire. In the letter, Kerouac makes Le Maître a promise for the future: "Someday, Madam, I shall write a French-Canadian novel, with the setting in New England, in French. It will be the simplest and most rudimentary French. If anybody wants to publish it, I mean Harcourt, Brace [the publisher of *The Town and the City*] or anybody else, they'll have to translate it" (*Selected Letters 1*, 228). As for his debut novel, "It was an American story. As I say, the French-Canadian story I have yet to attempt" (*Selected Letters 1*, 229). In acknowledging Le Maître's criticisms, he admits to succumbing to the pressure to assimilate to anglophone US culture: "But you were absolutely right in your few complaints on this score. Isn't it true that French-Canadians everywhere tend to hide their real sources" (*Selected Letters 1*, 229). He vows to begin treating his heritage and community with respect: "Believe me, I'll never hide it again" (*Selected Letters 1*, 229).

15.1 Hiding in French

He kept his word, more or less. Just a few months after writing to Le Maître, in February 1951, he composed a novella in French, *La Nuit est ma femme* [*The Night Is My Woman*], whose narrator-protagonist, Michel Bretagne, is overtly French-Canadian and lives his sense of cultural loss by wandering around the United States, extending the migration of his family and community. That is, Kerouac makes the very rootlessness that Le Maître discerns in *The Town and the City* the explicit theme of the novel in French he promised her. He extends the idea of rootlessness by writing *La Nuit est ma femme* in nonstandard French: his spelling is idiosyncratic, reflecting the pronunciation of peasants from Québec who had migrated to New England. His spelling sometimes shows the mark of anglophone phonetics, his way of indicating the mixture of languages that was occurring in his community; along these lines, he also uses a few English words.

Kerouac attended French-language parochial school until age eleven, then resumed studying the language during his year at the Horace Mann School in New York in preparation for Columbia University, where he also took French.[5] His choice to write in nonstandard French – the same French he uses in other writings, some published in his lifetime – is deliberate. His aim is to depict the language he grew up with, which was decreasingly spoken as the French-Canadian communities of the United States yielded to assimilation, to record it for posterity, to commemorate it – to honor the past of a migrant community, again the very thing Le Maître caught him not doing in *The Town and the City*. The distance of this language from standard French underscores the distance of Kerouac's community from the home they left in Québec, and the greater distance from the mother country, France, the result of the British conquest during the French and Indian War of 1754–1763. Kerouac put himself to the task of writing *La Nuit est ma femme* so as to exhibit his community, emphasizing its displacement and migration as it became less and less visible in the United States.

But even in this text he remains hidden: he never publicly revealed the existence of *La Nuit est ma femme*. It sat in his papers, which have long been housed in the New York Public Library's Berg Collection of English and American Literature. The archive was first opened to the public in 2006 and the novella first published in 2016, one of many previously unpublished French-language texts of varying length collected in *La Vie est d'hommage*, edited by Jean-Christophe Cloutier.[6] Nonetheless, as I've argued elsewhere, composing *La Nuit est ma femme* was integral to the major turning point in Kerouac's writing practices: the result was his three-week burst barely two months later, in April 1951, during which he wrote *On the Road* on a 120-foot scroll.[7] The road that is central to his best-known work is the place of migration, and in this draft he reveals himself by naming his narrator-protagonist Jack Kerouac, switching from the third-person narration of *The Town and the City* to first-person and drawing heavily on autobiography; he mentions the fact that this character speaks French with his mother. (In the 1957 version of *On the Road*, its first publication, the main character, Sal Paradise, is Italian-American and speaks Italian with his aunt.) In the scroll version, the road takes Jack all over the country as well as to Mexico, where he encounters different communities, most of which clearly result from migration: Latinx farmworkers in California, the African American neighborhood in Denver, the international harbor and Latin Quarter of New Orleans, inhabitants of Mexico of both European and indigenous heritage. Especially with regard to the lengthy section of *On the Road* that takes place in Mexico, which I'll return to later in this chapter, the road is a conduit across national borders, as it is for his French-Canadian community in its members' resettlement and visits back home.

Part of his aim in writing the novel all in a single burst, not pausing for revision – a procedure that was to crystalize as his famous "Spontaneous Prose" – is to capture language as it's spoken, complete with awkwardness and idiosyncratic, dialectal usage, just as it is in *La Nuit est ma femme*. I don't mean to say that he was trying to reproduce the "immediacy" of speech, but rather that he brings the irregularities of speech to writing in order to decrease the grammatical homogeneity of written American English and open it to larger possibilities of expression, which include nonnatives' use of it. Writing on a scroll that he assembled from sheets of architect's paper not only enhanced the process of uninterrupted language but also provided an image of the road.[8] As he wrote to Neal Cassady in May 1951, a few weeks after completing the scroll, "Went fast because road is fast … —just rolled it through the typewriter and in fact no paragraphs … rolled it out on floor and it looks like a road" (*Selected Letters 1*, 315–316). In the scroll version of the novel he describes traveling across Nebraska, the character of Neal Cassady at the wheel: "That magnificent car made the wind roar; it made the plains unfold like a roll of paper."[9] The typewriter and the car function in tandem: Kerouac is aware of both the newly developed US Numbered Highway System, which was begun in 1926 and made it possible to traverse the country in a few days, and the fairly new medium of the typewriter, which allowed him to write at his speed of a hundred words per minute.[10] Following the paths of migration and writing in order to commemorate them become part of the same technological task.

15.2 The Revealing Road

Despite the myth of the streamlining that editors supposedly imposed on the manuscript of *On the Road* and the consequent impurity of the 1957 version, Kerouac himself did several rewrites on his own initiative before publication, both subsequent drafts and variations on the theme of the road; this followed notes and partial drafts prior to the scroll. In one of the subsequent variations, he further pursues the intimate ties between his novel and his move into writing in French, another effort at revealing his French-Canadian heritage. In a notebook dated December 16, 1952 – almost a year and eight months after he typed the scroll – he composed thirty handwritten pages of a novella in dialectal French that he titled *Sur le chemin*. He added a second section in another notebook, additional phrases in other documents; when he partially translated the novella into English as *Old Bull in the Bowery* in 1954, he added more sections. The version published in 2016, masterfully reconstructed and translated by Cloutier, is over a hundred printed pages long.[11]

This novella is a bilingual text, a foray between languages as much as a story of travel. The phrase *sur le chemin* means "on the road," but it's not the more obvious *Sur la route*, the French title of *On the Road* used since the translation was first published in Paris in 1960. The word *chemin*, usually used for a smaller, more out-of-the-way road, as well as for a path, also has a religious connotation: the French for "the Way of the Cross" is *le chemin de la croix*, an all-important idea and symbol in the staunchly Catholic French-Canadian communities of New England. It's exemplified in the Stations of the Cross of the Grotto of Notre Dame de Lourdes in Lowell, with all captions in French, a durable monument to the community as well as the site of a haunting episode in Kerouac's novel *Doctor Sax*, first published in 1959.[12] The phrase *sur le chemin* also has the colloquial sense of "on the way."

This book tells a very different story from *On the Road*, a prehistory in which not only the two main characters but also their fathers meet for the first time. Its central event takes place in in New York City in 1935: Dean Pomeray is a drunk who drives from Denver with his nine-year-old son, also named Dean, and Leo Duluoz, a French Canadian, drives from Boston with his thirteen-year-old son Ti Jean (these ages match Kerouac's and Cassady's in 1935). "Ti Jean," meaning "Li'l Jean," was Kerouac's own nickname as a child. Duluoz is the surname Kerouac uses in most of his novels for his protagonist Jack or Jean Duluoz; he borrows his own father's first name, Leo, for the father of this family; his use of "Dean Pomeray" for the two characters based on the two Neal Cassadys, father and son, is in keeping with other versions of *On the Road*. In the Bowery, the Pomerays are greeted by Old Bull Balloon, a barely hidden rendition of William S. Burroughs (elsewhere Kerouac uses the same name for characters based on Burroughs), who turns out to be a French Canadian from Québec, an older relative of Leo. The French of this novella is similar to that of *La Nuit est ma femme* and that he writes in other works; here the sentences more strongly reflect English grammar and he puts more English words in his characters' mouths, especially Leo's.

Despite the distance between the plots of *Sur le chemin* and *On the Road*, Kerouac himself affirmed the close connection between the books. In a letter to Neal and Carolyn Cassady dated January 10, 1953, shortly after his return to his mother's home in Queens, he writes:

> In Mexico, after you [Neal] left, I in 5 days wrote, in French, a novel about me and you when we was kids in 1935 meeting in Chinatown with Uncle Bill Balloon, your father and my father and some sexy blondes in a bedroom with a French Canadian rake and an old Model T. You'll read it in print someday and laugh. It's the solution to the "On the Road" plots all of em and I will hand it in soon as I finish translating and typing. (*Selected Letters 1*, 395)

What Kerouac means by "all" the plots of *On the Road* is cryptic. But given the fact that one of the changes he made in *On the Road* between the initial 1951 composition and the 1957 publication was to slightly enhance the story of the futile search for Neal's lost father, the "solution" Kerouac finds probably has something to do with reaching for the ancestral past.[13] It probably also involves an attempt to link this past with the outsider's life he has found in adulthood through making his cultural mentor Burroughs a member of an extended French-Canadian family. The search for ancestry is a preoccupation that runs throughout his fiction and takes on allegorical dimensions: in most of his novels he emphasizes the sense of rootlessness that removal from an ancestral homeland entails. This removal is what drives him to remain hidden, as he describes it in the letter to Le Maître, while at the same time the quest for the past involves revelation of the self. The fact that Kerouac wrote both *La Nuit est ma femme* and *Sur le chemin* in Mexico suggests that they're connected to his experience of crossing borders: his family crossed a southern border when they left Québec for the United States, and in a reenactment of this migration, he crossed a southern border to travel to Mexico. These novels, a result of this reenactment, are part of his attempt to reveal an identity made distant in migration.

But as with *La Nuit est ma femme*, the revelation of *Sur le chemin* is partial: the book also remained hidden away in Kerouac's archive, more so for being scattered across different documents, until its 2016 publication. Once again, in the very act of revealing his true French-Canadian self, Kerouac hides. The narrator-protagonist named Jack Kerouac of the first *On the Road* manuscript becomes Jack Duluoz in *Sur le chemin*; no later than 1955, maybe as early as 1953, the character emerges as Sal Paradise, a name Kerouac came up with by misreading the words "sad paradise" in Allen Ginsberg's 1947 manuscript of the chapbook *Denver Doldrums*.[14] Even if Kerouac changed the names he had initially used in the 1951 manuscript of *On the Road* in response to his editor's concerns about liability (*Selected Letters 1*, 518–520), he chose to make his narrator-protagonist Italian-American, a member of a more widely known immigrant group. Sal is almost a generic immigrant child, a further concealment of Kerouac's own French-Canadian identity behind a broad American cultural category.

15.3 Traveling Languages

Just as Kerouac makes rootlessness a theme of *On the Road*, he makes the hiddenness of French-Canadian society and culture in the larger anglophone United States a theme of writing he undertook as he prepared *On the Road* for publication. Always aware of moving between languages, as he developed Spontaneous Prose he gave the English he wrote a foreign sound, adding the inflections and irregularities of a nonnative speaker. As Michel Bretagne puts it in *La Nuit est ma femme*, speaking for Kerouac, paraphrasing and enhancing the letter to Le Maître:

> J'ai jamais eu une langue a moi-même. Le Francais patoi j'usqua-six angts, et après ça l'Anglais des gas du coin. Et après ça—les grosses formes, les grands expressions, de poète, philosophe, prophète. Avec toute ça aujourd'hui j'toute melangé dans ma gum.[15]

In his translation, Cloutier renders the passage in an idiomatic American English that captures the French:

> I never had a language of my own. French patois until 6 years old, and after that the English of the guys on the corner. And after that—the big forms, the lofty expressions, of poets, philosophers, prophets. With all that today I'm all mixed up in my noggin.[16]

Kerouac literalizes this mix-up on the pages he writes in English; as he says to Le Maître, he will "refashion [English] to fit French images." The novels he wrote in this period, often set in the French-Canadian community he knew in childhood, include passages in French that he follows with English translations. The effects of this procedure are to bring English out of its homogeneity in order to show the many different ways it's spoken, to make English seem like a strange language to native speakers, and to bring the foreignness of his native French to the attention of his readers. He began doing this shortly after writing *La Nuit est ma femme* and around the time he wrote *Sur le chemin*. Two novels that he drafted in succession, *Doctor Sax* in 1952 and *Maggie Cassidy* in 1953, involve this procedure.[17] These are two of the three novels comprising the so-called Lowell trilogy, the third being *Visions of Gerard*, which he drafted in 1956. All three are depictions of his childhood and adolescence in Lowell, memorials to the French-Canadian community that was speaking less and less French, losing its strong sense of identity, dispersing in the dominant Anglophone culture. They all include passages in French.

In *Maggie Cassidy* he takes the process further by more deeply mixing the two languages in keeping with the way French was spoken in New England: his French always gives the impression of being affected by its proximity to English; it features words and phrases in English, spellings reflecting English phonetics, syntax influenced by English. In this novel he gave the English a foreign texture by first drafting long passages in French and then rendering them in English. Though *Maggie Cassidy* was first published in 1959, the original French-language parts of the manuscript were hidden in his archive; Cloutier includes them in *La Vie est d'hommage*. They consist of four complete chapters and eight partial chapters executed in four notebooks. As Cloutier points out in his introductory note to these texts, since the French-language manuscript begins at chapter 7, it's impossible to know whether Kerouac also composed any more of the manuscript in French.[18]

Nonetheless, the French-language sections of *Maggie Cassidy* are the basis for the novel's subsequent draft in English. A comparison of the very first passage, from the excerpt of chapter 7 in the notebooks, with the corresponding passage in the published version of the novel illustrates Kerouac's procedure.

> —We were scared; on s'morda de peine.
>
> Shta couchez sur mon bord avec mon bras alentour son coup, ma main grippez sur ses seins, et j lui manja les lèvres et elle les miennes. On ne sava plus loin allez sans s'batte. Apra ca on faisa inque s'assir pis en jazza dans la noirceur du salon tandis que la famille dorma et le radio joua bas. (*Maggie Cassidy: Sections en français*, 229)

> We were scared.
>
> I lay there on my side with my arm around her neck, my hand gripped on her rib, and I ate her lips and she mine. There were interesting crises.... No way to go further without fighting. After that we'd just sit and gab in the black of the parlor while the family slept and the radio played low.[19]

The French original showcases Kerouac's irregular spelling, partly phonetic (*shta* for *j'étais*), sometimes simply incorrect (as in *coup*, "blow" or "strike," for *cou*, "neck," two nouns with identical pronunciation), English influence showing in sounds: for example, in *shta* and *manja*, the terminal vowel almost like a short English *a* to approximate the Québécois pronunciation of the French *mangeais*, the form of *manger*, "to eat," in the imperfect tense. The word *grippez*, "gripped," is an archaism, used in Québécois French, though outmoded in metropolitan French,[20] maybe remaining in use partly under the influence of English. Kerouac ends some words with the letter *z*, a nonstandard spelling that recalls the use of the letter in late medieval and Renaissance French, which Kerouac had seen in the works of poet François Villon (1431–ca. 1463) and novelist François Rabelais (1483?–1553), both of whom he names repeatedly in his work. By echoing French from this period, Kerouac acknowledges the popular Québécois myth that the language there has changed little since colonization in the seventeenth century. He affirms this myth in *Satori in Paris* (1966), plunging its roots deeper by explicitly connecting it with Villon.[21] Its irregularities notwithstanding, this French is idiomatic and readable.

With small emendations, the English is a nearly word-for-word translation of the French, following its syntax, foreign sounding. Kerouac replaces "seins" – "breasts" – with "rib" in describing where his narrator's hands are, maybe to reduce the risk of censorship, probably also to make this story of teenage love seem a little more innocent. In the English Kerouac adds the cryptic phrase "These were interesting crises." Instead of translating *noirceur* as "darkness," which would be idiomatic in English, he renders it plain "black," preserving the *noir* of *noirceur*, allowing the French to tug on the English, as it does throughout the translated passages. The French is itself anglicized: the word *radio* in French is feminine, but here

Kerouac uses the masculine article *le*, which has historically been used as neutral for foreign words of indeterminate gender, also because the word *radio* ends with the more masculine-seeming *o*.

Kerouac writes in this English, gallicized through translation from a French that is itself anglicized, to emphasize the transition he and his community were undergoing to anglophone status, as well as the alterations to anglophone culture that this transition entails. He does so in a novel about his narrator-protagonist and alter ego Jack Duluoz taking steps to leave the community by getting romantically involved with a young anglophone woman, the Irish-American Maggie Cassidy. The young woman on whom this character is based was named Mary Carney; Kerouac gives the character the family name of his close friend Neal Cassady, using the more common spelling. Cassady often represented for Kerouac an Americanness that he himself wished to attain: for example, he dedicates his most experimental novel, *Visions of Cody*, a further rewrite of *On the Road* as a capacious portrait of Cassady under the character name Cody, "to America, whatever that is" (*Visions of Cody*, dedication page).

15.4 From Lowell to Global

The language and content of *Maggie Cassidy*, then, are a place where languages and cultures blend, cede their integrity, and become something else as they move. The novel features young characters of French-Canadian heritage and one friend of Greek heritage living in the ethnically mixed but predominantly anglophone world of Lowell. Accounts of French-Canadian assimilation, though, are only Kerouac's starting point: he proceeds in much of his work to meditations on how many cultures, migrating across the globe, encounter each other, interact, and change through the experience. *Doctor Sax*, the other Lowell novel he had just drafted when he wrote *Maggie Cassidy*, is an expansive vision of global culture, a fantastical picture of migrations traversing North America and the Atlantic over millennia. Though he initially drafted the novel in English, the text of *Doctor Sax* also includes passages in French; as is the case with *Maggie Cassidy*, its pages are an interlingual and intercultural zone.

At the very end of *Doctor Sax*, Kerouac names the place of its composition as "Mexico City, Tenochtitlan, 1952/Ancient Capital of Azteca" (*Doctor Sax*, 245): he emphasizes the novel's North American geography, extending across national borders as well as reaching through time to its indigenous heritage. Kerouac's mythical Lowell becomes the site of a battle between Doctor Sax and the Great Snake of the World, a creature combining medieval Christian imagery with Aztec mythology and embodying the destructiveness of war technology. Kerouac's title character is a composite of Christopher Marlowe's Doctor Faustus, Goethe's Faust, the Shadow of pulp magazines and radio, William S. Burroughs, and a few other figures, bearing the name of the saxophone, a key instrument from bebop, the improvisational form of jazz that captured Kerouac's imagination from the 1940s on. He builds the atmosphere of the novel through a syncretic mix of Québécois Catholicism and elements of Native American religion, with touches of Buddhism. Besides placing the United States in continental perspective, he recalls that North America was also a battlefield between the British and the French empires: the longest passage in French in the novel, a speech by a relative, the invalid Oncle Mike, on the Duluoz family's migration from France to New France, includes an account of the defeat of General Montcalm, the 1759 event that marked the fall of Québec and its eventual ceding to Great Britain at the conclusion of the French and Indian War (*Doctor Sax*, 118–119). Kerouac connects the people of Québec from whom he descends to more distant ancestry in Brittany: he writes of the eighteenth-century arrival of "the first of the American Armorican Duluozes" (*Doctor Sax*, 131). Using the adjectival form of the ancient name of Brittany in a pun he borrows from James Joyce, he brings the transatlantic dimension of the novel's geography into the person of his narrator-protagonist Jack Duluoz.[22]

Doctor Sax is a kaleidoscopic mix of cultures across historical time; Kerouac reaches for a global perspective, one of his goals when he began writing in the method that became Spontaneous Prose. The quest for this perspective is one of the purposes of *On the Road*: a major component of the cartography of North America that informs all his work, *On the Road* depicts explorations of the cultural variety of the United States and Mexico. He continued to work on it as he wrote *Doctor Sax* and several other novels: it's the start of a revelation of the multiethnic make-up of the United States and the multinational make-up of North America. As the conduit of migration, the road is also the place where the different cultures of North America interact.

Though Kerouac has been accused of perpetuating stereotypes in his depictions of different ethnic groups, his use of such images serves the purpose of conveying first impressions, and in each case his narrative makes them yield to a more complicated reality. In much of his writing, he presupposes that on first encounter, his traveling narrator-protagonist approaches people who are culturally different from himself as a tourist. In *On the Road*, Sal Paradise is aware of his affection for farmworkers in

California and his love for the Latinx woman Terry he meets; but he feels he can't be a part of their world because of the social status he's striving to achieve through college and a writing career. As someone of Italian immigrant heritage, Sal takes measures to become part of predominantly Anglo-Saxon white society. As he reflects later on, his "white ambitions" led him to abandon "a good woman like Terry" (*On the Road*, 180). From the start he approaches the Latinx people he meets in California as someone who remains partly outside dominant white culture yet doesn't want to lose his hold on it. Since he won't become a real part of the populations he encounters, he's a tourist. Kerouac makes sure his narrator and readers are aware of this, but also that his narrator's insights are about tourism as a cultural relationship.

15.5 Borders and Their Limits

Though tourism usually carries negative connotations, the idea of an opposition between the traveling yet entrenched philistine and the cosmopolitan observer has long been criticized. In his landmark 1976 study *The Tourist*, Dean MacCannell rejects any strict division between the two, instead seeing a continuum, each beginning an encounter with a new place with what he terms a "marker," a miniscule part of a vast cultural system. "Usually," MacCannell writes, "the first contact a sightseer has with a sight is not the sight itself but some representation thereof."[23] This could be a brochure, a plaque, a monument that over time has accrued significance on guided tours, or a mental image that has taken shape through exposure to many images from sources depicting supposedly key aspects of a place. In other words, travelers begin with stereotypes – like Kerouac, who approaches them with well-developed self-consciousness, rather than the unquestioning casual-to-brutal racism that too many critics have seen in superficial, often ridiculous appraisals of his work. When Sal, Dean, and their friends first cross the Mexican border, Sal observes, "To our amazement, it looked exactly like Mexico" (*On the Road*, 1957 version, 274). Through Sal, Kerouac reflects on the group's stereotypical images, confirmed through a first encounter at the site of countless previous first encounters.

As they drive on, they pass by a group of indigenous Mexicans in whose eyes Sal feels he and his friends are judged as "self-important moneybag Americans" (*On the Road*, 280). Freely admitting to being a tourist, he also speaks of seeing further: "These people were unmistakably Indians and were not at all like the Pedros and Panchos of silly civilized American lore" (*On the Road*, 280). Kerouac grants Sal full awareness of the tourist stereotypes he's packing. Though Sal may be substituting another set of images, it's a more complicated set, one gathered from study that dovetails with this experience. Some of this is Oswald Spengler's early twentieth century, two-volume warning, *The Decline of the West*, from which Kerouac (and presumably Sal) borrows the word "fellahin," the Arabic word for peasants. But Kerouac inverts Spengler's meaning: though Spengler also speaks of "peasants," meaning the groups of people who work the earth and eventually create civilization,[24] he reserves "fellahin" for those wandering aimlessly after the collapse of a civilization who produce nothing. The life of the fellahin (in German, *Fellachen*, in the translation spelled *fellaheen*) is "a planless happening without goal or cadenced march in time, wherein occurrences are many, but, in the last analysis, devoid of significance. The only historical peoples, the peoples whose existence is world-history, are the nations" (*On the Road*, 211).

But in this passage in *On the Road* and elsewhere in his writing, though Kerouac also uses the word *fellahin* to mean the people who remain after the fall of an empire, he means entirely productive, creative people, the ones who will usher in the next civilization, whatever form it will take. Implicitly criticizing Spengler's privileging of nations as the sole loci of history, Kerouac writes: "For when destruction comes to the world of 'history' and the Apocalypse of the Fellahin returns once more as so many times before, people will still stare with the same eyes from the caves of Mexico and the caves of Bali, where it all began and where Adam was suckled and taught to know" (*On the Road*, 280). Mexico has so far seen the Aztec Empire, which fell when the Spanish Empire arrived on the scene, which in turn fell and has now been replaced by Anglo-American domination of North America, "moneybag Americans" who feel free to gape as tourists. In his mention of Adam's birth, Kerouac rewrites the myth of human origin shared by Judaism, Christianity, and Islam. If Adam was "suckled," he wasn't created by divine fiat; hence human time is much longer than that of these major world religions. And if he was born in Mexico, Bali, and by implication everywhere there are fellahin – in short, everywhere on earth – then human origin is dislodged from the claim these religions place on it and scattered across the globe.

Earlier in the same passage, Sal describes the "Fellahin Indians of the world" as "the essential strain of the basic primitive, wailing humanity that stretches in a belt around the equatorial belly of the world," following with a series of locations outside Euro-America. Though it would be easy to accuse him of primitivism, he's proposing nothing less than the idea of a global culture that preceded and will follow the era of nation-states. Even his use of the word *primitive* here, rather than designating less developed cultures, suggests the fragility of predominantly white US-American civilization. And against the "white ambitions" that have driven his assimilation, he makes contact with the fellahin as part of himself: in the notebook in which he wrote the first part of *Sur le chemin* in Mexico City in 1952, he also sketched the genealogy of the Duluoz family, a mirror image of his own family, referring to the lineage as "Fellaheen."[25] He acknowledges his family and community's status as a population that has emerged from the imperial conquest of Québec, first by France and then by Britain. British domination contributed heavily to remaking the French settlers and their descendants into peasants or fellahin.[26] This status was maintained by the seigneurial system firmly in place until the Canadian Confederation of 1867, its aftereffects lasting decades more. The fall of Québec that Kerouac refers to in *Doctor Sax* is a pivotal event in the fellahin life of North America and its repeating apocalyptic events.

Beginning with his own situation as a multilingual migrant of peasant heritage, displaced from the national metropole of France and the drifting colony of Québec by the global shifts of empire, in his writing Kerouac extends his explorations to the many languages and peoples of North America and points to more remote geographies. As he becomes a writer, he becomes American, issuing the proverbial great American novel, first in *The Town and the City*, then in *On the Road*, with long trips through many other works in both prose and poetry, placing himself in the lineage of Wolfe, Twain, Whitman, and Melville, among others. But in his sense of springing from a borderless and nationless condition, he also reaches through the work of Goethe, Shakespeare, Proust, Rabelais, Dostoyevsky, Joyce, and Han-shan, among others. His writing is an appeal to a global literature that might not yet have existed in his time, that may still not yet exist, no less than a call to recognize and galvanize global culture.

Notes

1. Kerouac to Le Maître, in Jack Kerouac, *Kerouac: Selected Letters 1, 1940–1956*, ed. Ann Charters (New York: Viking, 1995), 228–229.
2. Jean-Philippe Warren, "The French Canadian Press in the United States," *The Journal of Modern Periodical Studies* 7, no. 1–2 (2016): 91–92.
3. Yvonne Le Maître, "The Town and the City," *Le Travailleur*, March 23, 1950 (my translation).
4. Jack Kerouac, *The Town and the City* (New York: Harcourt Brace, 1950), 111.
5. Joyce Johnson, *The Voice Is All: The Lonely Victory of Jack Kerouac* (New York: Viking, 2012), 45–46, 60.

6. The title *La Vie est d'hommage*, a phrase from the full-length version of Kerouac's highly experimental novel *Visions of Cody*, is a pun in French: the literal meaning is "Life is to be honored," but the pronunciation is the same as that of the phrase "La vie est dommage," meaning "Life is a pity." Jack Kerouac, *Visions of Cody* (1972; London and New York: Penguin, 1993), 362.
7. See Hassan Melehy, *Kerouac: Language, Poetics, and Territory* (New York: Bloomsbury, 2016), 45–58.
8. The best account of Kerouac's composition of *On the Road* is Isaac Gewirtz, *Beatific Soul: Jack Kerouac on the Road* (New York: New York Public Library, 2007), 109–147.
9. Jack Kerouac, *On the Road: The Original Scroll* (New York: Viking, 2007), 330. The phrase is nearly unchanged in the 1957 version: Jack Kerouac, *On the Road* (London and New York: Penguin, 2003), 234.
10. Dennis McNally, *Desolate Angel: Jack Kerouac, the Beat Generation, and America* (New York: Delta, 1979), 133.
11. Thanks to his remarkable abilities and efforts, Jean-Christophe Cloutier reconstructed and translated *Sur le Chemin* and *Old Bull in the Bowery*. In his introductory notes to these texts he provides explanations of the different documents and how he worked with them: Cloutier, introductory note, in Jack Kerouac, *Sur le chemin*, in *La Vie est d'hommage*, ed. Cloutier (Montreal: Boréal, 2016), 113–116; Cloutier, introductory note, in Kerouac, *Old Bull in the Bowery*, in *The Unknown Kerouac: Rare, Unpublished, & Newly Translated Writings*, ed. Todd Tietchen (New York: Library of America, 2016), 174.
12. Jack Kerouac, *Doctor Sax: Faust* Part Three (New York: Grove, 1959), 122–126.
13. Melehy, *Language*, 56–57.
14. Ann Charters, *Kerouac: A Biography* (1974) (New York: St. Martin's, 1994), 86; Jack Kerouac, "On the Road, second draft" (n.d.), Kerouac Papers, New York Public Library, 25.1; Kerouac "On the Road, third draft" (n.d.), Kerouac Papers, 26.1. Gewirtz dates the start of the second draft to 1955 and the third to 1953 (the third designated as such because it was completed after the second): Gewirtz, 112–118.
15. Jack Kerouac, *La Nuit est ma femme*, in *La Vie est d'hommage*, 55.
16. Jack Kerouac, *The Night Is My Woman*, trans. Jean-Christophe Cloutier and Kerouac, in *The Unknown Kerouac*, 66.
17. Ann Charters provides dates for the composition of all of Kerouac's work: "Chronology," in Jack Kerouac, *Kerouac: Selected Letters 2, 1957–1969*, ed. Charters (New York: Viking, 1999), 27–28.
18. Jean-Christophe Cloutier, introductory note to Jack Kerouac, *Maggie Cassidy: Sections en français*, in *La Vie est d'hommage*, 227.
19. Jack Kerouac, *Maggie Cassidy* (1959; London and New York: Penguin, 1993), 37.
20. Entry for *gripper*, Léandre Bergeron, *Dictionnaire de la langue québécoise* (Montreal: Typo, 1997); entry for *gripper*, *Le Petit Robert*, digital version 5.2 (Paris: Dictionnaires Le Robert, 2018).
21. Jack Kerouac, *Satori in Paris* (1966), in *Satori in Paris and Pic* (New York: Grove, 1985), 45–46. See also Kerouac to Whalen, *Selected Letters* 2, 373–374.

For an account of the myth of the Ancien Régime character of Québécois French, see Chantal Bouchard, *Obsessed with Language: A Sociolinguistic History of Québec*, trans. Louise von Flotow (Toronto: Guernica, 2008), 88–93.

22. The term "North Armorica" occurs in the second sentence of *Finnegans Wake*: James Joyce, *Finnegans Wake* (1939; London and New York: Penguin, 1999), 3.
23. Dean MacCannell, *The Tourist: A New Theory of the Leisure Class* (1976) (Berkeley and Los Angeles: University of California Press, 2013), 110.
24. Oswald Spengler, *The Decline of the West*, vol. 2 (1922), trans. Charles Francis Atkinson (London: Arktos, 2021), 109–113.
25. Jack Kerouac, "Workbook Mexicay" (1952), Kerouac Papers, New York Public Library, 39.10.
26. See Leslie Choquette, *Frenchmen into Peasants: Modernity and Tradition in the Peopling of French Canada* (Cambridge, MA: Harvard University Press, 1997), especially 279–305.

CHAPTER 16

The Two Phases of Jack Kerouac's American Buddhism

Sarah F. Haynes

During a December 1953 visit to Neal Cassady in California, Jack Kerouac walked into the San Jose Public Library in search of books on Buddhism. This was a seminal moment for Kerouac, as Buddhism would greatly influence his writing and impact his personal life up through the 1960s. Kerouac's introduction to Buddhism, and Asian thought more broadly, predated 1953. However, his trip to the library that December is identified as the beginning of his Buddhist period. This is a period during which Kerouac practiced Buddhism, intensely read Buddhist texts, incorporated Buddhist ideas into his novels and poetry, as well as completed Buddhist texts – specifically, *The Scripture of the Golden Eternity* (1960), the posthumously published *Some of the Dharma* (1997), and *Wake Up: A Life of the Buddha* (2008). This is in addition to his more famous, Buddhist-inspired works, *The Dharma Bums* (1958), *Mexico City Blues* (1959), and *Desolation Angels* (1965), which were also written during this period.[1] Traditionally, Kerouac's Buddhist period is viewed as ending in 1958, but a close reading of his unpublished writing reveals that Buddhism remained an important part of his life well into the mid-1960s.[2]

What follows is an examination of Kerouac's Buddhism informed by archival research of his unpublished Buddhist writing.[3] The aim is to provide a more complete understanding of Kerouac's Buddhism than what can be learned from his published works. A detailed analysis of his published and unpublished writing reveals that his Buddhist period should be separated into an Early Buddhist Period (1953–1958) and a Later Buddhist Period (1959–mid-1960s).[4] Kerouac's Early Buddhist Period is one of intense study and practice. And while his enthusiasm for the religion certainly decreased from 1959 to his death in 1969, it is inaccurate to state that he did not study Buddhism after 1958, as revealed by his unpublished diaries. Thus, 1959 through to 1967 should be identified as his Later Buddhist Period during which he continued his textual study, occasional meditation practice, and reworking of Buddhist texts. Additionally, it can be concluded that Kerouac believed himself to be a transmitter of Buddhism for Americans and that the Buddhism he believed helped his own suffering – and was, by extension, most useful for American practitioners – was largely rooted in the *Diamond Sūtra* (*Vajracchedikā Prajñāpāramitā Sūtra*) and in key *Mahāyāna* ideas.

Previous scholarship on Kerouac's Buddhism is limited to short examinations of his published works. While the corpus of literature on Kerouac is vast, little scholarship has focused on his Buddhist writing and practice. What does exist are a handful journal articles, unpublished theses, and the following three monographs: Carole Tonkinson's *Big Sky Mind: Buddhism and the Beat Generation*, John Lardas's *Bop Apocalypse: The Religious Visions of Kerouac, Ginsberg, and Burroughs*, and Benedict Giamo's *Kerouac, the Word and the Way: Prose Artist as Spiritual Quester*.

Each of these books provides an entry point into Kerouac's understanding and practice of Buddhism, thus, while all are useful, none offer a full and accurate account of his Buddhism that consider his unpublished works. However, more recently, John Whalen-Bridge and Kyle Garton-Gundling have offered more substantive chapters on the topic that begin to take Kerouac's engagement with Buddhism more seriously.[5]

While Kerouac is most famous for his 1957 novel *On the Road*, published during his Early Buddhist Period, this book was written well before Buddhism became a driving force in his life. For an understanding of Kerouac's Buddhism in his published works, one needs to consider *The Dharma Bums*, *Desolation Angels*, and *Mexico City Blues*. Subsequently, his overtly Buddhist books, *The Scripture of the Golden Eternity*, *Some of the Dharma*, and *Wake Up: A Life of the Buddha* are examined in conjunction with his unpublished Buddhist documents.[6]

16.1 *The Dharma Bums*

Conventional wisdom holds that the general ethos Kerouac cultivated in *On the Road* was a reaction to the conservatism and consumerism of post–Second World War America. Said ethos, carried through in *The Dharma Bums*, championed a life of nonconformity and simplicity while on the search for an authentic self and way of life, greatly influenced by alcohol and drug use. In *The Dharma Bums*, this ethos takes a decidedly Buddhist shape and Kerouac's vision for a Buddhist America shines through. *The Dharma Bums* was published in 1958 but was based on Kerouac's travels around the West Coast and North Carolina in 1955 and 1956, a period of intense Buddhist study.

The novel follows the exploits of Ray Smith (modeled on Kerouac) and the juxtaposition of his city life and mountain life. During his travels on the West Coast, Smith has his first real mountain experience as he's taken on a hike through the Sierra Nevada mountain range by one of the novel's main characters, Japhy Ryder.[7] Ryder best represents the Buddhist-inspired ethos Kerouac espouses in the novel, as evidenced in his call for a "rucksack revolution" led by Zen Lunatics. In the novel, Ryder opines, at length:

> I've been reading Whitman, know what he says, *Cheer up slaves, and horrifying despots*, he means that's the attitude for the Bard, the Zen Lunacy bard of old desert paths, see the whole thing is a world full of rucksack wanderers, Dharma Bums refusing to subscribe to the general demand that they consume production and therefore have to work for the privilege of consuming, all that crap they didn't really want anyway such as refrigerators, TV sets, cars, at least new fancy cars, certain hair oils and deodorants and general junk you finally always see a week later in the garbage anyway, all of them imprisoned in a system of work, produce, consume, work, produce, consume, I see a vision of great rucksack revolution thousands or even millions of young Americans wandering around with rucksacks, going up to mountains to pray, making children laugh and old men glad, making young girls happy and old girls happier, all of 'em Zen Lunatics who go about writing poems that happen to appear in their heads for no reason and also by being kind and also by strange unexpected acts keep giving visions of eternal freedom to everybody and to all living creatures ...[8]

For Kerouac, the rucksack revolution was a spiritual one envisioned as a coming together of East and West that would lead the Zen lunatic away from the staid postwar America.

The Dharma Bums presents Kerouac's understanding of Buddhism towards the end of his Early Buddhist Period. As a practitioner of Zen, Ryder presses upon Kerouac's character the wisdom of Zen Buddhism. Early in the book, tinged with frustration, Smith (Kerouac) says,

> "[l]issen Japhy," I said, "I'm not a Zen Buddhist, I'm a serious Buddhist, I'm an oldfashioned dreamy Hinayana coward of later Mahayanism," and so forth into the night, my contention being that Zen Buddhism didn't concentrate on kindness so much as on confusing the intellect to make it perceive the illusion of all sources of things. "It's *mean*," I complained. "All those Zen Masters throwing young kids in the mud because they can't answer their silly word questions" (*The Dharma Bums*, 8–9).

While Kerouac was inspired by Snyder's dedication to Buddhism, in both real life and the book they did not always agree, as is in the infamous *yabyum* scene. *Yabyum* in Tibetan Buddhism is the joining of male and female, the coming together of skillful means (*upāya-kauśalya*) and wisdom (*prajñā*) and as part of Tantric practice, *Yabyum* is the physical union of male and female through sexual ritual for the purposes of reaching enlightenment. For Kerouac, sexual ritual did not align with his understanding of a Buddhism steeped in the morality of the six perfections (*pāramitā*). Yet, as will be noted below, he had no problem omitting the precept regarding inappropriate use of intoxicants.

Thematically, *The Dharma Bums* covers much of the same material as Kerouac's Buddhist publications. Despite the undeniable Zen influence of Snyder on the book, Kerouac is able to bring his vision of Buddhism to the fore.[9] He provides lengthy expositions on the nature of existence in relation to emptiness (*śūnyatā*), particularly in the context of his favorite *Mahāyāna* text, the *Diamond Sūtra*. In a nod to the famous line from the *Diamond Sūtra* "form is emptiness, emptiness is form," Ryder states, "It's only through form that we can realize emptiness" (*The Dharma Bums*, 17). And later, "Diamond Sutra says 'Make no formed conceptions about the realness of existence nor about the unrealness of existence'" (*The Dharma Bums*, 73). Another major element of Kerouac's practice was the cultivation of the six perfections. *The Dharma Bums* pays particular attention to the ideas of kindness (*maitrī*) and charity (*dāna*). Early in *The Dharma Bums*, Kerouac's character hops a train out of Los Angeles where he encounters a "little bum" with whom he shares his food. Kerouac writes, "I reminded myself of the line in the Diamond Sutra that says, 'Practice charity without holding in mind any conceptions about charity, for charity after all is just a word'" (*The Dharma Bums*, 2). And later, reflecting upon Ryder, Smith thinks, "[t]here was another aspect of Japhy that amazed me: his tremendous and tender sense of charity. He was always giving thing, always practicing what the Buddhists call the Paramita of Dana, the perfection of charity" (*The Dharma Bums*, 56).

Kerouac's biggest concern as a Buddhist was suffering (*duḥkha*). In his search to alleviate his suffering, Kerouac was drawn to *Mahāyāna* concepts that taught enlightenment was within his grasp, merely needing to be awakened. Buddha-nature (*tathagatāgarbha*) and the figure of the bodhisattva appealed to him as the potential to overcome suffering seemed less daunting. The compassion (*karuṇā*) exhibited by bodhisattvas who suffer for the sake of others is exactly what Kerouac, still traumatized by his brother's death and his own destructive behavior, hoped to achieve. He wanted both to be saved and to save others. His character in *The Dharma*

Bums says, "'[e]verything is possible. I am God, I am Buddha, I am imperfect Ray Smith, all at the same time'" (*The Dharma Bums*, 93). Smith identifies his imperfect nature with the most divine of beings in Christianity and Buddhism.

Aligning with the idea of emptiness, Smith's journey in the novel is motivated by a desire to overcome his suffering. Kerouac introduces the topic of suffering, but from a more personal perspective, forewarning Ryder of where his interests lie. "I warned him at once I didn't give a goddamn about the mythology and all the names and national flavors of Buddhism, but was just interested in the first of Sakyamuni's four noble truths, *All life is suffering.* And to an extent interested in the third, *The suppression of suffering can be achieved*" (*The Dharma Bums*, 8). Suffering played a huge role in Kerouac's life for as long as he could remember, and although his struggle for absolution never bore any permanent fruit, his turn to the idea of reality as-it-is (*yathā-bhūta*) as a salve was frequent. Given the nature of reality as-it-is, perhaps it is unsurprising that Smith's spiritually driven rucksack revolution fails to gain ground and by the end of the novel he is on Desolation Peak working as a fire lookout.

Picking up where *The Dharma Bums* leaves off, *Mexico City Blues* and *Desolation Angels* follow Kerouac (as Jack Duluoz) through the remainder of his travels during 1955–1956.[10] Taking him from the East to West Coasts – including the mountains of the Pacific Northwest – down to Mexico, and eventually Tangier, the two novels and book of choruses reveal Kerouac's state of mind while he was in the middle of his Early Buddhist Period.

16.2 *Mexico City Blues*

Mexico City Blues best reflects how Buddhism inspired Kerouac's writing style and content. The book recounts, in chorus form, Kerouac's experiences living in Mexico City in 1955 with William S. Burroughs's friend, a morphine addict named Bill Garver, who enabled Kerouac and led to much of the book being written while inebriated.[11]

Mexico City Blues retains the spontaneity and stream of consciousness found in other Kerouac works, revealing the influence of jazz and Buddhism on him during this period. The form and style of *Mexico City Blues* present an unconventional and paradoxical poetic symbolism in its introduction of *Mahāyāna* ideas. Most prevalent is the idea of the emptiness as a characteristic of existence, opening the door for Kerouac to consider buddha-nature and the functioning of the mind. Chorus #67 reads:

Suchness
Is *Tathata*, the name,
Used,
to mean, Essence,
all things is made
of the same thing
essence

The thing is pure nature,
not Mother Nature

The thing is to express
the very substance of your thoughts
as you read this
is the same as the emptiness
of space
right now

and the same as the silence you hear
inside the emptiness
that's there
everywhere,
so nothing in the way
but ignorant sofas
and phantoms & chairs,
nothing there but the picture in the movie in your mind[12]

This chorus introduces the idea of emptiness by addressing the difficulties that ignorant, unenlightened people experience when trying to understand that even though aspects of reality appear different, they are all the same.

Kerouac turns to Buddhist philosophical ideas that focus on the suffering experienced by all sentient beings. Unsurprising, since for Kerouac, solace for his own suffering was found in Buddhism. The *Mahāyāna* idea of buddha-nature offered Kerouac guidance, and hope, that there would be an end to his own suffering caused by the trauma of his brother's death and how that grief manifested in addiction and attachment issues. Chorus #203 reads:

Heaven's inside you but there's no you.
What does that mean?
said the teacher,
The Great Holy the All Holy
Old Teacher: –

All you've got to do
Everytime you feel sick
Is stop (this madhouse
        shot of yours
        is not exactly
        the immemorial miel)

    stop – and stare
        through the things
        before your eyes
        with eyes unfocused
        and as soon as they move
        you will have seen
        that they move
        to illusion.

Seeing that all's illusion
You lose your mind
In meditation
And heal yourself well
        (AND WHAT'S BEEN HEALED?) (*Mexico City Blues*, 203)

Kerouac recognizes that buddha-nature (*tathāgatagarbha*) is inherent within all sentient beings and, following *Mahāyāna* philosophy, reiterates that illusory-like (*māyā*) nature of reality, complicated by our unenlightened mental process that is preventing ourselves from being healed. Worth mentioning is Kerouac's nod to the agency the individual has in bringing themselves to the recognition of their own buddha-nature.

Ultimately, *Mexico City Blues* is the finest example of the coming together of Kerouac's iconoclastic literary style, life experience, and early Buddhist interests. Kerouac viewed his stylistic innovations, as found in *Mexico City Blues*, as a challenge to the orthodoxy of postwar literature, as it so perfectly encapsulates his urgency, pursuit of experience, and Buddhist fervor. After reading the book, Snyder stated in an unpublished correspondence dated January 20, 1960, that *Mexico City Blues* would serve Kerouac well in the future, referring to the positive karma it would bring him.[13]

16.3 *Desolation Angels*

However, in many ways, *Desolation Angels* best represents Kerouac's engagement with Buddhism in a more traditional narrative form, as it was written over a five-year period starting in 1956 when he was deep into his study of Buddhism and extending into the 1960s and his Late Buddhist

Period. In particular, "Part One: Desolation in Solitude," provides a fictionalized account of Kerouac's time as a fire lookout on Desolation Peak in the North Cascade Mountains of Washington State, an experience he idealized and loathed.[14] Unsurprisingly, Kerouac had a romanticized vision for his two-month solitary experience. Kerouac's narrator, Jack Duluoz, takes the job after hearing of Jarry Wagner's (Snyder) experience as a lookout. Duluoz states,

> when I get to the top of Desolation Peak and everybody leaves on mules and I'm alone I will come face to face with God or Tathagata and find out once and for all what is the meaning of all this existence and suffering and going to and fro in vain' but instead I'd come face to face with myself, no liquor, no drugs, no chance of faking it but face to face with old Hateful Duluoz Me and many's the time I thought I die, suspire of boredom, or jump off the mountain, but the days, nay the hours dragged and I had no guts for such a leap, I had to *wait* and get to see the face of reality.[15]

Kerouac's expectation of a direct experience of God or the Buddha (referred to as *Tathagata*) was never realized. Though, in many ways, Kerouac reached a better understanding of himself during this period of sobriety and solitude. Duluoz comes to an acceptance of the Buddhist middle-path, recognizing that neither his life of constant sense-pleasing nor his life of ascetic deprivation on the mountain are likely to lead to enlightenment. What Duluoz wrestles with most in *Desolation Angels* is the difficulty of being at ease by himself, dwelling in his own thoughts, facing who he truly was, and accepting his grief and addictions. However, in reality Kerouac struggled just as much with the suffering brought about by his lifestyle off the mountain, despite the urgency he felt to return to it.

While on the mountain, Duluoz becomes disillusioned with the rucksack revolution. He writes of the

> idea we worked out together on long hikes concerning a 'rucksack revolution' with all over America 'millions of Dharma Bums' going up to the hills to meditate and ignore society O Ya Yoi Yar give me society, give me the beauteous-faced whores … Not that Jarry [Snyder] would deny this … I wanta go where there's lamps and telephones and rumpled couches with women on them … I'd rather undo the back straps of redheads dear God and roman the redbrick walls of perfidious samsara than this rash of rugged ridge full of bugs … In Desolation, Desolation is learned. (*Desolation Angels*, 69–70)

Here Kerouac's Duluoz expresses his yearnings for a conventional life and its materialism rather than what he then deemed the false pursuit of Ultimate Truth on Desolation Peak. Despite his desire to return to civilization and the things he used to avoid facing, *Desolation Angels* thematically situates Kerouac within much of his Buddhist-inspired writing. Following his interest in *Mahāyāna* philosophy, Kerouac writes at length about the nature of existence, its suffering, ignorance (*avidyā*), and emptiness – the void.

In *Desolation Angels*, like most of Kerouac's Buddhist-inspired works, a concern for the six perfections is interwoven amongst his discourses on emptiness and suffering. Duluoz manifests the kindness and charity that Kerouac focused upon in his own Buddhist practice, exemplifying the bodhisattva ethic of compassion so prevalent in the Indian *Mahāyāna* literature that Kerouac studied. Later in the book, Duluoz comments on his tendency towards kindness, "[a]nyway Irwin [Allen Ginsberg] doesnt take any bull from anybody, while me, I'm always sitting there with my Buddhist 'vow of kindness' (vowed alone in the woods) taking abuse with pent up resentment that never comes out" (*Desolation Angels*, 290). Here, Kerouac's character mirrors much of the internalized feelings seen in his diaries. The vows of kindness and generosity were Kerouac's guiding principles. Yet the above quote makes it clear that there was a bitterness he was unable to overcome.

Upon his descent and return to San Francisco, Duluoz quickly returns to his usual lifestyle. At the beginning of "Book One – Part Two: Desolation in the World," Duluoz notes,

> [w]hat I learned on the solitary mountain all summer, the Vision on Desolation Peak, I tried to bring down to the world and to my friends in San Francisco, but they, involved in the strictures of time and life, rather than the eternity and solitude of mountain snowy rocks, had a lesson to teach me themselves—Besides, the vision of the freedom of eternity which I saw and which all wilderness hermitage saints have seen, is of little use in cities. (*Desolation Angels*, 73)

Duluoz does not leave the mountain having a direct experience of enlightenment, though he comes to the realization that wilderness, solitude, and a lack of intoxicants do not suit him well. This, however, does not mean Kerouac left Buddhism on Desolation Peak.

16.4 *The Scripture of the Golden Eternity*

In 1956, Kerouac wrote the *sūtra* he published as *The Scripture of the Golden Eternity* (1960).[16] Encouraged by Snyder to compose a *sūtra*, *The Scripture of the Golden Eternity* is sixty-six verses that reflect Kerouac's interest in *Mahāyāna* ideas, namely emptiness, consciousness-only (*vijñapti-mātra*), and buddha-nature. Kerouac's confidence in his own ability to transmit the dharma through his composition of the *sūtra* stemmed from what he believed to be an experience of enlightenment that occurred in his backyard. In verse four, he writes, "I was awakened to show the way, chosen to die in the degradation of life, because I am the Mortal Golden Eternity."[17] Kerouac's perceived enlightenment was detailed as a direct experience of the Golden Eternity – what he equates with an enlightened being, a God, and emptiness. He writes,

> One that
> is what is, the golden eternity, or God, or,
> Tathagata—the *name*. The Named One.
> The human God. Sentient Godhood.
> Animate Divine. The Deified One.
> The Verified One. The Free One.
> The Liberator. The Still One.
> The Settled One. The Established One.
> Golden Eternity (*Scripture*, 23–24)

In the longest, and arguably most important verse of the *sūtra*, Kerouac details his encounter with the Golden Eternity:

> I was smelling flowers in the yard, and when
> I stood up I took a deep breath and the blood all
> rushed to my brain and I woke up dead on my
> back in the grass. I had apparently fainted,
> or died, for about sixty seconds. My neighbor
> saw me but he thought I had just suddenly
> thrown myself on the grass to enjoy the sun.
> During that timeless moment of unconsciousness
> I saw the golden eternity. I saw heaven. In it
> nothing had ever happened, the events of a
> million years ago were just as phantom and
> ungraspable as the events of now or of a million
> years from now, or the events of the next ten
> minutes. It was perfect, the golden solitude, the
> golden emptiness, Something-Or-Other, something
> surely humble. There was a rapturous ring of
> silence abiding perfectly. There was no question
> of being alive or not being alive, of likes, and
> dislikes, of near or far, no question of giving
> or gratitude, no question of mercy or judgment,
> or of suffering or its opposite of anything.
> It was the womb itself, aloneness, alaya vijnana
> the universal store, the Great Free Treasure, the

> Great Victory, infinite completion, the joyful
> mysterious essence of Arrangement. It seemed
> like one smiling smile, one adorable adoration,
> one gracious and adorable charity, everlasting
> safety, refreshing afternoon, roses, infinite
> brilliant immaterial golden ash, the Golden Age.
> The "golden" came from the sun in my eyelids,
> and the "eternity" from my sudden instant
> realization as I woke up that I had just
> been where it all came from and where it
> was all returning, the everlasting So, and
> so never coming or going; therefore I call it
> the golden eternity but you can call it anything
> you want. As I regained consciousness I felt sorry
> I had a body and a mind suddenly realizing I
> didnt even have a body and a mind and nothing
> had ever happened and everything is alright
> forever and forever, O thank you
> thank you thank you. (*Scripture*, 59–60)

In this seemingly direct experience of emptiness, Kerouac references the idea of buddha-nature and equates the experience with the *Yogācāra* concept of storehouse consciousness (*ālaya-vijñāna*).

Overall, *The Scripture of the Golden Eternity* offers the reader the most well thought out, semitraditional Buddhist discourse on Kerouac's understanding of Buddhism through the late 1950s that we have in publication. The book provides insight into his grasp of Buddhism by offering clarity regarding his construction of a traditional Buddhist text and his vision for an American Buddhism.

16.5 *Some of the Dharma*

Some of the Dharma is largely a collection of Kerouac's diary entries, musings, and poetry on Buddhism. Written during his Early Buddhist Period, particularly 1953–1956, the book was posthumously published in 1997. *Some of the Dharma* is an important work as it offers the reader insight into Kerouac's vision of Buddhism, as well as a glimpse into how his diaries and unpublished documents served as its foundation.

Some of the Dharma's ten chapters, referred to as books, mirror his diaries in both style and content, including his ups and downs and his vast knowledge of Buddhism. Kerouac believed in the importance of the book as a means of transmitting Buddhism to Americans and for his own study of the religion, and as such the book is an excellent representation of the diverse nature of his Buddhism during his early period. *Some of the Dharma* is often incoherent, moving from one topic to another, jumping among writing styles, and interweaving other religious ideas. In this way, it reflects the nature of his diaries. Despite its incoherence and fragmentary nature, several ideas can be identified as foundational to *Some of the Dharma*. Book One opens with definitions, a bibliography, and additional introductory Buddhist ideas. Kerouac introduces a variety of Buddhist literature, including *Pāli* and *Mahāyāna* texts. Despite the textual diversity, it quickly becomes apparent that Kerouac gravitates towards particular concepts and texts, namely those that are Indian *Mahāyāna* in provenance.

In Book One Kerouac identifies what he believes are key Buddhist concepts. He writes,

> [t]he great mystery and astonishing discovery of Indian Philosophy or Buddha is, that in reality there is only perfect emptiness … Now I remember: The state of my Mind was pure water before I was born…. Carefully strain off top for perfect purity and all things will be seen not in separateness but in unity wherein there is no place for evil passions to enter – This purity is in fully conformity with the mysterious and indescribable purity of Nirvana – This means that you must go, and devote yourself entirely to thought, for Two goals
>
> 1. Emptying yr mind, transmuting false Mind of death and re birth into true and clear Essence Mind, tranquilizing and straining off the pure, harmonizing starting point with Goal of perfect Enlightenment
> 2. Attain Bodhisattva-Mahasattvaship by abandoning all dependence upon conceptions of ego-selfness by running passionate desires thru the wringer of the 5 defilements and understanding the deceptiveness of the sense-organs and sense-minds and the discriminating thoughts[18]

When broken down, Kerouac's goals reveal what interested him about Buddhism. Focusing on *Mahāyāna*, Kerouac reveals that the way to reach enlightenment is through a direct realization of emptiness, as emptiness characterizes all things, including one's own self. For the suffering Kerouac, an understanding of emptiness helps to overcome the attachment to self, or ego, but also to realize the ephemeral nature of suffering itself. Kerouac takes a *Mahāyāna* approach through his second goal of attaining the status of a bodhisattva, as his understanding of Buddhism focuses on the *Mahāyāna* concepts of compassion and kindness, characteristics foundational to a bodhisattva, or the ideal figure in later Buddhism who is motivated to help others alleviate their suffering. In *Some of the Dharma* he comes to an understanding that the way to cease his own suffering is by addressing the functioning of his mind. For Kerouac, controlling the sense organs was the means to achieving any profound realization of the dharma, despite the fact that Duluoz seemingly chose a life of sense-pleasure in *Desolation Angels.*

Kerouac's focus on emptiness inevitably leads into a discussion of the *Mahāyāna* conception of the mental process. While he enters into the territory of Nāgārjuna and the *Mādhyamaka* school of Indian philosophy, his real affinity is for *Yogācāra* theories of the mind. Kerouac is looking to understand what causes his suffering, his attachments, and how his mind is perpetuating ignorance. In doing this, Kerouac attempts to accept the world for what it is, including his own suffering, and in doing so highlights the emptiness of all things which leads him to the ever-appealing idea of buddha-nature.

Kerouac's final words of Book Two of *Some of the Dharma* reflect this interest in *Yogācāra.* He writes,

> [b]y realizing that there is nothing to disappear into thin air except Mind Essence itself, which neither appears nor disappears, and so by realizing that the body and all its pain is Mind-only. By realizing that words and thoughts like these are ripples of Ignorance on the clear mirror surface of Mind Essence with its intrinsic unbroken Calm. For, emptiness is what it all is (*Some of the Dharma*, 90).

As mentioned above, Buddha-nature offers Kerouac an appealing alternative to a life of suffering. It informs him that within himself, amongst all the suffering, is the potential for enlightenment; he just needs to figure out how to awaken it.

Early in Book One the reader develops an understanding of how Kerouac's vision for Buddhism in America is to manifest itself. In the introductory material, Kerouac lists "The Four Precepts," which is significant because it suggests his Buddhism excludes the fifth precept (not to engage in inappropriate use of intoxicants). He accepts the precepts that require one not take life, not steal, not lie, and not engage in inappropriate sexual activity (*Some of the Dharma*, 8). Kerouac is always conflicted about his alcohol use. At times he believes it is his downfall and at other times he feels it is a useful tool on his religious journey. Here, it appears he is being more practical and accepts it as "reality as-it-is." That is, a part of his life, and that of Americans, that is not easily removed.

Kerouac believed the dharma could save the world, and truly thought it was his duty to bring the Buddha's teachings to Westerners, and *Some of the Dharma* was an important tool for making this happen (*Some of the*

Dharma, 16). Arguably, Westerners are still being introduced to Buddhism through *Some of the Dharma* and his other Buddhist works. For example, the introduction to Kerouac's life of the Buddha, *Wake Up*, is authored by well-known scholar of Buddhism Robert A. F. Thurman, who praises Kerouac for his knowledge and transmission of Buddhism. He writes, "it has become apparent to me that Jack Kerouac was the lead bodhisattva, way back there in the 1950s, among all of our very American predecessors."[19] And he later notes, that

> [i]t is likely that Kerouac understood the deeper, broader dimensions of Mahayana Buddhism better than his peers, either those like myself, who were strongly motivated to break away from their Christian background, or those who were receiving knowledge thru the prism of East Asian Chinese and Japanese cultures, and especially through Ch'an/Zen connection, where meditation and samurai-like hardball "no-thought" are emphasized.[20]

The criticisms against Kerouac's Buddhism – that he did not practice enough meditation, that his Buddhism was too literary in nature, and that its later iterations were too Christian in outlook – are all judgments that seemingly hint towards there being one true way to be a Buddhist, ignoring the rich diversity of the religion and discrediting the adaptations it has experienced in both the West and Asia. Kerouac was instrumental in adapting Buddhism for American audiences, as were D. T. Suzuki, Alan Watts, Chögyam Trungpa and so many more Asian and Western agents. To ignore Kerouac's impact does a disservice to his practice and development of the religion, as well as to the countless people who were introduced to Buddhism through his writing.

16.6 *Wake Up*

Wake Up: A Life of the Buddha, written in 1955, in the middle of his Early Buddhist Period, though not published until 2008, provides the reader with Kerouac's understanding of Buddhism through the life story of the Buddha. Kerouac's retelling of the Buddha's life story is not out of character when one considers his penchant for rewriting Buddhist texts and his preference for biographical narrative. Kerouac gravitated towards the life stories of various important Buddhist teachers, turning to them as models for how he should live.

Wake Up introduces readers to the various Buddhist texts Kerouac studied; he intersperses his prose with quotes from Buddhist texts in his retelling of the Buddha's life for a modern audience, and in particular he relies on the *Śūraṅgama Sūtra* (*Heroic March Sūtra*), a popular *Mahāyāna* text in East Asian Buddhism. The *sūtra* is largely a discussion between the Buddha and his cousin and attendant Ananda. The Buddha instructs Ananda on Indian *Mahāyāna* ideas, including the idea of buddha-nature, as well as logic and argumentation found in both the *Mādhyamaka* and *Yogācāra* schools of *Mahāyāna* philosophy.

The focus of Kerouac's *Wake Up* moves beyond the Buddha's life to highlight some of the ideas to which he kept returning in his own practice. Of course, the Buddha's own life experiences were appealing to Kerouac – Buddha's ability to independently change his life for the better resonated with solitary-inclined Kerouac, who was alone with little in the way of external guidance, as his own study of Buddhism was autodidactic in nature, much like a *pratyekabuddha* (solitary buddha). As he writes in *Wake Up*, "'I have no master,' replied the Enlightened One, 'no honorable tribe; no point of excellence; self-taught in this profoundest doctrine, I have arrived at superhuman wisdom'" (*Wake Up*, 44). If we consider this quotation in light of Kerouac's life at the time of writing *Wake Up*, it is evident that he recognized similarities between his life and the Buddha's, as he slowly alienated himself from his Beat Generation friends.

Wake Up integrates other ideas that drew Kerouac to Buddhism, including the suffering that characterizes existence and the need to break free from this conventional existence through the realization of emptiness. A little over half-way through the book, Kerouac employs passages from the *Śūraṅgama Sūtra* to support his discussion of emptiness. Quoting the Buddha in a teaching to disciples on the mind defiled by lust, Kerouac writes, "[a]ll is empty everywhere forever, wake up! The mind is fool and limited, to take these senses, petty thwartings in a dream, as reality; as if the deeps of the ocean were moved by the wind that ripples the waves. And that wind is ignorance" (*Wake Up*, 85). His discussion of emptiness continues in the vein of *Mahāyāna*. Kerouac's Buddha instructs:

> [l]ook carefully! Stare through the sight of things and you will only see the Great Heart of Compassion of all the Buddhas of Old beyond belief. This is Yathabhutam, the seeing of things truly.... Ananda, the intrinsic nature of earth is the real emptiness of space, the true vacuum; while the intrinsic nature of space is the real earth, the true essence. In the Tathagata's Womb of the un-bornness of the unborn essence of all things which is the Ultimate and Supreme Reality, space and sights are of perennial freshness and purity, permeating everywhere throughout the phenomenal universes, and are being forever manifested spontaneously and perfectly in accordance with the amount of Karma-need accumulated under the conscious activity of sentient beings who are but pitiful forms of ignorance in what is like a vision and a dream a long time already finished. (*Wake Up*, 130–131)

Here Kerouac brings together the emptiness of all things, in all the universes, in his understanding of reality as it truly is. As previously noted, Kerouac often returned to these ideas in response to his own daily struggles with fame and alcoholism. He evokes the quintessentially *Mahāyāna* concepts of compassion and buddha-nature and ends the passage with a reference to the ignorance that drives the mind of the unenlightened as though it were a dream or a vision. Overall, *Wake Up* offers a window into Kerouac's Early Buddhist Period and an illuminating introduction to the *Mahāyāna* Buddhist ideas that are fully formed in his later Buddhist writing.

When considering the corpus of Kerouac's works, several conclusions can be made about his study and interpretation of Buddhism. An examination of his published works and archival documents offers a more complete understanding of Kerouac's Buddhism and reveals that his engagement with the religion was far longer than what has previously been delineated. His study of Buddhism lasted well into the mid-1960s, and while it's true that the intensity of his interest in the dharma waned, he still turned to the teachings when he was especially suffering. An examination of the totality of Kerouac's Buddhist writing reveals he had a more nuanced understanding of Buddhism than previously thought. He greatly desired to share the teachings he deemed important for American audiences. Namely, how to alleviate suffering, how to understand of emptiness, and the importance of integrating kindness and generosity into one's life. Kerouac was not a fad practitioner of Zen Buddhism. He spent years studying Buddhist texts, attempting to integrate Buddhist principles into his life. And despite his constant struggles he believed himself to have experienced emptiness and felt compelled to share what he learned with his fellow Americans.

Notes

1. This is not an exhaustive list of Kerouac's Buddhist works.
2. The New York Public Library (NYPL) holds the vast Jack Kerouac Archive of largely unpublished writing.
3. I conducted over one hundred hours of archival research at the Kerouac Archive at the NYPL between 2017 and 2020. Unfortunately, permissions to quote unpublished materials were denied by the Kerouac Estate.
4. Kerouac's diary writing decreased significantly as his health deteriorated in the mid-1960s. However, in one of his last diary entries, written in 1967, mentions the importance of the Buddha's teachings in reference to his current health NYPL 58.17.
5. John Whalen-Bridge, "Buddhism and the Beats," *The Cambridge Companion to the Beats*, ed. Steven Belletto (New York: Cambridge University Press, 2017)

225–239; "The Dharma Bums, the Four Noble Truths, and the Problem of "Romantic" Buddhism," *Journal of Beat Studies* (Volume 10, 2022): 85–104. Kyle Garton-Gundling, *Enlightened Individualism: Buddhism and Hinduism in American Literature From the Beats to the Present* (Columbus: The Ohio State University Press, 2019).

6. For a more detailed examination see Sarah F. Haynes, *Jack Kerouac, Buddhism, and the American Search for Enlightenment* (New York: Bloomsbury, forthcoming).
7. Japhy Ryder is fictionalized version of Gary Snyder. Snyder is a Zen practitioner who greatly influenced Kerouac's Buddhism.
8. Jack Kerouac, *The Dharma Bums* (1958. New York: Penguin, 2006), 73–74.
9. Kerouac is often identified as a Zen Buddhist. I've argued elsewhere that this is a misrepresentation; see Sarah F. Haynes, "Sad Paradise: Jack Kerouac's Nostalgic Buddhism," *Religions* (April 10, 2019): 266–277.
10. *Mexico City Blues* (1959) was written in 1955. *Desolation Angels* (1965) was written at two different times, the first part in 1956 and the second in 1961.
11. For information on Garver see: allenginsberg.org/2019/02/46102/. Kerouac was in the middle of his Early Buddhist Period but continued to use intoxicants. His unpublished documents reveal that he turned to Buddhism when his lifestyle got out of control. For example, see NYPL 56.29.
12. Jack Kerouac, *Mexico City Blues* (1959. New York: Grove, 1994), 67.
13. NYPL 72.10.
14. Large sections of *Desolation Angels* were taken from his journals written on the mountaintop. These journals have recently been published in Jack Kerouac, *Desolation Peak: Collected Writings*, ed. Charles Shuttleworth (Lowell, MA: Sal Paradise Press, 2022).
15. Jack Kerouac, *Desolation Angels* (1965. New York: Riverhead Books, 1995), 4.
16. Other significant attempts to write Buddhist literature include his rewriting of the *Diamond Sūtra* and his original *Northport Sūtra*; the former is included in *Desolation Peak* as "The Diamondcutter of Perfect Knowing" (243–265), while the latter remains unpublished as of this writing.
17. Jack Kerouac, *The Scripture of the Golden Eternity* (New York: Cornith, 1960), 24.
18. Jack Kerouac, *Some of the Dharma* (1997. New York: Penguin, 1999), 11.
19. Robert A. F. Thurman, "Introduction" in Jack Kerouac, *Wake Up* (New York: Penguin, 2008), vii.
20. Thurman "Introduction," xvi.

CHAPTER 17

Jack Kerouac's Ambivalences as an Environmental Writer

Franca Bellarsi

The environmental humanities would not accurately discuss recent developments in Western ecological consciousness if they chose to exclude the contribution of Beat literature and art. Though much more attention has been paid to Gary Snyder's pioneering, Buddhist-inflected embrace of biocentrism than to other Beat(-affiliated) figures' individual engagement with anthropocentrism and its problematic appropriation of the biosphere, it is, nevertheless, the entire corpus of Beat texts, with their considerable diversity of environmental sensibilities, that matters when trying to understand changing philosophical and cultural approaches to the links binding the human to nonhuman creation.[1]

Jack Kerouac's writings are no exception: just as *The Dharma Bums* (1958) represents an iconic novel in relation to the willfully impure, unorthodox East–West syncretism at the heart of Beat spirituality, this work constitutes a central reference too when documenting the Beat effort to merge the sacred with the profane by resurrecting Romantic/Transcendentalist visions of nature.[2] However, if *The Dharma Bums* constitutes an excellent starting point, it cannot be a final stop on the road unravelling the author's ecological ambivalences, tensions which prove equally fascinating. Accordingly, my discussion will alternate between the frameworks of Deep and Dark Ecology.[3] It begins by examining *The Dharma Bums* through the lens of the Romantic/Transcendentalist models that inspired the novel's re-enchantment of nonhuman material creation. A second part turns to Kerouac's haiku and *The Scripture of the Golden Eternity* (1960) to show how the concept of Buddhist "Emptiness" considerably enriches his Romantic/Transcendentalist sense of "field-being." This section argues that the embeddedness of the human mind in the nonhuman *combined with* a serene acceptance of the latter's elusiveness actually constitutes one of Kerouac's important, if paradoxical, contributions to an understanding of the web of environmental continuities. By contrast, the third part moves from Kerouac's ecospiritual holism to his deep-seated ecophobia:[4] still insufficiently acknowledged, his darker sense of ecology borders on the ecogothic in several works,[5] not least the triptych formed by "Desolation Journal" (1956; pub. 2022), *Desolation Angels* (1965), and "Desolation Blues" (1956, pub. 1995).[6] A fourth and final section discusses how, despite his environmental angst, Kerouac nevertheless experiments considerably at the level of ecopoetics. A poem like "Sea" (1962) suggests that it is perhaps less at the thematic than at the aesthetic level that he radically opens up new, cutting-edge ecological ground, with his probing into a *wildness* of form that compensates, on the one hand, for the fear that untamed nature instills in his fiction and poetry, and on the other, for the limited presence of any wilderness in his city-inspired texts.

17.1 Transcendentalist Enchantment

When thinking about Kerouac and the natural environment, it should never be forgotten that he was urban-born and -bred, meaning that he would only gradually develop an enhanced attention to the particulars of the natural world. As romanticized as *The Dharma Bums* is, the opposition between Japhy Ryder and Ray Smith, Snyder's and Kerouac's respective fictional alter egos in the novel, remains true to life: as a city dweller, Kerouac genuinely needed a mentor to initiate him into the healing potential of what remains of the American wilderness.[7] Kerouac may update the myth of the American Frontier as a geographical pushing back leading to personal reinvention; all the same, both in life and fiction, urban reality is his most familiar environment, and living on the borderline between "civilization" and a residual primeval creation resisting its influence constitutes an acquired taste.

Tellingly, the greater biosphere does not even feature in Kerouac's first novel, *The Town and the City* (1950). Subsequently, *On the Road* (1957) begins to open up his prose to the diversity of America's landscapes. Nonetheless, it is only in the fourth section, when Sal Paradise is subsumed into the Mexican jungle, his body eerily growing one with it in a moment of literal ecstasy, that the nonhuman becomes the central focus of a narrative that remains, for the most part, anthropocentrically anchored in a succession of social interactions and urban environments.[8] In its *outré* search for spiritual transformation, *On the Road* may include the seeds of a re-enchantment of the profane everyday *via* material creation in its fleeting references to sunsets (*On the Road*, 17), clouds and skies (*On the Road*, 171), the Mississippi river (*On the Road*, 17, 99), as well as deserts, plains, and "jackpines in the moon" (*On the Road*, 54). However, these brief allusions make for a *spectral presence* of primeval creation – that is, they do not exactly cohere into a "painting-in-words" that would truly allow someone unfamiliar with certain regional landscapes of the US to form a precise mental image of them.[9]

Readers have to wait for *The Dharma Bums* to be offered Kerouac's first full-fledged *ecospiritual* novel, one that posits direct contact with the nonhuman "Other" as the very *precondition* to spiritual purification. In *The Dharma Bums* the nonhuman becomes the teacher and a return to primitive material creation offers a gateway to salvation, thereby all the more stridently revealing the loss incurred through an urban existence severed from the wider ecological web.

Inspired by the ecological-anarchist vision that Snyder would later develop in the essay collection *Earth House Hold* (1969), *The Dharma Bums* imaginatively recreates Kerouac's mountain-hiking in the Northwestern Cascade Range.[10] Thematically, the book idealizes Beat social disaffiliation from the never-ending cycle of work and consumption by fusing two countercultural lifestyles.[11] As suggested by the dedication to the seventh-century Ch'an/Zen Buddhist poet and mountain hermit Han-shan, Japhy and Ray return to nature to implement the Buddhist ideal of simplicity, like Han-shan freeing themselves from the constraints of codified life and from delusive addiction to the "illusory material."[12] Moreover, to flee the artificial consciousness of a society homogenized by its addiction to consumerism and the mass media (*The Dharma Bums*, 72), both heroes also revive the American model of countercultural simplicity recorded by Henry David Thoreau in *Walden, or My Life in the Woods* (1854). Japhy and Ray follow in the footsteps of the nineteenth-century Transcendentalist hermit who "dropped out" of the false consciousness generated by the city and consumerism because, as he puts it, "I wished to live deliberately, to front only the essential facts of life, and see if I could not learn what it had to teach, and not, when I came to die, discover that I had not lived."[13]

Transcendentalist voices like Thoreau's deeply influenced foundational figures of the American conservationist movement, including two explicitly identified by Ray when listing Japhy's heroes, namely: the Scottish-American explorer John Muir and the US naturalist John Burroughs (*The Dharma Bums*, 42). In fact, any reader familiar with Muir's work will see *The Dharma Bums* as a partial rewriting of *My First Summer in the Sierra* (1911), an autobiographical memoir documenting Muir's frugal, hermit-like lifestyle while exploring California's Sierra Nevada in 1869, as well as recording in great detail the landscapes, geology, fauna, and flora observed during his one-man expedition into the wild. Ray's realization of the beauty of the interconnected web of being revealed by the mountainscape often feels like a *composite recycling* of Muir's own: "And that roaring creek was a beauty by moonlight, those flashes of flying moon water, that snow white foam, those black-as-pitch trees, regular elfin paradises of shadow and moon" (*The Dharma* Bums, 68). Some of Ray's final ecstatic musings, with their "hundred of miles of pure snow-covered rocks and virgin lakes" and "[m]ad raging sunsets poured in seafoams of cloud through unimaginable crags, with every rose tint of hope beyond" (*The Dharma Bums*, 168; 172), recall not only the spiritually cleansing perfection of Muir's pantheistic material creation, but also the vitalistic view of nature that Muir shared with John Burroughs.[14]

In advocating a retreat into solitude to rediscover a more authentic self *via* nonhuman material creation, then, *The Dharma Bums* is not entirely original. Kerouac updates the disaffiliation from urban artificiality as handed down by Transcendentalism, an American philosophical sensibility that itself reworked the pastoralism of the German and English Romanticism that had inspired it. In *The Dharma Bums*, the *immersive* contemplation of the nonhuman to access a more genuine form of consciousness still resonates with William Wordsworth and his embrace of "emotion recollected in tranquility," since "Nature never did betray / the heart that loved her."[15] Likewise, Ray's assertion that "[t]he closer you get to real matter, rock air fire and wood, boy, the more spiritual the world is" (*The Dharma Bums*, 148) echoes the foundational credo of Ralph Waldo Emerson, the theoretical voice of Transcendentalism, who confidently claims that "Particular natural facts are symbols of particular spiritual facts," with the consequence that "Nature is the symbol of spirit."[16] Kerouac's ecospiritual vision, therefore, proves as *syncretic* as his Catholic–Buddhist religious one.

Philosophically, *The Dharma Bums* has thus inherited the idealism of American Transcendentalism, itself shaped in the idealistic Nature Philosophy of European Romanticism. Like them, Kerouac posits the environment as "something far more deeply interfused" (Wordsworth, "Tintern Abbey," 64, l. 97), with some sort of *circulation* between the human and the nonhuman: the human mind needs the agency of the nonhuman to awaken it out of its falsely assumed separation between self and other; but in reverse, the nonhuman cannot "exis[t] independently of the [human] subject that perceives it."[17] As Kerouac puts it in "Desolation Journal": "mind is matter and matter is mind."[18] From such a position, the next logical step is the belief in a universal "Mind" or energy coursing through all forms of the living, an "Oversoul," to use Emerson's vocabulary, whether this diffuse "Ultimate Principle" be theistic in kind or not.[19] Within such a holistic frame, the perceiver and the perceived *mutually constitute* one another: if the self can only know itself through its encounter with nonhuman forms of the living, physical-material creation, in turn, needs the thinking mind to be unveiled as more than an inert object and dead matter. In a nutshell, in contemporary environmental terms, *The Dharma Bums* inherited from Romanticism and Transcendentalism the intuition of "*field-being*."

17.2 Buddhist Acceptance of the Nonhuman

In *The Dharma Bums*, "field-being" is precisely the underlying notion that allows Kerouac to produce an ecospirituality seamlessly merging assumptions of Romanticism/Transcendentalism, ecology and Buddhism. Transcendentalism described "field-being" and the total fusion between self and environment that it supposes in terms of the individual experiencing him- or herself as a "transparent eyeball" (Emerson, "Nature," 39). Today, Deep Ecology explains this experience of a "*relational, total-field image*" as one that "dissolves not only the man-in-environment concept, but every compact thing-in-milieu concept."[20] Across its different schools, Buddhism has its own vocabulary too to express this nondual sense of being, in which a hierarchical vision of personhood defined as a solid, permanent self which exerts domination and control over its surroundings gets replaced, instead, by a *nonhierarchical* organization of phenomenal reality perceived in terms of a constantly shifting and mutual interdependence between inner and outer, self and other. Instead of "field-being," the original Sanskrit texts of Buddhism talk about *śūnyatā*, variously rendered in translation as "vacuity," "Emptiness," or "the Void."

Kerouac well understood that "Emptiness" does not imply a denial of the existence of phenomena as such, but rather refuses to see such phenomena, *human selfhood included*, as permanent at their core and completely separate and unaffected by other phenomena around them.[21] Importantly, Buddhist "field-being" goes further than Emerson's "transparent eyeball" by doubting the very veracity and solidity of what is perceived by the subject fusing with its surroundings in Transcendentalism (see, for instance, *Dharma Bums*, 105). In the foundational Buddhist text *Heart Sutra* (*Prajñāpāramitāhṛdaya*), "field-being" is cryptically encapsulated in the aphorism "form is emptiness and the very emptiness is form," a formulation that Kerouac loved so much as to produce a number of adaptations of it in contemporary American idiom, the most organized of these being the didactic poetic sequence *The Scripture of the Golden Eternity* (1960).[22] Comprising sixty-six variations on "Emptiness," *Scripture* partakes of the same paradoxical, elliptical quality as Kerouac's haiku writing. Like it, what *Scripture* adds to his Transcendentalist-style respiritualization of the human *via* the nonhuman material is an *epistemological humility removing the very grounds for ecophobia.*

As in classical Japanese haiku, Kerouac's compact vignettes dilute the centrality of the human by embedding references to it in the minute, ephemeral particulars of nonhuman natural creation. Often, haiku concentrate on unadorned and modest forms of sentient or nonorganic life easily overlooked by the inattentive observer. Overall, Kerouac conveys the serenity of the moment in a *biophilic* and minimalistic expression of the perceiving mind attuned to its surroundings: his paradoxical three-liners are punctuated by sparrows, crickets, flies, mosquitoes, or nondescript dogs, cats, and birds; besides generic animals, other unspectacular manifestations of nonhuman life are also included, such as rain, moss, leaves, frost, breezes, etc.[23]

Generally speaking too, even when he injects the realities of the city into a form traditionally linked to the nonurban, Kerouac's haiku continue to transmit what these condensed snapshots of the unique and ephemeral moment are supposed to exude: a capturing of things in their suchness while removing the usual hierarchies and predetermined order projected by the analytical mind upon the grid of reality; for example:

In back of the Supermarket,
in the parking lot weeds,
Purple flowers (*Book of Haiku*, 18)

As is typical of Kerouac's haiku, this one eschews metaphor to link apparently disconnected elements, relying instead on ellipsis, with the gap and tension between concrete elements implying hidden affinity beneath surface discrepancy.[24] Here, for instance, Kerouac's vignette suggests that there is continuity between the weeds and flowers, questioning whether flowers are indeed more valuable than weeds.

In its erasure of preconceived hierarchies, the haiku does away with fear, anxiety, and competition, three realities that feed ecophobia and stand in the way of deep-ecological relationship with the nonhuman. In Kerouac's haiku too, the tiny forms of nonhuman life do not represent any menace for the human and vice versa; nor do the larger forms of the living supplant and obliterate the more miniscule ones. Because the haiku privileges "suchness" over explicit relations rigidly ordering reality, Kerouac's haiku accept nonhuman forms of life as self-sufficient, letting them be in the world, without any sense of human entitlement over them or threat to the human emanating from their very existence.

Likewise, in *The Scripture of the Golden Eternity*, some of the simplest yet most effective passages refuse to adorn humble components of the biosphere. In addition, Kerouac's didactic poem evokes them first and foremost in terms of *relation* and *exchange*, not least with the perceiving human mind weaving an image of such particulars:

> #38. The world was spun out of a blade of grass: the world was spun out of a mind. Heaven was spun out of a blade of grass: heaven was spun out of a mind. Neither will do you much good, neither will do you much harm.[25]

If everything can be serenely accepted (stanza #53, in *Scripture*, 54) in the leveling matrix of "field-being" presupposed by the *Heart Sutra*'s "form is emptiness and the very emptiness is form," it is because, in keeping with Romantic/Transcendentalist belief, we are all made of the same "stuff" (stanza #10, in *Scripture*, 26) in "mortal animate form" (stanza #5, in *Scripture*, 24). Moreover, in line with subatomic physics, we amount to an innumerable quantity of "sun-motes," Kerouac holding each and every particle sacred (stanza #27, in *Scripture*, 34). Besides, in the "golden Eternity" of "Emptiness," humans not being distinct from the wildness of an "undisciplined" universe made of waves or particles (stanza #22, in *Scripture*, 32; stanza #39, in *Scripture*, 43) weakens the subject in a manner that indeed exceeds the "transparent eyeball" to which Emerson had assimilated the perceiver:[26] as emphasized in stanza #49, where mountains and trees are described as both "real" and "unreal," whatever the reality-weaving human sentience projects as preconceptions upon the nonhuman amounts to random, peremptory pronouncements never capturing the latter in its true essence (*Scripture*, 50).

In *Scripture*, environmental dread is, therefore, undercut by the skeptical view that a Buddhist Kerouac takes of a human "self" that would allegedly escape the mutability and fluctuation characterizing all other elements in the interdependent web of reality. Actually, in voiding our preconceptions of their solidity, "form is emptiness and the very emptiness is form" hollows out the very *alterity* of the nonhuman material: the associated epistemological humility nullifies the fear generated by the seeming "alien" character of the nonhuman, as shown by the happy coexistence with enigmatic Hozomeen Mountain in the more serene sections of the Desolation triptych. In short, by relativizing both the essence of the perceiving mind and its projections upon the nonhuman "Other," Buddhism enlarged the deep-ecological perspectives opened up for Kerouac by his Romantic/Transcendentalist assumptions.

17.3 Dark Ecological Alterity

However, deep ambivalences too affect Kerouac's syncretic ecospirituality. If the real-life confessions of "Desolation Journal" and its imaginative reworking in *Desolation Angels* and "Desolation Blues" extend the Deep Ecology of *The Dharma Bums*, they also clash with it. This collision is perhaps not totally unexpected in view of the unquestioning acceptance of Romantic/Transcendentalist pastoralism at the end of *The Dharma Bums*. Compounding a self-proclaimed "Enlightenment" revealing that he is actually not "detached" and "awakened" in the Buddhist sense (*The Dharma Bums*, 174), Ray's enchantment with nature's majesty too easily brushes aside the destabilizing encounters with forms of material creation resistant or indifferent to our pastoral expectations. Yet, the true test for any ecospirituality is precisely how it engages the *antipastoral* sides of untamable forms of matter and proposes to bridge the city/wilderness divide in a world where, for many, healing through nature can no longer take the form of a retreat into the uninhabited, primeval wild. *The Dharma Bums* and *Scripture* present an interfusion of microcosm and macrocosm that easily sits with "To see a World in a Grain of Sand/And a Heaven in a Wild Flower"; yet a number of passages from the Desolation triptych suggest a far more (eco)gothic kind of "Infinity" and "Eternity."[27]

Granted that the Desolation triptych is not made of uniformly dark compositions. In *Desolation Angels*, for instance, descriptions of the mountainscape alternate between the simply beautiful and the sublimely awesome. The first-person narrator variously evokes the picturesque character of the alpine meadow and the purity of the lake at the bottom of the slope, as well as misty chasms reminding him of Buddhist impermanence and vacuity.[28] Space is rendered in a manner that brings together the very vast with the very small, one of the most stunning, empathetic passages occurring when the narrator shifts his gaze from the peaks to a caterpillar. In the minute description poetically blending the anthropomorphic and biocentric, rarely has the world seen from a tiny insect's perspective appeared so complex and lyrical (*Desolation Angels*, 58–59). However, in contrast to *The Dharma Bums*, the enchanting web of creation is not sufficient to make the narrator forget about the weight of solitude and time. Significantly, the oppression of slowly unfolding temporality is already evoked at the very beginning of *Desolation Angels*: "every time I'd think of the Void I'd see [Mount] Hozomeen and understand—Over 70 days I had to stare at it" (*Desolation Angels*, 30). Significantly too, Kerouac's fictional alter ego is dying to return to the city, the stark duality between nature and culture affecting pastoralism never being resolved (*Desolation Angels* 32, 44, 52–53).

From the outset, nonhuman creation remains much more dual too:

> Hozomeen, Hozomeen, most beautiful mountain I ever seen, like a tiger sometimes with stripes, sunwashed rills and shadow crags wriggling lines in the Bright Daylight, vertical furrows and bumps and Boo! crevasses, boom, sheer magnificent Prudential mountain, nobody's even heard of it, and it's only 8,000 feet high, but what a horror when I first saw that void the first night of my staying on Desolation Peak waking up from deep fogs of 20 hours to a starlit night suddenly loomed by Hozomeen with his two sharp points, right in my window black— (*Desolation Angels*, 29–30)

Though Kerouac uses the term "beautiful," his description more readily brings to mind the "Sublime" as embodied by the uncanny energy of William Blake's "The Tyger" and as theorized by Edmund Burke (1729–1797). Indeed, the "sunwashed rills and shadow crags" of the mountain parallel "the fearful symmetry" of the hypnotic feline in Blake's *Songs of Experience* (1794), who, amongst other interpretations, symbolizes the irreducible and threatening alterity of the nonhuman realm of creation.[29] Besides the eerie animalization of mineral substance, the ecogothic mood in the opening of *Desolation Angels* also strikes a note of awe much akin to Burke's liminal state of "Astonishment": "that state of the soul, in which all its motions are suspended with some degree of horror … the mind being so entirely filled with its object, that it cannot entertain any other, nor by consequence reason on that object which employs it."[30]

Kerouac's description also enlists the perpendicular perspective combined with a rugged and broken surface, the shift between light and obscurity, the vastness, solitude, and silence that are so many triggers of sublimity-induced terror for Burke (see Part II, Sect. III, VI, VII, VIII, XIV, loc. 2488, 2672, 2700, 2708–2709, 2802).

Unsurprisingly, it is when Kerouac's Buddhism crumbles that Mount Hozomeen and other forms of the nonhuman become a source of ecophobia, be it for the real-life author or his fictional alter ego:

> Here I am on Desolation Peak not "coming face to face with God," as I sententiously predicted but myself, my shitty frantic screaming-at-bugs self—There is no God, there is no Buddha, there is nothing but just <u>this</u> and what name shall we give it? SHIT (*Desolation Peak*, 62)

On the peaks, the more desperate moments bordering on madness are not just generated by the Burkean Sublime forcing upon humans the contemplation of their transience and insignificantly small place in the world (see "Desolation Journal" 71, 97, 104).[31] Reaching even deeper, Kerouac's hopelessness touches upon the anguish bred by a nonhuman material realm of creation that eludes all human classifications, just facing observers with an "isness" that frustrates human perceivers, but from which they cannot ever detach themselves (*Desolation Peak*, 63).[32]

Further invalidating all mental projections upon them, the phenomena of the material world enshrining the human seem endowed with an agency of their own, as attested by the dynamic weather elements counteracting the apparent immobility of the mountains: "nothing but mist/as it rises ululatory responding/to every shift of wind" ("Desolation Blues," Chorus #5, 121). Yet, if they interact between them, these physical forces offer no more of a hold to the human imagination than does petrified matter, condemning the viewer to eternal separateness: "For the trouble with Desolation, is, no characters, alone, isolated, but is Hozomeen isolate?" (*Desolation Angels*, 39). All this contributes to a "life extend[ing] beyond the human to things and nonhumans that populate a world that is *not necessarily for or even with us*."[33] Repeatedly, in fact, Kerouac's Hozomeen and adjacent peaks come across as contemporary recyclings of Percy Bysshe Shelley's "Mont Blanc" (1816; pub. 1817) and its different takes on the nonhuman "everlasting universe of things."[34] In its exploration of the nonhuman's paradoxical mix of beauty and opacity, the Desolation triptych echoes Shelley's anxiety-generating hypothesis: "And what were thou [Mont Blanc], and earth, and stars, and sea,/If to the human mind's imaginings/Silence and solitude were vacancy?" ("Mont Blanc, Version A," 124, l. 142–144).

To understand Kerouac's fear and disappointment at nonhuman forms of material creation hindering the experience of "field-being," the dark ecological speculation of contemporary "object-oriented ontology" (OOO) and its attempt "to conceptualize this world without us, radically independent of the mind" prove particularly useful.[35] Timothy Morton's concept of the "hyperobject" especially helps to make sense of Kerouac's Hozomeen and Desolation Peak. Both are local realities, but the fear they instill by far exceeds their local anchorage in the material world; as conduits of *nonhuman natural alterity*, they transform the latter into a hyperobject, that is an object so "massively distributed in time and space in ways that baffle humans and make interacting with [it] fascinating, disturbing, problematic and wondrous."[36] The alterity of the nonhuman conveyed by Hozomeen and Desolation possesses typical "viscosity," since "[t]he more [you] struggle to understand hyperobjects, the more [you] discover that [you] are stuck to them."[37] This alien opacity of nonhuman nature is indeed experienced by Kerouac's narrator as "haunt[ing his] social and psychic space with an always-already."[38]

By contradicting the kind of interfused, mutually constitutive perceiver-perceived relationship that Romanticism/Transcendentalism takes for granted, the dark ecological lines in the Desolation triptych present an "ontological world of things [already always] without us."[39] Instead of Emerson's and Muir's belief in a spiritually significant and readable nature, a permanent sense of exile from and antagonism towards nonhuman material creation can repeatedly mark Kerouac's sense of his own physical environment. These are all traits of the "garrison mentality" associated with the nonindigenous Canadian sense of wild, primeval nature, suggesting that in connection with the biosphere too, Kerouac's Canadian roots run deep.[40]

17.4 An Ecopoetics of Alterity and Entanglement

Paradoxically, however, if some of his dark ecological texts center at the thematic level on the impossible interfusion between the human and nonhuman forms of the biosphere, Kerouac's aesthetics repeatedly re-establish a continuum between the human and nonhuman natural "Other." This proves especially true in his most experimental prose and poetry. An outstanding example of this is "Sea, Sounds of the Pacific at Big Sur," the wild-form poetic appendix to *Big Sur* (1962), a novel in which liquid, agentive materiality and the hermetic life forms of an ocean-facing canyon convey the disturbing sublimity of the nonhuman material "Other" threatening to engulf human identity.[41]

"Sea" reiterates the environmental dread of the Desolation triptych: only manifesting in fragments of sounds or images, the ever-mutable roaring waters never fully answer the bilingual call of the poetic narrator to unveil their mystery: "Parle, O, parle, mer, parle,/Sea, speak to me, speak."[42] However, the sea's enigmatic opacity is counterbalanced by an opening of poetic form to natural processes like *dissipative structures* and the *fluctuating randomness and design* found in nature. "Dissipative structures" relate to the *indeterminacy* that accompanies the potentially spontaneous emergence of "new structures of higher *order* and complexity" within open systems.[43] By analogy, what the open systems of nature and the open organism formed by a free-flowing, experimental poetic text share are so-called *points of bifurcation* or "points of instability at which new [unpredictable] structures and forms of order can emerge."[44] This is precisely why in its erratic oscillation between form and formlessness, "Sea" can be considered as an *ecopoetic* composition in the first place.

Over twenty pages, Kerouac's apparently chaotic aesthetics are strangely nondualistic too: if they preserve the sense of a fluctuating universe "that is not necessarily for or even with us,"[45] they nevertheless perform a twist on "field-being" by *entangling* the flux of nonhuman materiality with that of the human mind, Kerouac's imagery also embedding both in a sea of human artifacts:

> Hear over there the ocean motor?
> Feel the splawrsh of it?
> Six silly centepedes here, Machree—
> Ah Ratatatatatat—
> the machinegun sea, rhythmic
> balls of you pouring in (*Big Sur*, 187–188)

Allying soundscape and the graphic layout of a concrete poetry of ebb-and-flow, "Sea" thus interweaves physical and mental environments, the undulation of the waterbody overlapping with the breathing body of the poet and the poetic voice's waves of remembrance.

As such, "Sea" and its poetics still pursue the utopian quest for organicity and vitalism advocated early on in Kerouac's "Essentials of Spontaneous Prose" (1953). In seeking an all-encompassing rendition of an always fluctuating environment, "Sea" not only preserves the dark, raw energy of water, but also the mysterious energy of consciousness in "sketching composition" mode, whose "outfanning" mindflow runs over "jewel center" to arrive at the all-important "pivot," the bifurcation point where, as Jeremy Wastiaux notes, "the end of one creative loop ... requires that it be the beginning of another creative loop."[46] As a dark ecological poem, "Sea" may convey the ever-elusive liquidity of the material so that it becomes, once again, a hyperobject. However, its poetics combine the actual processes of physical nature with the rhythms of the human body-mind continuum, thereby generating a "literary ecotone" that erodes the inner/outer divide.

In short, "Sea" reveals a still different environmental facet of Kerouac: an author with a dark ecological sensibility often destabilized by the untamable wildness of the biosphere, but whose texts, nevertheless, radically re-enact the "wild" and its fluctuating energies through the *material texture* of his writing. Through the wildness of its aesthetics, "Sea" shows that despite his fears of the nonhuman, Kerouac too is capable of exploring a much more deep-seated, elemental animistic pendant to the Emersonian "Oversoul" of *The Dharma Bums*.

17.5 Ambivalences with Environmental Value

Kerouac's sense of the biosphere is anything but monolithic: an enchanting engagement with the nonhuman "Other" alternates with a far more anguished, if not downright ecophobic relationship with it, the thematic tensions between "field-being" and a feeling of permanent exile from one's environment never being resolved. Moreover, Kerouac's aesthetics confirm his conflicted ecological positioning: his organic form of wild entanglement in part corrects darker ecological distrust or more naïve ecospiritual facets, but still thrives on the elusiveness of the nonhuman natural "Other." Importantly, though, the tensions experienced by an author or narrator need not automatically generate discomfort in his readers. With their conflicted sense of materiality, Kerouac's writings should perhaps be read in the same way as Shelley's "Mont Blanc," a mosaic of challenging environmental hypotheses.

If Kerouac lacks a unified vision of the nonhuman, and if his ecospirituality vacillates before the hindering of "field-being" emanating from nature itself, this does not lessen the value of his work for contemporary readers seeking nonnaïve ways of bridging the human and nonhuman. On the contrary, the environmental ambivalences of Kerouac's voice may even, paradoxically, enhance its ecological value: a Hozomeen Mountain that inspires Transcendentalist-style beauty and reverence alternating with one that inflicts sublimity and fear shows that there is no "fast track" to Deep Ecology, raising the pivotal question of whether Deep Ecology can ever be reached even at the expense of Dark Ecology altogether. Kerouac's conflicted environmental stance invites us to ask whether there can be any solid ecospirituality without duly acknowledged ecophobia. His writings suggest that, in contrast with Ray Smith, we first need to come to terms with the deep and disturbing alterity of nonhuman material creation in order to meaningfully embrace it. By helping us understand that ecological dread may have to be a *precondition* to ecospirituality, the tensions between the human and nonhuman that to Jack Duluoz are a curse may be a blessing to us readers, Kerouac's environmental ambivalences helping us to pave our own road to ecological revelation.

Notes

1. In current ecological/ecocritical debates, "more-than-human" is often the preferred term as it adequately communicates the continuities between all living systems and avoids replicating the philosophical dualism at the root of today's environmental crisis. However, I will here systematically use "nonhuman" to better convey Kerouac's inability to overcome certain binary oppositions.
2. See, for instance, Gary Snyder's "Buddhism and the Coming Revolution," in *Earth House Hold* (New York: New Directions, 1969), 90–93.
3. Contrary to anthropocentric "shallow" ecology, which "views humans … as the source of all value, and ascribes only instrumental … value to nature,"

Deep Ecology "recognizes the intrinsic values of all living beings and views humans as just one particular strand in the web of life" (Fritjof Capra, "Deep Ecology: A New Paradigm," in *Deep Ecology for the Twenty-First Century*, ed. George Sessions [Boston & London: Shambala, 1995], 20).

Though biocentric, Dark Ecology rejects any gap-closing organicism between the human and nonhuman, doubting that human consciousness can access what is not identical with it: "dark ecology dances with the subject-object duality … Nature is *not* a mirror of our mind" (Timothy Morton, *Ecology without Nature. Rethinking Environmental Aesthetics* [Cambridge, Mass.: Harvard University Press, 2007], 185–186).

4. Contrary to "biophilia," our supposed innate need to "affiliate" with all life forms, "ecophobia" is humans' subconscious urge to destroy them. "Ecophobia" operates as "an irrational and groundless hatred (often fear) of the natural world that is as present and subtle in our daily lives and literature as homophobia and racism and sexism" (Simon C. Estok, *The Ecophobia Hypothesis* [New York and London: Routledge, 2018], 8–9, 10).
5. Rooted in ecophobia, ecogothic representations reflect the "unease, fear, and even contempt" experienced by humans confronting "the apparent 'blankness' of nature" and the seeming monstrosity of an environment challenging their normal sense of the body [Dawn Keetley and Matthew Wynn Sivils, eds., *Ecogothic in Nineteenth-Century American Literature* (New York and London: Routledge, 2018], 3–4).
6. Hereafter, Kerouac's diary, novel, and poem are referred to as the Desolation triptych.
7. Post Industrial Revolution and Hiroshima, in the so-called "Anthropocene" and "Plutocene," many doubt that true wilderness even still exists.
8. See Jack Kerouac, *On the Road* (Harmondsworth: Penguin, 1972 rpt.), 276–278.
9. Though a point hardly noted in criticism, landscape representation in *On the Road* heavily depends for its effectiveness on the ready-made iconic images of nature that readers themselves bring to the text.
10. See John Suiter's *Poets on the Peaks: Gary Snyder, Philip Whalen & Jack Kerouac in the North Cascades* (New York: Counterpoint, 2002).
11. Jack Kerouac, *The Dharma Bums* (London: Grafton, 1986 rpt.), 72.
12. "Han-shan," in *The Shambala Dictionary of Buddhism and Zen*, trans. Michael H. Kohn (Boston: Shambala, 1991), 82. In Buddhism, the "illusory material" means the illusions generated by attachment to material possessions as well as by clinging to wrong perceptions of reality.
13. Henry David Thoreau, *Walden and Civil Disobedience* (New York: Penguin Classics, 1986), 135.
14. Kerouac's lines resonate with entries made by Muir, for instance, on July 2, 17, 20 and August 26, 1869. See John Muir, *My First Summer in the Sierra,* in *Nature Writings*, ed. William Cronon (New York: The Library of America, 1997), 194, 223, 227, 291–292. On Burroughs, see in particular John Burroughs, *The Breath of Life* (Boston & New York: Houghton Mifflin, 1915), www.gutenberg.org/files/18335/18335-h/18335-h.htm.

15. William Wordsworth, "1802 Preface," in *William Wordsworth and Samuel Taylor Coleridge, Lyrical Ballads*, ed. Michael Mason (Harlow: Pearson Longman, 2007, 2nd edition), 82.; Wordsworth, "Lines Written a Few Miles above Tintern Abbey," in *Selected Poems*, ed. Stephen Gill (London: Penguin Classics, 2004), 65, l. 123–124.
16. Ralph Waldo Emerson, "Nature," in *Selected Essays*, ed. Larzer Ziff (New York: Penguin, 1982), 48.
17. Chris Washington and Anne C. McCarthy, "Introduction: Literature and Philosophy in the World without Us," in *Romanticism and Speculative Realism*, ed. Chris Washington and Anne C. McCarthy (New York & London: Bloomsbury Academic, 2019), 3.
18. Jack Kerouac, "Desolation Journal," in *Desolation Peak: Collected Writings*, ed. Charles Shuttleworth (Los Angeles: Rare Bird and Sal Paradise Press, 2022), 46.
19. Ralph Waldo Emerson, "The Over-Soul," in *Selected Essays*, 206–207.
20. Arne Naes, "The Shallow and the Deep, Long Range Ecological Movements" (1973), in *Deep Ecology for the Twenty-First Century*, 151 [original italics].
21. Peter Harvey, *An Introduction to Buddhism: Teachings, History and Practices* (Cambridge University Press, 1990), 51–53.
22. *Buddhist Wisdom. The Diamond Sutra and The Heart Sutra*, trans. Edward Conze (New York: Vintage/Random House, 2001), 86.
23. Jack Kerouac, *Book of Haiku*, ed. Regina Weinreich (New York: Penguin, 2003).
24. For characteristics of classical haiku, see R. H. Blyth, *A History of Haiku: From the Beginnings up to Issa*, (Tokyo: The Hokuseido Press, 1963).
25. Jack Kerouac, *The Scripture of the Golden Eternity* (San Francisco: City Lights, 1994), 42.
26. Emerson, "Nature," 39.
27. William Blake, "Auguries of Innocence," in *The Complete Poetry and Prose of William Blake*, ed. David Erdman (New York & London: Doubleday, 1988 revised ed.), 490, l. 1–4.
28. Jack Kerouac, *Desolation Angels* (London: Paladin, 1990), 51; 31.
29. For the dark ecological complexity of "The Tyger" (Erdman 24), see Franca Bellarsi, "'Without Contraries is no progression': Blake, My Teacher," *Vala. The Journal of the Blake Society* 3 (2022), 86–88.

    For Kerouac's interest in Blake (1757–1827), see Jack Kerouac, *Kerouac: Selected Letters 1, 1940–1956*, ed. Ann Charters (New York: Viking, 1995), 195, 204, 206, 497, 545, 565, 571.
30. Edmund Burke, *A Philosophical Enquiry Into The Origin Of Our Ideas Of The Sublime and Beautiful, and Other Pre-Revolutionary Writings*, ed. David Womersley (London: Penguin, 1998), loc. 2468.
31. Andrew Smith, *Gothic Literature* (Edinburgh University Press, 2007), 12.
32. See also 5th, 6th and 12th Chorus in "Desolation Blues," in Jack Kerouac, *Book of Blues* (New York: Penguin, 1995), 121–122, 128.
33. Washington and McCarthy, *Literature and Philosophy*, 5 [my emphasis].

34. Percy Bysshe Shelley, "Mont Blanc, Version A," in *The Major Works*, ed. Zachary Leader (Oxford University Press, 2003), 120, l. 1.
35. Washington and McCarthy, *Literature and Philosophy*, 3.
36. Timothy Morton, *Hyperobjects* (Minneapolis & London: University of Minnesota Press, 2013), loc. 1064. It is important to understand that for Morton, a hyperobject (like plastic, climate warming, etc.) may manifest locally, but its being is not reducible to the local.
37. Morton, *Hyperobjects*, loc. 550.
38. Morton, *Hyperobjects*, loc. 559.
39. Washington and McCarthy, *Literature and Philosophy*, 9.
40. "Garrison Mentality," en.wikipedia.org/wiki/Garrison_mentality, accessed April 2, 2023. The "garrison mentality" fundamentally clashes with the ecospiritual beliefs of many of Canada's First Nations.
41. In particular, see Chapters 3, 7, and 21, *Big Sur* (London: Paladin, 1992), 14, 30, 82.
42. Jack Kerouac, "Sea," in *Big Sur*, 171.
43. Fritjof Capra, *The Web of Life. A New Synthesis of Mind and Matter* (London: Flamingo, 1996), 187 [original emphasis].
44. Capra, *Web of Life*, 175, 187.
45. Washington and McCarthy, *Literature and Philosophy*, 5.
46. Jack Kerouac, "Essentials of Spontaneous Prose," in *The Penguin Book of the Beats* (New York: Penguin, 1992), 58; Jeremy Wastiaux, "The Ecopoetics of Jack Kerouac: Dissipative Structures in *Visions of Cody* and *Mexico City Blues*," MA thesis (Brussels: Université libre de Bruxelles, 2020), 42.

CHAPTER 18

The Essentials of Archival Prose

Jean-Christophe Cloutier

Former National Archivist of Canada Jean-Pierre Wallot once lyrically described archives as "houses of memory," while novelist and poet Jack Kerouac defined his own earthly task as "trying desperately to be a great rememberer redeeming life from darkness."[1] He even confessed to a friend that he had to "deal with my memory as if it were my single moral responsibility" and recall "every single thing" about his life.[2] Many critics have touched on the centrality of memory to Kerouac's style as a writer, and Gerald Nicosia's massive critical biography of Kerouac is aptly titled *Memory Babe* – a childhood nickname Kerouac's Lowell chums had bestowed upon him due to his knack for instant recall.[3] Kerouac's documented reputation for having a photographic memory often serves as an underlying explanation for his invention of "Spontaneous Prose" – his ability to blow down onto the page the fullness of his past within a moveable present – but this perspective has tended to downplay Kerouac's obsessive recordkeeping as memory aid. As he proudly announced to his bibliographer Ann Charters in 1966, "I've kept the neatest records you ever saw."[4] Indeed, contrary to popular belief, Kerouac was methodical in the management of his archive; he established an original alphanumeric classification system for the majority of his writings – arranging them in four series (A to D) – and "meticulously organized" much of his bulging personal papers.[5]

Today the Kerouac Archive stands as one of the most imposing sets of literary papers of the twentieth century. When the New York Public Library's Berg Collection acquired it in 2001, the *New York Times* reported:

> [T]he archive comprises more than 1,050 manuscripts and typescripts, including novels, short stories, prose pieces, poems and fragments, a handful of them in scroll form; 130 notebooks for almost all of his works, published and unpublished; and 52 journals, from 1934 to 1960 … Also included are 55 diaries created by Kerouac between 1956 and his death; about 1,800 pieces of correspondence … and 72 publishing contracts … and two sets

of more than 100 handwritten cards that he devised, at about 7, to play a fantasy baseball game of his own invention.[6]

Not listed here are the countless character charts, event logs, inventories, and hand-drawn maps that are also integral parts of Kerouac's painstaking process.

In light of this avalanche of evidence, I propose that Kerouac's oeuvre must be reassessed as a unique case of the literary deployment of the archival. "Spontaneous" names the author's instrument of choice because it serves his goals of leaving a "complete record" (*Visions of Cody*, 120) behind and becomes the means of (re)capturing the origins – or provenance – of the poetic insight and narrative structure of his innermost memories. As he himself once put it, "My life is like the sea, my memory the boat," positioning memory as the vessel through which he both survives and navigates the flows of his life.[7] Kerouac's Spontaneous Prose method is thus a technique in the service of the most archival of impulses; the wish to record and preserve all experience for posterity. Spontaneous poetics is where provenance meets recording eye. This thirst for capturing the moment is motivated by Kerouac's passion for origins – not just regarding his own ancestry and French-Canadianness but, as a writer, he further hopes to record the very inception of all epiphanies, emotions, sensations he experiences. Approaching Kerouac via the archive necessarily readjusts our sights not on the author's most popular book, *On the Road*, but rather on the one he rightly considered his masterpiece, *Visions of Cody* (written 1951–1952, published 1972), where his archival sensibility is most evident. The experimental novel recounts many of the same events as the more famous *On the Road*, but includes ornate details, doodles, letters, diary entries, and transcripts of recordings absent from the latter.[8] As Allen Ginsberg observed in his annotations to *Visions of Cody*, "many lacunae & unfinished explanations & facts of *On the Road* romanticisms are herein filled in & detailed roundly."[9] *Visions of Cody* both embodies the archival character of Kerouac's novelistic form while simultaneously serving an archival function of preservation.

Like the tape recorder of *Visions of Cody*, Kerouac's custodial practices create the ability to play back, again and again, what the eponymous Cody Pomeray calls the "skeletonized form" (*Visions of Cody*, 174) of a narrative's inception, before it has had the chance to be embellished and filled in with the flesh and muscles of emplotment. As such, *Visions of Cody* is itself the next lifecycle, or the sibling, of *On the Road* stripped to its essentials – a "skeleton" that is ironically much bulkier than its more famous, more traditional older brother. As Achille Mbembe puts it in "The Power of the

Archive and Its Limits," "[f]or a memory to exist, there first has to be the temptation to repeat an original act."[10] The repetitive nature of Kerouac's reinterpretation of the same events through multiple novelistic retellings is authorized by his redeployment of his own archive, all of which participates in his larger preservation project inspired by French Canadian *survivance*, the name given to a willed, systematic effort to sustain, maintain, and nurture Québécois culture and language amidst a hostile and aggressive assimilation program on both sides of the US border.[11] Indeed, Québec's motto is nothing less than "*Je me souviens*" [I remember]; originating in 1883 and made official in 1939, the same year Kerouac moved out of Lowell for New York.

The deeply personal nature of Kerouac's recordkeeping disrupts our sense that archival documenting need be objective. For Kerouac, objectivity was not only impossible but outdated, and thus undesirable.[12] He writes in his 1951 journal: "Modern times have produced a civilized mankind which is hopelessly and *luxuriantly* subjective—that's why in fact none of us has bothered to read all of the Comedy Humaine, which is an objective surface survey of the "chemistries of society."[13] Further forsaking the Balzacian model for the "introspective, secret, censorable & dark" subjectivity of "Proust, Joyce, Wolfe & Faulkner & James," Kerouac concludes: "my *lifework*, to keep with the times, & anyway to keep with how I secretly feel, is to be subjective—how everything appears to be *to me*. Now for a vast subjective form" (*Unknown Kerouac*, 122 [unless otherwise indicated, emphasis in original]). This "vast subjective form," Kerouac realized, has to be Proustian in its principles – to painstakingly pluck from private memory the makings of a grand literary work – but not in its practice.[14] As he put it in the preface to the 1960 New Directions edition of *Visions of Cody*: "My work comprises one vast book like Proust's *Remembrance of Things Past* except that my remembrances are written on the run instead of afterwards in a sick bed" (*Visions of Cody/Visions of Gerard Big Sur,* 762). The word "vast," present in both the 1951 journal entry ("vast subjective form") and the 1960 prefatory statement ("one vast book"), is an equally apt qualifier for the American continent and for Kerouac's archive, the latter of which represents the purest form his "lifework" luxuriously took on.

In what should rank among his most important texts, a journal he kept during the crucial months of September to November of 1951 – a document now published in *The Unknown Kerouac* as "Journal 1951," but humbly titled by its author as "More Notes" – Kerouac advances a theory of the archive that has since become central to my understanding of his literary project. His entry for September 10, 1951, opens by outlining his wish "to find a way of writing not just suitable for my "next book" but for all books that I will write from now till my dying days … —a form that'll fit me for life," a desire he quickly reformulates as a need "to find a *lifetime* form" (*Unknown Kerouac*, 122). The intermingling of life, literature, and form – all nestled within records created solely for the author's private organizational flow – aesthetically encapsulates the lifecycle model that dominates modern archival practice.[15] But the coalescing "jewel-center of interest"[16] comes in Kerouac's concluding thought in this same journal entry: "This journal using its losefulness" (*Unknown Kerouac*, 123). With that delightful formulation, Kerouac captures one of the paradoxical truths of the archival; using losefulness is precisely what an archive does. It rises against the unforgiving entropy of the physical world to take on new life out of the very loss of its creation. This sentiment is perfectly aligned with the one he expresses in his grandiose "Epilogue" to the journal, exclaiming that in "10 years, 50 years, 100 years from now … whether my children, historians, or that ancient-history worm reads this, I say it anyway, I hope it is true that a man can die and yet not only live in others but give them life, and not only life but that great consciousness of life" (*Unknown Kerouac*, 172). Kerouac's lifetime form, as I argue, is ultimately the meticulous, lifelong building of his archive, a labor informed by his visceral knowledge of life's ceaseless losefulness, and one that he put in the service of a grand literary project he called The Duluoz Legend.

Amongst all the works that constitute Legend, *Visions of Cody* is not only the novel that bears the mark of Kerouac's spontaneous method at its inception – one might say the novel cradles the method's very Nietzschean becoming – its wild inventory form is also a reflection of Kerouac's archival practices. Its contents were written before, during, and after the October 1951 "breakthrough" Kerouac had in the Kingsbridge VA hospital. The novel itself is a bulging repository of thoughts, visions, dreams, events, presented in the raw forms of their initial recording by Kerouac: complete and excerpted letters he sent and received, tape recordings that "are actual transcriptions [Kerouac] made of conversations with Cody," a few drawings and sketches, diary entries, notes and note-making acts – this is an archive wedged between a novel's covers. At the same time, the archive being pulled into the novel's form is transmogrified by the creative force of Kerouac's poetic prose; history becoming symbolic action, Kerouac's candor leads him to admit that he can only bear witness "through the keyhole of his eye … the eyes of poor Ti Jean (me)." (*Visions of Cody/Visions of Gerard/Big Sur*, 762).

Throughout this big burly novel, descriptions abound, vivid inventories incorporating smells, visuals, textures, thoughts new and remembered, taking advantage of the secret resources of literature as a more comprehensive human record of lived life and experience. In serving its archival function, the novel conjures a time already passed yet deserving of preservation via literary form. It opens in "AN OLD DINER like the one Cody and his father ate in," and repeatedly hammers that "old" note: the bread board is "worn down," there are "oldfashioned" windows that look like those in an "oldfashioned railroad car" or "old lunchcarts," the "[g]rill is ancient and dark," giving whiffs of "old ham or an old pastrami beef," the mugs are "brown and cracked" next to an "old pot" and a cash register "as old as the wood of a rolltop desk" (*Visions of Cody*, 5). "The newest things," the narrator lists, "are the steam cabinet, the aluminum coffee urns, the floor fans—But the marble counter," he adds, "is ancient, cracked, marked, carved, and under it is the old wood counter of the late twenties, early thirties … something suggesting decades of delicious greasy food. Ah!" (*Visions of Cody*, 5). Already with this "Ah!" we detect the exultation Kerouac obtains from his nostalgic recording. This diner contains a smell that is "curiously the hungriest in America," it is "nameless—memoried—sincere—makes the guts of men curl in October" (*Visions of Cody*, 5).

With the opening "sketch" on the diner, Kerouac establishes a mood of time regained, of a specific texture and sensual reality that also bears the marks of the moment's longevity, as with that ancient lunch counter being assimilated with American novelties. Even if some of what it evokes remains "nameless," it is nevertheless "memoried" – an important neologism I will expand on shortly. The prose is powerful and comprehensive enough to transport the reader into that place, that exact moment, yet as it does it reminds us that we are, as with archives, entering a storied site, one with a history of its own that we cannot witness save for the state in which it has survived and been made available. From the onset the novel thus establishes the struggle for historical legibility; so much of what surrounds the narrator seems to have "aged beyond recognition" (*Visions of Cody*, 7). Without a constant record, time becomes an inhibitor of recognition and threatens our ability to make connections and establish correspondences; already here we have a subtle logic behind a need for "spontaneous" recording. Crucially, for Kerouac, "the result" of spontaneous sketching "is not 'literature' and certainly not fiction but definitely something living" (*Unknown Kerouac*, 163). This fact is essential to understanding what is at stake for Kerouac, namely infusing his record-keeping with the animus of life.

What is also singularly interesting here is the fact that Kerouac had his breakthrough into spontaneous prose while sitting still, or rather, on a sick bed – he was staying at the VA Hospital in the Bronx due to a severe attack of thrombophlebitis. At his most Proustian, then, Kerouac finds the "solution of [his] lifework" (*Unknown Kerouac,* 125). Kerouac feels that he should "be forgiven for saying that it is not "fiction" or even "literature" in the literary & publishing sense," because he intends to move away from "so-called 'objectivity,' so-called 'story,' the *pretense* of it, the *smirk,*" and concludes, starting with a French term of endearment: "In effect, *mon vieux*, this might mean a *permanent complete daily journal*!!)." Out of this "permanent complete" recordkeeping will emerge, through his literary record management, a "legitimate" division of "people, places, confessions, sounds etc.—in other words, some way of *forming* the sketchings in major units" (*Unknown Kerouac*, 164). And each unit, Kerouac decides, must be filed in its proper place, as this will reflect his desired lifetime form. "The spirit of *pleasure* in solitary occupations is what I've got to recover from boyhood for manhood's work of art," Kerouac declares in the same journal, adding:

> the huge gray-day preoccupation with *files*, records, systems, small print, hoary histories in dusty ledgers. The confession of my entire life will get everybody off my chest … Shall I just *write my units* every day and file them in proper place?—for whoever told me that I was a *novelist* anyway! (*Unknown Kerouac*, 117)

The final sentence suggests how the "proper place" for Kerouac's "sketchings in major units" is not necessarily the novel as traditionally understood but may be the filing cabinet! He immediately clarifies what he means by "novelist": "Was NIETZSCHE a novelist? 'It is late afternoon; the grapes are turning brown!' Who cares that the man who said this was not a novelist?" (*Unknown Kerouac*, 117) Long before Karl Ove Knausgaard, Kerouac's archival sensibility demands a new understanding of what the novelistic can be; what counts is the recording of life and finding the proper place for each "living" unit. As such, Kerouac's truest writerly vocation is as archivist, not novelist; the archive is his *lifetime form.* It follows that Kerouac's challenge *as* a novelist was to figure out which of his units most belonged in novels, and his multiple attempts at filing the units across several texts, the proliferation of drafts and lifecycles for his sketches, animates the increasingly experimental nature of his style as a writer.

18.1 From Memory Chord to Memory Chord

Visions of Cody may be the boldest result of Kerouac's hospital breakthrough, a novel with "a crazy big shape" (*Visions of Cody*, 120) formed out of the archival nature of Kerouac's "huge gray-day preoccupation with *files*, records, systems" intended to give the reader a "living" sense of the "permanent complete." The novel's narrative voice is dedicated to this impossible task; nothing seems to escape our narrator's gaze – this Jack Duluoz spots everything, even "snow that's fallen on a twig" (*Visions of Cody*, 8). "The inclusion of everything or the desire to have everything in there," becomes so pronounced in *Visions of Cody* that "you get sections which are catalogues of things," as Clark Coolidge elucidates in his masterful piece on "Kerouac."[17] The inventories Kerouac piles into the novel threaten to overwhelm the speaker who sometimes even has to interrupt himself: "(and of course many more, why list any further, and besides we shall come back on other levels and more exhaustively)" (*Visions of Cody*, 94).

A few prose sketches after the extended Hector's diner sketch that opens the book, Kerouac qualifies the various "flashes" that are passing by his diner window as "memoried and human" (*Visions of Cody*, 22), just as he had described the diner smell as "memoried." Kerouac's invention of a new active verb for memory – "memorying" – is an integral part of his overall archival project. "Canuck Proust" that he is,[18] Kerouac extends the language of memory: not only memorying but rememberability as well. "Memorying" itself is akin to a process of "archivization;" it names how a memory travels into, and settles in, the palace of memory. Reflecting the dominant technologies of his day, Kerouac's memories sometimes take on the shape, in retrospect, of photographic records. Thinking back to a girl he once went on a date with, "poor little Rose with her Thirties style short dress" and "drinksad eyes," he remembers that she had a pimple on her "chin where you might kiss her and it would break and I hated to look at it though on her smooth face now in retrospect (and it's gone) it *memories* sexily like a beauty spot kind I used to see on chins of old movie queens in photos in front of theater—wondering if it was photo ink" (*Visions of Cody*, 16, my emphasis). Here, "memories" expresses how a particular detail is actively and erotically (thus, subjectively) remembered by Kerouac through a process of retrospection akin to reading photographs. He knows that the actual, real beauty spot/pimple is "gone," and that retrospection is merely its afterlife, archived in his "steeltrap brain."[19]

Yet despite possessing a "steeltrap" repository for a brain, Memory Babe often alludes to his need for notation to help him remember. While telling a story to Cody in "The Tape" section, he mentions, in passing, "I remember the name of the flophouse, in my notebooks, but I don't have it now" (*Visions of Cody*, 253). In other words, Duluoz considers his notebooks a living extension of his own memory; it is "I" who remembers, but the remembrance takes place "in my notebooks." In a remarkable phrase conflating notebook and memory, he declares, "all I gotta do is look back in my mind, like I look back on this page, to know what it was I said" (*Visions of Cody*, 387). When the narrator daydreams about how he will approach Cody's house when he finally gets out west, he sees himself "creep up the street taking in not only every aspect possible all the sensations round me," but "actually understanding in myriad rapid thought everything I sense as it stands in front of me and activates all around, in portable breast shirt-pocket notebooks slapping" (*Visions of Cody*, 52). His notebooks are an integral part of his self, slapping against his chest like a heartbeat, and the means through which he can record "every aspect possible." Notebooks pervade the narrative; he goes so far as to underscore the need to take notes: "The next time I've a dream about Cody and they're rare I will note it: but now just let the only other *rememberable* dream of Cody I have serve our growing purposes—this is going to be the complete Cody" (*Visions of Cody*, 45, my emphasis). As the record "grows," more and more memories will become "rememberable" – in other words, catalogued and made accessible to the rememberer/archivist/novelist.

Importantly, Kerouac's archival drive is also fueled by the fear, even terror, of forgetting. In "The Tape" section, Cody expresses this terror: "I can't remember man, it's a terrible thing not being able to remember" (*Visions of Cody*, 153). Later, Jack admits: "There is a stupid blur in my memory of the trip" (*Visions of Cody*, 445). The fear of amnesia is further compounded by the knowledge that all is fleeting and that not everything is made available to the recording eye. In this way, *Visions of Cody* – indeed, the whole Duluoz Legend – can take its place alongside James Joyce's *Ulysses* or Ford Madox Ford's *Parade's End* as examples of what Paul Saint-Amour calls a "truly counter-totalizing work," one that "avows the partiality of its totality claims without renouncing them, taking up totalization under the sign of its impossibility."[20] Indeed, it is during a brief conversation on Joyce that Cody warns Jack that his maniacal attempt to record everything is doomed: "You're not gonna get hardly any of this recorded you know." Jack seems to have already absorbed this fallen state of affairs when he replies, "Well, that's the sadness of it all" (*Visions of Cody*, 185). Even the tape recorder transcript does not represent a complete record of the events it depicts, and Kerouac is careful to reveal every instance when the "tape goes blank" (*Visions of Cody*, 185, 231) or "tape runs blank" (*Visions of Cody*, 192). These symbolically act like the inevitable gaps in any archive, which is, as Kerouac says, "the sadness of it all."

Still, the tape recorder is an example of the new technologies that Kerouac hoped could assist him in the fulfillment of his vocation; as he put it in "Journal 1951," "I need help – after all, these mechanical difficulties of writing by hand are over 50% of the trouble involved in swinging a thought from brain to paper" (*Unknown Kerouac*, 119). Moreover, since so often "the greatest perceptions come far from the desk, most while traveling, when the instruments of recording are not at hand and the poor human receiver is incapacitated to do any 'work'," he longed for a portable tape recorder.[21] "It's recording and explaining the visions and memories that rush across my brain, in narrative or otherwise logically connected sections," that prove difficult to recreate, "If I had a portable tape-recorder everything would be okay … just walk + talk" (*Unknown Kerouac*, 142).

In an unpublished essay composed while he was secretly writing his first French novel, *La nuit est ma femme*, Kerouac offers an astounding – and even scientific – reflection on the challenges of capturing the "stream of perceptions" into written form:

> This stream of perceptions, which is in the trance of waking-consciousness and not the "subconscious," is the most important level of any artist's mental endeavor, but because it is removed from the moral continuum which constitutes the image of a tale, just as is the electronic airborne signal, no one knows what to do with it. Faulkner has been most successful with it, Joyce the lesser: yet their works suffer from an over-density which is precisely like the over-density of the mind, the question being, shall we imitate nature or create our own images in the image of ourselves. It's all right for God but not us, and I would prefer imitating great nature once I truly found it as it travels in waves through my brain, as in a dream: I imagine then the tale would be of least significance, and there would come into existence the form of the natural story. But there has to be a continuity to any legitimate structure, and since the continuity of the stream of perceptions can never be recorded unless it is done as it waves-in particle by particle, which would require a tremendous trancelike discipline and better than that a mental recording machine (of impossible subtlety), stream-perception can only be used as the mine of images from which but a portion can ever be lifted—fished-out, as befits the old fashioned fisherman of the deep … A tremendous memory of the entire genesis and history of a perception is the first humanly possible requirement.[22]

The above passage, which so clearly positions Kerouac as a student and inheritor of Modernism (from Henri Bergson to Virginia Woolf to

William James' stream of consciousness), is one of his most sophisticated descriptions of the underlying purpose behind his imminent discovery: Spontaneous Prose – a "tremendous trancelike discipline" that allows for perceptions to be "recorded" as they wave in "particle by particle." The "mine of images" provides us with yet another metaphor for the archival repository of his memory. Moreover, as he realizes, if he can crack the code to capturing the stream "as it travels in waves" through his brain, "then the tale would be of least significance," in other words, as a novelist he can dispense with plot entirely, for it is merely "the *pretense* of it, the *smirk*."

Underlying Kerouac's concern with memory and its vicissitudes is his adamant desire to trace subjective perceptions – triggered as they are in the present – *back to their origins*, that is to recall "the entire genesis and history of a perception" has become a "requirement" – and this, incidentally, is the closest thing we get to a "plot" in *Visions of Cody*, peppered as it is with memory after memory being traced back. For example, sitting in a NY apartment in a narrative present, Kerouac's pipe smoke triggers the history of "a smell that I remembered just tonight again." He is transported back to the moment "the memory was instilled in me by the same forces eighteen years ago which now drive me obsessively to remember" (*Visions of Cody*, 32). Remembrance leads to a future drive to remember, and through careful examination of this "tremendous memory," the past – like drafts of a novel – becomes a mutable plane open to revision and new truths. He basks in "the (as Proust says God bless him) 'inexpressibly delicious' sensation of this memory," and excitedly pushes his theorizing further: "as memories are older they're like wine rarer, till if you find a real old memory, one of infancy, not an established often tasted one but a *brand new one!*, it would taste better than the Napoleon brandy Stendhal himself must have stared at … while shaving in front of those Napoleonic cannons" (*Visions of Cody*, 33). Herein lies part of Kerouac's archival magic: "jumping from memory chord to memory chord,"[23] as Coolidge puts it, he finds novelty in the old; the older the memory, the more chance it has of really being a "*brand new one!*" The pleasure he feels in scouring through "the entire genesis and history of a perception" is integral to his archive-based novelistic practice. Through the spontaneous recording of memory he finds the new in the already lived, transcending its losefulness by repeated re-examination, rerecording, renarrativizing.

For Kerouac, contemplative recall is tied to poetic inspiration; both wheels of time are interlocking gears in his steeltrap. The act of recording the above memory triggers in him "that so-seldom experience of seeing my whole life's richness swimming in a palpable mothlike cloud, a cloud I can really see and which I think is elfin and due to my Celtic blood—coming only in moments of *complete inspiration*. In my life I number them probably below five—at least on this level—" (*Visions of Cody*, 34). The rarity of such moments of complete inspiration underscores the difficulty of attaining the necessary "trancelike discipline" required to infuse the record with life. When this is achieved, his joy is palpable. For example, when Kerouac thinks about a particular tablecloth he once had in a Mexican apartment, he writes: "(that fleecy soft bed and soft table, what a joy to recall it! damn!—)" (*Visions of Cody*, 42). This joy is intimately tied to the character of Cody Pomeray, and thus serves as the underlying reasoning behind Duluoz's obsession with the former as he becomes his vehicle for total recall; Cody has him "hypnotized like a mad dream; I kept recalling my life" (*Visions of Cody*, 417). The recording of his recall is both artistic and deeply personal: "I must write down *books* too, story-novels," he tells himself, "and communicate to people instead of just appeasing my lone soul with a record of it—but this record is my joy" (*Visions of Cody*, 131). Here Kerouac really puts it quite simply; the building of his own archive, his record management, is his true joy. The labor, the craft it takes to "write down *books* too" comes only in the afterbirth of the record.

Thus, there is a matrix of interrelated dynamics constantly at play in Kerouac: his vocation, and his pleasure in life, is to make as exhaustive a record as possible, his steeltrap brain "memories" events and thoughts in anticipation of the recording activity whose delay is figuratively rectified by the "spontaneous" method. After all, the method is only as spontaneous as the archive can be said to be spontaneous. Through the act of recording Kerouac is then able to reach further back into the "mine" of memoried memories and thus find "brand new ones." *La mémoire rescapée à même l'écriture*; writing itself rescues the memory, and in so doing files it away for yet another possible lifecycle to come. Further, he is attracted to and obsessed with Cody Pomeray because the latter somehow has the capacity to assist him in the sincere total recall of his life. Finally, remembering Cody and making an analogous record of the "complete Cody" is ultimately a means of remembering himself and accessing his own memories from even before having met Cody, where his ancestry fuels his ancient elfin recall.

"I REMEMBER CODY" (*Visions of Cody*. 19), Duluoz declares early on, but Cody is not only a conduit to more memories for Duluoz; his friend's fast, frenzied existence is also a reminder of the fleetingness of life. Cody makes the narrator all too aware that the glumness of departure always follows the promise of arrival, that "the summation pinnacle possible in human relationships—lasts a second" (*Visions of Cody*, 19). Cody symbolically leads the narrator to see "that the moment is ungraspable, is already gone and if we sleep we can call it up again mixing it with unlimited other beautiful combinations—shuffle the old file cards of the soul in demented hallucinated sleep" (*Visions of Cody*, 20). In this impassioned turn of phrase, Kerouac demonstrates that the structure of his own memory is modeled on twentieth-century archival technology, its materiality akin to the "file cards" of a library.[24] As lived moments are memoried – thus becoming rememberable – they enter the filing cabinet of Kerouac's mind and become available for subsequent shuffling. Kerouac returns to the "file cards" image later in the novel when he fantasizes about such an organizational system for obtained ideas: "supposing each time you heard a delightfully original idea or were given such an image that makes the mind sing you immediately slapped it over like one of those new office roller files" (*Visions of Cody*, 49). Ideas and images are filed away in the great rolodex of Kerouac's mind, becoming a dynamic internal archive accessible via "tremendous trancelike discipline."

And yet – true to the internal struggle between the Eros and Thanatos of Kerouac's archive fever – the great swarming files in his mind have a certain spectrality that haunt the poor recorder: "I am conscious of my own personal tragedy," he admits, "my room itself is haunted by it at night when I sleep or wake from a series of restless desperate images, catching myself in the act of shuffling the file cards of the memory or the mind under the deck" (*Visions of Cody*, 51). Duluoz's greatest fear – tied, crucially, to "the persistent feeling that I'm gonna die soon" – is to be "throwing away something that I can't even find in the incredible clutter of my being but it's going out with the refuse en masse, buried in the middle of it, every now and then I get a glimpse" (*Visions of Cody*, 51). Kerouac provides here an embodied articulation of Jacques Derrida's "*mal d'archive*," that trouble, that evil, that insatiable passion. To have the fever, Derrida writes, "is to run after the archive, even if there's too much of it, right where something in it anarchives itself."[25] Kerouac narrativizes the same sentiment: catching himself "shuffling the file cards of the memory," he "glimpses" that place where it slips away and anarchives itself in "the clutter" of his being (where "there's too much of it"). In his desperate wager, he tries to "file" it all away in its "proper place," which simultaneously builds his archive and the basis of his novelistic output.

In "The Power of the Archive and its Limits," Mbembe emphasizes the archive's use as "proof that a life truly existed, that something actually happened, an account of which can be put together. The final destination of the archive," he adds, "is therefore always situated outside its own materiality, in the story that makes it possible."[26] Kerouac, however, suggests that the archive goes both ways: the recording of the event is what makes "something" happen; without the record, the memoried story never took place. The event awaits the record to become memory. Thus, we might say that the Spontaneous Prose method is an archival poetics *par excellence* in that it is simultaneously both product and process. If we recall that "for a memory to exist," as Mbembe suggests, "there first has to be the temptation to repeat an original act," then Kerouac's retellings become the very means of conjuring the memories he seeks to preserve. Once the writer loses the "willingness to repeat something," one falls instead into the "ritual of forgetting" Mbembe calls "commemoration."[27] The method becomes the "trancelike discipline" that safeguards against the falsity of 'commemoration' in favor of what Kerouac calls "memorying"; the creation and archiving of new memories for posterity. Fundamentally, then, the method is a pure manifestation of "*l'impatience absolue d'un désir de mémoire*," as Derrida puts it, the absolute impatience of a desire for memory.[28]

18.2 *IF I DON'T DO THIS, I LIE*

In 1951, Kerouac hoped to satiate this impatience by moving beyond notebooks and upgrading to the imagined greater immediacy of the tape recorder. In the passage below, Kerouac parenthetically reminds himself of his desire to purchase a tape recorder and, tellingly, again slips in an allusion to Proust:

> *do* need a recorder, *will* buy one … then I could keep the most complete record in the world which in itself could be divided into twenty massive and pretty interesting volumes of tapes describing activities everywhere and excitements and thoughts of mad valuable me and it would really have a shape but a crazy big shape yet just as logical as a novel by Proust. (*Visions of Cody*, 120)

Here, "Journal 1951" and *Visions of Cody* meet head on: the "lifetime form" he seeks seems at hand, though its shape will be radical and beyond accepted norms as befitting its exhaustive goal: "ALL of it or give up completely" (*Visions of Cody*, 121).

Initially, Kerouac excitedly warns his readers to "wait till *tape recorder*!" (*Visions of Cody*, 131), and then, as promised, Section 3 of the novel introduces us to "Frisco: The Tape," where the book – anticipating Andy Warhol's *a, A novel* (1968) and contemporary autofiction like Sheila Heti's

How Should a Person Be (2010) – now takes the form of transcripts of recorded conversations. After roughly 150 pages of unforgiving transcription, a new section begins entitled, "Imitation of the Tape." It is here that the novel's emphasis on "shape," or form, flaunts itself and takes on added importance. "Imitation of the Tape" reads like the metatextual enactment of Kerouac's wrestling with form; it must be both a recording of "ALL of it" and the "lifelong monologue" in Kerouac's mind. The result is a mishmash of all techniques previously used in the novel – "sketches" (or Kerouac's "file cards"), stream-of-consciousness rants, recollections, correspondence, audio tape transcripts, drawings, poetry, lists – with alternating velocity of change and metamorphosis, imitating the process of composing "on the run." In other words, "a crazy big shape yet just as logical as a novel by Proust."

"Journal 1951," written early in *Visions of Cody*'s compositional history, records Kerouac's vocational desire with even more raw verve, facing the problem of candor directly, and culminating, tellingly, in an exasperated French reprimand/imperative:

> Goddamit I want to use the Proustian method of recollection and amazement but *as I go along* in life, not after, so therefore why don't I allow myself to write about Neal and using his real name in my own private scribble book for my own joy?—doesn't my own work & joy belong to me anymore? *IF I DON'T DO THIS, I LIE*—Tonite's "work" consisted of nothing but expositions about "Dean" for the "reader"—*ASSEZ, maudit Christ de Batême—si tu va être un écrivain commence à ce soir ou commence jamais!!*
> ["ENOUGH, goddam Holy Batchism—if you're gonna be a writer start tonite or never start!!"] (*Unknown Kerouac*, 168)[29]

Through the above entry, we see how intermingled all these concerns are for Kerouac; first, the Proustian method must be used in medias res not post-facto which necessarily leads to a radical new form. Second, total candor – "100% personal honesty"[30] – is positioned as central to his poetics – simultaneously his "work & joy"; both are synonyms since "this record is my joy," he confesses. Moreover, this imperative to write as truthfully as possible, without accommodating "the reader," immediately leads Kerouac back to write in his first language – the outburst in which he challenges himself to be the writer he wants to become is in French, which in turn shows how entangled his mother tongue is to his goals as a revolutionary new kind of writer. It should be underscored that, at the time of writing the above entry, Kerouac had recently completed his first French novel, *La nuit est ma femme*.[31] That he kept this manuscript private yet carefully filed it away in his archive further suggests how Kerouac's most honest, lie-free, lifetime form is his archive itself (his "own private scribble book"), despite the disarming levels of candor that are nevertheless present in his published works.

In Derridean terms, Kerouac's lifetime form is motivated by "a compulsive, repetitive, and nostalgic desire for the archive, an irrepressible desire to return to the origin, a homesickness, a nostalgia for the return to the most archaic place of absolute commencement."[32] It is therefore not surprising that the Duluoz Legend chronologically concludes with *Satori in Paris*, the 1965 novel where Kerouac chronicles his feverish visits to the archives of the Bibliothèque Nationale de Paris, the Archives Nationale, and the Bibliothèque Mazarine in an effort to trace his French-Canadian and Breton origins. As I have shown, this impulse to seek and understand origins – his own, those of his close friends, or those of his own perception and memories – is the driving force behind Kerouac's lifelong, peripatetic quest. At the same time, plagued by "that horrible homelessness all French-Canadians abroad in America have"[33] as he was, Ti Jean Kérouac's *mal d'archive* was also a means of creating a home, of preserving and accessing the memories of that home. In other words, it is a practice of *survivance*, the rallying cry of French-Canadian diaspora. Kerouac's archive thus represents both concentrated material traces of this survivance while also representing an incredibly complex work of art in its own right. To archive to such extremes as Kerouac has done, you have to "be in love with yr life," as tells us in "Belief & Technique for Modern Prose."[34] You must think of yourself, as he puts it in *Visions of Cody*, as "mad valuable me" (120). This is what the Duluoz Legend ultimately cries out to the reader via "telepathic shock and meaning excitement" ("Essentials," 69): Love your life, use that losefulness; it's "the first humanly possible requirement."

Notes

1. Jean-Pierre Wallot, cited in Terry Cook, "What Is Past Is Prologue: A History of Archival Ideas Since 1898, and the Future Paradigm Shift," *Archivaria* 43 (Spring 1997), 18. Jack Kerouac, *Visions of Cody/Visions of Gerard/Big Sur* (New York: Library of America, 2015), 125.
2. Kerouac, letter to Neal Cassady (January 8, 1951), Jack Kerouac, *Jack Kerouac: Selected Letters 1, 1940–1956*, ed. Ann Charters (Viking: New York, 1995), 273.
3. See Gerald Nicosia, *Memory Babe: A Critical Biography of Jack Kerouac* (Berkeley: University of California Press, 1993). "Memory Babe" is also the title of a delightful, aborted manuscript that finally appeared in 2016's *The Unknown*

Kerouac: Rare, Unpublished, & Newly Translated Writings, ed. Todd Tietchen, Trans. Jean-Christophe Cloutier (New York: Library of America, 2016).

4. Jack Kerouac to Ann Charters (1966), Jack Kerouac, *Jack Kerouac: Selected Letters 2, 1957–1969*, ed. Ann Charters (New York: Viking, 1999), 424.
5. "New York Public Library Buys Kerouac Archive," *New York Times*, August 22, 2001. Accessed July 19, 2016. www.nytimes.com/2001/08/22/books/new-york-public-library-buys-kerouac-archive.html
6. "New York Public Library Buys Kerouac Archive," *New York Times*, August 22, 2001.
7. Jack Kerouac to Neal Cassady (January 9, 1951), *Selected Letters 1*, 285.
8. Selections from *Visions of Cody* were published in 1959 (New York: New Directions) but published in its entirety in 1972.
9. Allen Ginsberg, "Visions of the Great Rememberer," *Visions of Cody* (New York: Penguin, 1972), 418.
10. Achille Mbembe, "The Power of the Archive and Its Limits," trans. Judith Inggs, in *Refiguring the Archive*, ed. Carolyn Hamilton, Verne Harris, Jane Taylor, Michele Pickover, Graeme Reid, and Razia Saleh (Dordrecht, Netherlands: Kluwer, 2002), 24.
11. For more on "survivance" in relation to Kerouac, see Hassan Melehy, *Kerouac: Language, Poetics, and Territory* (New York: Bloomsbury, 2016) 11–16.
12. For a fascinating account of Kerouac's rejection of objectivity in relation to the politics of postwar historiography, see Steven Belletto, "Kerouac His Own Historian: Visions of Cody and the Politics of Historiography," *Clio* 37 (Spring 2008), 193–218.
13. Jack Kerouac, "Journal 1951," in *The Unknown Kerouac*, 122.
14. For an extensive study of the influence of modern French literature on the Beats, see Véronique Lane's *The French Genealogy of the Beat Generation: Burroughs, Ginsberg and Kerouac's Appropriations of Modern Literature, from Rimbaud to Michaux* (New York: Bloomsbury Academic, 2017).
15. For a summary of archival science's concept of the "lifecycle of records," see the introduction to Cloutier, *Shadow Archives: The Lifecycles of African American Literature* (New York: Columbia University Press, 2019).
16. Jack Kerouac, "Essentials of Spontaneous Prose," *Good Blonde & Others*, ed. Donald Allen (San Francisco: Grey Fox Press, 1993), 70.
17. Clark Coolidge, "Kerouac," *The American Poetry Review*, 24: 1 (January/February 1995), 49.
18. "Canuck Proust" phrase: *Unknown Kerouac*, 112.
19. *Conversations with Jack Kerouac*, ed. Kevin J. Haynes (Jackson: University Press of Mississippi, 2005), 70.
20. Paul Saint-Amour, *Tense Future: Modernism, Total War, Encyclopedic Form* (New York: Oxford University Press, 2015), 10.
21. Box 15, Folder 25, Jack Kerouac Papers, Henry W. and Albert A. Berg Collection of English and American Literature, The New York Public Library. Holograph essay dated March 13, 1951.

22. Box 15, Folder 25, Jack Kerouac Papers.
23. Coolidge, "Kerouac," 47.
24. For more on Kerouac's relation to libraries, see Jean-Christophe Cloutier, "Jack Kerouac's Love Affair with Libraries," *Journal of Beat Studies*, Volume 7, 2019; 5–18.
25. Jacques Derrida, *Archive Fever: A Freudian Impression*, trans. Eric Prenowitz (Chicago & London: The University of Chicago Press, 1995), 91.
26. Mbembe, "Power," 21.
27. Mbembe, "Power," 24.
28. Derrida, *Archive Fever*, 85.
29. My translation; "Holy Batchism" is how Kerouac himself elsewhere translates the same French Canadian expression, "Christ de Batême." As a sacrilegious exclamation of exasperation, it's like saying "goddammit" in American English.
30. Jack Kerouac to Allen Ginsberg (May 18, 1952), *Selected Letters 1*, 356.
31. This novel appears in Jack Kerouac, *La vie est d'hommage*, edited by Jean-Christophe Cloutier (Montreal: Boréal, 2016).
32. Derrida, *Archive Fever*, 91.
33. Jack Kerouac to Yvonne Le Maître (September 8, 1950), *Selected Letters, 1*, 228.
34. Jack Kerouac, "Belief & Technique for Modern Prose," *Good Blonde*, 72.

Further Reading

Books by Jack Kerouac

The Town and the City. Harcourt Brace, 1950.
On the Road. Viking, 1957.
The Subterraneans. Grove, 1958.
The Dharma Bums. Viking, 1958
Doctor Sax. Grove, 1959.
Maggie Cassidy. Avon, 1959.
Mexico City Blues. Grove, 1959.
Visions of Cody (excerpts). New Directions, 1959.
Lonesome Traveler. McGraw-Hill, 1960.
The Scripture of the Golden Eternity. Corinth, 1960.
Tristessa. Avon, 1960.
Book of Dreams. City Lights, 1961.
Pull My Daisy (text ad-libbed by Kerouac for the Robert Frank and Alfred Leslie film). Grove, 1961.
Big Sur. Farrar, Straus, and Cudahy, 1962.
Visions of Gerard. Farrar, Straus, and Cudahy, 1963.
Desolation Angels. Coward-McCann, 1965.
Satori in Paris. Grove, 1966.
Vanity of Duluoz. Coward-McCann, 1968.
Pic. Grove, 1971.
Scattered Poems. City Lights, 1971.
Visions of Cody. McGraw-Hill, 1972.
Trip Trap: Haiku on the Road (with Albert Saijo and Lew Welch). Grey Fox, 1973.
Heaven & Other Poems. Grey Fox. 1977.
Last Words & Other Writings. Zeta, 1985.
Pomes All Sizes. City Lights, 1992.
Good Blonde & Others. Grey Fox, 1993.
Old Angel Midnight. Grey Fox, 1993.
Book of Blues. Penguin, 1995.
San Francisco Blues. Penguin, 1995.
The Portable Jack Kerouac. Viking, 1995.
Some of the Dharma. Viking, 1997.

Atop an Underwood: Early Stories and Other Writings. Viking, 1999.
Orpheus Emerged. ibooks, 2000.
Book of Haikus. Penguin, 2003.
Departed Angels: The Lost Paintings. Thunder's Mouth, 2004.
Beat Generation: A Play. Thunder's Mouth, 2005.
Book of Sketches. Penguin, 2006.
On the Road: The Original Scroll. Viking, 2007.
Road Novels, 1957–1960 (*On the Road, The Dharma Bums, The Subterraneans, Tristessa, Lonesome Traveler*, Journal Selections). Library of America, 2007.
And the Hippos Were Boiled in Their Tanks (with William S. Burroughs). Grove, 2008.
Wake Up: A Life of the Buddha. Viking, 2008.
You're a Genius All the Time: Belief and Technique in Modern Prose. Chronicle, 2009.
The Sea Is My Brother: The Lost Novel. Da Capo, 2011.
Collected Poems. Library of America, 2012.
The Haunted Life and Other Writings. Da Capo, 2014.
Visions of Cody, Visions of Gerard, Big Sur. Library of America, 2015.
The Unknown Kerouac: Rare, Unpublished & Newly Translated Writings. Library of America, 2016.
La vie est d'hommage. Les Éditions du Boréal, 2016.
Desolation Peak: Collected Writings. Sal Paradise/Rare Bird, 2022.
Sur le chemin. Gallimard, 2023.
Truth and Beautiful Meaningful Lies: A Collection of Jack Kerouac Quotes. Sal Paradise/Rare Bird, 2023.
Self-Portrait: Collected Writings. Sal Paradise/Rare Bird, 2024.

Letters and Journals

Selected Letters, 1940–1956. Penguin, 1995.
Selected Letters, 1957–1969. Viking, 1999.
Door Wide Open: A Beat Love Affair in Letters, 1957–1958 (with Joyce Johnson). Viking, 2000.
Windblown World: The Journals of Jack Kerouac. Penguin, 2004.
Jack Kerouac and Allen Ginsberg: The Letters. Viking, 2010.

Secondary Work

Amram, David. *Offbeat: Collaborating with Kerouac*. New York: Thunder's Mouth, 2002.
Anctil, Pierre, Louis Dupont, Rémi Ferland, and Eric Waddell, eds. *Un Homme Grand: Jack Kerouac at the Crossroads of Many Cultures*. Ottawa: Carleton University Press, 1990.
Beaulieu, Victor-Levy. *Jack Kerouac: A Chicken-Essay*. Toronto: Coach House Books, 1975.

Belletto, Steven, ed. *The Cambridge Companion to the Beats*. New York: Cambridge University Press, 2017.
Belletto, Steven. *The Beats: A Literary History*. New York: Cambridge University Press, 2020.
Bloom, Harold, ed. *Jack Kerouac's On the Road*. Philadelphia: Chelsea House Publishers, 2004.
Cassady, Carolyn. *Off the Road: My Years with Cassady, Kerouac, and Ginsberg*. New York: William Morrow, 1990.
Charters, Ann. compiler. *A Bibliography of Works by Jack Kerouac*. New York: Phoenix Book Shop, 1967.
Charters, Ann, ed. *The Beats: Literary Bohemians in Postwar America, Parts I and II*. Detroit: Gale Research Company, 1983.
Charters, Ann. *Kerouac*. 1973. New York: St. Martin's, 1987.
Charters, Ann, ed. *Beat Down to Your Soul: What Was the Beat Generation?* New York: Penguin Books, 2001.
Charters, Ann and Samuel Charters. *Brother Souls: John Clellon Holmes, Jack Kerouac, and the Beat Generation*. Jackson: University Press of Mississippi, 2010.
Clark, Tom. *Jack Kerouac: A Biography*. New York: Marlowe & Company, 1984.
Coolidge, Clark. *Now It's Jazz: Writings on Kerouac & the Sounds*. Albuquerque: Living Batch Press, 1999.
Donaldson, Scott, ed. *On the Road: Text and Criticism*. New York: Penguin, 1979.
Ellis, R. J. *Liar! Liar! Jack Kerouac, Novelist*. London: Greenwich Exchange, 1999.
French, Warren. *Jack Kerouac: Novelist of the Beat Generation*. Boston: Twayne Publishers, 1986.
García-Robles, Jorge. *At the End of the Road: Jack Kerouac in Mexico*, trans. Daniel C. Schechter. Minneapolis: University of Minnesota Press, 2014.
Gewirtz, Isaac. *Beatific Soul: Jack Kerouac on the Road*. New York: New York Public Library, 2007.
Giamo, Ben. *Kerouac, the Word and the Way: Prose Artist as Spiritual Quester*. Carbondale: Southern Illinois University Press, 2000.
Gifford, Barry and Lawrence Lee. *Jack's Book: An Oral Biography of Jack Kerouac*. New York: St. Martin's, 1978.
Ginsberg, Allen. *The Visions of the Great Rememberer*. Amherst: Mulch Press, 1974.
Grace, Nancy M. *Jack Kerouac and the Literary Imagination*. New York: Palgrave, 2007.
Haynes, Kevin, ed. *Conversations with Kerouac*. Jackson: University Press of Mississippi, 2005.
Hemmer, Kurt, ed. *Encyclopedia of Beat Literature*. New York: Facts on File, 2007.
Hernandez, Tim Z. *Mañana Means Heaven*. Tucson: University of Arizona Press, 2013.
Hipkiss, Robert, *Jack Kerouac: Prophet of the New Romanticism*. Lawrence, KS: Regents Press, 1976.
Holladay, Hilary and Robert Holton, eds. *What's Your Road, Man? Critical Essays on Jack Kerouac's On the Road*. Carbondale: Southern Illinois University Press, 2009.

Holmes, John Clellon. *Gone in October: Last Reflections on Jack Kerouac*. Hailey, ID: The Limberlost Press, 1985.

Holton, Robert. *On the Road: Kerouac's Ragged American Journey*. New York: Twayne Publishers, 1999.

Hrebeniak, Michael. *Action Writing: Jack Kerouac's Wild Form*. Carbondale: Southern Illinois University Press, 2006.

Hunt, Tim. *Kerouac's Crooked Road: Development of a Fiction*. 1981. Berkeley: University of California Press, 1996.

Hunt, Tim. *The Textuality of Soulwork: Jack Kerouac's Quest for Spontaneous Prose*. Ann Arbor: University of Michigan Press, 2014.

Jarvis, Charles. *Visions of Kerouac: A Biography*. Lowell: Ithaca Press, 1974.

Johnson, Joyce. *Minor Characters: A Young Woman's Coming-of-Age in the Beat Orbit of Jack Kerouac*. 1983. New York: Penguin, 1999.

Johnson, Joyce. *The Voice Is All: The Lonely Victory of Jack Kerouac*. New York: Viking, 2012.

Johnson, Ronna C. and Tim Hunt, eds. *Journal of Beat Studies* 10 "The Special Kerouac Centenary Issue" (2022).

Jones, James T. *A Map of Mexico City Blues: Jack Kerouac as Poet*. Carbondale: Southern Illinois University Press, 1992.

Jones, James T. *Jack Kerouac's Duluoz Legend: The Mythic Form of an Autobiographical Fiction*. Carbondale: Southern Illinois University Press, 1999.

Jones, Jim [James T.] *Use My Name: Jack Kerouac's Forgotten Families*. Ontario: ECW Press, 1999.

Kerouac-Parker, Edie. *You'll Be Okay: My Life with Jack Kerouac*. San Francisco: City Lights Books, 2007.

Lane, Véronique. *The French Genealogy of The Beat Generation: Burroughs, Ginsberg and Kerouac's Appropriations of Modern Literature, from Rimbaud to Michaux*. New York: Bloomsbury Academic, 2017.

Lardas, John. *The Bop Apocalypse: The Religious Visions of Kerouac, Ginsberg, and Burroughs*. Urbana: University of Illinois Press, 2001.

Leland, John. *Why Kerouac Matters: The Lessons of On the Road (They're Not What You Think)*. New York: Viking, 2007.

Maher, Jr., Paul. *Kerouac: The Definitive Biography*. New York: Taylor Trader Publishing, 2004.

Maher, Jr., Paul, ed. *Empty Phantoms: Interviews and Encounters with Jack Kerouac*. New York: Thunder's Mouth, 2005.

Maher, Jr., Paul. *Jack Kerouac's American Journey: The Real-Life Odyssey of On the Road*. New York: Thunder's Mouth, 2007.

Martinez, Manuel Luis. *Countering the Counterculture: Rereading Postwar American Dissent from Jack Kerouac to Tomás Rivera*. Madison: University of Wisconsin Press, 2003.

McNally, Dennis. *Desolate Angel: Jack Kerouac, The Beat Generation, and America*. New York: Random House, 1979.

Melehy, Hassan. *Kerouac: Language, Poetics, and Territory*. New York: Bloomsbury Academic, 2016.

Milewski, Robert J., ed. *Jack Kerouac: An Annotated Bibliography of Secondary Sources: 1944–1979*. Metuchen, NJ: Scarecrow Press, 1981.

Mortenson, Erik. *Capturing the Beat Moment: Cultural Politics and the Poetics of Presence*. Carbondale: Southern Illinois University Press, 2011.

Nicosia, Gerald. *Memory Babe: A Critical Biography of Jack Kerouac*. 1983. Berkeley: University of California Press, 1994.

Nicosia, Gerald and Anne Marie Santos. *One and Only: The Untold Story of On the Road*. Berkeley: Viva, 2011.

Phillips, Rod. *"Forest Beatniks" and "Urban Thoreaus": Gary Snyder, Jack Kerouac, Lew Welch, and Michael McClure*. New York: Peter Lang, 2000.

Sandison, David. *Jack Kerouac: An Illustrated Biography*. Chicago: Chicago Review Press, 1999.

Sawczuk, Tomasz. *On the Road to Lost Fathers: Jack Kerouac in a Lacanian Perspective*. New York: Peter Lang, 2019.

Swartz, Omar. *The View from On the Road: The Rhetorical Vision of Jack Kerouac*. Carbondale: Southern Illinois University Press, 1999.

Theado, Matt. *Understanding Jack Kerouac*. Columbia: University of South Carolina Press, 2000.

Theado, Matt, ed. *The Beats: A Literary Reference*. New York: Carroll & Graf, 2003.

Turner, Steve. *Jack Kerouac: Angelheaded Hipster*. New York: Viking, 1996.

Tytell, John. *Naked Angels: Kerouac, Ginsberg, Burroughs*. New York: McGraw-Hill, 1976.

Warner, Simon and Jim Sampas, ed. *Kerouac on Record: A Literary Soundtrack*. New York: Bloomsbury Academic, 2018.

Weaver, Helen. *The Awakener: A Memoir of Kerouac and the Fifties*. San Francisco: City Lights Books, 2009.

Weinreich, Regina. *Kerouac's Spontaneous Poetics*. 1987. New York: Thunder's Mouth, 2002.

Index

Cambridge Companions To ...

AUTHORS

Edward Albee edited by Stephen J. Bottoms
Margaret Atwood edited by Coral Ann Howells (second edition)
W. H. Auden edited by Stan Smith
Jane Austen edited by Edward Copeland and Juliet McMaster (second edition)
Balzac edited by Owen Heathcote and Andrew Watts
Beckett edited by John Pilling
Bede edited by Scott DeGregorio
Aphra Behn edited by Derek Hughes and Janet Todd
Saul Bellow edited by Victoria Aarons
Walter Benjamin edited by David S. Ferris
William Blake edited by Morris Eaves
James Baldwin edited by Michele Elam
Boccaccio edited by Guyda Armstrong, Rhiannon Daniels, and Stephen J. Milner
Jorge Luis Borges edited by Edwin Williamson
Brecht edited by Peter Thomson and Glendyr Sacks (second edition)
The Brontës edited by Heather Glen
Bunyan edited by Anne Dunan-Page
Frances Burney edited by Peter Sabor
Byron edited by Drummond Bone (second edition)
Albert Camus edited by Edward J. Hughes
Willa Cather edited by Marilee Lindemann
Catullus edited by Ian Du Quesnay and Tony Woodman
Cervantes edited by Anthony J. Cascardi
Chaucer edited by Piero Boitani and Jill Mann (second edition)
Chekhov edited by Vera Gottlieb and Paul Allain
Kate Chopin edited by Janet Beer
Caryl Churchill edited by Elaine Aston and Elin Diamond
Cicero edited by Catherine Steel
John Clare edited by Sarah Houghton-Walker
J. M. Coetzee edited by Jarad Zimbler
Coleridge edited by Lucy Newlyn
Coleridge edited by Tim Fulford (new edition)
Wilkie Collins edited by Jenny Bourne Taylor
Joseph Conrad edited by J. H. Stape
H. D. edited by Nephie J. Christodoulides and Polina Mackay
Dante edited by Rachel Jacoff (second edition)
Daniel Defoe edited by John Richetti
Don DeLillo edited by John N. Duvall
Charles Dickens edited by John O. Jordan
Emily Dickinson edited by Wendy Martin
John Donne edited by Achsah Guibbory
Dostoevskii edited by W. J. Leatherbarrow
Theodore Dreiser edited by Leonard Cassuto and Claire Virginia Eby
John Dryden edited by Steven N. Zwicker
W. E. B. Du Bois edited by Shamoon Zamir
George Eliot edited by George Levine and Nancy Henry (second edition)
T. S. Eliot edited by A. David Moody
Ralph Ellison edited by Ross Posnock
Ralph Waldo Emerson edited by Joel Porte and Saundra Morris
William Faulkner edited by Philip M. Weinstein
Henry Fielding edited by Claude Rawson
F. Scott Fitzgerald edited by Ruth Prigozy
F. Scott Fitzgerald edited by Michael Nowlin (second edition)
Flaubert edited by Timothy Unwin
E. M. Forster edited by David Bradshaw
Benjamin Franklin edited by Carla Mulford
Brian Friel edited by Anthony Roche
Robert Frost edited by Robert Faggen
Gabriel García Márquez edited by Philip Swanson
Elizabeth Gaskell edited by Jill L. Matus
Edward Gibbon edited by Karen O'Brien and Brian Young
Goethe edited by Lesley Sharpe
Günter Grass edited by Stuart Taberner
Thomas Hardy edited by Dale Kramer
David Hare edited by Richard Boon
Nathaniel Hawthorne edited by Richard Millington
Seamus Heaney edited by Bernard O'Donoghue
Ernest Hemingway edited by Scott Donaldson
Hildegard of Bingen edited by Jennifer Bain
Homer edited by Robert Fowler
Horace edited by Stephen Harrison
Ted Hughes edited by Terry Gifford
Ibsen edited by James McFarlane
Kazuo Ishiguro edited by Andrew Bennett

Henry James edited by Jonathan Freedman
Samuel Johnson edited by Greg Clingham
Ben Jonson edited by Richard Harp and Stanley Stewart
James Joyce edited by Derek Attridge (second edition)
Kafka edited by Julian Preece
Keats edited by Susan J. Wolfson
Jack Kerouac edited by Steven Belletto
Rudyard Kipling edited by Howard J. Booth
Lacan edited by Jean-Michel Rabaté
D. H. Lawrence edited by Anne Fernihough
Primo Levi edited by Robert Gordon
Lucretius edited by Stuart Gillespie and Philip Hardie
Machiavelli edited by John M. Najemy
David Mamet edited by Christopher Bigsby
Thomas Mann edited by Ritchie Robertson
Christopher Marlowe edited by Patrick Cheney
Andrew Marvell edited by Derek Hirst and Steven N. Zwicker
Ian McEwan edited by Dominic Head
Herman Melville edited by Robert S. Levine
Arthur Miller edited by Christopher Bigsby (second edition)
Milton edited by Dennis Danielson (second edition)
Molière edited by David Bradby and Andrew Calder
William Morris edited by Marcus Waithe
Toni Morrison edited by Justine Tally
Alice Munro edited by David Staines
Nabokov edited by Julian W. Connolly
Eugene O'Neill edited by Michael Manheim
George Orwell edited by John Rodden
Ovid edited by Philip Hardie
Petrarch edited by Albert Russell Ascoli and Unn Falkeid
Harold Pinter edited by Peter Raby (second edition)
Sylvia Plath edited by Jo Gill
Plutarch edited by Frances B. Titchener and Alexei Zadorojnyi
Edgar Allan Poe edited by Kevin J. Hayes
Alexander Pope edited by Pat Rogers
Ezra Pound edited by Ira B. Nadel
Proust edited by Richard Bales
Pushkin edited by Andrew Kahn
Thomas Pynchon edited by Inger H. Dalsgaard, Luc Herman and Brian McHale
Rabelais edited by John O'Brien
Rilke edited by Karen Leeder and Robert Vilain
Philip Roth edited by Timothy Parrish
Salman Rushdie edited by Abdulrazak Gurnah
John Ruskin edited by Francis O'Gorman
Sappho edited by P. J. Finglass and Adrian Kelly
Seneca edited by Shadi Bartsch and Alessandro Schiesaro
Shakespeare edited by Margareta de Grazia and Stanley Wells (second edition)
George Bernard Shaw edited by Christopher Innes
Shelley edited by Timothy Morton
Mary Shelley edited by Esther Schor
Sam Shepard edited by Matthew C. Roudané
Spenser edited by Andrew Hadfield
Laurence Sterne edited by Thomas Keymer
Wallace Stevens edited by John N. Serio
Tom Stoppard edited by Katherine E. Kelly
Harriet Beecher Stowe edited by Cindy Weinstein
August Strindberg edited by Michael Robinson
Jonathan Swift edited by Christopher Fox
J. M. Synge edited by P. J. Mathews
Tacitus edited by A. J. Woodman
Henry David Thoreau edited by Joel Myerson
Thucydides edited by Polly Low
Tolstoy edited by Donna Tussing Orwin
Anthony Trollope edited by Carolyn Dever and Lisa Niles
Mark Twain edited by Forrest G. Robinson
John Updike edited by Stacey Olster
Mario Vargas Llosa edited by Efrain Kristal and John King
Virgil edited by Fiachra Mac Góráin and Charles Martindale (second edition)
Voltaire edited by Nicholas Cronk
David Foster Wallace edited by Ralph Clare
Edith Wharton edited by Millicent Bell
Walt Whitman edited by Ezra Greenspan
Oscar Wilde edited by Peter Raby
Tennessee Williams edited by Matthew C. Roudané
William Carlos Williams edited by Christopher MacGowan
August Wilson edited by Christopher Bigsby
Mary Wollstonecraft edited by Claudia L. Johnson
Virginia Woolf edited by Susan Sellers (second edition)
Wordsworth edited by Stephen Gill
Richard Wright edited by Glenda R. Carpio
W. B. Yeats edited by Marjorie Howes and John Kelly
Xenophon edited by Michael A. Flower
Zola edited by Brian Nelson

TOPICS

The Actress edited by Maggie B. Gale and John Stokes
The African American Novel edited by Maryemma Graham
The African American Slave Narrative edited by Audrey A. Fisch
African American Theatre by Harvey Young
Allegory edited by Rita Copeland and Peter Struck
American Crime Fiction edited by Catherine Ross Nickerson
American Gothic edited by Jeffrey Andrew Weinstock
The American Graphic Novel by Jan Baetens, Hugo Frey and Fabrice Leroy
American Horror edited by Stephen Shapiro and Mark Storey
American Literature and the Body by Travis M. Foster
American Literature and the Environment edited by Sarah Ensor and Susan Scott Parrish
American Literature of the 1930s edited by William Solomon
American Modernism edited by Walter Kalaidjian
American Poetry since 1945 edited by Jennifer Ashton
American Realism and Naturalism edited by Donald Pizer
American Short Story edited by Michael J. Collins and Gavin Jones
American Travel Writing edited by Alfred Bendixen and Judith Hamera
American Utopian Literature and Culture since 1945 edited by Sherryl Vint
American Women Playwrights edited by Brenda Murphy
Ancient Rhetoric edited by Erik Gunderson
Arthurian Legend edited by Elizabeth Archibald and Ad Putter
Australian Literature edited by Elizabeth Webby
The Australian Novel edited by Nicholas Birns and Louis Klee
The Beats edited by Steven Belletto
The Black Body in American Literature edited by Cherene Sherrard-Johnson
Boxing edited by Gerald Early
British Black and Asian Literature (1945–2010) edited by Deirdre Osborne
British Fiction: 1980–2018 edited by Peter Boxall
British Fiction since 1945 edited by David James
British Literature of the 1930s edited by James Smith
British Literature of the French Revolution edited by Pamela Clemit
British Romantic Poetry edited by James Chandler and Maureen N. McLane
British Romanticism edited by Stuart Curran (second edition)
British Romanticism and Religion edited by Jeffrey Barbeau
British Theatre, 1730–1830, edited by Jane Moody and Daniel O'Quinn
Canadian Literature edited by Eva-Marie Kröller (second edition)
The Canterbury Tales edited by Frank Grady
Children's Literature edited by M. O. Grenby and Andrea Immel
The City in World Literature edited by Ato Quayson and Jini Kim Watson
The Classic Russian Novel edited by Malcolm V. Jones and Robin Feuer Miller
Comics edited by Maaheen Ahmed
Contemporary African American Literature edited by *Yogita Goyal*
Contemporary Irish Poetry edited by Matthew Campbell
Creative Writing edited by David Morley and Philip Neilsen
Crime Fiction edited by Martin Priestman
Dante's 'Commedia' edited by Zygmunt G. Barański and Simon Gilson
Dracula edited by Roger Luckhurst
Early American Literature edited by Bryce Traister
Early Modern Women's Writing edited by Laura Lunger Knoppers
The Eighteenth-Century Novel edited by John Richetti
Eighteenth-Century Poetry edited by John Sitter
Eighteenth-Century Thought edited by *Frans De Bruyn*
Emma edited by Peter Sabor
English Dictionaries edited by Sarah Ogilvie
English Literature, 1500–1600 edited by Arthur F. Kinney
English Literature, 1650–1740 edited by Steven N. Zwicker
English Literature, 1740–1830 edited by Thomas Keymer and Jon Mee
English Literature, 1830–1914 edited by Joanne Shattock
English Melodrama edited by Carolyn Williams
English Novelists edited by Adrian Poole

English Poetry, Donne to Marvell edited by Thomas N. Corns

English Poets edited by Claude Rawson

English Renaissance Drama edited by A. R. Braunmuller and Michael Hattaway, (*second edition*)

English Renaissance Tragedy edited by Emma Smith and Garrett A. Sullivan Jr.

English Restoration Theatre edited by Deborah C. Payne Fisk

Environmental Humanities edited by Jeffrey Cohen and Stephanie Foote

The Epic edited by Catherine Bates

Erotic Literature edited by Bradford Mudge

The Essay edited by Kara Wittman and Evan Kindley

European Modernism edited by Pericles Lewis

European Novelists edited by Michael Bell

Fairy Tales edited by Maria Tatar

Fantasy Literature edited by Edward James and Farah Mendlesohn

Feminist Literary Theory edited by Ellen Rooney

Fiction in the Romantic Period edited by Richard Maxwell and Katie Trumpener

The Fin de Siècle edited by Gail Marshall

Frankenstein edited by Andrew Smith

The French Enlightenment edited by Daniel Brewer

French Literature edited by John D. Lyons

The French Novel: from 1800 to the Present edited by Timothy Unwin

Gay and Lesbian Writing edited by Hugh Stevens

German Romanticism edited by Nicholas Saul

Global Literature and Slavery edited by Laura T. Murphy

Gothic Fiction edited by Jerrold E. Hogle

The Graphic Novel edited by Stephen Tabachnick

The Greek and Roman Novel edited by Tim Whitmarsh

Greek and Roman Theatre edited by Marianne McDonald and J. Michael Walton

Greek Comedy edited by Martin Revermann

Greek Lyric edited by Felix Budelmann

Greek Mythology edited by Roger D. Woodard

Greek Tragedy edited by P. E. Easterling

The Harlem Renaissance edited by George Hutchinson

The History of the Book edited by Leslie Howsam

Human Rights and Literature edited by Crystal Parikh

The Irish Novel edited by John Wilson Foster

Irish Poets edited by Gerald Dawe

The Italian Novel edited by Peter Bondanella and Andrea Ciccarelli

The Italian Renaissance edited by Michael Wyatt

Jewish American Literature edited by Hana Wirth-Nesher and Michael P. Kramer

The Latin American Novel edited by Efraín Kristal

Latin American Poetry edited by Stephen Hart

Latina/o American Literature edited by John Morán González

Latin Love Elegy edited by Thea S. Thorsen

Literature and Animals by Derek Ryan

Literature and the Anthropocene edited by John Parham

Literature and Climate edited by Adeline Johns-Putra and Kelly Sultzbach

Literature in a Digital Age edited by Adam Hammond

Literature and Disability edited by Clare Barker and Stuart Murray

Literature and Food edited by J. Michelle Coghlan

Literature and the Posthuman edited by Bruce Clarke and Manuela Rossini

Literature and Religion edited by Susan M. Felch

Literature and Science edited by Steven Meyer

The Literature of the American Civil War and Reconstruction edited by Kathleen Diffley and Coleman Hutchison

The Literature of the American Renaissance edited by Christopher N. Phillips

The Literature of Berlin edited by Andrew J. Webber

The Literature of the Crusades edited by Anthony Bale

The Literature of the First World War edited by Vincent Sherry

The Literature of London edited by Lawrence Manley

The Literature of Los Angeles edited by Kevin R. McNamara

The Literature of New York edited by Cyrus Patell and Bryan Waterman

The Literature of Paris edited by Anna-Louise Milne

The Literature of World War II edited by Marina MacKay

Literature on Screen edited by Deborah Cartmell and Imelda Whelehan

Lyrical Ballads edited by Sally Bushell

Medieval British Manuscripts edited by Orietta Da Rold and Elaine Treharne

Medieval English Culture edited by Andrew Galloway

Medieval English Law and Literature edited by Candace Barrington and Sebastian Sobecki

Medieval English Literature edited by Larry Scanlon

Medieval English Mysticism edited by Samuel Fanous and Vincent Gillespie

Medieval English Theatre edited by Richard Beadle and Alan J. Fletcher (second edition)

Medieval French Literature edited by Simon Gaunt and Sarah Kay

Medieval Romance edited by Roberta L. Krueger

Medieval Romance edited by Roberta L. Krueger (new edition)

Medieval Women's Writing edited by Carolyn Dinshaw and David Wallace

Modern American Culture edited by Christopher Bigsby

Modern British Women Playwrights edited by Elaine Aston and Janelle Reinelt

Modern French Culture edited by Nicholas Hewitt

Modern German Culture edited by Eva Kolinsky and Wilfried van der Will

The Modern German Novel edited by Graham Bartram

The Modern Gothic edited by Jerrold E. Hogle

Modern Irish Culture edited by Joe Cleary and Claire Connolly

Modern Italian Culture edited by Zygmunt G. Baranski and Rebecca J. West

Modern Latin American Culture edited by John King

Modern Russian Culture edited by Nicholas Rzhevsky

Modern Spanish Culture edited by David T. Gies

Modernism edited by Michael Levenson (second edition)

The Modernist Novel edited by Morag Shiach

Modernist Poetry edited by Alex Davis and Lee M. Jenkins

Modernist Women Writers edited by Maren Tova Linett

Narrative edited by David Herman

Narrative Theory edited by Matthew Garrett

Native American Literature edited by Joy Porter and Kenneth M. Roemer

Nineteen Eighty-Four edited by Nathan Waddell

Nineteenth-Century American Literature and Politics edited by John Kerkering

Nineteenth-Century American Poetry edited by Kerry Larson

Nineteenth-Century American Women's Writing edited by Dale M. Bauer and Philip Gould

Nineteenth-Century Thought edited by Gregory Claeys

The Novel edited by Eric Bulson

Old English Literature edited by Malcolm Godden and Michael Lapidge (second edition)

Performance Studies edited by Tracy C. Davis

Piers Plowman by Andrew Cole and Andrew Galloway

The Poetry of the First World War edited by Santanu Das

Popular Fiction edited by David Glover and Scott McCracken

Postcolonial Literary Studies edited by Neil Lazarus

Postcolonial Poetry edited by Jahan Ramazani

Postcolonial Travel Writing edited by Robert Clarke

Postmodern American Fiction edited by Paula Geyh

Postmodernism edited by Steven Connor

Prose edited by Daniel Tyler

The Pre-Raphaelites edited by Elizabeth Prettejohn

Pride and Prejudice edited by Janet Todd

Queer Studies edited by Siobhan B. Somerville

Race and American Literature edited by John Ernest

Renaissance Humanism edited by Jill Kraye

Robinson Crusoe edited by John Richetti

Roman Comedy edited by Martin T. Dinter

The Roman Historians edited by Andrew Feldherr

Roman Satire edited by Kirk Freudenburg

The Romantic Sublime by Cian Duffy

Science Fiction edited by Edward James and Farah Mendlesohn

Scottish Literature edited by Gerald Carruthers and Liam McIlvanney

Sensation Fiction edited by Andrew Mangham

Shakespeare and Contemporary Dramatists edited by Ton Hoenselaars

Shakespeare and Popular Culture edited by Robert Shaughnessy

Shakespeare and Race edited by Ayanna Thompson

Shakespeare and Religion edited by Hannibal Hamlin

Shakespeare and War edited by David Loewenstein and Paul Stevens

Shakespeare on Film edited by Russell Jackson (second edition)

Shakespeare on Screen edited by Russell Jackson

Shakespeare on Stage edited by Stanley Wells and Sarah Stanton

Shakespearean Comedy edited by Alexander Leggatt

Shakespearean Tragedy edited by Claire McEachern (second edition)

Shakespeare's First Folio edited by Emma Smith

Shakespeare's History Plays edited by Michael Hattaway

Shakespeare's Language edited by Lynne Magnusson with David Schalkwyk

Shakespeare's Last Plays edited by Catherine M. S. Alexander

Shakespeare's Poetry edited by Patrick Cheney

Sherlock Holmes edited by Janice M. Allan and Christopher Pittard

The Sonnet edited by A. D. Cousins and Peter Howarth

The Spanish Novel: from 1600 to the Present edited by Harriet Turner and Adelaida López de Martínez

Textual Scholarship edited by Neil Fraistat and Julia Flanders

Theatre and Science edited by Kristen E. Shepherd-Barr

Theatre History by David Wiles and Christine Dymkowski

Transnational American Literature edited by Yogita Goyal

Travel Writing edited by Peter Hulme and Tim Youngs

The Twentieth-Century American Novel and Politics by Bryan Santin

Twentieth-Century American Poetry and Politics edited by Daniel Morris

Twentieth-Century British and Irish Women's Poetry edited by Jane Dowson

The Twentieth-Century English Novel edited by Robert L. Caserio

Twentieth-Century English Poetry edited by Neil Corcoran

Twentieth-Century Irish Drama edited by Shaun Richards

Twentieth-Century Literature and Politics edited by Christos Hadjiyiannis and Rachel Potter

Twentieth-Century Russian Literature edited by Marina Balina and Evgeny Dobrenko

Utopian Literature edited by Gregory Claeys

Victorian and Edwardian Theatre edited by Kerry Powell

The Victorian Novel edited by Deirdre David (second edition)

Victorian Poetry edited by Joseph Bristow

Victorian Women's Poetry edited by Linda K. Hughes

Victorian Women's Writing edited by Linda H. Peterson

War Writing edited by Kate McLoughlin

Women's Writing in Britain, 1660–1789 edited by Catherine Ingrassia

Women's Writing in the Romantic Period edited by Devoney Looser

World Literature edited by Ben Etherington and Jarad Zimbler

World Crime Fiction edited by Jesper Gulddal, Stewart King and Alistair Rolls

Writing of the English Revolution edited by N. H. Keeble

The Writings of Julius Caesar edited by Christopher Krebs and Luca Grillo

Printed in the USA
CPSIA information can be obtained
at www.ICGtesting.com
LVHW041314301124
797960LV00001B/50

* 9 7 8 1 0 0 9 4 2 3 5 6 4 *